CONTRAST AND CONTROVERSY IN MODERN PSYCHOLOGY

edited by
DANIEL P. KIMBLE
University of Oregon

Goodyear Publishing Company, Inc.,
Santa Monica, California

Library of Congress Cataloging in Publication Data

1. Psychology -- Addresses, essays, lectures.
2. Psychology, Pathological -- Addresses, essays, lectures.
3. Psychotherapy – Addresses, essays, lectures.
I. Kimble, Daniel Porter. [DNLM: 1. Behavior therapy.
II. Psychology. 3. Psychology, Social. BF121 C764]
BF149.C583 150'.8 76–46871
ISBN 0–87620–210–5

ISBN 0–87620–210–5
Y–2105–8

Currrent Printing (last digit):
10 9 8 7 6 5 4 3 2 1

Interior Design: Jacki Thibodeau
Cover Design: Don McQuiston

Printed in the United States of America

CONTENTS

INTRODUCTION 1

1. INTELLIGENCE: IS IT JUST WHAT INTELLIGENCE TESTS MEASURE? 3

Lost: Our Intelligence? Why? *Quinn McNemar* 4

Testing for Competence Rather Than for "Intelligence" *David C. McClelland* 22

2. PROCESSING VISUAL INFORMATION: AN EXAMPLE FROM THE STUDY OF APPARENT MOTION 44

Experiment 3: The Limiting Effect of Different Forms on the Perception of Apparent Movement *Jesse Orlansky* 45

Irrelevance of Figural Identity for Resolving Ambiguities in Apparent Motion *David Navon* 56

3. CONTROLLING OUR EMOTIONS: BIOFEEDBACK AS THERAPY—A PRESENT REALITY OR A PROMISE AS YET UNFULFILLED? 70

Biofeedback as Therapy: Some Theoretical and Practical Issues *Gary E. Schwartz* 71

Self-Control of Cardiac Functioning: A Promise as yet Unfulfilled *Edward B. Blanchard and Larry D. Young* 84

4. BEHAVIOR MODIFICATION: A BRAVE NEW WORLD OR 1984? 110

The End of Ideology in Behavior Modification *Perry London* 111

Behavior Theory and the Models of Man *Albert Bandura* 123

5. VIOLENCE ON TELEVISION: HOW HARMFUL? 141

Does Television Violence Cause Aggression? *Leonard D. Eron, Monroe M. Lefkowitz, L. Rowell Huesmann, and Leopold O. Walder* 143

Comment: Causal Analysis in R-R Studies: Television Violence and Aggression *Gilbert Becker* 161

Comment: On Television as a Cause of Aggression *Robert M. Kaplan* 164

Comment: Television and Aggression: A Counterargument *Dennis Howitt* 166

Comment: Weaknesses in the Television-Causes-Aggression Analysis by Eron et al. *Herbert Kay* 168

Comment: Television Violence and Aggression: The Causal Effect Remains *L. Rowell Huesmann, Leonard D. Eron, Monroe M. Lefkowitz, and Leopold O. Walder* 172

6. THE BATTERED CHILD: WHO IS REALLY TO BLAME? WHAT CAN BE DONE? 179

Physical Abuse of Children: Findings and Implications of a Nationwide Survey *David G. Gil* 180

The Child-abusing Parent: A Psychological Review *John J. Spinetta and David Rigler* 190

7. ON BEING SANE IN INSANE PLACES 203

On Being Sane in Insane Places *D. L. Rosenhan* 204

Schizophrenia, Language, and Reality *Roger Brown* 223

8. PSYCHOSURGERY: A MULTILEVEL CONTROVERSY 237

Psychosurgery: Perspective on a Current Issue *Bertram S. Brown, Louis A. Wienckowski, and Lyle W. Bivens* 239

Brain Surgery in Aggressive Epileptics *Vernon H. Mark* 260

INTRODUCTION

Modern psychology is a field that involves thousands of active researchers in laboratories, clinics, hospitals, and universities all over the world. The kinds of issues with which psychologists deal range from the treatment of schizophrenics to the function of individual brain cells. The subject matter is so diverse that it spills over into related fields such as biology, sociology, anthropology, philosophy, and law. In addition, many of the concerns of psychologists—for example, the effect on the viewer of violence on television or the use to which intelligence tests are put—are also of immediate concern to large numbers of nonpsychologists. Just about anything related to human behavior is being studied by some psychologist somewhere. The number of experiments and research reports grows continually, producing a torrent of new articles each year.

How can the beginning student gain a toehold in such a diverse field? I think that the best introduction is to read selected articles from the psychological literature. Thousands of articles are published each year in hundreds of periodicals in dozens of languages. Obviously, it is impossible for anyone to read more than a tiny fraction of these articles. What to do? Clearly, one must rely on some sort of sampling procedure, perhaps skimming many articles in order to select a more manageable number of key articles to read in greater depth. For the beginning student this is too often an insurmountable problem, as he or she does not have the experience or guidance to differentiate good from bad from indifferent research. Yet sooner or later (and I believe sooner is better) the serious student must come to grips with the original sources that form the mainstreams of modern psychological thought. Textbooks are useful for providing an organized approach to a field, but they must necessarily be general. Textbooks cannot be expected to provide the full flavor of the research on which they are based. This book is an attempt to provide the beginning student with a wedge into the current psychological literature. It is designed to be used in conjunction with any general introductory textbook but can, of course, be used in other ways as well.

The title of this collection of articles, *Contrast and Controversy in Modern Psychology*, reflects the hope that the selected articles represent areas of major concern to psychologists and others and are of more than simply historical or purely academic interest. Many of these articles deal with issues whose relevance spreads far beyond their origins, into therapy situations, into discussions concerning violence on television, and into the legislatures and courtrooms faced with decisions about psychosurgery. Thus one of the major biases in the selection of these articles was that they deal with issues that have widespread implications for our contemporary society. Informed citizens are necessary if we are to enact sensible laws and improve the quality of life, and the selection of the following articles reflects this concern.

There were other biases in the selection process too. I have tried to avoid the trivial but not the controversial. I have selected research that directly relates to human behavior, even though a substantial part of the psychological literature is based on work with experimental animals. I have tried to choose current issues rather than issues that are simply of historical importance. As I did this, it became apparent that many of the current issues are, in fact, "old wine in new bottles." That is, many of the concerns with which psychologists tried to come to grips in the past are still evident in these articles. This was a bonus, as there was not a conscious effort to achieve this end. I have tried to select articles that are, on the whole, well written and do not require advanced technical knowledge. If scientists stray too far in their writing and lose their nonscientist audience completely, there will be serious negative consequences. Of course, no one article will score 100% on all the preceding selection criteria. Finally, I have restricted the selections to articles published originally in English.

I sincerely hope this book will leave you frustrated. If so, you will want to get more of the available information, to dig deeper into one or more of the areas represented in these selections. If this book entices you into further reading, then it will have succeeded in its primary goal. Suggestions for further reading are to be found in the articles themselves and sometimes in the introductory remarks that precede each section.

I would like to acknowledge the help of the following individuals in the preparation of this book: Sheldon Cohen, Ann Elsner, Robert Grimm, Edward Lichtenstein, David Moody, Virginia Parr, and Wayne Wickelgren.

1. INTELLIGENCE:

Is It Just What Intelligence Tests Measure?

Perhaps no topic in psychology has been more controversial or explosive than intelligence testing. From the time of Francis Galton (1822–1911), controversies have raged over such questions as, What is intelligence? How do you measure it (assuming you can define it)? Is there a global general intelligence factor? Is it more realistic to try to measure individual skills and abilities? From the beginning of mental testing, the practical applications were apparent, and in fact, the development of many of the existing intelligence tests has occurred in the context of pressing practical needs. Current interest in intelligence testing is high. Arguments rage over almost every aspect of intelligence testing: how to do it, whether to do it at all, to what use to put the results. These arguments are not simply ivory-tower debates. Entry into colleges and universities and into numerous occupations currently depends, in part, on an individual's scores on some intelligence test.

The battle over intelligence testing is waged on several fronts, both theoretical and practical. On the theoretical side, Quinn McNemar in the first of the following two articles favors the concept that there is a general intelligence factor (or perhaps two fundamental factors, verbal and mathematical), while David McClelland comes out strongly against this concept, instead favoring tests that assess various competencies that differ according to real-life situations.

Woven into these articles are terms and concepts that may be unfamiliar to you. Such terms as *factor analysis* and *test validity* are used in these discussions. These should be good items for discussion with your instructor. Do not let jargon keep you from wrestling with these papers. While these two articles are remarkably free of the typical jargon of social scientists (one of the reasons they were selected), a certain amount of specialized vocabulary is unavoidable. I suspect there is simply no way to penetrate the scientific literature in any field without encountering a certain amount of new terminology. But we cannot let this terminology problem keep us away from this literature, or we will run the risk of a new priesthood of scientists who converse only with one another in their specialized secret language. This would be an intolerable situation for the great majority of people who are nonscientists (or scientists in only a narrow range of subjects). I think it would also be hazardous for the scientists in a specialized area to lose contact with the other branches of science and with their general audience. While this has already happened to some extent, we should resist further erosion of such important lines of communication.

LOST: OUR INTELLIGENCE? WHY?

Quinn McNemar, Stanford University

The Greeks had a word for it, but the Romans had a word with better survival properties. Regardless of the word, what is now called intelligence has been talked about for at least 2,000 years. And as long as 2,000 years before the advent of attempts to measure intelligence, there seems to have been recognition of the fact that individuals differ in intellectual ability.

The earlier attempts at measuring were based on either of two quite distinct conceptions: the Galton-Cattell idea that intellectual ability manifests itself in simple, discrimination functioning, and the Binet notion that cognitive ability reflects itself in more complex functioning. The Binet concept proved to be more fruitful, and by 1925 there was on the market, in addition to various versions of the Binet scale, a flood of group tests of so-called general intelligence.

A few words about definition may be in order. First, it might be claimed that no definition is required because all intelligent people know what intelligence is. It is the thing that the other guy lacks. Second, the fact that tests of general intelligence based on differing definitions tend to intercorrelate about as highly as their respective reliabilities permit indicates that, despite the diversity of definitions, the same function or process is being measured. Definitions can be more confusing than enlightening. Third, that confusion might have been anticipated is evident from a recent reexamination of the problem of definition by Miles (1957).

Address of the President to the Seventy-Second Annual Convention of the American Psychological Association, Los Angeles, September 5, 1964.

McNemar, Quinn. Lost: Our intelligence? Why? *American Psychologist*, 1964, *19*, 871–882.

This British chappie found himself struggling with the awful fact that the word "definition" itself has 12 definitions. Perhaps the resolution of this problem should be assigned to the newly formed Division of Philosophical Psychology, or maybe the problem should be forgotten since psychologists seem to have lost the concept of general intelligence.

Why has the concept been abandoned? Was it replaced by something else? By something better? Must we admit that the millions who have been tested on general intelligence tests were measured for a nonexistent function? If it is possible that the notion of general intelligence is not lost but merely gone astray, in what corners of what psychological fields should we search for it?

REASONS FOR DISCARDING THE IDEA OF GENERAL INTELLIGENCE

Apparently one reason why concepts are either discarded or modified beyond recognition is that too much is claimed for them. Among the supposed strikes against general intelligence are the following: the earlier false claims about IQ constancy; prediction failures in individual cases; unfounded claims that something innate was being measured by the tests; equally unfounded assertions that nothing but cultural effects were involved; the bugaboo that IQ tests reflect middle-class values; the notion that an IQ standing fosters undesirable expectations regarding school achievement; the idea that IQ differences are incompatible with democracy and lead to educational determinism; and finally, the great stress on general intelligence caused us to ignore other possible abilities.

This last point leads us right into the problem of factor analysis. Spearman died in battle defending his theory of *g*. Under pressure he reluctantly conceded that factors other than *g* might exist, and he frequently said, in effect, I told you so as long ago as 1906. Actually, Spearman was on the run before the invention of modern factor analysis, but it was not until Thurstone's (1938) first major application of his centroid factor method that Spearman's *g* became, seemingly, nonexistent. Thurstone said, "We have not found the general factor of Spearman," and "we cannot report any general common factor in the battery of fifty-six tests [p. vii]." As anticipated by some, Spearman was not prone to admit defeat. He reworked Thurstone's data, and a *g* was found, plus some group factors. He charged that Thurstone's rotational process had submerged the general factor.

American factorists found Thurstone convincing. The description of abilities in terms of seven primaries was an attractive package. The so-called primaries were more amenable to specific definition than the old hodgepodge called general intelligence. Despite the fact that Thurstone was able to replicate his findings on samples from two other populations, thus giving credence to his method and results, there were a couple of events that led to some turbulence in his seven-dimension rarified atmosphere. The first of these was a minor study by one of his own students, based on the intercorrelations Stanford-Binet items of 1916, in which the *g* refused to be rotated out. But rather than admit that this might be some kind of general intelligence, the author renamed it "maturational level." *Incidentally, this illustrates the first cardinal Principle of Psychological Progress: Give new names to old things.*

The second disturber of the neat little set of primaries, sans a *g*, resulted when Thurstone took the next logical step, that of constructing tests to measure the primaries. It was found that the primaries were themselves intercorrelated, whereas it had at the time been expected and hoped that they would be independent. The Thurstones (1941, p. 26) readily admitted that a general factor was needed to explain the interrelatedness of the primaries. This eventually led to the idea of oblique axes, which axes were regarded as representing the primaries as first-order factors, whereas the general factor pervading the primaries was dubbed a second-order factor. It began to look as though Spearman was being revisited, except for the little matter of labeling: anything called second-order could not possibly be regarded as of much importance. Furthermore, it could always be said that in the ability domain it is less difficult to attribute psychological meaningfulness to first-order than to second-order factors, so why pay much attention to the latter? Thus it was easy for most American factorists to drop the concept of general intelligence and to advocate that tests thereof, despite their proven usefulness over the years, should be replaced by tests of the primaries. Hence the emergence of differential aptitude batteries, about which more later.

Meanwhile, our British cousins did not tag along with the factor methods preferred on this side of the Atlantic. After all, it is possible to use factor methods that permit a sizable general factor, if such exists, to emerge as the very first factor. Being first, it is, presto, the most important, as indeed it is as a factor explaining, for the starting battery as a whole, more variance for more tests than attributable to any American-style primary factor. The methods preferred by the British also yield group factors, apt to bear the same name as the primaries, but of attenuated importance. Apparently, the British are skeptical of the multitude of ability factors being "discovered" in America. The structure of intellect that requires 120 factors may very well lead the British, and some of the rest of us, to regard our fractionization and fragmentation of ability into more and more factors of less and less importance as indicative of scatter-brainedness. This statement presumes that intellectual abilities are brain centered.

In practically all areas of psychological research, the demonstration of trivially small minutiae is doomed to failure because of random errors. Not so if your technique is factor analysis, despite its being based on the correlation coefficient—that slipperiest of all statistical measures. By some magic, hypotheses are tested without significance tests. This happy situation permits me to announce a Principle of Psychological Regress: *Use statistical techniques that lack inferential power.* This will not inhibit your power of subjective inference and consequently will progress you right back to the good old days when there was no strangling stat or sticky stix to make your insignificant data insignificant.

It may be a long time before we have an ivory-tower, strictly scientific resolution of the issue as to whether a scheme involving primary abilities plus a deemphasized *g* is preferable to one involving an emphasized *g* plus group factors. With bigger and better computers we will have bigger, though not necessarily better, factor-analytic studies, but it seems unlikely that such further studies will, in and of themselves, settle the issue under discussion. Until such time as some genius resolves the broader question, so ably discussed by Lee Cronbach in 1957, of the place, if any, of correlational method in a science that aspires to be experimental, we may have to turn to the criterion of social usefulness as a basis for judging whether it is wise to discard general intelligence. Like it or not, much of our heritage in this area is that earlier workers, from Binet on, had as their motivation the solution of social problems, and currently many in the area have a similar motivation.

THE BEARING OF SOCIAL USEFULNESS

In practice, if you believe that the concept of general intelligence has outlived its usefulness, you may choose from among several differential, or multiple, aptitude batteries which will provide measures of some of the so-called primary mental abilities. If you happen to believe that there is something to general ability, you can find tests to use. The novice looking for these latter tests may have to alert himself to the first Principle of Psychological Progress: *The test labels may have changed from "general intelligence" to "general classification" or "scholastic aptitude."* If you enjoy riding the fence, you might become a devotee of the practice of the College Board and others and measure just two abilities: Verbal and Quantitative.

This is certainly not the place to review the voluminous literature that amply demonstrates the practical utility of tests of general intelligence. Nor is it the place to catalog the misuses of the Stanford-Binet for purposes which Terman never claimed for it, or the misuses of the Wechsler scales for purposes which Wechsler *has* claimed for his scales. Neither the Binet nor the Wechsler provides a factorially pure, unidimensional measure of a *g*. The current Stanford-Binet was in reality constructed too early to benefit from the implication of factor analysis for test purity, whereas the Wechsler scales were based on the impossible premise that 10 or 11 subtests can simultaneously provide diagnostic subscores and a meaningful total score. Of the many group tests that apeared between 1920 and 1945 it can be said that few, if any, provide unidimensional measures of general intelligence. The chief difficulty is that most of them lead to a total score based on a mixture of verbal and mathematical material. Thus with two main sources of variance, marked qualitative differences can exist for quantitatively similar total scores. The College Board Educational Testing Service people have justifiably refrained from giving a total score involving verbal plus math, but there are those who question the usefulness of the Board's math score, and there are those who criticize the Educational Testing Service for failing to change over to a differential aptitude battery.

Let us next turn to a somewhat more detailed examination of the various so-called multiple aptitude batteries. What and who influenced whom in the development of these batteries is difficult to disentangle. At the risk of oversimplification, it might be said that two prime influences operated.

First, the early factor studies by the Thurstones, by Holzinger, and by Guilford are the progenitors of the Science Research Associates' Primary Mental Abilities (PMA) Test, the Holzinger-Crowder Unifactor Tests, the Guilford-Zimmerman Aptitude Survey, and the Segel-Raskin Multiple Aptitude Tests (MAT).

The second influence, which seems to have emerged from testing experience in the Armed Services during World War II, is the job-element approach, an approach which may or may not differ from the old job-analysis method. For whatever jobs you are dealing with, you study the activities involved in order to decide what aptitudes are called for. Whether or not these aptitudes have been previously isolated by factor analysis is totally irrelevant. It is hoped that some jobs will have aptitudes in common so that the needed number of tests will be less than the number of jobs. The one battery that is built on this approach is the Flanagan Aptitude Classification Tests, a battery that just happens to have the catchy abbreviation FACT. If we cannot muster any facts in psychology, we can at least have FACT scores!

A cross between testing for factorially defined abilities and job-element derived aptitudes is apparently involved in the General Aptitude Test Battery (GATB) of the United States Employment Service and the Differential Aptitudes Tests (DAT) of the Psychological Corporation, since in both batteries some of the tests seem to have sprung from factor-analysis results and some tests seem to have been thrown in as possible predictors of specific performances.

It is not our purpose to rank order the seven above-mentioned multi-test batteries, but a few remarks may be relevant as background for the sequel. Apparently the Employment Service's GATB was made available (but not put on the commercial market) with the idea that there would be a continuing program of validities studies. The accumulation is now impressive. For the DAT of the Psychological Corporation there is an over-abundance of data on validity, collected and analyzed prior to marketing the test. Both the Science Research Associates' PMA and FACT were made available without backing for the claimed usefulness of the tests. Belatedly, that is, six years after its appearance, some evidence on the predictive validity of FACT has been reported. Validity information for the other three batteries is not entirely lacking, though far from ample. Some will have noted that that fuzzy dodge called factor validity is being ignored here.

Now to get back to our main theme, to what extent have the 7 batteries contributed to the demise of general intelligence? In attempting to answer this, one encounters a paradox: Some test authors want to eat their cake and have it too. They attempt to measure factors and *g* with the same instrument. This is understandable in a couple of instances. Three of the 15 tests of the Employment Service's GATB were included to provide a measure of general intelligence, apparently because the authors still saw some merit in a *g* and were not committed to the factor schemata. Holzinger and Crowder suggest a weighted score for a measure of *g*, perhaps because of Holzinger's long-time alignment with Spearman. The real teaser is why Thurstone ever sanctioned, if he did, the summing of the Science Research Associates' PMA scores to obtain an IQ. One has the uncomfortable feeling that his publishers wished to *g* garnish the factor cake to make it more palatable in the marketplace.

Although Segel says nothing in his 1957 article about a general score from the Segel-Raskin MAT, the test publishers say that, in addition to yielding scores for four factors, it also provides a "Scholastic Potential" score. Perhaps Flanagan has not completely broken with tradition, since he states that four tests of the FACT battery measure "General College Aptitude"—a statement made with the same lack of empirical validity as the claim, which should be anxiety producing for those of you who fly a certain airline, that your highly paid pilot shares four of the aptitudes of a plumber!

Apparently, Guilford and Zimmerman and the test people at the Psychological Corporation are willing to stick to the sound principle that a differential test battery cannot provide factor scores that can be summed to obtain a meaningful IQ, or measure of a *g*.

Parenthetically, it might be said that the California Test of Mental Maturity (CTMM), which, according to the publisher's 1963 catalog, was originally "designed as a group test of intelligence patterned after the individual Stanford-Binet," serves as an illustration of factor icing a *g* cake. Some multitest batteries and the CTMM have a Madison Avenue advantage: The advertising claims the measurement of not only factors but also *g;* not only *g* but also factors. This measurement absurdity is all too apt to go unrecognized by many test users and hence a sales advantage for the aptitude battery that produces both factor scores and an IQ.

Just how successful have the multitest batteries been? Since by far the most extensive social use of tests has been, and continues to be, in the schools, let us look at the evidence of validity studies therein. As indicated previously, little is known about the predictive usefulness of some of the seven batteries discussed above. The DAT of the Psychological Corporation is the only battery for which adequate predictive (and concurrent) validity data, derived from school sources, are available. It is also the battery that has fared best in the hands of the test reviewers; therefore, if we allow the case for differential batteries to rest thereon, we will be looking at the best. So what is the story?

Recall that the hoped-for advantage of a multitest battery over the old-fashioned general intelligence test was that it would have greater predictive power, a power which could manifest itself in higher validity coefficients for specific subject matter and, perhaps, for overall achievement. It was hoped that such a battery would be truly differential in that particular factors (or subtests) would correlate higher with achievement in some areas than in other areas. Presumably each factor (or subtest) should have unique usefulness. If a battery were truly differential, it would be a boon to school guidance personnel.

Now the manual of the DAT of the Psychological Corporation contains a staggering total of 4,096—yes, I counted 'em—validity coefficients. With such a large pool to draw from, one could by gracious selection "show" that the DAT is the answer to the prayer of every counselor, male or female, or by malicious selection one could "prove" that the DAT is far worse than any test ever published. The validity coefficients range all the way down to −.37, which is presumably a chance deviation downward from 0, and all the way up to .90, which is likely not a chance deviation downward from unity. But ranges tell us nothing. After a careful perusal of the 4,096 correlations, it seems safe to summarize DAT validities as follows:

1. Verbal Reasoning (analogies to most of you) is the best single predictor; Language Usage, as represented by a sentence test dealing with grammar and word usage, and admittedly more achievement than aptitude, is a close second.
2. Numerical Ability, as measured by a test of simple arithmetic operations, designed to tap arithmetic reasoning without the usual verbal component, is the best predictor of achievement in school mathematics. It does not, however, correlate as well with grades in science as does Verbal Reasoning.
3. Aside from the Numerical Ability test, the only other test that shows differential power as a predictor is the Spelling test. If you cannot spell, you may have trouble learning shorthand.
4. The remaining five tests in the battery simply fail to show compelling evidence that they are good in the differential predictive sense. For the Mechanical Reasoning and the Clerical Speed and Accuracy tests this may be understandable in that little of school curricula for Grades 8 through 12 requires such abilities, but one would expect that Abstract Reasoning and Space Relations would fare better than they seem to.

Such data as we have been able to locate for the other six multitest batteries tend to support these findings on the DAT. Aside from tests of numerical ability having differential value for predicting school grades in math, it seems safe to conclude that the worth of the multitest batteries as differential predictors of achievement in school has not been demonstrated. Incidentally, the fact that the Verbal and Numerical tests stand out as the only two useful predictors tends to provide some support for the Educational Testing Service–College Board practice of providing scores for just these two abilities.

And now we come to a very disturbing aspect of the situation. Those who have constructed and marketed multiple aptitude batteries and advocated that they be used instead of tests of general intelligence seem never to have bothered to demonstrate whether or not multitest batteries provide better predictions than the old-fashioned scale of general intelligence. Be it noted that we are not discussing experimental editions of tests. Some say that insofar as a test publisher provides validity data for a new battery it is not necessary to show that the validities are, for the given school condition, better than those of other tests. With this, one can agree, but only in case no claims are made, explicitly or implicitly, regarding superior merits for the new battery.

It is far from clear that tests of general intelligence have been outmoded by the multitest batteries as the more useful predictors of school achievement. Indeed, one can use the vast accumulation of data on the validity of the Psychological Corporation's DAT to show that better predictions are possible via old-fashioned general intelligence tests. Consider the fact that a combination of the tests Verbal Reasoning (analogies) and Numerical Ability would be, in terms of content, very similar to many group tests of general intelligence. Consider also that an equally weighted combination of these two tests correlates in the mid-.80s with the Otis S-A, Higher Form. Then when you turn to a careful study of the empirical validities as reported in the DAT manual, you will not be surprised at the outcome of the application of a little arithmetic, which leads to the definite conclusion that a simple unweighted combination of the Verbal Reasoning and Numerical Ability tests predicts as well as or, in most instances, better than any subtest taken singly or in the differential sense.

The manual for the DAT contains the following statement (Bennett, Seashore, & Wesman, 1952):

> Apparently the *Verbal Reasoning* and *Numerical Ability* tests can serve most purposes for which a general mental ability test is usually given in addition to providing differential clues useful to the counselor. Hence, the use of the so-called intelligence test is apparently unnecessary where the *Differential Aptitude Tests* are already being used [p. 71].

Anyone who disagrees with this quotation could with better justification say that an intelligence test can serve nearly all, if not all, the purposes for which a multiple aptitude battery is given in the schools because the former, in general, is a better predictor and because, as we saw earlier, the differential clues are too fragmentary to be of use to the counselor. And there is a bonus: one classroom period of testing compared to six periods. A second bonus: much less costly. A third bonus: fewer scores to confuse the already confused minds of most school counselors.

Thus we come to the conclusion that general intelligence has not been lost in the trend to test more and more abilities; it was merely misplaced by a misplaced emphasis on a hope that a lot of us, including the speaker, once entertained, a hope that in turn was based on a misplaced faith in factor analysis: *the* hope that factors, when and if measured, would find great usefulness in the affairs of society. By the criterion of social usefulness, the multiple aptitude batteries have been found wanting. Now I have no desire to furnish ammunition for those test critics who would have us stop all testing merely because they find a trivially faulty item in a standardized test. At a time when there is shouting about the tyranny of the testers and the brass of the brain watchers, at a time when school people are showing resentment at the disruption caused by too many national testing programs, at a time when federal and state legislators are all too willing to write legislation that places restrictions on the use of tests, and at a time when both majorities and minorities are being denied the benefits of test-based guidance because certain well-intentioned persons fail to realize that scores for the underprivileged minorities are useful indices of *immediate,* or present, functioning—at a time when all these and other forces are operating to throw out the tests, it is high time for the profession to establish a bureau of standards to test the tests instead of coasting down a road that is tinged with some of the trappings of Madison Avenue. Better to have informed internal control than ignorant, hostile, external control.

INTELLIGENCE ELSEWHERE?

Aside from the near loss of the idea that progress in school may depend on general intelligence, one wonders whether intelligence has come to be regarded as unimportant in other areas.

Any of you who have money invested in stocks and wish some reassurance regarding the intelligence level of business and industry managers should read Edwin Ghiselli's (1963) Bingham Lecture. His summary of his own work indicates that the average intelligence of those in the upper and middle management levels falls at the ninety-sixth percentile of the population. Thomas Harrell (1961) came to a similar conclusion. Furthermore, management level is correlated with intelligence. You can be too dumb to succeed as a manager. Also you can be too bright to be a managerial success! Now it must be admitted that little, if anything, is known about whether management success might be better predicted by measures of factor-analytic defined abilities. On this you are free to guess. Most of you will have already guessed my guess.

A one-by-one cataloguing of what we know or do not know about what abilities contribute to success within various occupational and professional groups would merely add to the dullness of this presentation, so let us turn to some of the more esoteric fields of psychology to see whether the concept of general intelligence has or has had any relevance. One such field, and a very broad one, is creativity. Anyone who peeks over the fence into this field is apt to be astonished at the visible chaos. The definition of creativity is confounded by the diversity of subareas within the field; the criterion problems are far from licked; and so little is known about the creative process that measuring instruments are seemingly chosen on a trial-and-error basis.

We might presume that the role, if any, of general intelligence in creativity would increase as we pass from art to music, to architecture, to literature and drama, to science. Your presumption about the ordering may be different and more nearly correct. I would like to discuss briefly the extremes of my ordering.

At the risk of being called a heretic and a has-been statistician, I would like first to resort to the single case of a painter, examples of whose works were reproduced in color recently by Desmond Morris (1962) in a journal called *Portfolio and Art News Annual.* To my uncultured eye these paintings have the general appearance of the so-called school of modern art, and the running comment on the paintings involves what I must presume is the jargon of contemporary art critics: talk about self-rewarding activities, compositional control, calligraphic differentiation, thematic variation, optimum heterogeneity, and universal imagery. Since authors may use pen names, I would guess that this painter is using "Congon" as a "brush" name. Supposedly, by now some of you will be guessing that this single case is of interest in the context of this paper because of Congon's IQ. Well, because of this painter's underprivileged cultural background, no test scores are available. Congon, despite striking contribution to art, happens to be a chimp. Aside from a rather obvious conclusion, one wonders what would emerge from a blind (as to source) analysis of Congon's paintings by the personality boys. We might even tell them that Congon was breast fed.

Without in any way implying that creativity in the arts is unimportant, we hasten on to scientific creativity, a specific area in which it seems likely, because of the Sputnik-inspired spurt of interest, that we can learn something of the role, if any, of general intelligence. But immediately we encounter skulls that have been cracked on the criterion problem.

One elaborate study (C.W. Taylor, Smith, Ghiselin, and Ellison, 1961) on a sample of 166 physical scientists working at Air Force research centers came up with 150—yes, believe it or not—150 *criteria* of scientific productivity and creativity. By combining some scores and eliminating others, the number of criteria was reduced to 48. A factor analysis of the intercorrelations of the 48 reduced the number to 14 "categories." Apparently the 150 original criterion measures included everything except success at turning on a kitchen faucet, so one need not be surprised at the outcome of the factor analysis. For example, one factor-derived criterion of scientific productivity and creativity is "likableness"; another is "status seeking"; another is extent of membership in scientific and professional societies—the joiners, no doubt.

The fact that the intercorrelations among the 14 criterion categories derived from factor analysis range from −.08 to +.55, with a median of only .18, indicates either criterion complexity or else a whale of a lot of vagueness as to what is meant by productivity and creativity in science.

Now this criterion mess emerged from a study of interview results of 166 physical scientists, but nearly half of these so-called scientists were engineers, and the education of the total group indicates only two years of graduate work on the average; so when is a scientist a scientist a scientist?

The next step in this study was to collect data on 107 of these so-called scientists, for a whopping total of 130 potential predictors, which, when pitted against 17 criterion measures, produced 2,210 validity coefficients. The distribution of these, excluding 30 values involving un-cross-validated empirical keys, almost restores one's faith in the random-sampling distribution of correlation coefficients around zero! There were 16 predictors based on aptitude tests, hence 16 × 17, or 272, validities for this area. Since only 4% of them reach the 5% level, we can do no more than accept the null hypothesis: Aptitude ain't important in scientific productivity and creativity. The idea that some scientists are more equal in ability than others apparently is not true.

But this criterion-based study did not contribute to my worry about the role of general intelligence. The failure to include a general intelligence measure as a potential predictor may be interpreted as indicating that the authors already had the answer.

Let us turn to another criterion-based study (D.W. Taylor, 1961). The criterion measures for creativity and productivity were based on the checking by supervisors of statements that had been scaled by Thurstone's equal-appearing interval method. Creativity and productivity, so gauged, correlated .69 with each other on a sample of 103 researchers (electronics scientists and engineers). For this same group, intelligence as measured by the Terman Concept Mastery Test (CMT) correlated only .20 or less with the criteria. Two Psychological Corporation tests and an American Institute for Research test did a little better. Creativity is slightly more predictable than productivity. Insofar as these two criteria are themselves valid, the findings indicate that within a group of research workers, precious little of the variance in creativity, and still less in productivity, can be predicted by the tests.

A third study (MacKinnon, 1962) based on criterion (rated) measures of performance was concerned with the creativity of architects. Although the author reports that *within* a creative sample the correlation is essentially zero between intelligence (CMT) and rated creativity, it is not clear from the context what is meant by "within" sample. If this means within the sample of 40 creative architects selected as the "most creative" in the country, then we indeed have such a drastic restriction in range on the *criterion* variable that little, if any, correlation can be expected for any and all predictors. Now the author says, without presenting any evidence, that "over the whole range of intelligence and creativity there is, of course, a positive relationship between the two variables [p. 488]." One wonders just what is meant by creativity in architecture as rated either by fellow architects or by editors of architectural journals. If judged creativity reflects engineering-structural innovation, then intelligence would likely be a correlate; if judged creativity depends on new artistic designs, then the intelligence component would likely be of less importance. It would seem that when the author says we "may have overestimated . . . the role of intelligence in creative achievement" [p. 493], he should have included some marked qualifications as to what type of creativity he had in mind.

That such qualification is indeed necessary is supplied by a funding of still another investigator (Barron, 1963). For a group of highly creative writers it was estimated, by way of the Terman CMT, that their average IQ is about 140, which we interpret as meaning that a high IQ is a necessary though not sufficient condition for outstanding success as a writer. On the basis of his own studies and those of other persons, this same investigator suggests that "over the total range of intelligence and creativity a low positive correlation" of .40 probably obtains. This sweeping generalization is for all areas of creativity.

And speaking of sweeping generalizations, consider the suggestion in a 1961 study (Holland, 1961) that "we need to use nonintellectual criteria in the selection of students for scholarships and fellowships [p. 146]." The author did not say so, but presumably he meant in addition to intellectual ability; maybe he did not, since he had previously concluded that "intelligence has little or no relationship to creative performance in arts and science [p. 143]" at the high school level. His data back up this conclusion, as might have been expected when correlations are based on groups restricted in range to the top 1%!

If the foregoing examples of criterion-based studies of creativity seem to indicate that general intelligence is relatively unimportant for creativity, it should be remembered that drastic but unknown or unspecified curtailment of range exists for both ability and criteria. Why do correlational studies under such adverse circumstances?

Next, we turn to a few studies of creativity which cannot be criticized because of restriction of range on the criteria. These studies simply avoid this problem by never having actual criterion information. The approach is to claim that certain tests, which typically are scored for novel responses or novel solutions to problems, *are* measures of creativity, with no evidence whatsoever that the tests have predictive validity for nontest, real-life creative performance. This bit of ignorance does not prove to be a handicap to those who think that creativity can be studied without the nuisance of obtaining criterion measures. We reluctantly accept the test-based criteria solely for the sake of seeing what happens to general intelligence as a part of the picture. Time permits only three examples.

We first note that general intelligence has not manifested itself as a correlate of so-called creativity tests in the factor-analytic studies of creativity. The explanation for this is easily found—no measures of general intelligence are used in these studies. When discussing his plans for studying creativity, a certain author (Guilford, 1950) said that "we must look well beyond the boundaries of the IQ if we are to fathom the domain of creativity [p. 448]." He went on to say the conception "that creative talent is to be accounted for in terms of high intelligence or

IQ . . . is not only inadequate but has been largely responsible for lack of progress in the understanding of creative people [p. 454]." With a part of this, one can agree, but does it follow that one should prejudge the role of general intelligence as a source of variance in creativity tests or factors derived therefrom? Does the failure to include an IQ test help one learn the extent to which one must go beyond the boundaries of the IQ to fathom creativity? Apparently the author, although willing to predict that the correlations between IQ and the many types of creativity tests "are only moderate or low," was unwilling to include an IQ test for the sake of finding out. However, negation by omission is not very convincing.

That at least one test bearing the label "creativity" is correlated more than moderately with IQ is evidenced by the value of .67 (average for boys and girls) for the carefully chosen sample of 15-year-olds in Project Talent (Shaycoft, Dailey, Orr, Neyman, & Sherman, 1963). This sample-stable r (based on a total N of 7,648) becomes .80 when corrected for attenuation.

In a recent extensive study (Getzels & Jackson, 1962), already extensively criticized, creativity is defined as the sum of scores on five tests (median intercorrelation of only .28). Although the investigators use the sum score for most of their analyses, they do not bother to report the correlation of creativity, so defined, with IQ. From the published report, I have ascertained (via the correlation-of-sums formula) that creativity and IQ correlate to the extent of .40 for the total of 533 cases. Now this r of .40 has been greatly attenuated because of three things: first, the usual measurement errors; second, the cases were highly selected on IQ (mean of 132); third, the IQs are a mixture from the Stanford-Binet, Henmon-Nelson, and Wechsler Intelligence Scale for Children (the use of regression-estimated Binet IQs from the other two scales aggravates rather than improves the mixture). We deduce that intelligence and the creativity tests used here have far more common variance than the authors believe.

Much is made of the finding that the creativity tests tended to correlate higher than did IQ with verbal-content school achievements. Again the IQ comes in for an unfair drubbing because of the same mixture of IQ scores and, what is more pertinent, because of explicit selective curtailment on the IQ variable and only incidental selection on the creativity variable.

Of more importance to the present paper is the analysis, by these same authors, based on a high IQ group and a high creative group, these groups being selected as the top 20% for each variable but excluding those who were in the top 20% on both variables. These two selected groups were then contrasted on total school achievement (and a host of other variables that are of no interest here). The mean IQ for the high IQ group was 150, whereas the mean IQ for the high creative group was 127, yet the achievement means of the two groups were "unexpectedly" equally superior to the school population mean despite the 23-point difference in mean IQ.

The authors say that it "*is* quite surprising" that the high creativity group achieved so well. From this it is concluded that the "creative instruments account for a significant portion of the variance in school achievement [p. 24]," and the subsequent argument implies that creativity is more important for ordinary school achievement than is the IQ. Now anyone who is at all familiar with a three-variate problem will not be "unexpectedly" surprised at the foregoing results. Indeed, if the authors had bothered to give the three basic correlations among the three variables (IQ, creativity, and total school achievement) for the entire group, any person versed in simple multivariate analysis could deduce the results. Furthermore, he could deduce a further result (and this one has been overlooked by the critics) which might be unpleasantly surprising to the thesis of these authors: namely, the high IQ and the high creative groups did equally well in school achievement despite an unreported difference in mean creativity that is of the same order as the much stressed difference in IQ.[1] Utilizing the half-blind logic of the authors, one can say that creative ability is not as important as IQ for school achievement—just the opposite of their proposition.

Now the fact that seven of nine replications of this study confirm the original findings merely indicates that repetition of the same faulty design and false logic will lead to the same false conclusions. The design being used is such that if two variables are equally correlated with a third, the conclusion will be reached that the two are actually unequally correlated with the third. This is the neatest trick of the decade for supplying educationists with an antidote for the IQ virus. I cannot refrain from saying at this point that, although discouraged, I am still hopeful that people who do statistical studies will first learn a modicum of elementary statistics!

Time does not permit a discussion of other studies in which creativity is defined in terms of test performance instead of being based on actual creativity of the sort prized by society. In summary of this brief on creativity studies, I would like to offer a few dogmatic-sounding observations. First, one need not be surprised at the fact that so-called creativity tests do not yield high correlations with IQ tests—but the correlations are generally far higher than those found in typical studies with range restrictions. I would anticipate that for normalized scores, the uncurtailed scatters for IQ versus creativity tests will be bivariate normal. Second, if we have honest to goodness criterion measures of literary or architectural or scientific creativity, the scatter diagram between IQ and such creativity (not normalized, since it makes sense to expect askewed distribution for actual creativity) will be triangular in shape for unselected cases. That is, at the high IQ levels there will be a very wide range of creativity, whereas as we go down to average IQ and on down to lower levels, the scatter for creativity will be less and less. Having a high IQ is not a guarantee of being creative; having a low IQ means creativity is impossible. Third, it remains to be seen whether or not the so-called creativity tests and/or factors derived therefrom have appreciable value as predictors of actual creative performance. Such tests may or may not yield better predictions than a test of general intelligence. Fourth, as far as I am concerned, to claim factorial validity for creativity tests, along with definitions of creativity in terms of tests, is an unwarranted avoidance of the fundamental problem of validity.

The recently renewed interest in gifted children, along with the flurry of creativity studies, has led to a reexamination of methods for identifying the gifted. It has long been recognized that identification in terms of high IQ is too narrow—those gifted in such areas as art and music would be overlooked. The argument against the IQ is now (Torrance, 1962) being reinforced by the claim that the selection of the top 20% on IQ would mean the exclusion of 70% of the top 20% on tested creativity. This startling statistic, which implies a correlation of only .24 between IQ and creativity, is being used to advocate the use of creativity tests for identifying the gifted. Be it noted that these creativity tests will also miss those gifted in art and music.

We are being told that it is important "to identify creative talent early in life." Hence you need not be surprised that the search goes down to the kindergarten level, with claims of successful identification. The creativity tests are presumed to be better for this purpose than the IQ tests because of the failure of the IQ to be constant, an argument that completely overlooks the fact that the IQ does have some constancy whereas absolutely nothing is known about the stability of standings on creativity tests. The IQ tests, known to be imperfectly valid as predictors of outstanding achievement in life, are to be replaced by the creativity tests, known to be of unknown validity as predictors. Anyway, progress, defined as change, is in the offing.

The IQ is being linked with *learning* as an outmoded educational objective; the new objective involves an emphasis on *thinking*. Somehow or other creativity, not general intelligence, is being associated with thinking. The horrible idea of underachievers and overachievers, in terms of expectancies based on the IQ, will be abolished. But no thought is given to the fact that the use of creativity tests will simply define a new crop of under- and overachievers.

In an apparent zeal to rid us of general intelligence, it is argued that measured creativity is significantly related to ordinary school achievement. Maybe so, but never, never does one find complete data reported as to the relative sizes of validity coefficients. And as we have seen, the technique being used will show that equal coefficients are unequal. Why not the full facts, free of fantasy?

An additional difficulty is not being faced by those who would replace IQ tests by creativity tests, or creative-thinking tests. The factor-analytic studies indicate either no, or a trivially small, general creativity factor in these tests, yet these self-characterized "bold, adventurous" reformers (see Torrance, 1963) do not hesitate to advocate a total score which is nearly devoid of meaning. Changing the curriculum to the teaching of creativity and creative thinking will not overcome this measurement difficulty. Again, I express the hope that the IQ is replaced by something better rather than by something worse.

There are other areas, such as reasoning, problem solving, and concept formation, in which one might expect to find some consideration of intelligence as an aspect. One might also expect that investigators of thinking would have something to say about individual differences in thinking being dependent upon intelligence, but for some unintelligent reason, these people seem never to mention intelligence. Surely it cannot be inferred that thinking about thinking does not involve intelligence!

IN CONCLUSION

It has been the thesis of this paper that the concept of general intelligence, despite being maligned by a few, regarded as a second-order function by some, and discarded or ignored by others, still has a rightful place in the science of psychology and in the practical affairs of man. It has not been argued that the nature of general intelligence is well understood. Much, however, has been written about its nature. Over 40 years ago (*Intelligence,* 1921a, 1921b) an editor secured and published the reasoned views of 13 well-known test psychologists. Later Spearman set forth his speculations about the nature of *g*. Prior to these, Binet had, of course, given much thought to the problem.

More recent discussions exist. Hebb (1949) has considered the problem from the viewpoint of neurology and brain functioning. Cyril Burt (1955), always a vociferous defender of the concept of general intelligence, has reviewed the evidence for a *g* and restated the idea, dreadful to some, that intelligence is innate. Perhaps it was inevitable that Raymond Cattell (1963), who has camped with the general intelligence contingent, should gaze into his crystal *n*-dimensional factor ball and find evidence for crystallized as opposed to fluid general intelligence. Joseph McVicker Hunt's (1961) book on *Intelligence and Experience* is in large part devoted to questions pertaining to the nature of intelligence.

By far the most provocative recent discussion that I have encountered is the closely reasoned 44-page paper by Keith Hayes (1962). He puts forth a motivational-experiential theory of intelligence. In essence, he presumes that there are hereditary differences in motivation. "Experience-producing drives" and environmental differences produce differences in experience, which in turn, by way of learning, lead to differences in ability. Therefore, differences called intellectual are nothing more than acquired abilities. I think that Hayes has ignored the possibility of individual differences in learning ability, but if such a formulation leads to experimental manipulation of variables, we may eventually make progress in an area that has too long been dominated by ever increasing fractionization by factor analysis, with little thought as to how the fractured parts get put together into a functioning whole.

Abilities or capacities or aptitudes or intellectual skills or whatever you choose to call them, are measured in terms of response products to standardized stimulus situations. The *stimulus* is presented to an *organism* which by some *process* comes up with a *response;* thus any attempt to theorize and/or study intellect in terms of a simple stimulus-response (S-R) paradigm seems doomed to failure unless drastically modified and complicated by the insertion of O for organism and P for process.

There have been thousands of researches on the multitudinous variations from organism to organism, and the results fill books on individual differences. These studies can be roughly classified into two types. First, those that ascertain the intercorrelations among scaled response products to various stimulus situations, known as tests, have to do with the structure of intellect; and whether the resulting factors are anything more than dimensions for describing individual differences need not concern us here. The second type of study seeks the nontest correlates of test performance, and whether or not any of the found correlates can be regarded as explaining individual differences is not of interest here. Both types of studies certainly force one to stress the overwhelming diversity exhibited among the organisms.

But these studies of individual differences never come to grips with the *process*, or operation, by which a given organism achieves an intellectual response. Indeed, it is difficult to see how the available individual difference data can be used even as a starting point for generating a theory as to the process nature of general intelligence or of any other specified ability.

As a basis for a little speculation, let us conceive of a highly hypothetical situation in which the two members of a pair of identical twins, with identical experiences, find themselves cast up on an uninhabited tropical island. Let us assume that they are at the supergenius level, far beyond that of your favorite man of genius. Let us also assume that, though highly educated in the sciences, they have been fortunate enough to have had zero exposure to psychology. In addition, we presume that, being highly involved and abstracted in the pursuit of science, they have never noticed what we call individual differences in abilities.

A quick exploration of the island assures them that food is plentiful, that shelter is available, and that clothing is not a necessity. To allay the boredom that they foresee as an eternity in this laborless heaven, they decide to spend their time in the further pursuit of science, but the lack of the wherewithal for constructing gadgets rules out any research in the physical sciences. Having had a college course in Bugs and Bites, they proceed to study the life of the island's insects, then the habits of the birds, and the antics of a couple of monkeys. The manner in which the monkeys adjust to the environment leads them to set up some trial situations for more systematic observation. Needless to say, the monkeys show evidence of what we call learning and what we call problem solving.

Eventually they decide that attempting to outwit each other might be more fun than being outwitted by the monkeys, so they begin to cook up and use games and problems for this purpose. This activity leads each to speculate and introspect about how problems are invented and how solved. Then by cleverly designed experiments, preceded of course by theory, they set forth highly developed laws and principles about what we call reasoning and problem solving. Incidentally, they switch back and forth between the roles of experimenter and subject, there being no college sophomores available. They continue for years the study of their own mental operations, constantly on the alert for new phenomena to investigate.

And now with apologies to the ancient Greeks, who did have some ideas along these lines, we leave with you the 64-million drachma question: Will our two identical supergeniuses, being totally unaware of individual differences, ever hit upon and develop a concept of intelligence?

REFERENCES

Barron, F. *Creativity and psychological health.* Princeton, N.J.: Van Nostrand, 1963.

Bennett, G. K., Seashore, H. G., & Wesman, A. G. *Differential aptitude tests, manual* (2nd ed.). New York: Psychological Corporation, 1952.

Burt, C. L. "The evidence for the concept of intelligence." *British Journal of Psychology,* 1955, *25,* 158–177.

Cattell, R. B. Theory of fluid and crystallized intelligence: A critical experiment. *Journal of Educational Psychology,* 1963, *54,* 1–22.

Cronbach, L. J. The two disciplines of scientific psychology. *American Psychologist,* 1957, *12,* 671-684.

Getzels, J. W., & Jackson, P. W. *Creativity and intelligence.* New York: Wiley, 1962.

Ghiselli, E. E. Managerial talent. *American Psychologist,* 1963, *18,* 631–642.

Guilford, J. P. Creativity. *American Psychologist,* 1950, *5,* 444–454.

Harrell, T. H. *Manager's performance and personality.* Cincinnati, Ohio: South-Western, 1961.

Hayes, K. J. Genes, drives, and intellect. *Psychological Report,* 1962, *10,* 299–342.

Hebb, D. O. *The organization of behavior.* New York: Wiley, 1949.

Holland, J. L. Creative and academic performance among talented adolescents. *Journal of Educational Psychology,* 1961, *52,* 136–147.

Hunt, J. McV. *Intelligence and experience.* New York: Ronald Press, 1961.

Intelligence and its measurement: A symposium. *Journal of Educational Psychology,* 1921a, *12,* 123–147.

______. *Journal of Educational Psychology,* 1921b, *12,* 195–216.

MacKinnon, D. W. The nature and nurture of creative talent. *American Psychologist,* 1962, *17,* 484–495.

Miles, T. R. On defining intelligence. *British Journal of Educational Psychology,* 1957, *27,* 153–165.

Morris, D. The biology of art. *Portfolio and Art News Annual,* 1962, No. 6, 52–63, 122–124.

Segel, D. The multiple aptitude tests. *Personnel Guidance Journal,* 1957, *35,* 424–432.

Shaycoft, M. F., Dailey, J. T., Orr, D. B., Neyman, C. A., Jr., & Sherman, S. E. *Project talent: Studies of a complete age group—age 15.* Pittsburgh: Univ. of Pittsburgh Press, 1963. (Mimeograph)

Taylor, C. W., Smith, W. R., Ghiselin, B., & Ellison, R. Explorations in the measurement and predictions of contributions of one sample of scientists (Technical Report No. 61-96). USAF ASD, 1961.

Taylor, D. W. Variables related to creativity and productivity among men in two research laboratories. In C. W. Taylor & F. Barron (Eds.), *Scientific creativity.* New York: Wiley, 1961.

Thurstone, L. L. *Primary mental abilities.* Chicago: Univ. of Chicago Press, 1938.

Thurstone, L. L., & Thurstone, T. G. *Factorial studies of intelligence.* Chicago: Univ. of Chicago Press, 1941.

Torrance, E. P. *Guiding creative talent.* Englewood Cliffs, N.J.: Prentice-Hall, 1962.

______. *Education and the creative potential.* Minneapolis: Univ. of Minnesota Press, 1963.

Yamamoto, K. Role of creative thinking and intelligence in high school achievement. *Psychological Record,* 1964, *14,* 783–789.

NOTES

1. Since this was written, the replication study of Yamamoto (1964) gives data that corroborate this deduction.

TESTING FOR COMPETENCE RATHER THAN FOR "INTELLIGENCE"

David C. McClelland, Harvard University

The testing movement in the United States has been a success, if one judges success by the usual American criteria of size, influence, and profitability. Intelligence and aptitude tests are used nearly everywhere by schools, colleges, and employers. It is a sign of backwardness not to have test scores in the school records of children. The Educational Testing Service alone employs about 2,000 people, annually administers Scholastic Aptitude Tests to thousands of aspirants to college, and makes enough money to support a large basic research operation. Its tests have tremendous power over the lives of young people by stamping some of them "qualified" and others "less qualified" for college work. Until recent exceptions were made (over the protest of some), the tests have served as a very efficient device for screening out black, Spanish-speaking and other minority applicants to colleges. Admissions officers have protested that they take other qualities besides test achievements into account in granting admission, but careful studies by Wing and Wallach (1971) and others have shown that this is true only to a very limited degree.

This article contains the substance of remarks made at a public lecture given at the Educational Testing Service, Princeton, New Jersey, January 4, 1971. Requests for reprints should be sent to David C. McClelland, Department of Psychology and Social Relations, Harvard University, William James Hall, Cambridge, Massachusetts 02138.

McClelland, David C. Testing for competence rather than for "intelligence." *American Psychologist,* 1973, *28,* 1–14.

Why should intelligence or aptitude tests have all this power? What justifies the use of such tests in selecting applicants for college entrance or jobs? On what assumptions is the success of the movement based? They deserve careful examination before we go on rather blindly promoting the use of tests as instruments of power over the lives of many Americans.

The key issue is obviously the *validity* of so-called intelligence tests. Their use could not be justified unless they were valid, and it is my conviction that the evidence for their validity is by no means so overwhelming as most of us rather unthinkingly had come to think it was. In point of fact, most of us just believed the results that the testers gave us, without subjecting them to the kind of fierce skepticism that greets, for example, the latest attempt to show that ESP exists. My objectives are to review skeptically the main lines of evidence for the validity of intelligence and aptitude tests and to draw some inferences from this review as to new lines that testing might take in the future.

Let us grant at the outset that brain-damaged or retarded people do less well on intelligence tests than other people. Wechsler (1958) initially used this criterion to validate his instrument, although it has an obvious weakness: brain-damaged people do less well on almost *any* test so that it is hard to argue that something unique called lack of intelligence is responsible for the deficiency in test scores. The multimethod, multitrait criterion has not been applied here.

TESTS PREDICT GRADES IN SCHOOL

The games people are required to play on aptitude tests are similar to the games teachers require in the classroom. In fact, many of Binet's original tests were taken from exercises that teachers used in French schools. So it is scarcely surprising that aptitude test scores are correlated highly with grades in school. The whole Scholastic Aptitude Testing movement rests its case largely on this single undeniable fact. Defenders of intelligence testing, like McNemar (1964), often seem to be suggesting that this is the only kind of validity necessary. McNemar remarked that "the manual of the Differential Aptitude Test of the Psychological Corporation contains a staggering total of 4,096—yes, I counted 'em—validity coefficients." What more could you ask for, ladies and gentlemen? It was not until I looked at the manual myself (McNemar certainly did not enlighten me) that I confirmed my suspicion that almost every one of those validity coefficients involved predicting grades in courses—in other words, performing on similar types of tests.

So what about grades? How valid are they as predictors? Researchers have, in fact, had great difficulty demonstrating that grades in school are related to any other behaviors of importance—other than doing well on aptitude tests. Yet the general public—including many psychologists and most college officials—simply has been unable to believe or accept this fact. It seems so self-evident to educators that those who do well in their classes *must* go on to do better in life that they systematically have disregarded evidence to the contrary that has been accumulating for some time. In the early 1950s a committee of the Social Science Research Council of which I was chairman looked into the matter and concluded that while grade level attained seemed related to future measures of success in life, performance within grade was related only slightly. In other words, being a high school or college graduate gave one a credential that opened up certain higher level jobs, but the poorer students in high school or college did as well in life as the top students. As a college teacher I found this hard to believe until I made a simple check. I took the top eight students in a class in the late 1940s at Wesleyan University, where I was teaching—all straight-A students—and contrasted what they were doing in the early 1960s with what eight really poor students were doing—all of whom were getting barely passing averages in college (C− or below). To my great surprise, I could not distinguish the two lists of men 15–18 years later. There were lawyers, doctors, research scientists, and college and high school teachers in both groups. The only difference I noted was that those with better grades got into better law or medical schools, but even with this supposed advantage they did not have notably more successful careers as compared with the poorer students who had had to be satisfied with second-rate law and medical schools at the outset. Doubtless the C− students could not get into even second-rate law and medical schools under the stricter admissions testing standards of today. Is that an advantage for society?

Such outcomes have been documented carefully by many researchers (cf. Hoyt, 1965) both in Britain (Hudson, 1960) and in the United States. Berg (1970) in a book suggestively titled *Education and Jobs: The Great Training Robbery* has summarized studies showing that neither amount of education nor grades in school are related to vocational success as a factory worker, bank teller, or air traffic controller. Even for highly intellectual jobs like scientific researcher, Taylor, Smith, and Ghiselin (1963) have shown that superior on-the-job performance is related in no way to better grades in college. The average college grade for the top third in research success was 2.73 (about B−) and for the bottom third, 2.69 (also B−). Such facts have been known for some time. They make it abundantly clear that the testing movement is in grave danger of perpetuating a mythological meritocracy in which none of the measures of merit bears significant demonstrable validity with respect to any measures outside of the charmed circle. Psychologists used to say as a kind of an "in" joke that intelligence is what the intelligence tests measure. That seems to be uncomfortably near the whole truth and nothing but the truth. But what's funny about it, when the public took us more seriously than we did ourselves and used the tests to screen people out of opportunities for education and high-status jobs? And why call excellence at these test games intelligence?

Even further, why keep the best education for those who are already doing well at the games? This, in effect, is what the colleges are doing when they select from their applicants those with the highest Scholastic Aptitude Test scores. Isn't this like saying that we will coach especially those who already can play tennis well? One would think that the purpose of education is precisely to improve the performance of those who are not doing very well. So when psychologists predict on the basis of the Scholastic Aptitude Test who is most likely to do well in college, they are suggesting implicitly that these are the best bets to admit. But in another sense, if the colleges were interested in proving that they could educate people, high-scoring students might be poor bets because they would be less likely to show improvement in performance. To be sure, the teachers want students who will do well in their courses, but should society allow the teachers to determine who deserves to be educated, particularly when the performance of interest to teachers bears so little relation to any other type of life performance?

DO INTELLIGENCE TESTS TAP ABILITIES THAT ARE RESPONSIBLE FOR JOB SUCCESS?

Most psychologists think so; certainly the general public thinks so (Cronbach, 1970, p. 300), but the evidence is a whole lot less satisfactory than one would think it ought to be to justify such confidence.

Thorndike and Hagen (1959), for instance, obtained 12,000 correlations between aptitude test scores and various measures of later occupational success on over 10,000 respondents and concluded that the number of significant correlations did not exceed what would be expected by chance. In other words, the tests were invalid. Yet psychologists go on using them, trusting that the poor validities must be due to restriction in range due to the fact that occupations do not admit individuals with lower scores. But even here it is not clear whether the characteristics required for entry are, in fact, essential to success in the field. One might suppose that finger dexterity is essential to being a dentist and require a minimum test score for entry. Yet it was found by Thorndike and Hagen (1959) to be related negatively to income as a dentist! Holland and Richards (1965) and Elton and Shevel (1969) have shown that no consistent relationships exist between scholastic aptitude scores in college students and their *actual accomplishments* in social leadership, the arts, science, music, writing, and speech and drama.

Yet what are we to make of Ghiselli's (1966, p. 121) conclusions, based on a review of 50 years of research, that general intelligence tests correlate .42 with trainability and .23 with proficiency across all types of jobs? Each of these correlations is based on over 10,000 cases. It is small wonder that psychologists believe intelligence tests are valid predictors of job success. Unfortunately, it is impossible to evaluate Ghiselli's conclusion, as he does not cite his sources and he does not state exactly how job proficiency was measured for each of his correlations. We can draw some conclusions from his results, however, and we can make a good guess that job proficiency often was measured by supervisors' ratings or by such indirect indicators of supervisors' opinions as turnover, promotion, salary increases, and the like.

What is interesting to observe is that intelligence test correlations with proficiency in higher status jobs are regularly higher than with proficiency in lower status jobs (Ghiselli, 1966, pp. 34, 78). Consider the fact that intelligence test scores correlate −.08 with proficiency as a canvasser or solicitor and .45 with proficiency as a stock and bond salesman. This should be a strong clue as to what intelligence tests are getting at, but most observers have overlooked it or simply assumed that it takes more general ability to be a stock and bond salesman than a canvasser. But these two jobs differ also in social status, in the language, accent, clothing, manner, and connections by education and family necessary for success in the job. The basic problem with many job proficiency measures for validating ability tests is that they depend heavily on the *credentials* the man brings to the job—the habits, values, accent, interests, etc.—that mean he is acceptable to management and to clients. Since we also know that social class background is related to getting higher ability test scores (Nuttall & Fozard, 1970), as well as to having the right personal credentials for success, *the correlation between intelligence test scores and job success often may be an artifact*, the product of their joint association with class status. Employers may have a right to select bond salesmen who have gone to the right schools because they do better, but psychologists do not have a right to argue that it is their *intelligence* that makes them more proficient in their jobs.

We know that correlation does not equal causation, but we keep forgetting it. Far too many psychologists still report average-ability test scores for high- and low-prestige occupations, inferring incorrectly that this evidence shows it takes more of this type of brains to perform a high-level than a low-level job. For instance, Jensen (1972) wrote recently:

> Can the I.Q. tell us anything of practical importance? Is it related to our common-sense notions about mental ability as we ordinarily think of it in connection with educational and occupational performance? Yes, indeed, and there is no doubt about it. . . . The I.Q. obtained after 9 or 10 years of age also predicts final adult occupational status to almost as high a degree as it predicts scholastic performance. . . . The *average* I.Q. of persons within a particular occupation is closely related to that occupation's standing in terms of average income and the amount of prestige accorded to it by the general public [p. 9].

He certainly leaves the impression that it is "mental ability as we ordinarily think of it" that is responsible for this association between average IQ scores and job prestige. But the association can be interpreted as meaning, just as reasonably, that it takes more *pull*, more opportunity, to get the vocabulary and other habits required by those in power from incumbents of high-status positions. Careful studies that try to separate the *credential* factor from the *ability* factor in job success have been very few in number.

Ghiselli (1966) simply did not deal with the problem of what the criteria of job proficiency may mean for validating the tests. For example, he reported a correlation of .27 between intelligence test scores and proficiency as a policeman or a detective (p. 83), with no attention given to the very important issues involved in how a policeman's performance is to be evaluated. Will supervisors' ratings do? If so, it discriminates against black policemen (Baehr, Furcon, & Froemel, 1968) because white supervisors regard them as inferior. And what about the public? Shouldn't their opinion as to how they are served by the police be part of the criterion? The most recent careful review (Kent & Eisenberg, 1972) of the evidence relating ability test scores to police performance concluded that there is no stable, significant relationship. Here is concrete evidence that one must view with considerable skepticism the assumed relation of intelligence test scores to success on the job.

One other illustration may serve to warn the unwary about accepting uncritically simple statements about the role of ability, as measured by intelligence tests, in life outcomes. It is stated widely that intelligence promotes general adjustment and results in lower neuroticism. For example, Anderson (1960) reported a significant correlation between intelligence test scores obtained from boys in 1950, age 14–17, and follow-up ratings of general adjustment made five years later. Can we assume that intelligence promotes better adjustment to life as has been often claimed? It sounds reasonable until we reflect that the "intelligence" test is a test of ability to do well in school (to take academic-type tests), that many of Anderson's sample were still in school or getting started on careers, and that those who are not doing well in school or getting a good first job because of it are likely to be considered poorly adjusted by themselves and others. Here the test has become part of the criterion and has introduced the correlation artificially. In case this sounds like special reasoning, consider the fact, not commented on particularly by Anderson, that the same correlation between intelligence test scores and adjustment in girls was an insignificant .06. Are we to conclude that intelligence does *not* promote adjustment in girls? It would seem more reasonable to argue that the particular ability tested, here associated with scholastic success, is more important to success (and hence adjustment) for boys than for girls. But this is a far cry from the careless inference that intelligence tests tap a general ability to adapt successfully to life's problems because high-IQ children (read "men") have better mental health (Jensen, 1972).

To make the point even more vividly, suppose you are a ghetto resident in the Roxbury section of Boston. To qualify for being a policeman you have to take a three-hour-long general intelligence test in which you must know the meaning of words like "quell," "pyromaniac," and "lexicon." If you do not know enough of those words or cannot play analogy games with them, you do not qualify and must be satisfied with some such job as being a janitor for which an intelligence test is not required yet by the Massachusetts Civil Service Commission. You, not unreasonably, feel angry, upset, and unsuccessful. Because you do not know those words, you are considered to have low intelligence, and since you consequently have to take a low-status job and are unhappy, you contribute to the celebrated correlations of low intelligence with low occupational status and poor adjustment. Psychologists should be ashamed of themselves for promoting a view of general intelligence that has encouraged such a testing program, particularly when there is no solid evidence that significantly relates performance on this type of intelligence test with performance as a policeman.

THE ROLE OF POWER IN CONTROLLING LIFE-OUTCOME CRITERIA

Psychologists have been, until recently, incredibly naive about the role of powerful interests in controlling the criteria against which psychologists have validated their tests. Terman felt that his studies had proved conclusively that "giftedness," as he measured it with psychological tests, was a key factor in life success. By and large, psychologists have agreed with him. Kohlberg, LaCrosse, and Ricks (1970), for instance, in a recent summary statement concluded that Terman and Oden's (1947) study "indicated the gifted were more successful occupationally, maritally, and socially than the average group, and were lower in 'morally deviant' forms of psychopathology (e.g., alcoholism, homosexuality)." Jensen (1972) agreed:

> One of the most convincing demonstrations that I.Q. is related to "real life" indicators of ability was provided in a classic study by Terman and his associates at Stanford University. . . . Terman found that for the most part these high-I.Q. children in later adulthood markedly excelled the general population on every indicator of achievement that was examined: a higher level of education completed; more scholastic honors and awards; higher occupational status; higher income; production of more articles, books, patents and other signs of creativity; more entries in *Who's Who;* a lower mortality rate; better physical and mental health; and a lower divorce rate. . . . Findings such as these establish beyond a doubt that I.Q. tests measure characteristics that are obviously of considerable importance in our present technological society. To say that the kind of ability measured by intelligence tests is irrelevant or unimportant would be tantamount to repudiating civilization as we know it [p. 9].

I do not want to repudiate civilization as we know it, or even to dismiss intelligence tests as irrelevant or unimportant, but I do want to state, as emphatically as possible, that Terman's studies do *not* demonstrate unequivocally that it is the kind of ability measured by the intelligence tests that is responsible for (i.e., causes) the greater success of the high-IQ children. Terman's studies *may* show only that the rich and powerful have more opportunities, and therefore do better in life. And if that is even possibly true, it is socially irresponsible to state that psychologists have established "beyond a doubt" that the kind of ability measured by intelligence tests is essential for high-level performance in our society. For, by current methodological standards, Terman's studies (and others like them) were naive. No attempt was made to equate for *opportunity* to be successful occupationally and socially. His gifted people clearly came from superior socioeconomic backgrounds to those he compared them with (at one point all men in California, including day laborers). He had no unequivocal evidence that it was "giftedness" (as reflected in his test scores) that was responsible for the superior performance of his group. It would be *as* legitimate (though also not proven) to conclude that sons of the rich, powerful, and educated were apt to be more successful occupationally, maritally, and socially because they had more material advantages. To make the point in another way, consider the data in Table 1, which are fairly representative of findings in this area. They were obtained by Havighurst, Bowman, Liddle, Matthews, and Pierce (1962) from a typical town in Middle America. One observes the usual strong relationship between social class and IQ and between IQ and college-going—which leads on to occupational success. The traditional interpretation of such findings is that more stupid children come from the lower classes because their parents are also stupid which explains why they are lower class. A higher proportion of children with high IQ go to college because they are more intelligent and more suited to college study. This is as it should be because IQ predicts academic success. The fact that more intelligent people going to college come more often from the upper class follows naturally because the upper classes contain more intelligent people. So the traditional argument has gone for years. It seemed all very simple and obvious to Terman and his followers.

Table 1

Numbers of Students in Various IQ and SES Categories (Sixth Grade) and Percentage Subsequently Going to College

IQ	SOCIOECONOMIC STATUS			
	High	*% to College*	*Low*	*% to College*
High	51	71	57	23
Low	33	18	96	5

Note, x^2 = 11.99, $p < .01$, estimated tetrachoric r = .35, SES × IQ. (Table adapted from Havighurst et al., 1962. Copyrighted by Wiley, 1962.)

However, a closer look at Table 1 suggests another interpretation that is equally plausible, though not more required by the data than the one just given. Compare the percentages going to college in the "deviant" boxes—high socioeconomic status and low IQ versus high IQ and low socioeconomic status. It appears to be no more likely for the bright children (high IQ) from the lower classes to go to college (despite their high aptitude for it) than for the "stupid" children from the upper classes. Why is this? An obvious possibility is that the bright but poor children do not have the money to go to college, or they do not want to go, preferring to work or do other things. In the current lingo, they are "disadvantaged" in the sense that they have not had access to the other factors (values, aspirations, money) that promote college-going in upper-class children. But now we have an alternative explanation of college-going—namely, socioeconomic status, which seems to be as good a predictor of this type of success as ability. How can we claim that ability as measured by these tests is the critical factor in college-going? Very few children, even with good test-taking ability, go to college if they are from poor families. One could argue that they are victims of oppression: they do not have the opportunity or the values that permit or encourage going to college. Isn't it likely that the same oppressive forces may have prevented even more of them from learning to play school games well at all?

Belonging to the power elite (high socioeconomic status) not only helps a young man go to college and get jobs through contacts his family has; it also gives him easy access as a child to the credentials that permit him to get into certain occupations. Nowadays, those credentials include the words and word-game skills used in Scholastic Aptitude Tests. In the Middle Ages they required knowledge of Latin for the learned professions of law, medicine, and theology. Only those young men who could read and write Latin could get into those occupations, and if tests had been given in Latin, I am sure they would have shown that professionals scored higher in Latin than men in general, that sons who grew up in families where Latin was used would have an advantage in those tests compared to those in poor families where Latin was unknown, and that these men were more likely to get into the professions. But would we conclude we were dealing with a general ability factor? Many a ghetto resident must or should feel that he is in a similar position with regard to the kind of English he must learn in order to do well on tests, in school, and in occupations today in America. I was recently in Jamaica, where all around me poor people were speaking an English that was almost entirely incomprehensible to me. If I insisted, they would speak patiently in a way that I could understand, but I felt like a slow-witted child. I have wondered how well I would do in Jamaican society if this kind of English were standard among the rich and powerful (which, by the way, it is not) and therefore required by them for admission into their better schools and occupations (as determined by a test administered perhaps by the Jamaican Testing Service). I would feel oppressed, not less intelligent, as the test would doubtless decide I was because I was so slow of comprehension and so ignorant of ordinary vocabulary.

When Cronbach (1970) concluded that such a test "is giving realistic information on the presence of a handicap," he is, of course, correct. But psychologists should recognize that it is those in power in a society who often decide what is a handicap. We should be a lot more cautious about accepting as ultimate criteria of ability the standards imposed by whatever group happens to be in power.

Does this mean that intelligence tests are invalid? As so often when you examine a question carefully in psychology, the answer depends on what you mean. Valid for what? Certainly they are valid for predicting who will get ahead in a number of prestige jobs where credentials are important. So is white skin: it too is a valid predictor of job success in prestige jobs. But no one would argue that white skin per se is an ability factor. Lots of the celebrated correlations between so-called intelligence test scores and success can lay no greater claim to representing an ability factor.

Valid for predicting success in school? Certainly, because school success depends on taking similar types of tests. Yet neither the tests nor school grades seem to have much power to predict real competence in many life outcomes, aside from the advantages that credentials convey on the individuals concerned.

Are there *no* studies which show that general intelligence test scores predict competence with all of these other factors controlled? I can only assert that I have had a very hard time finding a good carefully controlled study of the problem because testers simply have not worked very hard on it: they have believed so much that they were measuring true competence that they have not bothered to try to prove that they were. Studies do exist, of course, which show significant positive correlations between special test scores and job-related skills. For example, perceptual speed scores are related to clerical proficiency. So are tests of vocabulary, immediate memory, substitution, and arithmetic. Motor ability test scores are related to proficiency as a vehicle operator (Ghiselli, 1966). And so on. Here we are on the safe and uncontroversial ground of using tests as criterion samples. But this is a far cry from inferring that there is a general ability factor that enables a person to be more competent in anything he tries. The evidence for this general ability factor turns out to be contaminated heavily by the power of those at the top of the social hierarchy to insist that the skills they have are the ones that indicate superior adaptive capacity.

WHERE DO WE GO FROM HERE?

Criticisms of the testing movement are not new. The Social Science Research Council Committee on Early Identification of Talent made some of these same points nearly 15 years ago (McClelland, Baldwin, Bronfenbrenner, & Strodtbeck, 1958). But the beliefs on which the movement is based are held so firmly that such theoretical or empirical objections have had little impact up to now. The testing movement continues to grow and extend into every corner of our society. It is unlikely that it can be simply stopped, although minority groups may have the political power to stop it. For the tests are clearly discriminatory against those who have not been exposed to the culture, entrance to which is guarded by the tests. What hopefully can happen is that testers will recognize what is going on and attempt to redirect their energies in a sounder direction. The report of the special committee on testing to the College Entrance Examination Board (1970) is an important sign that changes in thinking are occurring—if only they can be implemented at a practical level. The report's gist is that a wider array of talents should be assessed for college entrance and reported as a profile to the colleges.

This is a step in the right direction if everyone keeps firmly in mind that the criteria for establishing the validity of these new measures really ought to be not *grades in school* but grades in life in the broadest theoretical and practical sense.

But now I am on the spot. Having criticized what the testing movement has been doing, I feel some obligation to suggest alternatives. How would I do things differently or better? I do not mind making suggestions, but I am well aware that some of them are as open to criticism on other grounds as the procedures I have been criticizing. So I must offer them in a spirit of considerable humility, as approaches that at least some people might be interested in pursuing who are discouraged with what we have been doing. My goal is to brainstorm a bit on how things might be different, not to present hard evidence that my proposals are better than what has been done to date. How would one test for competence, if I may use that word as a symbol for an alternative approach to traditional intelligence testing?

1. *The best testing is criterion sampling.* The point is so obvious that it would scarcely be worth mentioning if it had not been obscured so often by psychologists like McNemar and Jensen, who tout a general intelligence factor. If you want to know how well a person can drive a car (the criterion), sample his ability to do so by giving him a driver's test. Do not give him a paper-and-pencil test for following directions, a general intelligence test, etc. As noted above, there is ample evidence that tests which sample job skills will predict proficiency on the job.

Academic skill tests are successful precisely because they involve criterion sampling for the most part. As already pointed out, the Scholastic Aptitude Test taps skills that the teacher is looking for and will give high grades for. No one could object if it had been recognized widely that this was *all* that was going on when aptitude tests were used to predict who would do well in school. Trouble started only when people assumed that these skills had some more general validity, as implied in the use of words like "intelligence." Yet even a little criterion analysis would show that there are almost no occupations or life situations that require a person to do word analogies, choose the most correct of four alternative meanings of a word, etc.

Criterion sampling means that testers have got to get out of their offices where they play endless word and paper-and-pencil games and into the field where they actually analyze performance into its components. If you want to test who will be a good policeman, go find out what a policeman does. Follow him around, make a list of his activities, and sample from that list in screening applicants. Some of the job sampling will have to be based on theory as well as practice. If policemen generally discriminate against blacks, that is clearly not part of the criterion because the law says that they must not. So include a test which shows the applicant does not discriminate. Also sample the vocabulary he must use to communicate with the people he serves since his is a position of interpersonal influence—and not the vocabulary that men who have never been on a police beat think it is proper to know. And do not rely on supervisors' judgments of who are the better policemen because that is not, strictly speaking, job analysis but analysis of what people think involves better performance. Baehr et al. (1968), for instance, found that black policemen in Chicago who were rated high by their superiors scored high on the Deference scale of the Edwards Personal Preference Test. No such relationship appeared for white policemen. In other words, if you wanted to be considered a good cop in Chicago and you were black, you had to at least talk as if you were deferent to the white power system. Any psychologist who used this finding to pick black policemen would be guilty of improper job analysis, to put it as mildly as possible.

Criterion sampling, in short, involves both theory and practice. It requires real sophistication. Early testers knew how to do it better than later testers because they had not become so caught up in the ingrown world of intelligence tests that simply were validated against each other. Testers of the future must relearn how to do criterion sampling. If someone wants to know who will make a good teacher, they will have to get videotapes of classrooms, as Kounin (1970) did and find out how the behaviors of good and poor teachers differ. To pick future businessmen, research scientists, political leaders, prospects for a happy marriage, they will have to make careful behavioral analyses of these outcomes and then find ways of sampling the adaptive behavior in advance. The task will not be easy. It will require new psychological skills not ordinarily in the repertoire of the traditional tester. What is called for is nothing less than a revision of the role itself—moving it away from word games and statistics toward behavioral analysis.

2. *Tests should be designed to reflect changes in what the individual has learned.* It is difficult, if not impossible, to find a human characteristic that cannot be modified by training or experience, whether it be an eye blink or copying Kohs' block designs. To the traditional intelligence tester this fact has been something of a nuisance because he has been searching for some unmodifiable, unfakeable index of innate mental capacity. He has reacted by trying to keep secret the way his tests are scored so that people will not learn how to do them better, and by selecting tests, scores on which are stable from one administration to the next. Stability is supposed to mean that the score reflects an innate aptitude that is unmodified by experience, but it could also mean that the test is simply insensitive to important changes in what the person knows or can do. That is, the skill involved may be so specialized, so unrelated to general experience, that even though the person has learned a lot, he performs the same in this specialized area. For example, being able to play a word game like analogies is apparently little affected by a higher education, which is not so surprising since few teachers ask their students to do analogies. Therefore, being able to do analogies is often considered a sign of some innate ability factor. Rather, it might be called

an achievement so specialized that increases in general wisdom do not transfer to it and cause changes in it. And why should we be interested in such specialized skills? As we have seen, they predictably do not seem to correlate with any life-outcome criteria except those that involve similar tests or that require the credentials that a high score on the test signifies.

It seems wiser to abandon the search for pure ability factors and to select tests instead that are valid in the sense that scores on them change as the person grows in experience, wisdom, and ability to perform effectively on various tasks that life presents to him. Thus the second principle of the new approach to testing becomes a corollary of the first. If one begins by using as tests samples of life-outcome behaviors, then one way of determining whether those tests are valid is to observe that the person's ability to perform them increases as his competence in the life-outcome behavior increases. For example, if excellence in a policeman is defined partly in terms of being even-handed toward all minority groups, then a test of fair-mindedness (or lack of ethnocentrism) might be used to select policemen and also should reflect growth in fair-mindedness as a police recruit develops on the job. One of the hidden prejudices of psychology, borrowed from the notion of fixed inherited aptitudes, is that any trait, like racial prejudice, is unmodifiable by training. Once a bigot, always a bigot. There is no solid evidence that this trait or any other human trait cannot be changed. So it is worth insisting that a new test should be designed especially to reflect growth in the characteristic it assesses.

3. *How to improve on the characteristic tested should be made public and explicit.* Such a principle contrasts sharply with present practice in which psychologists have tried hard—backed up by the APA Ethics Committee—to keep answers to many of their tests a secret lest people practice and learn how to do better on them or fake high scores. Faking a high score is impossible if you are performing the criterion behavior, as in tests for reading, spelling, or driving a car. Faking becomes possible the more indirect the connection is between the test behavior and the criterion behavior. For example, in checking out hundreds of items for predicting flight training success, it may turn out that something like playing the piano as a boy has diagnostic validity. But no one knows exactly why: perhaps it has something to do with mechanical ability, perhaps with a social class variable, or with conscientiousness in practicing. The old-fashioned tester could not care less what the reason was as long as the item worked. But he had to be very careful about security because men who wanted to become pilots easily could report they had played the piano if they knew such an answer would help them be selected. If playing the piano actually helped people become better pilots—which no psychologist bothered to check out in World War II—then it might make some sense to make this known and encourage applicants to learn to play. That would be very like the criterion-sampling approach

to testing proposed here, in which the person tested is told how to improve on the characteristic for which he will be tested.

Or to take another example, doing analogies is a task that predicts grades in school fairly well. Again no one knows quite why because schoolwork ordinarily does not involve doing analogies. So psychologists have had to be security conscious for fear that if students got hold of the analogies test answers, they might practice and become good at analogies and fake high aptitude. What is meant by faking here is that doing well on analogies is *not* part of the criterion behavior (getting good grades), or else it could hardly be considered faking. Rather, the test must have some indirect connection with good grades, so that doing well on it through practice destroys its predictive power: hence the high score is a fake. The person can do analogies, but that does not mean any longer that he will get better grades. Put this way, the whole procedure seems like a strange charade that testers have engaged in because they did not know what was going on, behaviorally speaking, and refused to take the trouble to find out as long as the items worked. How much simpler it is, both theoretically and pragmatically, to make explicit to the learner what the criterion behavior is that will be tested. Then psychologist, teacher, and student can collaborate openly in trying to improve the student's score on the performance test. Certain school achievement tests, of course, follow this model. In the Iowa Test of Basic Skills, for instance, both pupil and teacher know how the pupil will be tested on spelling, reading, or arithmetic, how he should prepare for the test, how the tests will be scored, etc. What is proposed here is that *all* tests should follow this model. To do otherwise is to engage in power games with applicants over the secrecy of answers and to pretend knowledge of what lies behind correlations, which does not in fact exist.

4. *Tests should assess competencies involved in clusters of life outcomes.* If we abandon general intelligence or aptitude tests, as proposed, and move toward criterion sampling based on job analysis, there is the danger that the tests will become extremely specific to the criterion involved. For example, Project ABLE (Gagné, 1965) has identified over 50 separate skills that can be assessed for the exit level of millman apprentice (job family: woodworker and related occupations). They include skills like "measures angles," "sharpens tools and planes," and "identifies sizes and types of fasteners using gauges and charts." This approach has all of the characteristics of the new look in testing so far proposed: the tests are criterion samples; improvement in skill shows up in the tests; how to pass them is public knowledge; and both teacher and pupil can collaborate to improve test performance. However, what one ends up with is hundreds, even thousands, of specific tests for dozens of different occupations. For some purposes it may be desirable to assess competencies that are more generally useful in clusters of life outcomes, including not only occupational outcomes but social ones as well, such as leadership, interpersonal skills, etc. Project ABLE has been excellent at identifying

the manual skills involved in being a service station attendant, but so far it has been unable to get a simple index of whether or not the attendant is pleasant to the customers.

Some of these competencies may be rather traditional cognitive ones involving reading, writing, and calculating skills. Others should involve what traditionally have been called personality variables, although they might better be considered competencies. Let me give some illustrations.

(a) Communication skills. Many jobs and most interpersonal situations require a person to be able to communicate accurately by word, look, or gesture just what he intends or what he wants done. Writing is one simple way to test these skills. Can the person put together words in a way that makes immediate good sense to the reader? Word-game skills do not always predict this ability, as is often assumed. I will never forget an instance of a black student applicant for graduate school at Harvard who scored in something like the fifth percentile in the Miller Analogies Test, but who obviously could write and think clearly and effectively as shown by the stories he had written as a reporter in the college paper. I could not convince my colleagues to admit him despite the fact that he had shown the criterion behavior the Analogies Test is supposed to predict. Yet if he were admitted, as a psychologist he would be writing papers in the future, not doing analogies for his colleagues. It is amazing to me how often my colleagues say things like: "I don't care how well he can write. Just look at those test scores." Testers may shudder at this and write public disclaimers, but what practically have they done to stop the spread of this blind faith in test scores?

In Ethiopia in 1968 we were faced with the problem of trying to find out how much English had been learned by high school students who had been taught by American Peace Corps volunteers. The usual way of doing this there, as elsewhere, is to give the student a "fill in the blanks," multiple-choice objective test to see whether the student knows the meaning of words, understands correct grammatical forms, etc. We felt that this left out the most important part of the criterion behavior: the ability to use English to communicate. So we asked students to write brief stories, which we then coded objectively, not for grammatical or spelling correctness, but for complexity of thought which the student was able to express correctly in the time allotted. This gave a measure of English fluency that predictably did correlate with occupational success among Ethiopian adults and also with school success, although curiously enough it was significantly negatively related to a word-game skill (English antonyms) that more nearly approximates the usual test of English competence (Bergthold, 1969).

Important communication skills are nonverbal. When the proverbial Indian said, "White man speak with forked tongue," he doubtless meant among other things that what the white man was saying in words did not jibe with what he was doing or expressing nonverbally. The abilities to know what is going on in a social setting and to set the correct emotional tone for it are crucial life-outcome criteria. Newmeyer (1970), for instance, has found a way to measure success at enacting certain emotions so that others receive them correctly and to measure success at receiving the correct emotions over various enactors. He found that black boys at a certain age were consistently better than white boys at this particular kind of communication skill, which is a far more crucial type of criterion behavior than most paper-and-pencil tests sample.

(b) Patience, or response delay as psychologists would call it, is a human characteristic that seems essential for many life outcomes. For instance, it is desirable for many service occupations where clients' needs and demands can be irritating. It would seem particularly desirable in a policeman who has the power and authority to do great damage to people who irritate him. Kagan, Pearson, and Welch (1966) have shown that it is an easily measured human characteristic that is relatively stable over time and can be taught directly.

(c) Moderate goal setting is important in achievement-related games, as I have explained fully elsewhere (McClelland, 1961). In most life situations, it is distinctly preferable to setting goals either too high or too low, which leads more often to failure. Many performance situations have been devised which measure the tendency to set moderate, achievable goals and help the person learn how to set more realistic goals in the future (Alschuler, Tabor, & McIntyre, 1970; McClelland & Winter, 1969).

(d) Ego development. Many scholars (see Erikson, 1950; Loevinger & Wessler, 1970; White, 1959) have reasoned that there is a general kind of competence which develops with age and to a higher level in some people than in others. Costa (1971a) recently has developed a Thematic Apperception Test code for ego development which appears to have many of the aspects sought in the new measurement direction proposed here. The thought characteristics sampled represent criterion behavior in the sense that at Stage 1, for example, the person is thinking at a passive conformist level, whereas at Stage 4, he represents people in his stories as taking initiative on behalf of others (a more developed competency). The score on this measure predicts very well which junior or high school students will be perceived by their teachers as more competent (even when correlations with intelligence and grade performance are removed), and furthermore a special kind of education in junior high school moves students up the ego development scale significantly. That is, training designed to develop a sense of initiative produced results that were reflected sensitively in this score. Pupils and teachers can collaborate in increasing this kind of thinking which ought to prepare students for competent action in many spheres of life.

5. *Tests should involve operant as well as respondent behavior.* One of the greatest weaknesses of nearly all existing tests is that they structure the situation in advance and demand a response of a certain kind from the test taker. They are aimed at assessing the capacity of a person to make a certain kind of response or choice. But life outside of tests seldom presents the individual with such clearly defined alternatives as "Which dog is most likely to bite?" or "Complete the following number

series: 1 3 6 10 15 ___," or "Check the word which is most similar in meaning to *lexicon.*" If we refer to these latter behaviors as respondents in the sense that the stimulus situation clearly is designed to evoke a particular kind of response, then life is much more apt to be characterized by operant responses in the sense that the individual spontaneously makes a response in the absence of a very clearly defined stimulus. This fact probably explains why most existing tests do not predict life-outcome behaviors. Respondents generally do not predict operants. To use a crude example, a psychologist might assess individual differences in the *capacity* to drink beer, but if he used this measure to predict actual beer consumption over time, the chances are that the relationship would be very low. How much beer a person can drink is not related closely to how much he does drink.

Testers generally have used respondent behaviors to save time in scoring answers and to get higher test-retest reliability. That is, the person is more likely to give the same response in a highly structured situation than in an unstructured one that allows him to emit any behavior. Yet slavishly pursuing these goals has led to important lacks in validity of the tests because life simply is not that structured and often does not permit one to choose between defined-in-advance responses. The n Achievement measure, which is an operant in the sense that the subject emits responses (tells stories) under only very vague instructions, has predicted over a 12–14-year period in three different samples those who will drift into entrepreneurial business occupations (McClelland, 1965). Here an operant is predicting an operant—the tendency to think spontaneously about doing better all the time predicts a series of spontaneous acts over time which leads the individual into an entrepreneurial occupation. But predicting from operants to respondents or vice versa does not work, at least for men (McClelland, 1966). The n Achievement score is not related to grades or academic test scores (respondent measures), nor do grades relate to entering entrepreneurial occupations (see McClelland, 1961).

Even within fairly structured test situations it is possible to allow for more operant behavior than has been the usual practice. Not long ago we tried to find an existing performance test on which a person with high n Achievement ought to do well because such a test might be a useful substitute for the Thematic Apperception Test storytelling measure in certain situations. Theoretically, such a test should permit operant behavior in which the individual generates a lot of alternatives for solving a problem in search of the most efficient solution. But to our surprise, we could find no such test. Tests of divergent thinking existed that counted the number of operants (e.g., original uses for a paper clip) an individual could come up with, but they did not require the person to find the best alternative. Most other tests simply required the person to find the one correct answer the test maker had built into the item. What was needed were test items to which there were many correct answers, among which one was better than others in terms of some criteria of efficiency that the person would have to apply. This task seemed more lifelike to us and certainly more like the type of behavior characteristic of people with high n Achievement. So we invented an Airlines Scheduling Test (Bergthold, 1969), in which the person is faced with a number of problems of getting a passenger from City A to City B by such and such a time at minimum expenditure in time, energy, money, and discomfort. From schedules provided, several alternative routes and connections can be generated (if the test taker is energetic enough to think them up) that will solve the problem, but one is clearly the most efficient. The test has promise in that it correlates with the n Achievement score at a low level. But the main point is that it requires more lifelike operant behavior in generating alternative solutions, and therefore it should have more predictive power to a variety of situations in which what the person is expected to do is not so highly structured as in standard respondent tests.

6. *Tests should sample operant thought patterns to get maximum generalizability to various action outcomes.* As noted already, the movement toward defining behavioral objectives in occupational testing can lead to great specificity and huge inventories of small skills that have little general predictive power. One way to get around this problem is to focus on defining thought codes because, almost by definition, they have a wider range of applicability to a variety of action possibilities. That is, they represent a higher order of behavioral abstraction than any given act itself which has not the capacity to stand for other acts the way a word does. And in empirical fact this is the way it has worked out. The n Achievement score—an operant thought measure—has many action correlates, from goal setting and occupational styles to color and time-span preferences (McClelland, 1961), which individually have little power as "actones" to predict each other. A more recent example is provided by an operant thought measure of power motivation which has very low positive correlations with four action characteristics: drinking, gambling, accumulating prestige supplies, and confessing to having many aggressive impulses that are not acted on (McClelland, Davis, Kalin, & Wanner, 1972). These action characteristics are completely unrelated to each other so that they would be unlikely to come out on the same dimension in a factor analysis. But what is particularly interesting is that they appear to be alternative outlets for the power drive because the power motivation score correlates much higher with the maximum expression of *any one* of these alternatives than it does with any one alone or with the sum of standard scores on all of them. The thought characteristic—here the desire to have impact, to make a big splash—is the higher order abstraction that gives the test predictive power for alternative ways of making a big splash in action—by gambling, drinking, etc. The tester of the future is likely to get further in finding generalizable competencies of characteristics across life outcomes if he starts by focusing on thought

patterns rather than by trying to infer what thoughts must lie behind the clusters of action that come out in various factors in the traditional trait analysis.

However, I have been arguing for this approach for over 20 years, and as far as I can see, the testing movement has been affected little by my eloquence. Why? There are lots of reasons: People keep insisting that the n Achievement score is invalid because it will not predict grades in school—which is ironic since it was designed precisely to predict life outcomes and not grades in school. Or they argue it does not predict all types of achievement (Klinger, 1966)—when, of course, it is not supposed to, on theoretical grounds. But the practical problem (outside the tedium of content coding) is the unreliability of operant thought measures. Many of them are unreliable, though not all. Costa's (1971b) ego development score has a test-retest stability coefficient over a year of .66, $N = 223$. Unreliability is a fatal defect if the goal of testing is to *select* people, let us say, with high n Achievement. For rejected applicants could argue that they had been excluded improperly or that they might have high scores the next time they took the test, and the psychologist would have no good defense. One could just imagine beleaguered psychologists trying to defend themselves against irate parents whose children had not gotten into a preferred college because their n Achievement scores were too low.

But the emphasis in the new testing movement should be as much on evaluating educational progress as it is on identifying fixed characteristics for selection purposes. The operant thought measures are certainly reliable enough for the former objective. The educator can use them to assess whether a certain class or an innovative approach to teaching has tended, on the average, to promote ego development in thought as assessed by Costa's measure. The educator does not care *which particular child* is high in the measure since he does not plan to use the measure to select the child for special treatment. So its unreliability does not matter. He, as an administrator, can use the test information to decide whether the goals of the school are being forwarded by one educational approach or another. In a sense, the very unreliability of the thought measures may be a virtue if they encourage educators to stop thinking only about selection and start thinking more about evaluating educational progress.

Does this mean that test reliability is always unimportant? Not at all. Sometimes it will be important to diagnose deficiencies reliably that are to be made up. On other occasions, tests will have to be used to pick out those most likely to be able to do a particular job well. So something will have to be done about reliability. Thus a man with a high n Achievement score is a better bet for a sales job than a man with a low n Achievement score, but the measure of n Achievement from content coding of thought samples is not very defensible for selection purposes because it is unreliable. In this instance, the thought code can be used as the criterion against which more reliable performance measures can be validated. For example, the Airlines Scheduling Test score is reliable, and if it turns out to be related consistently to the n Achievement score based on thought sampling, it can be used as a substitute for the latter in selection. In fact, the thought codes can be considered devices for finding the clusters of action patterns that can be measured more reliably to get indexes of various competency domains central to various life outcomes. For example, if it turns out that an elevated socialized power (s Power) score (McClelland et al., 1972) characterizes successful policemen more than unsuccessful ones—as would be expected—then the action correlates of socialized power, such as capacity to lead or be influential in social groups, can be used to select potentially good policemen. The s Power score itself could not be so used because it is unreliable and fakeable if you learn the scoring system, but it is essential as a validating criterion for more reliable measures because its wide network of empirical and theoretical relationships helps find the action characteristics that will be useful for selection purposes.

While the six principles just enumerated for the new testing movement may affect occupational testing, the fact remains that testing has had its greatest impact in the schools and currently is doing the worst damage in that area by falsely leading people to believe that doing well in school means that people are more competent and therefore more likely to do well in life because of some real ability factor. Concretely, what would an organization like the Educational Testing Service do differently if it were to take these six principles into account? As a start, it might have to drop the term "intelligence" from its vocabulary and speak of scholastic achievement tests that are more or less content specific. The non-content-specific achievements (formerly called aptitudes) do predict test-taking and symbol manipulation competencies, and these competencies are central to certain life-outcome criteria—like making up tests for others to pass or being proficient as a clerk (Ghiselli, 1966). But it is a serious practical and theoretical error to label them general intelligence, on the basis of evidence now available.

Once the innate intelligence philosophy is discarded, it becomes apparent that the role of such a testing service is to report to schools a profile of scholastic and nonscholastic achievements in a number of different areas. Then in the case of selection it is for the college to decide whether it has the educational programs that will promote growth in given areas of low performance. If performance is already high, say in mathematics, then the college probably can produce little improvement in that area and should ask itself in what other areas it can educate such a student, as shown by his lower levels of accomplishment at the outset. The profile particularly should include measures of such general characteristics as ego development or moral development (Kohlberg & Turiel, 1971) based on thought samples, because these general competencies ought to be improved by higher educational systems anyway.

The profile of achievements should be reported not only at entrance but at various points throughout the schooling to give teachers, administrators, and students feedback on whether growth in desired characteristics actually is occurring. Test results then become a device for helping students and teachers redesign the teaching-learning process to obtain mutually agreed-on objectives. Only then will educational testing turn from the sentencing procedure it now is into the genuine service it purports to be.

REFERENCES

Alschuler, A. S., Tabor, D., & McIntyre, J. *Teaching achievement motivation.* Middletown, Conn.: Educational Ventures, 1970.

Anderson, J. E. The prediction of adjustment over time. In I. Iscoe and H. Stevenson (eds.), *Personality development in children.* Austin: Univ. of Texas Press, 1960.

Baehr, M. E., Furcon, J. E., & Froemel, E. C. *Psychological assessment of patrolman gratifications in relation to field performance.* Washington, D.C.: U.S. Government Printing Office, 1968.

Berg, I. *Education and jobs: The great training robbery.* New York: Praeger, 1970.

Bergthold, G. D. *The impact of Peace Corps teachers on students in Ethiopia.* Unpublished doctoral dissertation, Harvard Univ., 1969.

College Entrance Examination Board. *Report, special committee on testing.* Princeton, N.J.: Educational Testing Service, 1970.

Costa, P. *Introduction to the Costa ego development manual.* Department of Social Relations, Harvard Univ., 1971a. (Mimeograph)

______. *Working papers on ego development validation research.* Harvard Univ., 1971b. (Mimeograph)

Cronbach, L. J. *Essentials of psychological testing.* (3rd ed.) New York: Harper, 1970.

Elton, C. F., & Shevel, L. R. *Who is talented? An analysis of achievement.* (Research Report No. 31) Iowa City, Ia.: American College Testing Program, 1969.

Erikson, E. H. *Childhood and society.* New York: Norton, 1950.

Gagné, R. M. *The conditions of learning.* New York: Holt, Rinehart & Winston, 1965.

Ghiselli, E. E. *The validity of occupational aptitude tests.* New York: Wiley, 1966.

Havighurst, R. J., Bowman, P. H., Liddle, G. P., Matthews, C. V., & Pierce, J. V. *Growing up in River City.* New York: Wiley, 1962.

Holland, J. L., & Richards, J. M., Jr. *Academic and nonacademic accomplishment: Correlated or uncorrelated?* (Research Report No. 2) Iowa City, Ia.: American College Testing Program, 1965.

Hoyt, D. P. *The relationship between college grades and adult achievement, a review of the literature.* (Research Report No. 7) Iowa City, Ia.: American College Testing Program, 1965.

Hudson, L. Degree class and attainment in scientific research. *British Journal of Psychology,* 1960, *51,* 67–73.

Jensen, A. R. The heritability of intelligence. *Saturday Evening Post,* 1972, *244*(2), 9, 12, 149.

Kagan, J., Pearson, L., & Welch, L. The modifiability of an impulsive tempo. *Journal of Educational Psychology,* 1966, *57,* 359–365.

Kent, D. A., & Eisenberg, T. The selection and promotion of police officers. *The Police Chief,* February 1972, pp. 20–29.

Klinger, E. Fantasy need achievement as a motivational construct. *Psychological Bulletin,* 1966, *66,* 291–308.

Kohlberg, L., LaCrosse, J., & Ricks, D. The predictability of adult mental health from childhood behavior. In B. Wolman (Ed.), *Handbook of child psychopathology.* New York: McGraw-Hill, 1970.

Kohlberg, L., & Turiel, E. *Moralization research, the cognitive development approach.* New York: Holt, Rinehart & Winston, 1971.

Kounin, J. S. *Discipline and group management in classrooms.* New York: Holt, Rinehart & Winston, 1970.

Loevinger, J., & Wessler, R. *Measuring ego development* (2 vols.). San Francisco: Jossey-Bass, 1970.

McClelland, D. C. *The achieving society.* New York: Van Nostrand-Rheinhold, 1961.

———. *N* Achievement and entrepreneurship: A longitudinal study. *Journal of Personality and Social Psychology,* 1965, *1,* 389–392.

———. Longitudinal trends in the relation of thought to action. *Journal of Consulting Psychology,* 1966, *30,* 479–483.

———. Education for competence. In H. Heckhausen & W. Edelstein (Eds.), *Proceedings of the 1971 FOLEB Conference.* Berlin: Institut für Bildungsforschung in der Max-Planck-Gesellschaft, in press.

McClelland, D. C., Baldwin, A. L., Bronfenbrenner, U., & Strodtbeck, F. L. *Talent and society.* Princeton N.J.: Van Nostrand, 1958.

McClelland, D. C., Davis, W. N., Kalin, R., & Wanner, H. E. *The drinking man.* New York: Free Press, 1972.

McClelland, D. C., & Winter, D. G. *Motivating economic achievement.* New York: Free Press, 1969.

McNemar, Q. Lost: Our intelligence? Why? *American Psychologist,* 1964, *19,* 871–882.

Newmeyer, J. A. *Creativity and non-verbal communication in pre-adolescent white and black children.* Unpublished doctoral dissertation, Harvard Univ., 1970.

Nuttall, R. L., & Fozard, T. L. Age, socioeconomic status and human abilities. *Aging and Human Development,* 1970, *1,* 161–169.

Taylor, C., Smith, W. R., & Ghiselin, B. The creative and other contributions of one sample of research scientists. In C. W. Taylor & F. Barron (Eds.), *Scientific creativity: Its recognition and development.* New York: Wiley, 1963.

Terman, L. M., & Oden, M. H. *The gifted child grows up.* Stanford: Stanford Univ. Press, 1947.

Thorndike, R. L., & Hagen, E. *10,000 careers.* New York: Wiley, 1959.

Wechsler, D. *The measurement and appraisal of adult intelligence* (4th ed.). Baltimore: Williams & Wilkins, 1958.

White, R. W. Motivation reconsidered: The concept of competence. *Psychological Review,* 1959, *66,* 297–333.

Wing, C. W., Jr., & Wallach, M. A. *College admissions and the psychology of talent.* New York: Holt, Rinehart & Winston, 1971.

2. PROCESSING VISUAL INFORMATION

An Example from the Study of Apparent Motion

Unlike intelligence testing, the subject treated in the following pair of articles has not stirred up any great debates outside psychology. Yet within the field of experimental psychology, particularly in the field of human visual perception, there is considerable interest in how we perceive motion. We know, of course, not only that we can perceive real motion but also that a compelling illusion of motion can be readily achieved, an illusion that has led to the development of movies. But there is still some uncertainty about the stimulus features that are important in creating the phenomenon of apparent motion. The following two articles take different sides on the question of whether the shape of the stimuli is of any significance in the perception of apparent motion.

The two articles are instructive in other ways as well. They represent two different generations of research—Jesse Orlansky exemplifying the older, BC (before computers) researcher, and David Navon, the new generation of experimental psychologists skilled in the use of both sophisticated experimental design and the latest in computer-aided stimulus presentation.

The results of these experiments have some implications for our theories about the stages in which we seem to process information. Perhaps an interesting class discussion could be generated on how one might go about examining other stages in the processing of visual information than the ones discussed here.

EXPERIMENT 3: THE LIMITING EFFECT OF DIFFERENT FORMS ON THE PERCEPTION OF APPARENT MOVEMENT

Jesse Orlansky, Institute for Defense Analysis, Washington, D.C.

The problem of this experiment was to determine whether extreme difference in form of the stimulus figures would invalidate conditions otherwise normal for the perception of movement. An implicit problem was whether conditions making for the complete absence of figure-similarity could be achieved. On the basis of information reported earlier in this investigation, one would suspect that extreme difference in form should tend to reduce the range and, if all figure-similarities were entirely abolished, to eliminate movement.

About 1910, in Berlin, Linke commercially produced a toy stroboscope by means of which a triangle could be seen transformed into a man. In his experiments *(8, 9)* he finds that one form may change, as may one color, into another. Linke reported that movement occurred. Our concern is an investigation of the conditions under which movement may or may not appear.

The stimulus pairs were figures chosen to resemble each other as little as possible. These pairs were composed of simple figures as in the previous experiments. No brief is held that an acme of difference was achieved; the contemplation of what such extreme differences would be, reduced the experimenter to vacuous thoughts. It is held, without fear of contradiction, that they were "pretty different."

Five series of figure combinations, which appear in an accompanying illustration, were eventually chosen. They comprise Series III–VII.

While the figures in Series VII were chosen primarily because they are different, they pose an interesting sub-problem, revolving mainly about the fact that the area of the four-squares figure in combination A is 2.40 sq. in.; the figures in all other series total the usual 3 sq. in. The result in Series VII makes the super-position of both figures in the A pair (unequal in area) form a perfect square, as shown. The super-position of the equal-area figures of combination B would form an irregular figure, also shown. Actually, most subjects never noticed the difference in area between A and B.

PROCEDURE

Surely disastrous for the morale of an experiment would be to invite a subject to perceive the motion of extravagant figure combinations for

Orlansky, Jesse. Excerpt from The effect of similarity and difference in form on apparent visual movement. *Archives of Psychology*, 1940, *246*, 1–85. Reprinted with permission.

a period of an hour. Particularly if movement failed to be perceived under these conditions, it would never be known whether these subjects could have seen movement with ordinary figures. A resolution of this difficulty lay in presenting these series separately; each of them could be completed

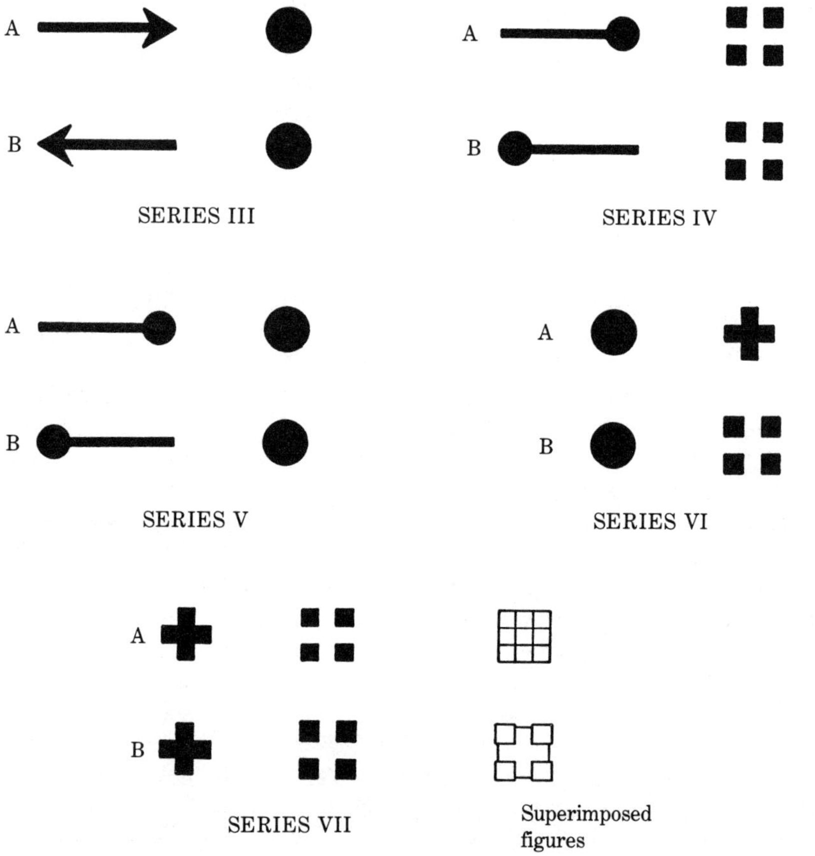

within 10 minutes. . . . We know, therefore, that these subjects readily perceived apparent motion. And from Gilbert's study *(4)* and our own observations we know that whatever slight practice effects there were over the period of an hour generally act to increase rather than decrease the range of movement.

The apparatus which has already been described was again used. [Apparatus from earlier section of this article is shown in box.—*Ed.*]

APPARATUS

a. The Exposure Apparatus

A rectangular wooden box was constructed, with these outside dimensions: length 26 in., height 18 in., and width 10 in. (see Figure 1). A vertical partition divided the interior into equal-sized, light-

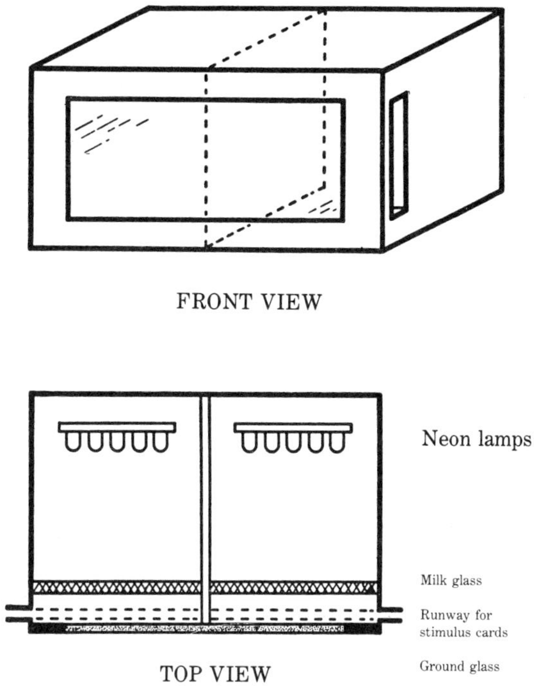

FIGURE 1: The apparatus.

proof compartments. The front of this box was cut away and a ground glass screen, 10 by 20 in., inserted so that each compartment could be used to illuminate its half of the ground glass. A slot and guide were built into the right and left sides of the box. An opaque cardboard inserted into either guide cut off the light (of the neon bulbs in each compartment) from reaching the ground glass. Therefore, any figure cut out of the cardboard could be seen on the ground glass only when illuminated from behind. There being two such compartments, independent control of their lights could be used to present first one figure and then another.

Neon bulbs were used for illumination because their lag in striking and extinction is practically negligible. Each compartment had a bank of five neon bulbs. These are standard 3-watt, 120-volt G.E. lamps; their light is an orange glow. In our experiment, the lamps were operated by direct current. In each compartment, a sheet of flash opal glass was inserted to diffuse the light evenly before it reached the ground glass.

b. The Timer

The apparatus which produced the alternation of the exposed figures was the same as that used by Gilbert in another experiment and a complete description may be found in his published paper (*10*). In brief, the time-interval between the figures presented depended on the adjustable speed of a motor and commutator. Motor speed was controlled by a sliding rheostat and was constantly registered by a Weston electrical tachometer, calibrated in r.p.m. These readings were then calculated into sigma units (1/1000 sec.), which gave absolute time readings of the interval between the serial stimulations. The duration of each stimulation (exposure-time) was always one-half the blank period between presentations (time-interval).

The procedure was the same as that followed in the previous experiments to control the factors of area, distance, position, order of appearance, duration, and illumination.

SUBJECTS

The subjects in this experiment were the same individuals who served in the other parts of this study. There were 16 subjects for each of the five series of this experiment, none of whom appear here twice, making for a combined total of 80 different individuals so examined.

RESULTS

a. Range

The average ranges of time-intervals between successive stimuli presentations over which apparent movement was observed for the several series of this experiment may be found in Table 1. Inspection of these average ranges immediately shows that they are exceedingly restricted. Half of these ranges are under 40, and 80% are under 47; above

Table 1
The Ranges of Movement for the Combinations in Series III–VII in Experiment 3: Reliabilities of the Differences by Fisher's Method. 16 Cases. To Yield a Significant Difference, t Should Equal 2.13.

SERIES	COMBINATION	AVERAGE RANGE	FISHER'S t FOR DIFFERENCE A–B
III	A	30.2	1.01
	B	41.7	
IV	A	39.8	0.61
	B	33.8	
V	A	76.0	0.32
	B	78.3	
VI	A	45.1	0.86
	B	33.5	
VII	A	33.0	0.95
	B	46.4	

47 there are two at about 75; including all ranges, the mean falls at 45.8, and if the highest two were excluded, the mean would be 37.9

These should be compared to the ranges found in Experiment 1, where the ranges of the 25 combinations ran from 99.9 to 211.1. The mean of these values, which includes all the identical and nonidentical combinations, equals 146.6. The mean of the 5 identical combinations alone equals 180.3. In Experiment 2 the ranges ran from 100.6 to 158.2, averaging 129.4; the mean of the 4 highest (the identical pairs) equals 146.2. Remembering that differences as low as 23 points between the ranges of the second experiment were statistically reliable, there can be no question that the reduction from these ranges to the ones of Experiment 3 is enormous.

Fisher's test *(3)* for the significance of small samples was applied to these data. This was done only for those combinations seen by the same subjects, which indicates the intraseries comparisons. Within each series, Fisher's t never reaches here above 1.01, and it would have to be at least 2.13 to be significant. This means that in every case the two pairs of each series are low and do not significantly differ from each other. It may be noticed that the ranges of Series V are the highest of all the nonsense patterns. The critical ratio between the ranges of figures III A and V A (30.2 and 76.0) indicates that this difference is reliable, being equal to 4.35. This is probably due to the fact that the small and large circles in Series V are actually similar figures, thus differing from the figures comprising Series III. We will return to this combination in a later experiment.

b. Analysis of the Types of Movement Effects

In some ways the most interesting types of movements in the whole experiment were observed with these dissimilar patterns. This material is too bulky and unwieldy to be completely presented as a table in the paper. A summary of this material appears in Table 2, and there will be, in addition, a general discussion of its meaning.

When movement is easily observed, there is little ambiguity in the subject's report, and generally the movements can be categorized under a few headings. The inability to perceive movement is reported on only a few trials. . . .

Quite the reverse is the situation in the present experiment, where the figure combinations make it difficult to perceive movement. An attempt to elucidate this condition is the basis of Table 2. When movement is difficult of perception, the subject apparently organizes the stimuli into many different phenomenal appearances. The result is that many different kinds of movements are observed, as shown in the last column of the table. As the number of categories necessary to classify the movement effects increases, each category must necessarily occupy a smaller percent of the total occurrence. Of interest, therefore, is the percent of occurrence for that type of movement most frequently observed with

Table 2
Summary of the Analysis of Types of Movements Observed in Series III–VII, Experiment 3

SERIES COMBINATION		PERCENT OF TRIALS IN WHICH MOST COMMON TYPE OF MOVEMENT OCCURRED	PERCENT OF TRIALS IN WHICH NO MOVEMENT WAS OBSERVED	NUMBER OF DIFFERENT TYPES OF MOVEMENT OBSERVED
III	A	25.0	30.0	14
	B	25.1	19.6	8
IV	A	19.6	23.2	8
	B	32.1	33.9	7
V	A	50.0	10.0	5
	B	55.0	10.0	8
VI	A	17.7	48.4	6
	B	26.7	56.7	3
VII	A	32.0	20.0	7
	B	22.0	22.0	8

each stimulus. There is, finally, the related index of the percent of trials in which no movement was perceived.

The last column of this table shows that a large number of different kinds of movements were occasioned by this experiment, the median being 7.5 types. The median of this simple index was 3 in Experiment 2, and there was no value higher than 5. In the present case the greatest number of different categories of movement observed for any combination was 14. The critical ratio of the difference between the means in Experiments 2 and 3 is 5.37. The number of categories necessary to describe the diversity of movements in Experiment 3 is reliably greater than the number in Experiment 2.

Another sign of this diversity may be found in the third column of the present table. No single type of movement occurs with greater frequency than in 55% of the trials, and in one case the modal type falls as low as 18%. The average of these modal frequencies is 30.5%, and it would be 25.1 if the highest values were excluded. The corresponding average in Experiment 2 is 71.8%. Compared to Experiment 2, therefore, there is a sharp drop in the frequency with which the most commonly observed type of movement occurs.

Finally, there is the matter of the number of trials in which there was a complete failure of movement to occur. In Experiment 2 this occurred in 2.9% of the trials for all combinations; the greatest failure of a single combination to exhibit movement was in 9% of its trials. Compare this with an average failure of movement in 27.4% of the trials in Experiment 3. In every combination at least 10% of the trials failed to show any movement; and for one stimulus-combination, movement was not reported in

56.7% of the trials. There was certainly a marked inability to perceive movement in this experiment.

Almost every conceivable type of movement effect and a good number that were incredible until they were actually reported may be found in this experiment. Fusion effects, besides those previously recorded, were experienced in plane, third-dimensional, and angular varieties. Expansion-contraction was a general category of high frequency within which occurred many novel transformations of one figure into another and back again; these were also complicated by variability in the plane of the movements.

Figures were reported as independent objects circling each other in space, almost as binary stars. A phenomenon similar to this presented a revolving cube on the four faces of which the two exposed figures alternated with two blank spaces. In the cases of stimuli involving an arrow or a half-dumbbell a frequent report was that this figure crashed through or was shot out of the other. Series III bore reports that the arrowhead actually appeared conical, so when this figure pivoted 90 degrees in the third dimension, the subject saw only the largest circumference of the cone, a circle which was the other figure. Had the actual dimensions of the widest part of the arrowhead (the base of the assumed cone) and the diameter of the circle been respected, this would have necessitated a report that the arrowhead expanded to approximate the size of the circle. But this was overlooked, leading one to suspect that the real diameters were adjusted to apparent equality.

A noteworthy effect observed in all cases, though most common in Series VI, was the report that the figures became blurred and fuzzy. This was particularly the case when subjects reported that a combination was rarely conducive to movement. The figures then appeared to lose their contour characteristics, and the subject would report movement that changed one indistinct figure into another indistinct figure, this change taking place through a nebulous haze. From the point of view of the functional relation between such forms, the indistinct figures actually looked much more like each other than they did with sharp contours. The possibility that a change of accommodation may have contributed to this effect will be considered in the discussion.

c. Subjective Estimates of the Relative Ease for the Perception of Apparent Movement

Subjects were asked to designate which of the two combinations were observed to move more readily. Since there were different groups of subjects for each of the five series of this experiment, every subject was prepared to estimate only those he observed; thus, inter-series comparisons cannot be made. Within each series, however, the pattern is perfectly obvious. And this is practically a chance choice, the meaning of which must be that subjects could not consistently agree that some combinations moved more readily than others. As a matter of fact, there was probably very little choice. These results may be found in Table 3. In

Table 3
Averages of the Subjects' Estimates, by Ranking, of the Ease with Which the Combinations of Series III–VII Appeared to Move

SERIES	COMBINATION	AVERAGE RANK
III	A	1.7
	B	1.3
IV	A	1.4
	B	1.6
V	A	1.3
	B	1.7
VI	A	1.6
	B	1.4
VII	A	1.5
	B	1.5

any case, the view could very easily be entertained that these results comply more with the subjects' polite attempt to satisfy a request by the experimenter than they do with any phenomenal differences.

DISCUSSION

There can be little doubt that when figures widely different from each other are repeatedly presented under conditions ordinarily conducive to the apprehension of apparent movement, there is only a slight range (if there be any at all) over which movement is perceived. It is an academic question whether the differences in the forms of each combination actually probe the ultimates of such form differences as may exist. One interpretation may be, therefore, that had the differences been absolutely antithetical, there would have been no movement at all. This is an a priori assertion, though there is merit in the position. Had still other differences between the figures been introduced in their areas, brightness, color, number, and spatial separation, it is quite possible that these difficulties would have inhibited any perception of movement.

An alternative, not incompatible with the first, may be that the lower limit beyond which the increasing difference in form does not further restrict the range lies at or close below the lowest range observed by us, under our constant conditions of area, color, brightness, and so on.

Movement was certainly restricted, though not eliminated. The question which remains to be answered, then, concerns the fact that movement was not completely repudiated. The rationale of the answer will, it is thought, resolve the suggested alternatives into a single explanation.

The diversity between the figures had other effects in addition to reducing the ranges to the smallest values yet observed. One such effect was the inability to perceive movement on one trial in every four; for one combination it was more often than one in two trials. To this extent, then, were expectations met in fact. Among the observed movements no single type was quite stable, the sign of this being the large number of different types of movement. The same influence makes even the most prominent type of movement appear infrequently as compared with other combinations.

The key to the whole situation may be the interesting fact that the figure combinations for which it was most difficult to perceive motion lost their sharp outlines and became blurred. The result of this blurring was to make the indistinct masses more like each other, the condition under which movement was perceived. This blurring effect might not be the case with greater exposition times. When there was no movement, blurring was not often reported.

It would appear that there is a strong tendency to make the figures appear equal in movement. When the forms differ, most such similarities are ruled out. Then fusion may appear. Beyond that, certain differences are overlooked in the setting up of apparent working constancies for which there is no complete basis in fact, e.g., the cases of the conical arrowhead (Series III) and the four-squares figure (Series VII B). Should the actual differences be too awkward to be overlooked in this manner, certain releases from the immediate contexts were reported. Here, reference is made to the appearance of the two figures independently circling each other in space and the invention of a revolving figure on whose four faces the two figures alternated with the blank spaces. These effects would, of course, be complicated by the lack of stability of any particular movement, so that the subject would report two or three types of movement on a single trial, the patternization of which is very likely influenced by the time-interval. And then a final resolution of different figures into a movement relationship might require the actual obliteration of the differences (never complete) through appearances which by their very indistinctness made possible some similarities. When no similarity of form exists, the effects which occur seem to disclose fictitious similarity. From an analysis of the reported phenomena, subjects attempt to set up some fictitious similarity.

A change in visual accommodation may have produced the blurring of figural characteristics which accompany perceived movement under those conditions. The experiment was conducted in the dark, and there was neither the opportunity nor apparatus to determine the involvement of convergence or accommodation in the phenomena. The suggestion of an accommodation effect, therefore, is speculative and inferential. Should it prove that accommodation is involved, it implies that a stimulus characteristic (the figure received is a blurred one) and not a perceptual rendering (the blurring of a clear figure) would explain the phenomenon. A complete explanation is not to be found in the fact that accommodation is implicated. Thus remaining unaccounted [for] would be the fact that accommodation was imperfect only on trials for which blurring occurred—and that it did not ordinarily change for similar figures. The present explanation poses no antagonism between the alternative hypotheses, and the observation that marked form-differences are accompanied by blurring (however produced) may remain uncontested.

An explanation placing the perception of blurred movement solely on the peripheral changes of accommodation would be as untenable as the position that eye movements explain apparent movement. Wertheimer *(10)* never said that eye movements were not involved in the perception of movement. He did say, however, that an explanation solely in these terms would be insufficient. To this he adduced evidence that the time-intervals over which movement was observed were too short to permit eye movements as explanations; this also applied to after-images. His classic demonstration was that any explanation involving eye movements would also require the eye to move in opposite directions at the same time; and this is impossible. Likewise, the breakdown of visual sensitivity as in flicker-fusion could not explain the phi phenomenon. When movement may no longer be perceived at the upper threshold (simultaneity) flicker may still be observed. Langfeld *(7)* separately stimulated each eye and still got the impression of movement. This corroborated the assertion that movement depended on central rather than on peripheral factors. In two experiments, eye movements were measured directly, and it was shown that apparent movement occurred even while the eyes were stationary. This was independently shown by Guilford and Helson *(5)* and by Hulin and Katz *(6)*. Eye movements are, therefore, thought not to provide a probable explanation. Dimmick and Scahill *(2)* and Bartley *(1)* even asserted that there was no difference between apparent and real movement.

The same reasoning may be applied to the suggested accommodation effect. It is not denied that accommodation may be involved. Fortunately, this may be directly determined with the proper instruments available for its measurement. But the important point, as with eye movements, is that it may not always occur. It would, therefore, seem that accommodation is not a peripheral effect but that it is a central effect to help the subject blur the figures when this may aid in the perception of movement. It would be an instance in which central factors under certain conditions mediate peripheral adjustments.

Only the inability to predict the results of this experiment permitted the premature assertion that complete form-difference should destroy movement. Theoretically, this should be true. But then, other objective similarities still remain. The figures are equal in area, color, brightness, and duration of presentation; as mere blobs of light, disregarding form, they could still be considered alike. Then they are continuously presented under conditions where even the least impressionable subject understands that he is likely to perceive apparent movement.

The two alternatives of a few pages ago really rest on a common base. As regards the first, a complete lack of similarity between the forms (and other aspects) of figures presented for apparent movement may in all probability result in the failure to apprehend such movement. It may be said, in respect to the second, that our failure to completely eliminate movement (though it was seriously restricted) may be due to residual features of similarity in area, color, brightness, and duration of presentation. And to this must be added the import of the present discussion. The real differences tend to be disregarded or actively reduced, and novel organizations may resolve them by creating new figures.

SUMMARY

This experiment set the problem of studying the possible breakdown of apparent movement by combinations of markedly dissimilar figures. The range of movement was considerably reduced by such combinations, but movement was not completely eliminated. Many different types of movements were observed and analyzed, and there were many trials on which movements could not be perceived. Subjects were not able to judge that some combinations rendered movement more easily than others. An explanation was offered for the occurrence of the residual movement effects which held the apprehension of apparent movement to be a perceptual process, actually a constancy effect, whereby objective differences tend to be disregarded or actively reduced.

REFERENCES

1. Bartley, S. H. The relation of retinal illumination to the experience of movement. *Journal of Experimental Psychology*, 1936, *19*, 475–485.
2. Dimmick, F. L., and Scahill, H. G. Visual perception of movement. *American Journal of Psychology*, 1925, *36*, 412–417.
3. Fisher, R. A. *Statistical techniques for research workers* (6th ed.). Edinburgh: Oliver and Boyd, 1936.
4. Gilbert, G. M. Dynamic psychophysics and the phi phenomenon. *Archives of Psychology*, 1939, No. 237.
5. Guilford, J. P., and Helson, H. Eye movements and the phi-phenomenon. *American Journal of Psychology*, 1929, *41*, 596–606.
6. Hulin, W. S., and Katz, D. Eye movements and the phi-phenomenon. *American Journal of Psychology*, 1934, *46*, 332–334.
7. Langfeld, H. S. Apparent visual movement with a stationary stimulus. *American Journal of Psychology*, 1927, *39*, 343–355.
8. Linke, P. Die stroboskopische Täuschungen und das Problem des Sehens von Bewegungen. *Psychologische Studien*, 1907, *3*, 393–545.
9. ———. *Grundfragen der Wahrnehmungslehre-Untersuchungen über die Bedeutung Phänomenologie für die experimentelle Psychologie*. Munich: Reinhardt, 1918.
10. Wertheimer, M. Experimentelle Studien über das Sehen von Bewegung. *Zeitschrift für Psychologie*, 1912, *61*, 161–265.

IRRELEVANCE OF FIGURAL IDENTITY FOR RESOLVING AMBIGUITIES IN APPARENT MOTION

David Navon, University of California, San Diego

In order to examine the degree to which form perception affects the formation of apparent-motion experience, subjects were presented with nine ambiguous apparent-motion situations, where the elements of each single flash were various figures. One of the interpretations of each situation preserved the figural identity of the figures across flashes. It was found that figural identity does not have any effect on determining the type of motion experienced, except when the figural analysis involved is relatively simple.

In the vast literature about apparent motion only little attention is given to the effect of figural identity on perceived motion. The question is whether a subject may experience a sensation of motion when presented with a flash of a certain figure followed by another flash of a *different* figure in a different location. Early studies (mentioned in Kolers, 1972, p. 43) show that figural identity is by no means a necessary condition for perceiving motion. However, Orlansky (1940) concluded from the results of his experiments that although disparity of shape does not rule out illusory motion, it may make it less compelling and narrow the range of its appearance. The notion, implied by Orlansky's conclusions, that sensation of motion is determined to some degree by the visual similarity between the figures in the alternating flashes, was strongly opposed by Kolers (1972). On the basis of the results of Kolers and Pomerantz (1971) and Kolers (1972, pp. 51–53), he argued that disparity in shape cannot be expected to affect illusory motion, because figural analysis is completed only after the impression of motion is either created or not, so that the perceived motion can intervene in the figural analysis but not vice versa. In Kolers' words, "the visual system responds to locations of stimulation and infers or creates changes of figure to resolve that disparity" (Kolers, 1972, p. 57).

Most of the evidence that Kolers relies on are demonstrations that "given the choice of retaining a figure but moving it to a new location, or

This project was supported in part by Grant NS07454 from the National Institutes of Health. I thank Donald Norman very much for his careful review and his useful comments. Requests for reprints should be sent to David Navon, who is now at the Department of Psychology, University of Haifa, Haifa 31999, Israel.

Navon, David. Irrelevance of figural identity for resolving ambiguities in apparent motion. *Journal of Experimental Psychology: Human Perception and Performance*, 1976, *2*, 130–138.

retaining a location and building a new figure within it, the visual system performs the latter task" (Kolers, 1972, p. 54). For example, when he showed (Figure 46, Array 5) in succession the stimuli displayed here in A and B of Figure 1, no motion was perceived; rather, the extreme figures changed shape, and the innermost ones blinked on and off. Kolers' demonstrations indicate that the visual system exhibits *location inertia* rather than *preservation of figural identity*. To complete this line of argumentation, one should show that preservation of identity does not affect the perception of motion even when it does not conflict with maintenance of locations.

For this purpose I designed several situations of ambiguous apparent motion, each with several interpretations. Each interpretation involves the same degree of change of locations. One interpretation of each situation satisfies the principle of preservation of figural identity. The others do not. If figural identity has any effect at all on the formation of motion impression, then the interpretation in which figural identity is preserved should be the one most likely to be perceived. A failure of figural identity to bias perception would be another indication of its irrelevance in determining perceived motion.

METHOD

Stimuli

Each different situation of apparent motion can be called an *episode*. An episode is characterized by the appearance of a cycle of two or six consecutive different displays, and it consists of a number of iterations of this cycle. Each display was presented for 150 msec with a 30-msec time interval between any two consecutive displays as well as between

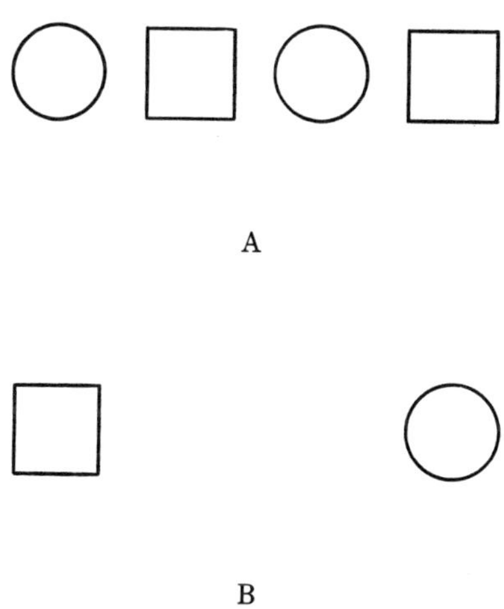

FIGURE 1. The displays alternated by Kolers (adapted from Kolers, 1972, Figure 46, Array 5).

any two consecutive cycles. Each of the individual displays will be called an *array*. An array consisted of two or six elements taken out of either of the sets presented in Figure 2. Each set of elements is called a *vocabulary*. The vocabularies differ in the degree of difficulty for the subject to identify (or, more generally, to perform figural analysis on) their members. Presumably the simplest are the line segments, and the most difficult for an American student are the Hebrew letters.

The arrays in one cycle of each of the nine episodes used in this experiment and possible interpretations for the episodes are shown in Figure 3. (The elements shown in the figure are taken from the English-letters vocabulary.)

The names of the episodes follow the type of motion that would have been perceived had the identity of elements been preserved across flashes.

The "crossing slides" episode. The identity-preserving interpretation of this episode is that of crossed diagonal motion. The other likely interpretation is that of simultaneous vertical movement in both sides of the display. It was already found (Kolers, 1972, pp. 76–79) that subjects do not see simultaneous motion in two diagonal crossing paths, even when the interpretation of crossed motion preserves the identity of the elements while the alternative one does not. This episode is meant to replicate Koler's finding with the vocabularies used in this experiment.

The "seesaw" episodes. In these episodes the most likely interpretations are that of two simultaneous motions along one dimension in opposite directions and that of a seesaw oscillation about either the vertical or horizontal axis. The identity-preserving interpretations in the "vertical seesaw" episode are the ones which involve horizontal motion of the elements, whereas in the "horizontal seesaw" episode they are the ones which involve vertical motion of the elements.

The "cha-cha-cha" episodes. The locations of the elements of the second array in these episodes are halfway between two adjacent locations of the elements of the first array on the circumference of the imaginary circle connecting the elements. The intercycle time interval was the same as the interarray time interval. Thus there are two possible interpretations: either that of a circular motion (of the configuration as a whole or of the six elements individually), which can be either clockwise or counterclockwise, or that of a 30° back-and-forth tilting motion (again of the configuration as a whole or of the six elements individually). The "identi-

vocabulary	figures						
English letters	E	Z	M	T	L	H	◊
Hebrew letters	ש	ב	פ	ד	ה	ט	◊
Line segments	—	|	⟍	/	⟋	\	◊

FIGURE 2. The elements used to construct arrays tabulated according to vocabularies.

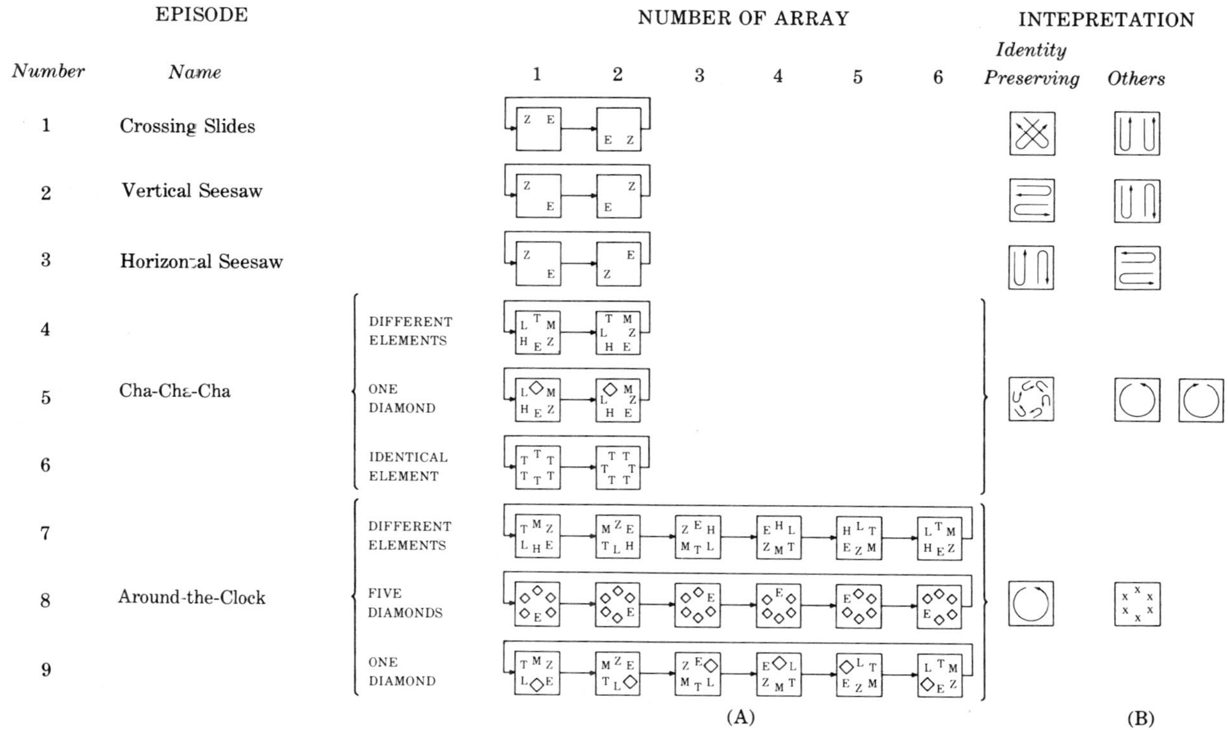

FIGURE 3. The arrays in one cycle of each of the nine episodes and possible interpretations of the episodes. (The arrays of the different episodes are presented in (A) in order of their appearance. An arrow going from one array to another denotes that the second immediately follows the first. Several possible interpretations of the episodes are presented in (B). A perceived motion is represented by an arrow tracing its direction and approximate location. A stationary element is represented by an x at its location. Size relationships are slightly distorted due to space limitations. The fixation point is omitted from the figure.)

cal element" version of these episodes enables the testing of the prior bias toward each of these possible interpretations, because each of them would preserve the identity of the elements. The "one diamond cha-cha-cha" episode introduces a different aspect of disparity between elements, namely size disparity; the size of the diamond is three times as large as the average size of a letter.

The "around-the-clock" episodes. Kolers demonstrated that restimulation of the same locations produces no apparent motion regardless of the change in identity of the elements shown in those locations, but to show it he used an episode (Kolers, 1972, Figure 46, Array 6) in which identity-preserving apparent motion was a priori unlikely because it would have involved crossed motion, which was shown to be practically impossible (Kolers, 1972, pp. 76–79). The "different elements around-the-clock" episode circumvents this difficulty: The identity-preserving interpretation is that of a counterclockwise circular motion of the configuration as a whole or of the six elements individually. No path is crossing any other one, so during the identity-preserving apparent motion there is never more than one element at a given location at the same time. The other versions of the around-the-clock episodes are variations on the same theme. In the "five diamonds" episode, five elements are identical. The "one diamond" version differs from the "different elements" version in a way analogous to the one by which Episode 5 differs from Episode 4, namely introduction of size disparity.[1]

Ferris wheel versus roulette. The arrays of the cha-cha-cha and the around-the-clock episodes as depicted in Figure 3 correspond to a condition that was called the *Ferris wheel* arrangement. It is characterized by presenting all the elements in their upright position, such that a perceived circular motion resembles the motion of a Ferris wheel. In fact some of the stimuli used in these episodes correspond to another condition called the *roulette* arrangement, in which each element is erect with respect to the radius connecting it to the center of the display, such that a perceived circular motion resembles the motion of a roulette. As an example for this arrangement the arrays of Episode 4 under the roulette arrangement are presented in Figure 4.

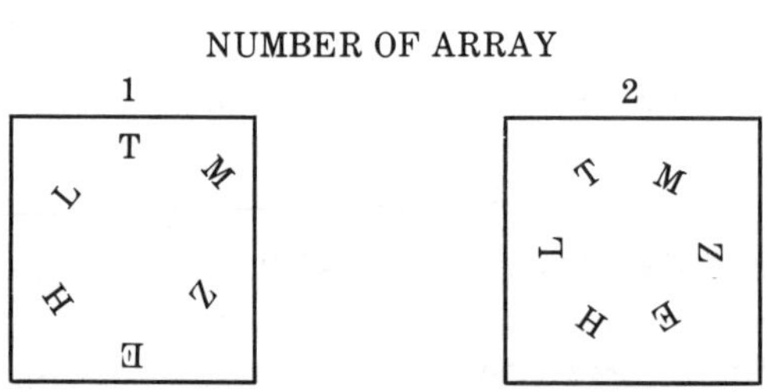

FIGURE 4. The arrays of Episode 4 under the roulette arrangement. (The fixation point is omitted from the figure.)

Subjects and Response Mode

In contrast with the convention in apparent-motion studies to present few experienced subjects with many repetitions of the same stimuli (possibly with a change of some of the display parameters), I used naive subjects and presented them with an episode only once. My consideration was that if a visual ambiguity is really ambiguous, that is to say, the different interpretations are perceptually possible and likely, then once one is familiar with all the interpretations, he may be inclined to impose one of them on the visual field according to considerations which are not perceptual. For example, he may try to force himself to see the identity-preserving motion, because it reconciles best his percept with his conjecture about the process of generating the stimuli. Therefore, the subjects saw an episode only until their first interpretation was superseded by a second one, if at all. They reported their first interpretation (and the second one if there was any). The approximate duration for which the first interpretation persisted was recorded in a way described in the Procedure section.

Subjects were 26 nonpaid undergraduates at the University of California, San Diego, who participated in the experiment as part of their course requirement in the department of psychology. Eight subjects were unable to experience ordinary beta horizontal motion in the preliminary stage of the experiment, so although they did participate in the rest of the experiment (to avoid the need for a cover story), their data were not included in the analysis. No subjects were familiar with the Hebrew alphabet.

Design

The episodes were classified into three groups: (a) Episodes 1, 2, 3; (b) Episodes 4, 5, 6; and (c) Episodes 7, 8, 9 (see Figure 2). Episodes of one group were presented consecutively; thus the sequence of trials may be conceived as forming blocks of three trials each. Groups and vocabularies were paired and assigned to blocks according to a 3×3 Graeco-Latin square. The episodes were ordered within blocks according to three orthogonal Latin squares, one for each block. Each subject was assigned to one sequence of the Graeco-Latin square which dominated the three orthogonal Latin squares, and in addition to one of the arrangement conditions.

Apparatus and Setting

The main equipment consisted of a display Tektronix oscilloscope (which decayed completely in .9 msec at the luminance level used) and a typewriter keyboard, both controlled by a PDP-9 computer in an acoustically isolated booth. The subject sat in the booth in front of a table. The keyboard was positioned on the table at about elbow level directly in front of the subject. The display oscilloscope was positioned in front of the subject at about eye level. Viewing distance was about 45 cm.

The length of an element was about 4 mm, and the diameter of the imaginary circle circumscribing the elements in Episodes 4–9 was about 60 mm. Thus the longer side of an element subtended about 0°30′ visual angle for the subject, and the whole relevant visual field subtended about 7°40′ visual angle. The illumination of the booth was dim but sufficient for reading and writing. The brightness of the display was sufficient for perfect recognition of the elements. A small model of a Ferris wheel, constructed of an Erector Set, was set on the table so that the subject was able physically to demonstrate the motion experienced by him. The "seats" of the Ferris wheel could be fixed to stimulate the roulette arrangement as well.

Procedure

Each trial, including the pretest trials, was preceded by a 1-sec warning beep. From the onset of the beep until the termination of the trial display, a small dot was seen at the visual field. A trial started immediately after the onset of the beep. Subjects were run individually. The experimenter sat in the booth with the subject, recorded the subject's verbal responses after the trial was over, and initiated the trials by depressing a key on the keyboard. At the beginning of the experiment the experimenter read general instructions and asked the subject to attend to his immediate impression rather than to try to describe the episode analytically. The subject was also asked to fixate at the center dot when watching an apparent-motion trial.

Preliminary stage. The subject was presented with six letter-recognition pretest trials. In each of them a different upright English letter was displayed for 150 msec in one of the elements locations of Array 1 of Episode 4. In the first three pretest trials the subject did not know where the letter was about to appear; in the last three trials he was told the position beforehand. Then the subject was exposed to a 150-msec display of Array 1 of Episode 4. He was required to draw schematically whatever he had managed to see. Then the subject was presented with two demonstrations: The first one was the ordinary horizontal beta motion of the letter E moving between the locations of Z and H in Array 1 of Episode 4. The second one was a counterclockwise circular motion of the letter T appearing sequentially in the elements locations of Array 1 of Episode 4. (It appeared always upright for subjects under the Ferris wheel condition and rotated while revolving for subjects under the roulette condition.) Each of the demonstrations was presented until the experimenter made sure whether the subject could experience a steady sensation of motion. Then the sequence of nine test trials was presented.

Test stage. The subject was instructed to watch an episode as long as he could maintain his first steady interpretation of the episode and to depress a certain key on the keyboard as soon as the first interpretation switched to a second one, if it ever happened. Depressing the key caused immediate termination of the display. In case the subject did not depress the key, the display was terminated after 10.7 sec. The time the subject took before depressing the key, if at all, was measured. After the termination of the display, the subject described verbally his interpretation(s) of the episode, and in case of difficulties in verbal communication the subject could use the Erector Set pieces to physically demonstrate his experience.

As said earlier, exposure time was about [2] 150 msec, and ISI (interstimulus interval: interarray and intercycle intervals) was about 30 msec. Those parameters were selected on the basis of both former findings (Kolers, 1964) and some informal studies with myself and several other colleagues as subjects.

RESULTS AND DISCUSSION

The arrangement condition (i.e., Ferris wheel versus roulette) did not seem to affect the results at all, so data are pooled across conditions. The type of vocabulary interacts with the results only in one case, so data are pooled across vocabularies except for that single case.

The crossing slides episode. Seventeen subjects reported a vertical motion in at least one of their interpretations. No subject reported a crossing diagonal motion in either of the two interpretations. One subject reported a seesaw motion. The result is highly significant, $\chi^2(2) = 26.86$, $p < .001$. Thus on the basis of both the present result and Kolers' similar finding (Kolers, 1972, pp. 76–79), it can be concluded that the failure to see crossing diagonal apparent motion is a pervasive phenomenon that is probably not affected at all by preservation of identity. Although interesting, this is somewhat weak evidence for the unimportance of the principle of preservation of identity because it may be argued that effective as this principle may be, it may still fail if it leads to a perceptual absurdity, such as the presence of two visual objects at the same location at a certain moment, which is implied by the crossing paths. The failure to see diagonal motion can also be attributed to the size difference between the vertical and the diagonal paths. More direct evidence is provided by the results of the other episodes.

The seesaw episodes. The preservation of figural identity should resolve the ambiguity of Episode 2 in favor of the opposite horizontal motion (or seesaw motion about the vertical axis) and the ambiguity of Episode 3 in favor of the opposite vertical motion (or seesaw motion about the horizontal axis). If the effect of identity is partial but is still present, several possibilities exist. First, both motions will be seen alternately, but the first to appear or the more compelling will be the one preserving the identity of the elements. Second, one type of motion is a priori more likely to be experienced; thus it will be the only interpretation in the episode in which the motion preserves the identity of the elements. In the episode in which the other type of motion preserves the identity, however, both motions will be experienced. Third, both motions will be experienced in both episodes, and the first interpretation will be the same in both episodes, but the first interpretation will switch sooner to the second one in the episode in which the second one preserves the identity. In the analysis of the subjects' reports, each occurrence of any of these events was considered as an indication in favor of preservation of identity; if neither of them occurred, it was considered as an indication against preservation of identity. Fifteen indications were counted against preservation of identity and only 3 for it, χ^2 (1) = 12, $p < .001$. Furthermore, among the 15, 3 were examples of the opposite of the prediction from preservation of identity; for example, the first interpretation in both episodes was that of a vertical motion, superseded by a sensation of horizontal motion merely in Episode 3 (and not in Episode 2, as it should have been, had figural identity the expected effect). Actually the vertical motion is much more likely to be perceived regardless of the identity of the elements. Only 1 of the 16 subjects saw first a horizontal motion. One may argue that the tendency to see vertical motion outweighs the identity effect which may still exist. However, an additional finding refutes this argument. If it had been true, one should not have experienced horizontal motion at all in Episode 3; in fact, the frequency of sensing both motions is equal for the two episodes.

It should be noted that subjects frequently identify the elements and are often aware of the change in identity. If this, nevertheless, fails to affect the type of motion perceived, although preservation of figural identity does not conflict in this case with any other known perceptual principle, then the formation of the sensation of motion cannot be mediated to any extent by results of figural analysis.

The cha-cha-cha episode. The most prevalent report about this type of episode is a counterclockwise circular motion[3] abruptly changing to a clockwise circular motion.[4] The direction of motion failed to switch only rarely; and strangely enough, the clockwise direction never preceded the counterclockwise one. In either of the different elements and identical element versions, 17 subjects saw a circular motion, 1 had some eccentric sensation, and nobody saw a tilt. The result is highly significant, χ^2 (2) = 30.34, $p < .001$. Thus the identical element version shows that the tilting interpretation (the identity-preserving interpretation) is a priori unlikely relative to the circular interpretations, and the different elements version shows that figural identity cannot increase its likelihood. One may contend that figural identity might have been the cause for the instability of the direction of movement. However, the frequency of switch of directions is the same in both episodes. In 10 out of 15 cases the switch in the identical element version is sooner than the switch in the different elements one.

The picture is somewhat different in the one diamond version, where one of the elements is about three times as large as the others. In this episode, to sense circular motion one has to ignore not only shape disparity but size disparity as well. In three cases the conflict was solved by perceiving the diamond as being stationary (and not tilting) while the other elements moved around the circle. However, in some others a back-and-forth tilt was seen by the subjects in at least one of their two interpretations. Here there seems to be an effect to the vocabulary of the elements. As can be seen in Table 1, the disparity between the diamond and the letters was not sufficient to override the tendency to see circular motion, whereas the diamond was different enough from the line segments to induce the tilting interpretation. (Fisher's exact probability after eliminating "other interpretations" is .004.) It thus appears that although strict identity of shapes is unnecessary and even irrelevant for perceiving motion between successive stimuli, nevertheless some sort of similarity between the stimuli has to be maintained. A more thorough discussion of the possible aspects of that similarity will be presented later.

The around-the-clock episodes. Here the figural identity of the elements is preserved by a counterclockwise circular motion of all the elements. An alternative interpretation is that of the elements staying in the same location but changing shapes. This is a clear instance of superiority of location inertia over preservation of figural identity. In still other interpretations the perceived identity of one of the elements induces just a circular motion of itself while the other elements are seen as stationary.[5] This often happened in the five diamonds and one diamond versions, where one element was clearly discernible from the other five. Any subject that saw any kind of circular motion in at least one of his interpretations of an episode is classified under the heading "Circular" in Table 2; subjects who did not see any motion at all are classified under the heading "Stationary." As can be seen, the impact of shape preservation that almost does not exist in the different diamonds version is considerably effective in the five diamonds version and even more so in the one diamond version, Cochran's Q (3) = 20.46, $p < .001$. In view of this finding and of the result described in Table 1, it seems that the type of motion perceived is sometimes, although not often, affected by the output of processes which identify the objects in the scene of an episode. So the observed impotence of the principle of preservation of figural identity probably cannot be explained by a process in which figural analysis necessarily succeeds motion analysis.

In order to gain better understanding of the possible interaction between these two types of analysis, let us examine carefully the properties

Table 1
Frequency of Different Interpretations of the "One Diamond Cha-Cha-Cha" Episode According to Type of Vocabulary

VOCABULARY	INTERPRETATION		
	CIRCULAR	TILTING	OTHER
Letters	9	0	3
Line segments	1	5	0

Table 2
Frequency of Different Interpretations of the "Around-the-Clock" Episodes

EPISODE	INTERPRETATION	
	STATIONARY	CIRCULAR
Different elements	15	3
Five diamonds	6	12
One diamond	2	16

of the diamond episodes that are not shared by the different elements around-the-clock episode. In the latter the number of elements whose identities are preserved only by the counterclockwise circular motion but not by the stationary impression is greater than their number in the five diamonds version. Nevertheless figural identity has no effect in the different elements episode and some effect in the five diamonds episode. Hence the "amount" of identity preservation must be unrelated to its potential impact. On the other hand, the load that the different elements episode imposes on figural analysis processes is much heavier than the load imposed by the five diamonds one. To put it another way, whereas in the first one each array introduces six concurrent changes in the shape of stimuli at given locations with respect to the immediately preceding array, in the second one there is only one such change to be noticed by the figural analysis mechanisms. The relative load on the processes for form analysis and motion analysis must thus have a critical function in determining the direction of interdependence between them, namely which is going to affect the other.

The one diamond around-the-clock episode and the line segments version of the one diamond cha-cha-cha episode suggest that size of objects is much more likely to be preserved in apparent motion than their contours and internal structure. This is not surprising if we closely inspect the issue of location inertia versus preservation of identity. What do we mean when we say that the visual system retains a location and builds a new figure within it (Kolers, 1972, p. 54)? Clearly, most of the points subsumed in the different figures do not overlap. So there must be some obscure sense of "occupying the same place" that the visual system is responsive to. It is not exhausted by information about the origin or the center of gravity of a figure; it seems to contain information about "average visual angle subtended by the different diameters of the figure," or "maximal diameter," or the like. In this sense, size disparity violates not only the preservation of identity but the persistence of location. To put it differently, the difference between an array and its successor in the one diamond around-the-clock episode lies not just in the identity of the elements at the given position but also in the global configuration. The identity of the overall spatial arrangement may well affect motion perception, although the identity of the elements usually does not.

Attneave (1974), Breitmeyer, Love, & Wepman (1974), and Kolers and Pomerantz (1971) discussed the relationship between ISI and the degree to which apparent motion is affected by shape. However, the phenomena demonstrated in this article appear to be unaffected by changes in ISI. In informal observations made on several colleagues and myself with ISI values of 0, 150, 200, and 300 msec, the motion appeared less compelling but essentially unchanged. At an ISI of 400 msec, one can hardly see any continuous motion at all.

Anstis (1970) proposed that in apparent motion "each point in the field at time t_1 is perceived as moving towards the nearest point that happens to have the same brightness at time t_2" (p. 1428). In an informal study I presented several colleagues with an episode similar to Episode 2, except that the figures were two diamonds, one of which was three times as intense as the other one. The favored motion was a vertical one over a wide range of intensity settings. Thus in this case, figural identity is not the only attribute which is not preserved; brightness is also not preserved.

Some Theoretical Implications

Finally, some hypothesis about the processes involved in perceiving motion may explain most of the discussed findings. First, it should be noted that the exposure time of 150 msec used in the experiment was certainly sufficient for figure identification, as evidenced both by the pretests in which subjects by and large did not fail to recognize any of the probe letters and by the fact that subjects identified elements during the presentation of the episodes. Thus figural analysis *is* performed, although it usually does not bear on the motion perceived. Any model of motion perception will have to take this into consideration. Kolers accounts for it by hypothesizing two functionally independent systems, one for pattern analysis and one for space-and-motion analysis, whose outputs are coordinated by a higher order assessor (Kolers, 1972, pp. 114–116). This assumption is unnecessary because a unified system can also yield the same phenomena.

Assume that the formation of motion perception is a process of looking for the best account for disparities in consecutive static displays. The decision must be made very fast in order to maintain a continuous and coherent percept, even at the cost of ignoring some information that is slowly obtained or interpreted. To explain the precedence of location information over figural identity, one should simply consider the kind of information the process which determines the motion receives. Suppose that the process of determining shape takes longer to perform than the process of determining location (e.g., as suggested by results of Fehrer & Raab, 1962, and Thorson, Lange, & Biederman-Thorson, 1969). Then the process which is analyzing motion would receive information about location or global configuration before it would receive information about shape. Figural information may arrive too late to be useful. That is probably why location inertia is more potent than figural identity and also why size disparity is more effective than figural disparity. Nevertheless, when the load on the figural recognition processes is smaller (as it presumably is in Episode 8 when compared with Episode 7), figural analysis may be completed sooner, so that it is more likely to affect the perception of motion.

In sum, the observation that motion perception is unaffected by pattern recognition does not necessarily entail that those processes reside in separate systems. It may be that the motion detectors use whatever has been processed by the visual system up to the time of their operation, including intermediary results of the figural analysis processes. However, the rate of figural analysis is slow and seldom keeps up with the rate of motion analysis, hence the relative irrelevance of figural identity in perceiving apparent motion.

REFERENCES

Anstis, S. M. Phi movement as a subtraction process. *Vision Research*, 1970, *10*, 1141–1430.

Attneave, F. Apparent movement and the what-where connection. *Psychologia—An International Journal of Psychology in the Orient*, 1974, *17*, 108–120.

Breitmeyer, B., Love, R., & Wepman, B. Contour suppression during stroboscopic motion and metacontrast. *Vision Research*, 1974, *14*, 1451–1456.

Brown, J. F., & Voth, A. C. The path of seen movement as a function of the vector-field. *American Journal of Psychology*, 1937, *49*, 543–563.

Fehrer, E., & Raab, D. Reaction time to stimuli masked by metacontrast. *Journal of Experimental Psychology*, 1962, *63*, 143–147.

Kolers, P. A. The illusion of movement. *Scientific American*, 1964, *211* (4), 98–106.

———. *Aspects of motion perception*. Oxford, Eng.: Pergamon Press, 1972.

Kolers, P. A., & Pomerantz, J. R. Figural change in apparent motion. *Journal of Experimental Psychology*, 1971, *87*, 99–108.

Orlansky, J. The effect of similarity and difference in form on apparent visual movement. *Archives of Psychology*, 1940, *246*, 85.

Thorson, J., Lange, G. D., & Biederman-Thorson, M. Objective measure of the dynamics of a visual movement illusion. *Science*, 1969, *164*, 1087–1088.

NOTES

1. There was a slight imperfection in Array 1 of the one diamond around-the-clock episode: The plotting routine trimmed the bottom edge of the diamond and placed it at the top of the visual field. The defect was hardly visible and seemed not to affect the perceived motion at all.

2. Some imprecision is unavoidable because it takes the plotting routine from 1 to 3 msec to plot the stimuli.

3. In all the circular episodes, including the pretest demonstration of circular motion, subjects mostly reported a circular, although jerky, motion, rather than motion along the sides of a hexagon. This was more compelling under the roulette condition than under the Ferris wheel condition. This phenomenon, previously observed by Brown and Voth (1937), indicated that perception of motion is not independent of the global context, be it the figural

properties of the global configuration in the array itself or the short-term history of changes of locations from array to array.

4. Five subjects (four of them in the roulette condition) reported that the circle seemed to expand before switching directions of movement.

5. Actually some subjects reported seeing an element going around a stationary circle made out of other elements, which entail that it occludes different parts of the circle while moving. This observation is inconsistent with Kolers' claim (Kolers, 1972, p. 81) that illusory motion, which allows for two objects to occupy the same place at the same time, is impossible.

3. CONTROLLING OUR EMOTIONS:

Biofeedback as Therapy — a Present Reality or a Promise as yet Unfulfilled?

One of the most interesting and controversial developments in the last 10 to 15 years has been the introduction of corrective feedback in the control of "automatic" functions of the body such as heartbeat, blood pressure, and electrical activity recorded from the scalp, known as the electroencephalogram (EEG). In the following two articles the issue is raised as to whether current biofeedback technology has progressed to the point where it can be widely applied by clinical psychologists and others in an outpatient setting or whether the procedures and techniques are still too experimental and unreliable for such use.

Neither of these articles gives a complete go-ahead signal for the widespread use of such techniques, but the article by Edward Blanchard and Larry Young seems to be more conservative in its conclusions than the article by Gary Schwartz.

What are some of the procedural issues that are important in thinking about biofeedback? What are the main differences between biofeedback techniques and those of progressive relaxation or yoga? These articles are relevant to discussions about the ancient (but still honorable) topic of the interactions of the phenomena we call mental and those we call physiological. One approach to this old mind-body problem is to view both changes in rate of heartbeat and anxiety as two different manifestations of a single process, the operation of a complex biological organism that has the ability to monitor its own functions. What are the various implications of different views about the mind-body problem? Which models are most useful in thinking about behavior? While these questions may seem somewhat philosophical (as, indeed, they are), the history of both psychology and physiology has been profoundly affected by the attitudes that have been dominant at a given time. How would you characterize your own attitude on these questions? How about the attitudes of the authors of the following articles?

BIOFEEDBACK AS THERAPY: SOME THEORETICAL AND PRACTICAL ISSUES

Gary E. Schwartz, Harvard University

A central component in psychotherapy is the use of corrective feedback. This has been especially evident during the past 15 years, with the emergence of many new approaches to treatment, including behavior therapy, sensitivity and encounter groups, and what have sometimes been called "video" therapies. In all of these approaches, the patient receives some form of augmented feedback about his own behavior, be it gradual shaping using contingent reinforcement, the reaction of other people in a group setting to the patient's feelings and actions, or the images and sounds of the patient—therapist interaction using videotape replays. Under the right conditions with suitable motivation or incentives the patient may develop awareness or insight into his own behavior and may learn new ways of experiencing and dealing with his environment.

In a similar vein the growth of biofeedback can be seen as the development of new, more refined techniques for providing an individual with feedback for specific physiological processes, and with appropriate incentives these procedures enable him to modify and control what were once considered involuntary and automatic functions, such as heart rate, blood pressure, and brain waves. Actually, the growth of biofeedback simultaneously came out of two somewhat different traditions. One was operant conditioning, where early researchers (in the 1960s) such as Shapiro, Kimmel, Miller, and DiCara viewed the goal of research as demonstrating that operant control of visceral and glandular processes could be obtained in humans using contingent reinforcers such as money and in animals with reinforcers such as electrical stimulation of reward centers in the brain. At about the same time, Kamiya, Brown, and others became interested in seeing whether human subjects could learn to discriminate higher nervous system activity and associated subjective states by providing them with external feedback such as brief lights or

This article is based on an invited address presented at the Third Annual Brockton Symposium on Behavior Therapy, April 1972. Requests for reprints should be sent to Gary E. Schwartz, Department of Psychology and Social Relations, Harvard University, 1444 William James Hall, Cambridge, Massachusetts 02138.

Schwartz, Gary E. Biofeedback as therapy: Some theoretical and practical issues. *American Psychologist*, 1973, *28*, 666–673.

tones for specific electroencephalogram changes. It was reasoned that through the feedback and resulting discrimination, subjects would be able to develop voluntary control over these functions.

It is important to consider the history and scope of the issues raised by this research in order to more fully appreciate its implications and applications to clinical treatment. In particular, biofeedback has stimulated renewed interest in concepts such as voluntary control and consciousness and in the central question of the degree to which man can modify and control his behavior in the face of opposing forces in the environment. Consequently, the role of the individual patient in taking responsibility for the maintenance and control of his own health becomes of paramount importance. Although biofeedback is a form of behavior therapy, this does not alter the basic issues involved, especially since questions of self-control and cognition are becoming central issues in current behavioral approaches to treatment.

Over 250 papers have been published on the use of operant-feedback techniques in the control of physiological processes, and four volumes reprinting much of this work are now available (Barber et al., 1971; Kamiya et al., 1971; Stoyva et al., 1972: Shapiro et al., 1973). My wish is not to review this work nor to cover all the potential clinical applications to date, since this material has been recently reviewed elsewhere (Shapiro & Schwartz, 1972).[1] Rather, this article considers some of the important issues or problems involved in clinically applying biofeedback techniques to the individual patient. Toward this end I will discuss some of our basic and clinical research on the voluntary control of human cardiovascular responses, for it illustrates many of the problems involved.

BASIC RESEARCH

The possible application of biofeedback to the control of essential hypertension (high blood pressure of unknown etiology) first requires the development of a suitable blood pressure measurement and feedback system. A prerequisite for any biofeedback application is the accurate sensing and processing of physiological activity, and not surprisingly, one of the reasons why the field took so long in developing was that readily available biomedical technology, including accurate programming equipment, has only appeared in the past 15 years.

Actually, the technology for sensing and recording human blood pressure on a continuous basis was already available, but it was not practical for routine laboratory work since it required surgical insertion of a pressure-transducing tube into an artery. On the other hand, while the traditional stethoscope and blood pressure cuff procedure used by the physician was neither aversive nor dangerous, it was too intermittent (one could only obtain about two readings per minute) and too inaccurate to make it satisfactory as a feedback device. However, using new pressure-regulating devices and solid-state circuitry (coupled with an extension of blood pressure measurement theory), it was possible to modify and automate a constant cuff pressure system to accurately measure median blood pressure (±2 millimeters of mercury) and at the same time provide the subject with binary (yes-no) feedback at each heart beat for increases or decreases in blood pressure (Tursky, Shapiro, & Schwartz, 1972). The details of this system need not concern us here—the point is to highlight the general problem of being able to detect and measure the function in question so that it can be easily and practically used by the patient.

In our basic research (as well as clinical) studies to date, we have typically used the procedure of giving the subject binary feedback for small, desired changes in blood pressure (or heart rate) at each beat of the heart and, after producing a certain number of correct responses, of giving the subject a reward or incentive in the form of a slide.[2] The slides might be landscapes of Boston, pictures from around the world, photos of nude women, or numbers reflecting monetary bonuses. As will be seen, in multisession work involving patients, maintaining interest and motivation can become an important problem, one not easily solved by using simple extrinsic rewards.

In the first two studies (Shapiro, Tursky, Gershon, & Stern, 1969; Shapiro, Tursky, & Schwartz, 1970a) the basic question was whether healthy college students could learn to raise or lower their systolic blood pressure in a single session. All subjects received the same general instructions, and only the contingency of the feedback and reward was varied between groups. To control for possible instructional effects, subjects were not told what the bodily function was, nor were they told in what direction the function was to change. The results indicated that subjects reinforced for increases in blood pressure were able to raise or maintain their pressure, while subjects reinforced for decreases in systolic pressure were able to lower their pressure over the session. Another group given random reinforcement showed that its average pressure fell about midway between the increase and decrease groups, suggesting that the two contingent groups controlled their pressure above and beyond the nonspecific effects of the instructions, the stimulation afforded by the feedback and reward, and quiet sitting in a lounge chair for 40 minutes (Crider, Schwartz, & Shnidman, 1969). Interestingly, postexperimental questionnaires revealed that subjects were not aware they had actually controlled their blood pressure, nor did they realize the direction their pressure had changed.

Some questions consistently raised by this research were, What were the subjects doing or thinking to control their blood pressures? Were they getting excited or relaxed? Were they thinking specific thoughts or possibly tensing their muscles in some way? Hence, questions of cognitive or somatic mediation were considered to be important, especially by those researchers interested in the theoretical question of whether operant conditioning of autonomic activity per se had in fact taken place (Katkin & Murray, 1968). As it turned out, the blood pressure data proved to be convincing in this regard, because when heart rate (a related cardiovascular function) was analyzed, no differences were found between groups. In other words, the subjects had not learned simply to raise or lower overall autonomic arousal, even within the cardiovascular system. In a later study (Shapiro, Tursky, & Schwartz, 1970b), when subjects were trained to raise and lower their heart rate using a similar binary feedback and reward technique, the subjects now learned to control their heart rate, without similarly affecting their systolic blood pressure. Altogether, findings of specificity of learning such as these were seen as important prerequisites for the application of biofeedback training to clinical problems (Shapiro & Schwartz, 1972), since alleviation of the symptom was desired without corresponding side effects such as those sometimes produced by drugs.

However, questions of mediation and specificity are more complex than originally envisioned (Schwartz, 1972) and have important implications for therapy (Schwartz, in press). On the one hand, the therapist is not usually concerned with obtaining a pure effect from a scientific point of view, but wants any combination of factors that will produce large, long-lasting, generalizable, and safe effects. Thus, if for a given hypertensive patient it was found that training in general muscle relaxation alone produced the most rapid and massive decreases in pressure, this would be clinically valuable. Cognitive and somatic mediation, if useful, is of significance to the therapist.

On the other hand, the therapist may be concerned with what else is changing when a person is given biofeedback for a particular function. In fact, there are instances where the therapist may be interested in *patterns* of responses. For example, the desired goal for those hypertensive patients having normal heart rates may be to lower stroke volume and/or peripheral resistance rather than to change heart rate per se. However, in reducing pain in patients suffering from angina pectoris, the desired goal may not be to lower just blood pressure, or heart rate, but rather to lower both functions simultaneously, since by decreasing rate and pressure, the heart requires less oxygen, which in turn leads to reduced pain (Braunwald, E., Epstein, Glick, Wechsler, & Braunwald, N. S., 1967). In other words, it becomes important not only to be able to predict under what conditions side effects may occur but also how one might produce them in specific cases.

One approach to this problem is to analyze carefully what else is simultaneously being reinforced when feedback and reward are given (Schwartz, 1972, in press). Returning to the blood pressure–heart rate example, if systolic blood pressure and heart rate were so related over time that increases in one of them were always associated with increases in the other, and vice versa, then when an experimenter chose to give feedback and reward for one, he would unwittingly provide the identical contingency for the other as well. Therefore, from learning (or feedback) theory we would expect that both functions should in fact be learned simultaneously and in the same direction. If these two functions were so related that whenever one increased the other simultaneously decreased, and vice versa, then if feedback and reward were given for one, the other would simultaneously receive the opposite contingency. Both functions should also be learned, only now in opposite directions. However, since neither of these results was empirically obtained, it would follow that systolic blood pressure and heart rate are unrelated in such a way that binary feedback for one results in some form of simultaneous random reinforcement of the other.

Assuming for the moment that this conclusion is true, the next question that arises is, How could a person be taught to control both of them? One approach that follows from the above analysis is to give the feedback and reward only when the desired pattern of responses occurs. In theory, it should be possible to teach a person to voluntarily integrate his systolic blood pressure and heart rate (make both functions increase or decrease together), or to differentiate them (make them go in opposite directions) by providing feedback and reward for the desired pattern. In subsequent studies, it has been verified that systolic blood pressure and heart rate are only integrated 50% under resting conditions (they spontaneously change from beat to beat in the same direction only half of the time) and that subjects can learn voluntarily to make them go together (Schwartz, 1972; Schwartz, Shapiro, & Tursky, 1971) or apart (Schwartz, 1972) when given feedback for the appropriate pattern.

Thus the interrelationships among bodily functions over time, as well as the exact nature of the contingency (feedback) involved, control the degree to which learned specificity or patterning occurs. Although this type of formulation may provide a useful first step in the prediction and control of multifunctions using biofeedback, it must be incomplete, for it treats physiology as if it operated in a vacuum, without constraints. However, physiological (and associated cognitive) constraints do exist and must be taken into account (Schwartz, 1972). The extent to which simple predictions from learning or feedback theory fail can reveal the exact nature of the constraints involved.

For example, it is easier for subjects to learn to make their systolic blood pressure and heart rate go together than to make them go apart (Schwartz, 1972). Furthermore, feedback for integrating these functions produces somewhat larger effects and more rapid learning than feedback for either single function alone. In addition, when subjects are taught to lower both functions simultaneously, they now begin to report feelings of relaxation and calmness, states one would expect to be associated with more general autonomic relaxation. Altogether, it would seem that in the process of trying to understand and extend biofeedback techniques to patterns of responses, the research uncovers more about the nature of the physiological systems themselves and their relation to cognition.[3]

The combined behavioral-biological approach to biofeedback outlined here has a number of implications for treatment. One is that the clinician should carefully evaluate exactly how he administers feedback to an individual patient so that he is better able to precisely determine and control what the patient will and will not learn. Understandably, this applies not only to simple discrete-digital feedback but to more complex forms of continuous-analog feedback as well. For example, if a patient is receiving analog feedback for beat by beat changes in heart rate, and he has sinus arrhythmia (heart rate rising and falling with each breath), the subject will be simultaneously receiving feedback for respiration, and he may modify it accordingly. The clinician should be aware of this possibility and should make a rational decision as to whether or not such learning is desirable.

For applications involving the self-control of more complex states like anxiety or fear, it becomes important to determine what function or pattern of functions occurs in these states for the individual patient. It is well known that individuals differ in their autonomic specificity and that situations may evoke different patterns (Lacey, 1967); thus it makes good sense that the feedback be selected so as to optimize its integration (correlation) with the problem in question.

As for the question of constraints, it follows that if it is possible to clinically evaluate the flexibility or variability of the function(s) in question, it may be possible to assess whether biofeedback will ultimately work for a given patient. For example, if a patient with fixed hypertension (possibly due to excessive hardening of the arteries) has blood pressure levels constantly elevated above normal, it seems unlikely that biofeedback will have any significant effect on purely physiological grounds. Evaluating the potential for organ change (e.g., by taking sleep measurements) may be a useful screening technique. It follows that early diagnosis of the individual for preventive feedback training before the organ system is seriously damaged may be the most meaningful application to psychosomatic medicine.

Before considering further issues raised by clinical work, it may be useful to show how this model applies to animal biofeedback research, where curare is used to paralyze the muscles. Miller (1969) and DiCara (1970) have argued that by paralyzing the muscles with curare, the question of somatic mediation is eliminated. However, all the curare procedure (using moderate doses) does is eliminate potential feedback from actual muscle contraction; it does not stop the rat from struggling and tensing his muscles "in his head." According to the model, to the extent that heart rate and muscle activity are naturally integrated at the level of the brain, reinforcement for the former will result in consistent reinforcement of the latter as well, regardless of the actual state of the muscles.[4] A. H. Black (personal communication, 1971) has found that when he teaches a curarized dog to "move in his head," that is, to produce or inhibit theta waves from the hippocampus (in a nonparalyzed dog, theta occurs when the dog makes voluntary movements), heart rate simultaneously increases or decreases as well. Recently, Goesling and Brener (1972) have found that teaching a rat to tense or relax prior to curare greatly influences his later ability to raise or lower his heart rate while under curare. Hence, the question of mediation is complex, especially at the level of the brain, and one must evaluate *(a)* relations between responses, *(b)* the nature of the reinforcement contingency, and *(c)* natural biological, environmental, and "state" constraints in order to understand and predict exactly what is being learned (Schwartz, in press).

PRELIMINARY CLINICAL APPLICATIONS TO ESSENTIAL HYPERTENSION AND RAYNAUD'S DISEASE

We have attempted to apply the general procedures developed in the basic research to patients diagnosed with essential hypertension (Benson, Shapiro, Tursky, & Schwartz, 1971). First, the seven patients participated in from 5 to 16 control sessions, during which blood pressures were taken under resting conditions. Then systolic blood pressure feedback and reward sessions were initiated and continued until no further reductions in blood pressure occurred for 5 consecutive sessions. The number of conditioning sessions varied from 8 to 34, with a mean of about 22 sessions. The results showed that six of the seven patients decreased their pressure by as little as 3.5 millimeters of mercury and by as much as 33.8 millimeters of mercury (mean decrease for all patients was 16.5 millimeters of mercury). Interestingly, the one patient who failed to show any decrease in blood pressure was later diagnosed to have renal artery stenosis, which relates back to the question of biological constraints.

Although these findings are encouraging, they are a long way from demonstrating that biofeedback can be a clinical treatment for hypertension. First, it is not known whether patients can control their pressure without the feedback or even if the feedback was the significant factor in the research. Placebo variables may have been operating and can only be evaluated by the use of the appropriate control groups (Shapiro & Schwartz, 1972). On the other hand, as in all forms of therapy, positive expectations on the part of the patient may well be a prerequisite for positive gains, especially in behavioral therapies where patient cooperation and practice are necessary for change.

Related is the general question of patient motivation. As described in the review of the clinical research (Shapiro & Schwartz, 1972):

> Central to all forms of psychotherapy is patient motivation and involvement. The question, at the simplest level, is how to motivate patients to spend the necessary time practicing the desired behavior. With severely retarded and/or emotionally disturbed children, reinforcers such as food, candy, or other desired objects (e.g., watching a fan spin) are often necessary for modifying the behavior. However, with less severe problems, therapist praise, praise from significant others in the patient's environment, or self-reinforcement (a sense of competence) may be more than sufficient. One predictor of success in psychotherapy is the extent to which the patient's problems are causing him pain or suffering. With regard to biofeedback, Miller has suggested that feedback, for controlling the function in and of itself may be all that is necessary. However, as progress is made, and the novelty of the situation wears off, what will keep the patient working at the task? In our experience with patients suffering from essential hypertension, a potpourri of rewards was successful, including money for participating and for succeeding (most of these patients were on welfare and thus the money they earned was quite significant), slides of scenes around the world, and general, non-specific praise from the physician and research

> assistant running the sessions. However, this was an experiment, and the patients were receiving a sizeable monetary reward. One wonders whether they would have spent the same number of hours trying to control their blood pressure in the absence of such incentives, which are impractical on a large-scale basis. In this respect, learning to control physiologic processes is like any other self-control procedure (e.g., dieting) since sacrifice on the patient's part may be necessary for the sake of health [p. 180].

Actually, the hypertensive patient may be a special case, more similar to the average cigarette smoker than to the headache patient. Although the pain caused by tension or migraine headaches is relatively immediate, as is its relief, it may be years before the potential harm from high blood pressure or smoking is experienced directly by the patient. Hence it is understandable why headache patients are willing to pay for experimental biofeedback treatment (T. Budzynski, personal communication, 1971), while we must pay our research hypertensive patients to potentially help themselves.

The question of motivation leads to another important problem: namely, whether the patient is able or willing to control his bodily functions in the hectic, rapidly changing environment outside of the laboratory. It is well known that environmental stressors can augment or even cause psychosomatic disorders, and it should not be surprising if many patients desire biofeedback for their blood pressure, just as they take medicine for their stress-related stomachaches. Simply put, the typical patient would rather change his body than change his life-style or his environment, the two factors which together augment or cause the bodily dysfunctions in the first place. In this context it would seem reasonable that biofeedback should be viewed as but one approach to the treatment of the total person, realizing that to cure a problem such as hypertension will require more than just the patient consciously attempting to lower his pressure. Similar views concerning behavioral therapies in general have been stressed by Lazarus (1971).

A good example of this point comes from one of our hypertension patients who during the feedback sessions was successful in lowering his pressure. Over the five daily sessions of a typical week, he might lower his pressure by 20 millimeters of mercury and thus earn a total of over $35. However, we consistently noticed that after the weekend he would enter the laboratory on Monday with elevated pressures again. In interviews with the patient, the problem became clear. After earning a sizable amount of money, the patient would go to the race track on the weekend, gamble, and invariably lose. The likelihood of teaching this patient to "relax" while at the race track through simple laboratory blood pressure feedback would seem slim, indicating that there is a need to work on other aspects of the patient's behavior (e.g., by changing the contingencies of reward) and personality which are related to the high pressure.

Depending on the particular function, dysfunction, and patient involved, biofeedback training may take many sessions. Getting the patient committed to spending this amount of time is difficult enough; getting him to travel to the laboratory for each session often becomes a formidable problem. For this reason the development of home feedback devices, coupled with weekly consultation with the physician and/or therapist, appears to be a fruitful direction in which to move. In addition, the use of portable feedback devices makes it possible for the patient to evaluate his progress under different environmental conditions outside of the laboratory, and this may significantly enhance the potential for generalization.

Whether or not the patient can learn to control these processes without feedback is still an open and important question. Procedures for weaning the patient from the feedback need to be worked out (Weiss & Engel, 1971). However, patients may be able to learn certain cognitive or somatic strategies which they then can use without feedback. One example of this comes from a patient we were experimentally treating for Raynaud's disease, a problem of peripheral constriction and reduced blood flow that under extreme conditions can lead to gangrene in the hands and feet. Symptoms of Raynaud's disease include a feeling of cold in the afflicted area that can be quite painful. The patient was a man in his early sixties with very cold feet; this patient was somewhat unusual in that he was a practicing psychoanalyst who came for behavioral treatment of his problem. Briefly, blood volume was recorded simultaneously from the big toes of each foot, and the patient was given binary feedback for each heart beat that was followed by a small increase in blood volume. The feedback and reward procedure was modeled after the blood pressure work, and similar slides were used. Although placebo and expectancy effects cannot be discounted (and were probably operating), over 10 sessions he began to show large increases in blood volume, particularly in the left foot, the foot initially selected for feedback and reward. In the middle of a later session we then switched to providing feedback and reward for the right foot, which subsequently reached similar increases in overall blood volume. This finding of relative specificity was not surprising because it was observed on the polygraph that spontaneous dilations and constrictions frequently occurred in one foot and not the other, and therefore the feedback was really contingent to the particular foot controlling the programming equipment, while the other simultaneously received a form of random reinforcement.

This particular patient was unusually inclined toward free association and interpreted the purpose of the slides as diverse material for him to covertly free associate to. In one of the later sessions the slide projector accidentally jammed and, rather than showing a slide, flashed just a white, bright light on the screen. This proved to be a fortunate accident, for the patient began free associating to the sun, warmth, beaches, and so forth, and he reported that these thoughts were particularly helpful in warming his feet. Furthermore, these "hot thoughts," as the patient described them, were the images he used to control his feet outside of the laboratory. Interestingly, this procedure proved to be highly adaptive for him since if his feet got cold, even while he was doing therapy with patients, he reported that all he had to do was "turn on his hot thoughts" for a few moments and he felt relief. Whether or not he actually was able to control his feet out of the laboratory is not known, nor is it known if these images were really the significant mechanisms by which he controlled his blood volume. Nonetheless, the case illustrates the potential use of cognitive mediation in the development of self-control of bodily processes.[5] While this patient remained symptom free for about a year and a half, he later contacted us indicating that his symptoms had returned and that he desired further training.

This patient was highly educated (and high up on the socioeconomic ladder), experienced and comfortable in laboratory situations, and greatly desirous and expectant of success. The other Raynaud's patient we have tried to work with so far was from a lower-middle-class background, inexperienced and wary of the laboratory setting, and of questionable motivation and expectancy concerning exactly what the feedback really was and what it was supposed to help her to do. This woman was seen for fewer than 10 sessions, and there was little indication of clinically meaningful (as opposed to statistical) increases in blood volume in her hands. Although it is not known if further training would have yielded large enough changes to constitute therapeutic success, this seems unlikely since she appeared to have a severe case of the disease (she was being considered for a sympathectomy); and on top of this, we had little success in improving her attitude and reactions toward the whole situation. Her experience illustrates how personality and individual differences make it impossible to provide a simple "cookbook" approach to questions such as, What should I tell the patient? or What kinds of incentives should I provide? On the other hand, to the extent that specific instructions direct a patient's attention to certain aspects of his behavior or lead him to utilize certain strategies in learning control, it can be speculated that what the patient is told and what he is asked to do may depend on both the specific nature of the desired function(s) to be changed and the personality of the patient.[6]

SUMMARY AND CONCLUSIONS

Biofeedback is clearly an important discovery, one that may prove to have some value in medical and psychological treatment. However, there are many problems that need to be solved, particularly when applied to the individual patient. Biofeedback, if used in conjunction with other medical and psychological techniques, may be useful with certain patients. However, in the face of specific biological and environmental constraints, I am somewhat pessimistic about its application to chronic physical disease, particularly in the absence of other therapeutic procedures.[7] Emphasizing the problems involved is not meant to discourage experimental attempts at clinical application. Although a combined behavioral-biological approach that emphasizes *(a)* the natural relations between responses, *(b)* the exact manner that the feedback and reward is given, and *(c)* biological, cognitive, and environmental constraints is indicated, it is not implied that all of these factors need to be taken into account before using biofeedback in a specific case. Rather, the purpose of the article is to illustrate potential areas of inquiry and evaluation that may be clinically useful.

Even if direct voluntary control of certain bodily functions or patterns of functions proves to have little therapeutic value, biofeedback per se can still serve an important function—to signal both the therapist and the patient that the patient is currently thinking, feeling, or doing specific things that are detrimental to his physical or emotional health. In the same way that a scale helps direct the therapist and his obese patient in learning how to reduce food consumption and/or increase exercise in order to control weight, biofeedback for visceral and neural disorders may be so employed as well. By means of immediate, augmented feedback (with its associated increased bodily awareness), the patient may be able to learn new ways of coping *behaviorally* with his environment, or he may be able to alter his *lifestyle* in such a way as to keep his physiological processes within safer limits. In this respect, biofeedback is really similar to current psychotherapies, for they all provide corrective feedback.[8]

REFERENCES

Barber, T. X., DiCara, L. V., Kamiya, J., Miller, N. E., Shapiro, D., & Stoyva, J. (Eds.) *Biofeedback and self-control, 1970: An Aldine annual on the regulation of bodily processes and consciousness.* Chicago: Aldine-Atherton, 1971.

Benson, H., Shapiro, D., Tursky, B., & Schwartz, G. E. Decreased systolic blood pressure through operant conditioning techniques in patients with essential hypertension. *Science*, 1971, *173*, 740–742.

Braunwald, E., Epstein, S. E., Glick, G., Wechsler, A. S., & Braunwald, N. S. Relief of angina pectoris by electrical stimulation of the carotid-sinus nerves. *New England Journal of Medicine*, 1967, *227*, 1278–1283.

Crider, A., Schwartz, G. E., & Shnidman, S. R. On the criteria for instrumental autonomic conditioning: A reply to Katkin and Murray. *Psychological Bulletin*, 1969, *71*, 455–461.

DiCara, L. V. Learning in the autonomic nervous system. *Scientific American*, 1970, *222*, 30–39.

Goesling, W. J., & Brener, J. Effect of activity and immobility conditioning upon subsequent heart rate conditioning in curarized rats. *Journal of Comparative and Physiological Psychology*, 1972, *81*, 311–317.

Kamiya, J., DiCara, L. V., Barber, T. X., Miller, N. E., Shapiro, D., & Stoyva, J. (Eds.) *Biofeedback and self-control: An Aldine reader on the regulation of bodily processes and consciousness.* Chicago: Aldine-Atherton, 1971.

Katkin, E. S., & Murray, E. N. Instrumental conditioning of automatically mediated behavior: Theoretical and methodological issues. *Psychological Bulletin*, 1968, *70*, 52–68.

Lacey, J. Somatic response patterning and stress: Some revisions of activation theory. In M. H. Appley & R. Trumbull (Eds.), *Psychological stress.* New York: Appleton-Century-Crofts, 1967.

Lazarus, A. A. *Behavior therapy and beyond.* New York: McGraw-Hill, 1971.

Maslach, C., Marshall, G., & Zimbardo, P. G. Hypnotic control of peripheral skin temperature: A case report. *Psychophysiology*, 1972, *9*, 600–605.

Miller, N. E. Learning of visceral and glandular responses. *Science*, 1969, *163*, 434–445.

Obrist, P. A., Webb, R. A., Sutterer, J. R., & Howard, J. L. The cardiac-somatic relationship: Some reformulations. *Psychophysiology*, 1970, *6*, 569–587.

Schwartz, G. E. Cardiac responses to self-induced thoughts. *Psychophysiology*, 1971, *8*, 462–467.

______. Voluntary control of human cardiovascular integration and differentiation through feedback and reward. *Science*, 1972, *175*, 90–93.

______. Toward a theory of voluntary control of response patterns in the cardiovascular system. In P. A. Obrist, A. H. Black, J. Brener, & L. V. DiCara (Eds.), *Cardiovascular psychophysiology*. Chicago: Aldine, in press.

Schwartz, G. E. Cardiac responses to self-induced thoughts. *Psychophysiology*, 1971, *8*, 462–467.

Schwartz, G. E., & Shapiro, D. Biofeedback in essential hypertension: Current findings and theoretical concerns. *Seminars in Psychiatry*, in press.

Schwartz, G. E., Shapiro, D., & Tursky, B. Learned control of cardiovascular integration in man through operant conditioning. *Psychosomatic Medicine*, 1971, *33*, 57–62.

______. Self-control of patterns of human diastolic blood pressure and heart rate through feedback and reward. *Psychophysiology*, 1972, *9*, 270 (abstract).

Schwartz, G. E., Shaw, G., & Shapiro, D. Specificity of alpha and heart rate control through feedback. *Psychophysiology*, 1972, *9*, 269 (abstract).

Shapiro, D., Barber, T. X., DiCara, L. V., Kamiya, J., Miller, N. E., & Stoyva, J. (Eds.) *Biofeedback and self-control, 1972: An Aldine annual on the regulation of bodily processes and consciousness*. Chicago: Aldine, 1973.

Shapiro, D., & Schwartz, G. E. Biofeedback and visceral learning: Clinical applications. *Seminars in Psychiatry*, 1972, *4*, 171–184.

Shapiro, D., Schwartz, G. E., & Tursky, B. Control of diastolic blood pressure in man by feedback and reinforcement. *Psychophysiology*, 1972, *9*, 296–304.

Shapiro, D., Tursky, B., Gershon, E., & Stern, M. Effects of feedback and reinforcement on the control of human systolic blood pressure. *Science*, 1969, *163*, 588–589.

Shapiro, D., Tursky, B., & Schwartz, G. E. Control of blood pressure in man by operant conditioning. *Circulation Research*, 1970a, *26* (supplement 1), *27*, I–27 to I–32.

______. Differentiation of heart rate and blood pressure in man by operant conditioning. *Psychosomatic Medicine*, 1970b, *32*, 417–423.

Stoyva, J., Barber, T. X., DiCara, L. V., Kamiya, J., Miller, N. E., & Shapiro, D. (Eds.) *Biofeedback and self-control, 1971: An Aldine annual on the regulation of bodily processes and consciousness*. Chicago: Aldine-Atherton, 1972.

Tursky, B., Shapiro, D., & Schwartz, G. E. Automated constant cuff pressure system to measure average systolic and diastolic blood pressure in man. *IEEE Transactions on Biomedical Engineering*, 1972, *19*, 271–275.

Wallace, R. K. Physiological effects of transcendental meditation. *Science*, 1970, *167*, 1751–1754.

Weiss, T., & Engel, B. T. Operant conditioning of heart rate in patients with premature ventricular contractions. *Psychosomatic Medicine*, 1971, *33*, 301–321.

NOTES

1. Potential applications discussed in this article include essential hypertension, cardiac arrhythmias, tension and migraine headaches, rumination, Raynaud's disease, anxiety and fear reduction through relaxation and systematic desensitization, pain reduction through alpha training, meditation and yoga, attention and learning, and sexual behavior.

2. An analysis of contingent reinforcement as a stimulus containing both information (feedback) and incentive (reward) value is discussed in Schwartz (in press) and Schwartz and Shapiro (in press), the latter completed just prior to publication.

3. These findings have been extended, and predictions of the model replicated, in current research on the voluntary control of diastolic blood pressure and heart rate (Schwartz, Shapiro, & Tursky, 1972; Shapiro, Schwartz, & Tursky, 1972). The approach also has been applied to the voluntary control of EEG alpha and heart rate (Schwartz, Shaw, & Shapiro, 1972), but this material will not be reviewed here.

4. Although there is good psychophysiological evidence for believing that heart rate and somatic activity are centrally integrated (Obrist, Webb, Sutterer, & Howard, 1970), this does not imply that other autonomic responses are also so integrated.

5. Specific cognitive control of skin temperature (relative dilation in one hand and constriction in the other through hypnosis and imagery of warmth and cold) has recently been reported by Maslach, Marshall, and Zimbardo (1972). Further evidence for cognitive control of cardiovascular activity due to specific thought processes can be found in Schwartz (1971) and Schwartz and Higgins (1971).

6. For example, if a subject is instructed to close his eyes and to think a neutral word over and over in a relaxed fashion, a reduction in a number of psychophysiological responses (a pattern) may occur, such as those seen in certain forms of meditation (Wallace, 1970).

7. Learning to relax a chronically tense (but otherwise healthy) muscle with biofeedback, for example, would seem to be a more likely candidate for success. Also, in this case the response in question is likely to be already under some voluntary control since it is part of the motor system. This point would similarly apply to learning to control certain electroencephalographic rhythms, to the extent that they involve self-regulatory sensorimotor processes.

8. It might be noted that this approach to the use of biofeedback removes the negative clinical implications suggested by recent difficulties in replicating large magnitude effects in the curarized rat (N. E. Miller & L. V. DiCara, personal communication, 1972). Rather than trying to eliminate those overt somatic "mediators" capable of producing large autonomic changes, the goal here is to deliberately use them to produce more physiologically adaptive reactions (e.g., through breathing exercises or other yoga procedures).

SELF-CONTROL OF CARDIAC FUNCTIONING: A PROMISE AS YET UNFULFILLED

Edward B. Blanchard, Tennessee Psychiatric Hospital

Larry D. Young, Harvard University

The research in the operant conditioning or self-control of four cardiac functions—heart rate level, heart rate variability, blood pressure, and cardiac arrhythmias—is reviewed. Although the fact of the self-control of these functions seems well established, with few exceptions the magnitude of change is statistically significant rather than clinically significant. A few studies, all involving numerous training sessions, have reported large magnitude changes. Several methodological issues are raised and discussed. Finally, alternative modes of achieving self-control of cardiac function, such as progressive relaxation and Yoga exercises are discussed.

Since the mid-1960s an increasing number of articles on the topic of the operant conditioning and/or establishment of self-control of cardiovascular processes in humans have appeared in the literature. These articles hold out the promise, either implicitly or explicitly, of being able to treat cardiovascular disorders by psychological rather than pharmacological means. However, a critical examination of this literature, which is the principal purpose of the present article, reveals that, for the most part, this promise is, as yet, unfulfilled. With rare exceptions the results are reported for changes in cardiovascular functioning of normal subjects instead of patients, and the magnitude of change reported has been of a *statistically* significant rather than *clinically* significant magnitude.

The research is summarized in terms of the four cardiovascular responses studies, with particular emphasis on the magnitude of change obtained. From this summarization several methodological issues become apparent and are subsequently discussed.

HEART RATE

In Table 1 are summarized the studies involving change in heart rate as the dependent variable. Omitted from this table and from intensive

Preparation of this manuscript was supported in part by Grant 1R01HL14906-01 from the National Heart and Lung Institute, Robert W. Scott, principal investigator. The authors wish to thank W. Stewart Agras and Mischel Hersen for their critical comments on earlier versions of this manuscript.

Blanchard, Edward B., and Young, Larry D. Self-control of cardiac functioning: A promise as yet unfulfilled. *Psychological Bulletin*, 1973, *79*, 145–163.

Table 1
Summary of Self-Control of Heart Rate

AUTHORS	INDEPENDENT VARIABLES								RESULTS
	Desired Response	*Reinforcement*	*Feedback Type*	*Subjects Informed of Response*	*Trial Length*	*Trials per Session*	*Number of Sessions*	*Controls*	*Magnitude of Heart Rate Change*
Engel & Hansen, 1966	Decrease HR	½¢ per second of correct response	Binary visual	No	25 minutes	1	6	Yoked	E: —.5 BPM (range: 2.6 to −2.6 BPM) C: 5.6 BPM
Engel & Chism, 1967b	Increase HR	½¢ per second of correct response	Binary visual	No	25 minutes	1	6	Yoked	E: 5.9 BPM (range: 4.2 to 9.8 BPM) C: 3.0 BPM
Levene, Engel, & Pearson, 1968	Alternately increase and decrease HR	None	Binary visual	No	1 minute	25	Varied from 2–4 (until response was learned)	None	E: 4.8 BPM on increase trials (2 of 5 subjects showed consistent alternation) −2.5 BPM on decrease trials
Brener & Hothersall, 1966	Alternately increase and decrease HR	None	Binary auditory	No	50 IBIs (50 seconds)	8	1	None	E: HR>base line on 85% of beats on increase trials HR<base line on 55% of beats on decrease trials (HR<base line on 80% of beats on post decrease trial)

Table 1 (Continued)

AUTHORS	INDEPENDENT VARIABLES								RESULTS
	Desired Response	*Reinforcement*	*Feedback Type*	*Subjects Informed of Response*	*Trial Length*	*Trials per Session*	*Number of Sessions*	*Controls*	*Magnitude of Heart Rate Change*
Brener & Hothersall, 1967	Alternately increase and decrease HR	None	Binary auditory	No	50 IBIs (50 seconds)	22	2	None	E: 8–10 BPM difference between increase and decrease trials
Brener, Kleinman & Goesling, 1969	Alternately increase and decrease HR	None	None	Yes	50 IBIs (50 seconds)	29	1	None	E: 1–3 BPM difference between increase and decrease trials
	Alternately increase and decrease HR without feedback	None	Binary auditory for 100%, 50%, and 0% of trials	Yes	50 IBIs (50 seconds)	18	2	None	100% feedback significantly better (by 2–3 BPM difference between increase and decrease trials) than 0% feedback; 100% feedback showed 10 BPM difference at second trial; second session performance significantly better than first session

Johns, 1970	Increase and decrease HR	None	Binary auditory	E: Yes	70 seconds	19	1		E: raise: 4.6 BPM; lower: no change
				C1: Yes				C1: Information no feedback	C1: raise: no change; lower: −2.3 BPM
				C2: No				C2: No information feedback	C2: no change
				C3: No				C3: No information no feedback	C3: no change
Finley, 1971	Decrease HR	None	Proportional visual	No	5 minutes	11	1	Inaccurate feedback	E: −1.7 BPM feedback versus no feedback E versus C: −1.5 BPM
Sroufe, 1971	Increase HR	None	Proportional visual	Yes	5 minutes	3	1	None	E: 10 BPM for shallow versus deep respiratory volume
Peters, Scott, & Gillespie, 1971	Increase HR	Contingent commercial television	None	No	20 minutes	1	13	Single subject	19 BPM
	Decrease HR						10	Single subject	−19 BPM

Table 1 (Continued)

AUTHORS	INDEPENDENT VARIABLES								RESULTS
	Desired Response	*Reinforcement*	*Feedback Type*	*Subjects Informed of Response*	*Trial Length*	*Trials per Session*	*Number of Sessions*	*Controls*	*Magnitude of Heart Rate Change*
Headrick, Feather, & Wells, 1971	Alternately increase and decrease HR	None	Proportional auditory	No	1 minute	10	1	None	E: raise 3.3 BPM; lower; no change
	Increase and decrease HR	None	Proportional visual	Yes	1 minute		12	Single subject	E: raise: 30 BPM; lower: −5 BPM
Bergman & Johnson, 1971	Increase and decrease HR	None	None	Only experimental subjects	6 IBIs (5 seconds)	30	1	Uninformed subjects	raise: E>C, +1.5 BPM lower: no difference E versus C
Blanchard, Young, & McLeod, 1972	Increase and decrease HR	None	Proportional visual	Yes	1 minute	10	1	None	Low aware subjects could raise (2.9 BPM) and lower (−2.8 BPM) HR from own base line
Blanchard & Young, 1972	Increase and decrease HR	None	Proportional visual and proportional auditory	Yes	1 minute	8	2	No feedback	E combined: raise: +4.2 BPM; C: .3 BPM; lower: −3.3 BPM; C: −2.2 BPM
Scott, Blanchard, Edmunson, & Young, 1972	Increase HR	Contingent commercial television or	Binary visual	No, then yes	20 minutes	1	34	Single subject	16 BPM with contingent money

	Decrease HR	1¢/10 second correct response		Yes			52		−16 BPM, decided clinical improvement
	Increase HR			No			18		30 BPM
Stephens, Harris, & Brady, 1972	Increase and decrease HR	½¢/second of correct response	Proportional visual and proportional auditory	Yes	5 or 30 minutes	8 or 1	17	Single subject	Increase = 23 BPM decrease = 5 BPM
					5 or 60 minutes	4 or 1	18		Increase = 24 BPM
					5 minutes	8	10		Increase = 15 BPM decrease = 6 BPM
					5 or 60 minutes	8 or 1	12		Increase = 29 BPM
Bergman & Johnson, 1972	Increase HR	None	Binary visual for half of subjects in all groups E_1 = none E_2 = heart sounds	E_1 and E_2 = yes; C = no	20 seconds	30	1	Uninformed, no feedback	Binary visual feedback ineffective as reinforcer; informed, instructed subjects E_1 & $E_2 > C$: 1.8 BPM $E_1 = E_2$

Note: Abbreviations: E = experimental, C = control, BPM = beats per minute, HR = heart rate, IBI = interbeat interval.

consideration by this review are studies by Shearn (1962), Frazier (1966), and Brener (1966), all of which used a shock avoidance procedure. Basically, these studies allowed the subject to avoid mild but painful electrical shocks by emitting a heart rate of the appropriate magnitude. These studies, which did show that subjects could learn some degree of heart rate control, are omitted because such a paradigm was not thought to be relevant for clinical practice.

Inspection of Table 1 reveals that each experimenter has tended to use his own individual method of determining if subjects can change their heart rate. Although with three exceptions the magnitude of the change in heart rate achieved is quite small, ranging 1–7 beats per minute, nevertheless it seems fairly well established that small but statistically significant changes in heart rate can be obtained through giving subjects feedback or reinforcement. However, these changes, though of sufficient magnitude to be statistically significant, are not clinically significant. For the purpose of this review, a change in response is considered to be clinically significant if it is equal to either 20% of the base rate or, in the case of an abnormally high response, the change is such as to return the response to the normal range.

The three studies which have demonstrated large magnitude changes in heart rate include a single subject whom Headrick, Feather, and Wells (1971) ran for 14 sessions and who demonstrated within-trial increases in heart rate of 30 beats per minute for the short 1-minute trial. Recently Stephens, Harris, and Brady (1972) have reported on four normal subjects who were run under a complex combination of feedback and reinforcement conditions for 10–18 sessions of trials varying 5–60 minutes. In all four subjects clinically significant within-trial increases in heart rate were obtained, ranging 15–29 beats per minute; moreover, two of the subjects were able to decrease their heart rate 5–8 beats per minute from base line. A final study by Scott et al. (1972)[1] reported clinically significant increases in heart rate of 16 and 25 beats per minute in two normal subjects which were maintained over three consecutive daily sessions. More importantly, a stable (over daily sessions) 16 beats per minute decrease in heart rate was obtained in a patient suffering from tachycardia. Coincident with the decrease in heart rate (in the latter subject) were several clinical improvements including obtaining gainful employment. This last case is the only reported direct clinical application of the studies of heart rate conditioning to date.

The methodological issues and conflicts which have arisen in this area are presented next.

Operant Conditioning Versus Self-Control

The first issue is one of terminology, yet it extends beyond mere semantics. Engel and his associates refer to their operations as operant conditioning. In addition to visual feedback, their subjects were given small sums of money for accumulated experimental time during which their heart rate was in the appropriate direction relative to a criterion heart rate. Stephens, Harris, and Brady (1972) followed a similar procedure.

Most of the other studies of heart rate change are described in terms of self-control established through external sensory feedback. It is possible, of course, to construe all of these studies as examples of operant conditioning in which the reinforcement is knowledge of having successfully emitted the correct response. On the other hand, it is equally possible to construe the reinforcement, especially that used by Bergman and Johnson (1972), in informational terms as binary feedback, since subjects receive reinforcement if they are correct and do not receive it if they are not making the correct response.

If one considers knowledge of results to be a reinforcer, feedback and reinforcement are inextricably confounded in the feedback studies. Therefore, it is not possible to settle the question by merely giving one group of subjects feedback and a second group reinforcement and then comparing their performance. However, it would be possible to determine if the reinforcement used by Engel has an effect above that achieved by feedback by comparing the performance of groups of subjects run in Engel's paradigm with an without monetary reinforcement.

Type of Feedback

There are two dimensions in the classification of types of feedback used. The first is sensory modality. Feedback has been given to subjects by either auditory or visual means, or by both, with no apparent rationale given for preferring one mode to the other. Blanchard and Young (1972), in their study of the relative efficacy of these two modes, made both within- and between-subject comparisons and found no statistical advantage for one sensory modality over the other. Thus it would seem that the decision as to which sensory modality one should use, particularly in a clinical procedure, must rest on factors other than efficacy.

In describing the second classification dimension, we have introduced some new terminology which may require explanation. By *binary* feedback we refer to a situation such as that in studies by Engel and his associates and by Brener and his associates wherein the subject's heart rate in terms of interbeat intervals, the reciprocal of heart rate, is compared to some criterion on a beat-by-beat basis. After each comparison the subject is automatically informed as to whether or not he has met or exceeded the criterion by the presence or absence of the feedback signal, respectively. This class of feedback has been delivered in either the auditory mode (Brener, Kleinman, & Goesling, 1969) or the visual mode (Engel & Chism, 1967b; Engel & Hansen, 1966).

By *proportional* feedback we refer to a situation such as that in studies by Finley (1971), Sroufe (1971), Blanchard, Young, and McLeod (1972) in which the subject is provided with direct knowledge of heart rate on a beat-by-beat basis. With this kind of feedback the subject is told not only if he is right or wrong as in binary feedback but also by how much. At the time of this review, no one has compared binary and proportional feedback with regard to relative efficacy.

Knowledge of Response by the Subject

Whether or not the subjects should be informed of the particular response which they are to change is an issue in the field of heart rate control which provokes almost as much mixed opinion as the particular feedback arrangement to use. From Table 1 one can see that researchers are fairly well divided as to whether or not to inform the subjects of the nature of the response. For example, Brener changed his policy on informing the subjects: in his first two studies (Brener & Hothersall, 1966, 1967) the subjects were not informed; in his later study (Brener et al., 1969) they were informed.

This difference of opinion seems to date back to the early work of Engel and his associates. For reasons which are unclear in their reports, they elected not to inform subjects what response was related to the feedback and reinforcement. Engel and Hansen (1966) found, post hoc, that subjects who did not correctly infer the response that was related to the feedback and reinforcement contingency showed evidence of learning the heart-rate-slowing response whereas four of their five nonlearners correctly guessed that heart rate was the response. In a second study (Engel & Chism, 1967b), although all five subjects showed evidence of heart rate speeding, four of the five subjects did not know the nature of the response.

Bergman and Johnson (1972) have taken a step toward resolving this issue by treating awareness of the response as an independent variable. Of two groups of subjects receiving no feedback of heart rate, those informed of the response raised it significantly higher ($\Delta\overline{X} = 1.8$ beats per minute) than uninformed subjects trying to control an unspecified response. Interestingly, a third group of subjects who were both informed and given feedback in the form of heart sounds did no better than the informed, no-feedback subjects.

One would hope that further research in this area will show that knowledge of the response being changed, at the very least, has no detrimental effect since in a clinical application of these procedures one would prefer to be able to inform patients fully about the procedure.

Types of Control Groups

Several different policies on control groups have been followed in these studies. One policy has been to use no formal control group but instead to use subjects as their own controls by comparing heart rate during experimental trials to that recorded during some other period. This within-subject control policy was followed by Blanchard et al., 1972; Brener and Hothersall, 1966, 1967; Brener et al., 1969; Headrick et al., 1971; Levene, Engel, and Pearson, 1968; and Stephens et al., 1972.

A second policy on control groups, which has been followed by Engel and Hensen (1966) and Engel and Chism (1967b), is the use of yoked controls. In this procedure the control subject receives the same feedback signal as the experimental subject to whom he is yoked. A similar form of false feedback has been used by Finley (1971).

Church (1964) has pointed out the statistical and methodological fallacies inherent in the use of yoked controls. Examination of the results for subjects given some form of false feedback reveals that the performance of these yoked control subjects tends to deteriorate, that is, their responses are in the wrong direction. For example, in the study of heart rate slowing by Engel and Hansen (1966) the control subjects achieved a mean increase in heart rate of 5.6 beats per minute. Furthermore, Finley's (1971) control subjects showed an increased heart rate ($\Delta \overline{X}$ = .8 beats per minute) when they received false feedback as contrasted to times when they received no feedback. Comparisons of changes in heart rate for experimental and control subjects thus yield spuriously large effects because of capitalizing on differences which include the deterioration of the controls.

The appropriate control condition would be one in which subjects receive the same instructions as the experimental subjects but no feedback. The inclusion of an instructed, no-feedback control has been followed by Blanchard and Young (1972), Bergman and Johnson (1972), Brener et al. (1969), Johns (1970), and Sroufe (1971).

Changes in Heart Rate in the Absence of Feedback or Reinforcement

The use of a no-feedback condition enables one to detect if subjects can significantly change their heart rate in the absence of external feedback or reinforcement. The results on this point are mixed. Bergman and Johnson (1971) found both significant increases and decreases for very brief (4–6 seconds) trials in the absence of any feedback. In a later study, described above, Bergman and Johnson (1972) found that subjects instructed to increase heart rate but given no feedback did as well as similarly instructed subjects who received a form of auditory feedback.

Although the subjects of Brener et al. (1969) who received feedback on 100% of the trials showed significantly greater heart rate control than those subjects who received no feedback, the latter group did show a small ($\Delta \overline{X}$ = 2.4 beats per minute) but significant difference between raise and lower trials. However, since the results were reported as differences, no directional statement can be made from their data. Both Johns (1970) and Blanchard and Young (1972) found that their no-feedback control subjects could lower heart rate but could not raise it ($\overline{X}$ = −2.3 beats per minute, $\overline{X}$ = −2.2 beats per minute, respectively). At this point, one cannot conclude definitely that feedback enables subjects to change heart rate in either direction more than subjects who are similarly instructed but receive no feedback.

Another way of viewing this question is to examine how well subjects who have been trained to control heart rate with feedback can control their heart rate in the absence of feedback. This is a point of considerable clinical significance since transfer of the self-control that patients learn in an experimental setting to their natural environment is essential. Brener et al. (1969) found significantly greater generalized self-control for subjects given feedback on 100% of trials than to subjects given no feedback.

Sroufe (1971), working primarily with heart rate variability (to be discussed later), has achieved similar results. His subjects, who were taught to control heart rate variability through paced respiration and who were given proportional visual feedback, showed significant transfer of self-control to a no-feedback state after only a brief (5-minute) training period.

Respiratory Effects

An issue in the field of self-control of cardiac function surrounded by much controversy is the relative importance of mediational variables. Although mediation by means of cognitive or unspecified skeletal muscular mechanisms has been suggested, the primary focus of the mediation controversy has been on the effects of respiratory variables. Experimental procedures designed to answer whether or not the obtained heart rate change resulted from respiratory changes fall into four general categories. Although no investigator failed to monitor respiration, some did little else. Brener and Hothersall (1966) and Brener et al. (1969) report monitoring respiration but do not mention any instructions concerning breathing, nor do they report any analyses of the observed differences.

Blanchard and his associates (Blanchard et al., 1972; Blanchard & Young, 1972) and Engel and his associates (Engel & Chism, 1967b; Engel & Hansen, 1966; Levene et al., 1968) gave all subjects in their investigations the explicit instructions not to change their breathing pattern from normal. Again, however, only monitoring and visual inspection of the data were used to reach the conclusions that respiration did not change significantly and that the observed heart rate differences did not result from respiratory changes. Levene et al. (1968) did carry the investigation a step further, however, by teaching two subjects whose respiration rates were variable to duplicate their earlier respiration rate through a pacing technique. This resulted in changes in heart rate variability but not in overall heart rate.

The third approach to the problem, namely, manipulation of respiration rate to ensure its constancy during heart-rate-conditioning sessions, was employed by Brener and Hothersall (1967), Johns (1970), and Sroufe (1969) and basically consists of having subjects pace their respiration to a metronome or rhythmic puff of air set at their adaptation respiration rate. Even with respiration rate held constant experimentally, subjects were still able to alter their heart rate significantly in the appropriate direction. However, as Sroufe pointed out, ability to control heart rate appears to deteriorate with any session when the subject is attempting to control two systems simultaneously.

The final method used (Finley, 1971; Headrick et al., 1971; Hnatiow & Lang, 1965; Lang, Sroufe, & Hastings, 1967) to ensure that changes in heart rate were not the result of respiratory differences is to monitor, analyze, and control statistically through covariance analyses any systematic variations in respiration that are found. There have been no significant relationships between heart rate change and respiratory changes with two minor exceptions: Headrick et al. (1971) found a significant correlation between breathing amplitude and heart rate for only one subject; and Hnatiow and Lang's (1965) single significant correlation was between average heart rate deviation during the final no-feedback period and the average inspiration to total cycle ratio for the final feedback period.

A summary of cardiorespiratory relations is not complete without the inclusion of two studies which focus specifically on them. In the earlier investigation (Engel & Chism, 1967a) 20% changes in respiration rate sustained for a 10-minute period did not cause changes in average heart rate. However, an inverse relation was noted between respiration rate and heart rate variability. Sroufe's (1971) series of three experiments was broader in scope since he manipulated respiratory volume in addition to respiration rate. His results confirmed the earlier finding of Engel and Chism (1967a) that changes in respiration rate affect only heart rate variability with increases in respiration rate producing a more stable heart rate. However, changes in respiratory volume affected both the level and variability of heart rate with deeper breathing producing a higher but more variable heart rate.

In light of the evidence, monitoring of respiratory variables seems mandatory for those investigations attempting to show heart rate control. However, monitoring alone is not sufficient; the effects of respiratory changes must be controlled either experimentally or statistically to eliminate this possible source of confounding. As Sroufe (1971) has so aptly observed, "The fact that cardiac control is possible with respiration experimentally controlled merely suggests that subjects *can* control rate independent of respiration, not that respiration is of minor importance [p. 654]."

Sroufe's (1971) research carries several implications and suggestions for subsequent research in the area of heart rate self-control, particularly clinical studies: Since respiration and skeletal muscle activity are more discriminable than cardiac activity, they might profitably be used early in training and gradually faded as the desired response is acquired. As Sroufe (1971) showed, utilization of these or similar techniques improved the transfer of the learned cardiac control from periods where feedback is present to periods where it is absent: ultimately, utilization improved the first step in establishing generalization from the experimental chamber to the natural environment.

HEART RATE VARIABILITY

Lang and his associates have been the principal researchers investigating the self-control of heart rate variability. All of their studies have used the same basic experimental procedure: The experimental subjects are given proportional visual feedback of their heart rate and asked to keep it within ±3 beats per minute of a set point (their mean preexperimental heart rate). Dependent measures are the standard deviation of the distribution of interbeat intervals and time on target (within the ± beats per minute range).

In the first study (Hnatiow & Lang, 1965) experimental subjects performed significantly better than yoked controls who received false feedback and who were told only to track the visual display, with no mention of controlling it.

The second study (Lang et al., 1967) was a refinement of the first to include additional controls. Subjects in the experimental group again received proportional visual feedback of heart rate, were told what the feedback display represented, and were instructed to try to keep their heart rate within a 6 beat per minute range. Those in one control group received the same instructions but the feedback display of their yoked experimental partner. The other two control groups were not informed concerning what the visual display represented and were told only to track the visual display.

The experimental group was significantly better at reducing heart rate variability than any of the controls. Of special note are the within-subject analyses which showed that the experimental subjects improved significantly from no-feedback to feedback-available conditions. The control subjects yoked to the experimental subjects, who were also supposed to control heart rate, did poorest, supporting our previous criticism of this control procedure.

In the third study of this series (Sroufe, 1969) subjects again were given either true or false proportional visual feedback of heart rate and told to keep it within a specified range. The purpose of the study was to control for respiration effects and the possibility that subjects were reducing heart rate variability through respiratory means. Thus three groups were taught over several sessions to breathe at a fixed rate, while a fourth group had no restrictions placed on their breathing. All subjects received two training sessions before data were collected in a third session of 1-minute trials. Again, subjects given true feedback showed significant reductions in heart rate variability during times it was available compared both to no-feedback periods and to subjects receiving false feedback. For subjects breathing at fixed rates, performance tended to deteriorate over time while no such deterioration was found for subjects not under respiratory restriction.

Interestingly, a final study in this series (Hnatiow, 1971) failed to replicate the early findings of better control by subjects receiving feedback than the yoked controls in spite of using identical equipment and procedures.

To date, Lang and his associates have reported no clinical application of their procedure. In fact, all of their work has been with normal college students.

BLOOD PRESSURE

In Table 2 are summarized the studies involving change in blood pressure as the dependent variable.

In all of their blood pressure control studies, Shapiro and his colleagues at Harvard have used the same basic experimental procedure: A subject receives binary feedback, both visual and auditory, as to whether his blood pressure is at or in the appropriate direction away from a criterion blood pressure value on each heart beat; in addition to this sensory feedback the subject receives a reinforcement of a brief presentation of a slide of either a nude, a landscape, or an indication of small financial reward on some fixed-ratio schedule for a blood pressure response in the appropriate direction.

The method of delivering this feedback involves inflating an arm cuff to a pressure very close to either systolic or diastolic blood pressure, depending on which is of interest, then varying the pressure in small increments and noting the presence or disappearance of Korotkoff sounds within a specified time interval after each heart beat. Feedback delivery is dependent upon the appropriate response. For example, in trying to shape a decrease in systolic blood pressure, feedback would be given the subject if no Korotkoff sound was detected following the R wave of the electrocardiogram. Had a sound been detected, indicating that the systolic pressure was above the cuff pressure, no feedback would be given. Typically, subjects are given 25 trials per session, with a trial being 50 interbeat intervals long.

As can be seen in Table 2, with the exception of their recently completed clinical trial (Benson, Shapiro, Tursky, & Schwartz, 1971) the magnitude of change in blood pressure has been rather small, averaging less than 1 millimeter of mercury per trial for subjects who were increasing blood pressure and about 2–3 millimeters of mercury per trial for subjects lowering their blood pressure. Using as an index of the efficacy of their procedure the average blood pressure on the final block of five trials, the average amount of increase in blood pressure has been 1–2 millimeters of mercury while the average decrease in subjects lowering blood pressure has been 4–6 millimeters of mercury.

Despite their impressive series of studies many of the criticisms previously leveled at the research on self-control of heart rate can be supplied to the blood pressure self-control studies. First and foremost, it is not possible to tell what are the active ingredients in the Shapiro procedure since subjects receive both binary auditory and visual feedback as well as reinforcement on some fixed ratio schedule. Whether reinforcement contributes to the efficacy of the procedure is not known, nor are the relative efficacies of the types of feedback.

Table 2
Summary of Self-Control of Blood Pressure

AUTHORS	INDEPENDENT VARIABLES								RESULTS
	Desired Response	*Reinforcement*	*Feedback*	*Subjects Informed of Response*	*Trial Length*	*Trials per Session*	*Number of Sessions*	*Controls*	*Results: Magnitude of Blood Pressure Change*
Shapiro, Tursky, Gershon, & Stern, 1969	E_1 = Increase systolic BP E_2 = Decrease systolic BP	Slides of nudes FR 20	Binary auditory and visual	No	65 seconds	25	1	None	E_1: −.8 millimeter Hg $E_1 > E_2$ E_2: −4.8 millimeters Hg
Shapiro, Tursky, & Schwartz, 1970a	E_1 = Increase systolic BP E_2 = Decrease systolic BP	Slides (1/3 nudes, 1/3 landscapes, 1/3 money . . . 10–25¢) FR 20	Binary auditory and visual	No	50 IBI	25	2	Random reinforcement (50% probability for each IBI)	1. E_1:2.3 millimeters Hg; C:0 millimeters Hg $E_1 > C = E_2$
	E_1, C, E_2 = Decrease systolic BP								2. E_1: −2.0 millimeters Hg; C: −2.0 millimeters Hg; E_2: −4.5 millimeters Hg $E_1 = C > E_2$
Shapiro, Tursky, & Schwartz,	E_1 = Increase HR	Slides of nudes FR 20	Binary visual for all subjects plus	Yes	50 IBI	25	1	None	E_1: HR = .8 BPM; BP = .5 millimeter Hg

1970b	E_2 = Decrease HR		half received binary auditory and other half proportional auditory						E_2: HR = 5.0 BPM; BP = −.5 millimeter Hg For BP $E_1 = E_2$
Schwartz, 1972	HR-BP Integration & differentiation	Slides (landscapes, nudes, money) FR 12	Binary auditory and visual	No	50 IBI	25	1	None	HR = BP integration easier to achieve than HR = BP differentiation
Shapiro, Schwartz, & Tursky, 1972	E_1 = Increase diastolic BP E_2 = Decrease diastolic BP	Slides (landscapes, nudes, money) FR 20	Binary auditory and visual	No	50 IBI	35	1	None	E_1: 7/10 increased BP $\overline{X}$ = 4.0 millimeters voluntary control maintained in extinction E_2: 8/10 decreased BP $\overline{X}$ = −2.0 millimeters
Schwartz, Shapiro, & Tursky, 1971	E_1 = Increase HR and systolic BP E_2 = Decrease HR and systolic BP	Slides (landscapes, nudes, money) FR 12	Binary auditory and visual	No	50 IBI	40	1	None	E_1: HR = 1.2 BPM; BP = 2.2 millimeters Hg E_2: HR = −6.0 BPM; BP = −4.8 millimeters Hg $E_1 > E_2$

Table 2 (Continued)

AUTHORS	INDEPENDENT VARIABLES								RESULTS
	Desired Response	*Reinforcement*	*Feedback*	*Subjects Informed of Response*	*Trial Length*	*Trials per Session*	*Number of Sessions*	*Controls*	*Results: Magnitude of Blood Pressure Change*
Benson, Shapiro, Tursky, & Schwartz, 1971	Decrease systolic BP	Slides (landscapes, nudes, money) 5¢/slide FR 20	Binary auditory and visual	Yes	50 IBI	30	8–34 conditioning sessions $\overline{X}$ = 21.7	None	$\bar{X} = -16.5$ millimeters Hg (Range: = .9 to −33.8 millimeters Hg)
Brener & Kleinman, 1970	Decrease systolic BP	None	Proportional visual	Yes	50 seconds	20	2	To pay attention to feedback display	E (Session 1): −16 millimeters Hg; (Session 2): −10 millimeters Hg C (Session 1): No change; (Session 2): No change
Hnatiow, 1971	Decrease systolic BP variability	None	Proportional visual	E Yes C No	5 minutes	3	1	Track display of yoked partner	E = C on blood pressure variability reduction E reduced blood pressure more than C (but this was not the task)

Note: Abbreviations: E = experimental, Hg = mercury, IBI = interbeat interval, HR = heart rate, BP = blood pressure, FR = fixed ratio.

A second problem with these studies has been the failure to include a no-feedback control in order to evaluate the efficacy of their combination of procedures over merely instructing subjects to lower their blood pressure. In one study (Shapiro, Tursky, and Schwartz, 1970a) a group reinforced on a random basis was included. Results showed that groups reinforced for raising or lowering blood pressures, while different from each other, did not differ from this group which was reinforced randomly. Thus to date, this group of investigators has shown primarily that subjects reinforced for raising blood pressure are different from subjects reinforced for lowering blood pressure.

Despite the methodological problems with these studies, the Shapiro group certainly deserves praise for their pioneering work in this area. Recently they have focused on self-control of diastolic blood pressure (Shapiro, Schwartz, and Tursky, 1972) and the degree of integration and differentiation of the cardiovascular system (Schwartz, 1972; Schwartz, Shapiro, & Tursky, 1971). The former line of research, using the same basic experimental paradigm, has shown that diastolic blood pressure can be altered significantly by this procedure and, of much interest from a clinical point of view, that the changes show some degree of stability after the feedback and reinforcement are no longer available. In the latter research area a fair degree of independence of heart rate and blood pressure have been shown.

The study by Benson et al. (1971) answers one of our major criticisms leveled at the blood pressure self-control research, namely, the exclusive reliance on normal subjects. Benson applied Shapiro's basic blood pressure control procedure to a group of seven hypertensive patients. Their average systolic blood pressure during the final base-line periods was 165 millimeters of mercury. Clinically significant decreases in blood pressure were obtained in five of the seven patients ($\overline{X} = 22.6$ millimeters of mercury).

As with the heart rate studies which showed large scale changes in that response, numerous trials were necessary to obtain this magnitude of change ($\overline{X} = 21.7$ conditioning sessions of 25 trials each). While no data are available on the stability of the change when the feedback was no longer available or on the degree of transfer of the decreased blood pressure outside of the laboratory, these results are provocative enough to warrant following up and certainly to increase the clinical promise held out by this research.

As can be seen in Table 2, there has been only one important study of blood pressure self-control conducted by an investigator outside of the Shapiro group at Harvard, and that is by Brener and Kleinman (1970). This study, which utilized a form of proportional visual feedback, has several commendable features: The size of the change in blood pressure, approximately 15 millimeters of mercury in the first session and approximately 12 millimeters of mercury in the second, is considerably larger than that reported by Shapiro and his colleagues with normal subjects and is of a magnitude which could be clinically significant. Second, control subjects who received the same type of feedback of their own blood pressure but were not instructed to change their blood pressure were used and showed no overall change in blood pressure. A further control group is needed, however, in which subjects, who are instructed to try to lower blood pressure, receive no feedback.

The form of feedback used within the classification system presented previously is closest to proportional visual feedback. Subjects were able to view a manometer which continuously displayed pressure in the occluding staff. The cuff pressure,, and hence the feedback received by subjects, oscillated about the individual subject's systolic blood pressure. An interesting aspect of this procedure was the taking of blood pressure on the left index finger rather than upper arm. Such a procedure minimizes the problem ischaemia.

The size changes in blood pressure obtained by Brener and Kleinman's procedure are much larger than those obtained by Shapiro and his colleagues in a similar length of time on a similar population of normotensive college-age males. One could speculate that the major reason for this difference is that Brener and Kleinman's subjects received a form of proportional feedback whereas Shapiro's subjects received binary feedback delivered both visually and aurally.

CARDIAC ARRHYTHMIAS

Although there have been several brief reports (Engel & Melmon, 1968; Weiss & Engel, 1971) on the operant conditioning of cardiac arrhythmias, most of the data seem to be summarized in one article (Weiss & Engel, 1971). The latter study contains detailed reports on eight patients suffering from premature ventricular contractions who were all treated in approximately the same experimental paradigm.

The paradigm was, for the most part, a replication of the procedures used in Engel's three previous studies. Patients were given binary visual feedback as to whether their heart rate was at or beyond the desired heart rate in the appropriate direction. In this study, contrary to the previous work with normals, patients were fully informed of all the details of the experiment, especially the response being monitored and also were not given monetary rewards for time accumulated in the correct direction. Despite the omission of this tangible reinforcer, the authors still describe their study in terms of "operant conditioning" rather than self-control through feedback.

Most patients were run under four conditions and some under a fifth. These were, in the usual order, heart rate speeding, heart rate slowing, alternately speeding and slowing heart rate for 1-to-4-minute trials, and then control of heart rate variability. In this final condition, subjects received binary feedback (light onset) when their heart rate stayed within a 10-beat range. The nature of this feedback arrangement also provided subjects with feedback of the occurrence of each premature ventricular contraction. The fifth condition, in which four of the patients were run, consisted of a gradual removal of feedback. Feedback was alternately presented and removed; the initial ratio of 1 minute of feedback to 1 minute without was extended to 1 minute on and 7 minutes off. Interestingly, in this final phase, subjects did as well without feedback as with it, indicating that true self-control had been learned.

Four of the eight patients had a significantly reduced frequency of premature ventricular contractions after the training procedure as measured in the ward and at a follow-up 3–21 months afterward. A fifth patient did not have a significant reduction in premature ventricular contractions rate but did learn to recognize their occurrence and was able to control them at home through resting. The other three patients showed no evidence of learning to control premature ventricular contractions.

Total number of training sessions ranged 22–77 with a mean of 57.5. The five cases which can be considered successes all had 47 or more training sessions. Our reanalysis of these results show that improvement is significantly (by $p = .05$, Fisher's exact probability test) related to receiving 47 or more training sessions.

Weiss and Engel deserve commendation for the following two related techniques for extending their procedures into the area of clinical application: first, eliminating the necessity for external feedback to control the cardiac dysfunction, and more importantly, monitoring premature ventricular contraction rate outside the experimental chamber. The degree of generalization observed in this latter procedure is especially encouraging. Generalization of learned control of cardiac functioning to the natural environment, true self-control, is the desired clinical terminal behavior.

There are two obvious criticisms which can be leveled at this otherwise excellent clinical study. The first is the lack of a controlled group of patients who were either untreated or given some equally time-consuming and involving placebo task. This criticism is obviated to some degree because of the prolonged base-line period prior to the experimental phase during which premature ventricular contractions were noted. The documented history of premature ventricular contractions ranged 3 months–8 years with a mean of 3.0 years. Despite this, one would hope that a next step would be a controlled outcome study of the procedure.

The second criticism is the obvious confounding of several aspects of the training procedure. One does not know whether the entire sequence of training procedures is necessary or only part of it. Thus a next step would be to isolate which parts of the training procedure are necessary, facilitative, or superfluous, in order to improve efficiency.

ALTERNATIVE METHODS OF CARDIAC CONTROL

There are at least two additional lines of research which are related to the area of self-control of cardiac function: *(a)* the use of progressive relaxation as developed by Jacobson (1938) and *(b)* the use of various yogic exercises and related forms of meditation. In both of these a significant degree of change in various cardiac functions has been produced.

Progressive Relaxation

Jacobson (1939) reported on the effects on blood pressure of training in and subsequent use of his system of muscle relaxation. His conclusions, which tended to be more qualitative than quantitative, were that there is a general relation between decreases in blood pressure and decreases in muscle activity as shown by the electromyogram and that training in progressive relaxation results in greater decreases in electromyogram activity than self-induced relaxation without training. He presented blood pressure data on 14 normotensive subjects, 9 of whom had been trained in progressive relaxation. These data, both systolic and diastolic blood pressure, were collected after a 15-minute adaptation period during which the subjects rested in a supine position and again after 45 minutes of self-induced relaxation. Analyses of these data by the present authors revealed significant decreases in both systolic blood pressure ($\Delta\overline{X} = 8.0$ millimeters of mercury; $F = 19.9$, $df = 1/12$, $p < .01$) and diastolic blood pressure ($\Delta\overline{X} = 7.8$ millimeters of mercury; $F = 11.5$, $df = 1/12$, $p < .01$), but no differences between the trained and untrained subjects in degree of reduction achieved. It should be noted that the magnitude of change in blood pressure in this study exceeds that reported by Shapiro and his colleagues in any of their studies of normotensive subjects (see Table 2) and compares favorably with the results reported by Brener and Kleinman (1970).

In a second study, Jacobson (1940) reported decreases in heart rate associated with relaxation training. Heart rate was measured initially after a 15-minute adaptation period during which the subjects rested in a supine position and later after 45 minutes of progressive relaxation. The average decrease in heart rate was 6.5 beats per minute. Analysis of this data *by the present authors* shows this change to be highly significant ($t = 5.59$, $p < .001$).

In a more recent study, Paul (1969) reported on physiological changes in college-age females who were treated for 30 minutes by either *(a)* a brief form of progressive relaxation training, *(b)* hypnosis induction and suggestions of relaxation, or *(c)* self-instructed relaxation. Heart rate data were collected during a 10-minute adaptation period and at the end of training. The progressive relaxation training group showed significantly greater changes in heart rate than the other two groups with reductions of approximately 8 beats per minute occurring in both sessions. It seems possible that Paul's subjects were not completely adapted when the initial heart rate recording was made, which could account for part of the magnitude of change.

In a later report, Paul and Trimble (1970) compared subjects given training in brief progressive relaxation either by tape recording or by a therapist present in the room. The latter condition led to significantly greater decreases in heart rate; however, the tape-recorded relaxation treatment did result in a group mean decrease in heart rate of approximately 4 beats per minute, which is comparable to the results reported by most other investigators.

It thus seems that training in deep muscle relaxation, even of an abbreviated form, can lead to decreases in heart rate comparable to those achieved by most of the studies in the biofeedback area. This finding leads us to speculate that the operant conditioning or self-control procedures are possibly only inefficient methods of teaching subjects to relax.

Yoga

Although many claims of phenomenal degrees of self-control among Yogis had been made, few scientific data were collected on this subject until the 1950s when Wenger and his associates (Wenger & Bagchi, 1961; Wenger, Bagchi, & Anand, 1961) made systematic autonomic recordings from over 50 Yogis in India. In one study of three Yogis who claimed to be able to stop their hearts, Wenger et al. (1961) found *(a)* absence of radial pulse, *(b)* absence of most heart sounds, *(c)* blood pressure radically increased, but *(d)* no stoppage of the heart and, in fact, *(e)* very little slowing in heart rate. They concluded that these subjects were utilizing thoracic muscle interference with venous return which led to a radical decrease in blood flow.

A fourth Yogi claimed only to be able to slow his heart rate and did so, demonstrating increases in interbeat intervals from a base line of approximately 1.0 second to slightly over 2 seconds for several beats (equivalent to changes in heart rate from 60 beats per minute to 30 beats per minute.) The authors concluded that no muscle interference was apparently used; rather, the alterations seemed to be due to vagal innervation.

A similar example of voluntary cardiac arrest was reported by McClure (1959) in the case of a 44-year-old Caucasian male. This patient, who showed no cardiac irregularities, could voluntarily go into cardiac arrest for periods of approximately 5 seconds, increasing the interbeat interval of his heart rate from normally 1.0 second to over 5 seconds. Although the patient did not know the mechanism involved, McClure concluded that it was due to vagal innervation and was entirely unrelated to respiration rate.

Three systematic studies of the effects of Yoga exercises and meditation on cardiac function have recently been reported. Datey, Deshmukh, Dalvi, and Vinekar (1969) studied the effects of training in the yogic exercise called Shavasan on 47 hypertensive patients. The patients, whose original blood pressures were in the range 160–270/90–145, all received training in Shavasan for unspecified lengths of time. The typical training course was described as requiring 3 weeks of daily 30-minute sessions. Results were reported for three groups of patients; *(a)* 10 not on medication; *(b)* 22 whose hypertension was controlled by drugs; and *(c)* 15 whose hypertension was not adequately controlled by drugs. In all cases, blood pressure was reported as the diastolic pressure plus one-third of the pulse pressure. For those not on medication, blood pressure was reduced in 9 out of 10 cases with the average reduction being 27 millimeters of mercury ($p < .05$). In the second group, the effects of training in Shavasan were evaluated in terms of the reduction in patients' drug dosage necessary to keep their blood pressure under control. In 13 of 22 patients the drug dosage was decreased by 33% or more, with an average reduction for those 13 patients of 68%. In the third group, the effects were evaluated in the same fashion, and drug dosage was reduced by at least 33% in 6 of 15 patients. This study seems to show that a chronic course of training in yogic exercise had a clinically significant effect on a majority of the hypertensive patients studied and would warrant investigation in a controlled-outcome study.

In the first of two studies of similar design, Wallace (1970) studied the physiological effects of transcendental meditation, as taught by the Maharishi Mahesh Yogi. Physiological responses of 15 normal college students, who had been practicing transcendental meditation for from 6 months to 3 years, were monitored both for 30 minutes prior to a 20–30 minute meditation period and during the latter period. In the five subjects for whom heart rate was measured, an average decrease of 5 beats per minute was observed. It was not stated, however, whether or not the magnitude of change was statistically significant.

In a more elaborate study of similar design, Wallace, Benson, and Wilson (1971) monitored physiological responses of 36 subjects who had been practicing transcendental meditation for an average of 29 months. The principal results of comparisons between the meditation period and the 30 minutes immediately preceding, during which subjects were resting comfortably, were significant changes in electroencephalogram and oxygen consumption. There was also a small but significant ($p < .05$) decrease in heart rate ($\Delta\overline{X} = -.3$ beats per minute), but no change in blood pressure.

These studies, though not of the controlled-outcome format in which a no-treatment or attention-placebo group is monitored, are highly suggestive that Yoga and other Eastern forms of exercise-meditation training can have important clinical application in the field of cardiac self-control. Certainly the changes achieved are of sufficient magnitude to warrant exploring this line of research as well as the ones discussed previously.

CONCLUSIONS

The self-control of several cardiac functions—acceleration, deceleration, and variability of heart rate and increases and decreases in blood pressure—has been amply demonstrated in normal subjects. However, with few notable exceptions the magnitude of change obtained has been small; the duration for which control was manifested has been brief, and the generalization of the changes obtained in the experimental chamber rarely demonstrated. Future research in this area must follow two directions if the promise it holds out is to be fulfilled: *(a)* there is now a need for chronic studies involving many trials to obtain large-scale changes; *(b)* there is also a need for more direct application of this work to clinical populations. Finally, as was pointed out in the final section of this paper, alternative modes of obtaining changes in cardiac functioning—such as training in progressive relaxation, transcendental meditation, or various Yoga exercises—may prove to be more fruitful approaches to obtaining clinically significant changes than the operant-conditioning-feedback techniques reviewed in the main body of this paper. Only comparative outcome studies, conducted on a chronic basis, can answer this question, but certainly it is deserving of an answer.

REFERENCES

Benson, H., Shapiro, D., Tursky, B., & Schwartz, G. E. Decreased systolic blood pressure through operant conditioning techniques in patients with essential hypertension. *Science*, 1971, *173*, 740–742.

Bergman, J. S., & Johnson, H. J. The effects of instructional set and autonomic perception on cardiac control. *Psychophysiology*, 1971, *8*, 180–190.

______. Sources of information which affect training and raising of heart rate. *Psychophysiology*, 1972, *9*, 30–39.

Blanchard, E. B., & Young, L. D. Relative efficacy of visual and auditory feedback for self-control of heart rate. *Journal of General Psychology*, 1972, *87*, 195–202.

Blanchard, E. B., Young, L. D., & McLeod, P. G. Awareness of heart activity and self-control of heart rate. *Psychophysiology*, 1972, *9*, 63–68.

Brener, J. Heart rate as an avoidance response. *Psychological Record*, 1966, *16*, 329–336.

Brener, J., & Hothersall, D. Heart rate control under conditions of augmented sensory feedback. *Psychophysiology*, 1966, *3*, 23–28.

______. Paced respiration and heart rate control. *Psychophysiology*, 1967, *4*, 1–6.

Brener, J., & Kleinman, R. A. Learned control of decreases in systolic blood pressure. *Nature*, 1970, *226*, 1063–1064.

Brener, J., Kleinman, R. A., & Goesling, W. J. The effects of different exposures to augmented sensory feedback on the control of heart rate. *Psychophysiology*, 1969, *5*, 510–516.

Church, R. M. Systematic effect of random error in the yoked control design. *Psychological Bulletin*, 1964, *62*, 122–131.

Datey, K. K., Deshmukh, S. N., Dalvi, C. P., & Vinekar, S. L. "Shavasan": A yogic exercise in the management of hypertension. *Angiology*, 1969, *20*, 325–333.

Engel, B. T., & Chism, R. A. Effect of increases and decreases in breathing rate on heart rate and finger pulse volume. *Psychophysiology*, 1967a, *4*, 83–89.

______. Operant conditioning of heart rate speeding. *Psychophysiology*, 1967b, *3*, 418–426.

Engel, B. T., & Hansen, S. P. Operant conditioning of heart rate slowing. *Psychophysiology*, 1966, *3*, 176–187.

Engel, B. T., & Melmon, L. Operant conditioning of heart rate in patients with cardiac arrhythmias. *Conditional Reflex*, 1968, *3*, 130.

Finley, W. W. The effect of feedback on the control of cardiac rate. *Journal of Psychology*, 1971, *77*, 43–54.

Frazier, T. W. Avoidance conditioning of heart rate in humans. *Psychophysiology*, 1966, *3*, 188–197.

Headrick, M. W., Feather, B. W., & Wells, D. T. Unidirectional and large magnitude heart rate changes with augmented sensory feedback. *Psychophysiology*, 1971, *8*, 132–142.

Hnatiow, M. Learned control of heart rate and blood pressure. *Perceptual and Motor Skills*, 1971, *33*, 219–226.

Hnatiow, M., & Lang, P. J. Learned stabilization of cardiac rate. *Psychophysiology*, 1965, *1*, 330–336.

Jacobson, E. *Progressive relaxation*, Chicago: Univ. of Chicago Press, 1938.

———. Variation of blood pressure with skeletal muscle tension and relaxation. *Annals of Internal Medicine*, 1939, *12*, 1194–1212.

———. Variation of blood pressure with skeletal muscle tension and relaxation. II. The heart beat. *Annals of Internal Medicine*, 1940, *13*, 1619–1625.

Johns, T. R. Heart rate control in humans under paced respiration and restricted movement: The effect of instructions and exteroceptive feedback. *Dissertation Abstracts International*, 1970, *30*, 5712–5713.

Lang, P. J., Sroufe, L. A., & Hastings, J. E. Effects of feedback and instructional set on the control of cardiac rate variability. *Journal of Experimental Psychology*, 1967, *75*, 425–431.

Levene, H. I., Engel, B. T., & Pearson, J. A. Differential operant conditioning of heart rate. *Psychosomatic Medicine*, 1968, *30*, 837–845.

McClure, C. M. Cardiac arrest through volition. *California Medicine*, 1959, *90*, 440.

Paul, G. L. Physiological effects of relaxation training and hypnotic suggestion. *Journal of Abnormal Psychology*, 1969, *74*, 425–437.

Paul, G. L., & Trimble, R. W. Recorded vs. "live" relaxation training and hypnotic suggestion: Comparative effectiveness for reducing physiological arousal and inhibiting stress response. *Behavior Therapy*, 1970, *1*, 285–302.

Schwartz, G. E. Voluntary control of human cardiovascular integration and differentiation through feedback and reward. *Science*, 1972, *175*, 90–93.

Schwartz, G. E., Shapiro, D., & Tursky, B. Learned control of cardiovascular integration in man through operant conditioning. *Psychosomatic Medicine*, 1971, *33*, 57–62.

Shapiro, D., Schwartz, G. E., & Tursky, B. Control of diastolic blood pressure in man by feedback and reinforcement. *Psychophysiology*, 1972, *9*, 296–304.

Shapiro, D., Tursky, B., Gershon, E., & Stern, M. Effects of feedback and reinforcement on the control of human systolic blood pressure. *Science*, 1969, *163*, 588–590.

Shapiro, D., Tursky, B., & Schwartz, G. E. Control of blood pressure in man by operant conditioning. *Circulation Research*, 1970, *26*, (Supplement 1:27–32.)

———. Differentiation of heart rate and systolic blood pressure in man by operant conditioning. *Psychosomatic Medicine*, 1970b, *32*, 417–423.

Shearn, D. W. Operant conditioning of heart rate. *Science*, 1962, *137*, 530–531.

Sroufe, L. A. Learned stabilization of cardiac rate with respiration experimentally controlled. *Journal of Experimental Psychology*, 1969, *81*, 391–393.

———. Effects of depth and rate of breathing on heart rate and heart rate variability. *Psychophysiology*, 1971, *8*, 648–655.

Stephens, J. H., Harris, A. H., & Brady, J. V. Large magnitude heart rate changes in subjects instructed to change their heart rates and given exteroceptive feedback. *Psychophysiology*, 1972, *9*, 283–285.

Wallace, R. K. Physiological effects of transcendental meditation. *Science*, 1970, *167*, 1751–1754.

Wallace, R. K., Benson, H., & Wilson, A. F. A wakeful hypometabolic physiologic state. *American Journal of Physiology*, 1971, *221*, 795–799.

Weiss, T., & Engel, B. T. Operant conditioning of heart rate in patients with premature ventricular contractions. *Psychosomatic Medicine*, 1971, *33*, 301–321.

Wenger, M. A., & Bagchi, B. K. Studies of autonomic functions in practitioners of Yoga in India. *Behavioral Science*, 1961, *6*, 312–323.

Wenger, M. A., Bagchi, B. K., & Anand, B. K. Experiments in India on "voluntary" control of the heart and pulse. *Circulation*, 1961, *24*, 1319–1325.

NOTES

1. R. W. Scott, E. B. Blanchard, E. Edmundson, & L. D. Young. An improved shaping procedure for clinical cardiac control. Paper presented at Southeastern Psychological Association meeting, Atlanta, 1972.

4. BEHAVIOR MODIFICATION:

A Brave New World or 1984?

In the last few years there has been a concerted effort on the part of psychologists to make explicit something that has been known but not always understood: that behavior will usually change as a function of its result. In the field of psychology, behavior modification (or, as it is often referred to, behavior mod) has developed into a somewhat controversial topic, raising both blood pressures and issues perhaps out of proportion to the underlying controversy. As Perry London points out in the first of the following two articles, perhaps there were reasons for behavior modifiers to develop an in-group mythology, but because "the borders are secure now, the settlers are thriving. . . . it is time . . . to build this domain, not defend it." While this sounds like a noncontroversial proposal by London, he actually is proposing that *behavior modification is and should be a technology rather than a science*. One major difference between a technology and a science is that a science has a theoretical base from which research develops and to which the results are relevant. While in some stages of science the theoretical base may be modest, London is proposing that in a technology there need be no theoretical base at all: "The question with respect to behavior modification is twofold: First, is current theory very good (scientifically) in this case? Second, is any theory very useful for the current development of this field at this time? I think the answer to both questions is no."

According to London, behavior therapists never really had much of a therapy, just an "ideology." What does he mean by this? After reading both London's and Albert Bandura's articles, do you tend to agree or disagree with London's assertion that behavior modifiers are psychotechnicians, not scientists? Are psychotechnicians good or bad things to be?

Bandura, on the other hand, is concerned about the "views about the nature of man" implied by behavior *theory*, the same theory that London dismisses as not very good, not very useful—actually not even theory! No wonder behavior modification is a controversial topic! As Bandura points out, what we believe about human nature is very important, both for future research and for current applications: "What we believe man to be affects which aspects of human functioning we study most thoroughly and which we disregard. Premises thus delimit research and are, in turn, shaped by it. As knowledge gained through study is put into practice, the images of man on which social technologies rest have even vaster implications."

Do you think Bandura would accept London's view that behavior modification is and should be a form of psychotechnology? Why? Is there something more to be gained from probing the results of behavior modification research than simply better ways to eliminate bed-wetting? Or is merely finding the best technology for a variety of behavior problems the sum and substance of behavior modification? And what about the models of man that Bandura refers to? Society as a whole seems to require such models. These change with time, sometimes rapidly, but is society as a whole likely to abandon such models and operate as a vast, complicated but model-less technology?

Bandura also discusses several situations in which external reinforcers do not have the expected result on behavior (as with principled dissenters and nonconformists). What would a psychotechnologist think of these situations?

Lurking not too far beneath the surface of Bandura's argument is another ageless debate in psychology, that of free will versus determinism. How does Bandura deal with this issue? What do *you* think about it?

THE END OF IDEOLOGY IN BEHAVIOR MODIFICATION

Perry London, University of Southern California

When little "behavior modifiers" sit at their professional daddies' knees and ask, "Where did I come from?" they are usually told a story about the "principles of learning" that spawned them, the evil clinicians who left them to perish on a hillside, and the kindly shepherd doctors who found

Requests for reprints should be sent to Perry London, Department of Psychology, University of Southern California, 734 West Adams Boulevard, Los Angeles, California 90007.

London, Perry. The end of ideology in behavior modification. *American Psychologist*, 1972, *27*, 913–920.

them, raised them as their own, and eventually restored them to their rightful positions as the benefactors of behavior. When they grow up, confer their own benefits, and spawn their own little behavior modifiers, they become disabused of the myth. But not entirely—there remains, at the very least, a tradition of deferring to the principles of learning as the ultimate source of all good modifications and a parallel ritual of knocking psychoanalysts, Rogerians, existentialists, and general psychiatrists who have not yet mastered or endorsed the jargon of respondents, operants, and reinforcements.

Like most myths this tale has been based on some true events and has proved useful for the promotion of behavioristic patriotism and for extending the frontiers of experimentation and the clinical and technical growth of the field. And it makes a good story. But enough is enough. The borders are secure now, the settlers are thriving, the dark untrammeled forests are trammeled and cut down, the stumps blown, the fields plowed. It is time now to build this domain, not defend it.

Building it requires three things: first, abandoning strife with other modalities and developing peaceful commerce to see what they have to offer and exchange; second, examining the constructs that underlie modifying operations and that give clues for the design of new ones; and finally, devoting ourselves to *criterion validity*, that is, to building treatment methods that work. The entire field has been moving in these directions during the past few years, but only partly, I think, as a result of the intelligent pressures of people making these recommendations. The shift results also from technological changes in related disciplines and from attitude changes in the entire society that supports them. New equipment brings new possibilities for use and a new social readiness to use it, and the speed with which it gets advertised and talked about pushes advances in practice that no theory is likely to keep up with. This article argues that it is probably just as well.

For public purposes, behavior modifiers of the 1960s usually described their activities as logically inevitable corollaries of theorems or principles of learning and of ongoing discoveries about how they applied to disordered human behavior. Actually, there were only about three principles that they ever referred to, all of which can be reduced to one or one and a half principles—namely, that learning depends on the connections in time, space, and attention between what you do and what happens to you subsequently (Franks, 1969; Lazarus, 1971). In addition, the special application to human behavior was predicated less on ongoing scientific discoveries about learning or about people than on the idea that human neuroses are probably about the same as animal neuroses (Wolpe, 1958). The critical principles of learning involved had all been spelled out rather elaborately between 1898 and 1938, and the business about animal neuroses was posited by Pavlov in the same period. During that period, in fact, Pavlov, Watson, Jones, Mowrer, and Guthrie pretty much spelled out all of the major behavior therapy methods that became popular for treating people since 1958, with the possible exception of desensitization and operant behavior shaping (London, 1964). And they are exceptions only because the former is not derived from the usual learning principles, and cannot be, and because the latter is something everybody knew about anyhow but never applied ingeniously until Skinner laboriously spelled out its monumental implications.

EVOLUTION OF BEHAVIOR MODIFICATION

The early growth of behavior modification as a professional specialty was largely polemical and political, not theoretical, and most of its scientific hoopla evolved to serve the polemical needs of the people who made it up—not all of it, however, and not only polemical needs.

The study of learning for behavior therapists, in fact, was always more for the purpose of metaphor, paradigm, and analogy than for strict guidance about how to operate or about what it all means. Whatever value theory may have for dictating laboratory procedures, therapeutic operations have been essentially seat-of-the-pants affairs, and still are, because they address immediate practical problems that require solutions in fact, not in principle. The disregarding of principles to see what really works, in this connection, reflects the intelligence and scientific good sense of therapists. The search for principles to explain what works, on the other hand, reflects their integrity and their anxiety—integrity because only fools would accept their own results without question, anxiety because therapists seek principles as much to increase their confidence as to reduce their ignorance. People also look for principles to help fight intellectual battles. Conventional therapies could be assaulted for their ineffectiveness, but the basis for offering new ones had to be more than complaints about the old ones. And in the case of behavior modification, it had to be more than a simplistic appeal to "what works." Of all popular therapies, psychoanalysis in particular was based on a pretentious, respectable, and smart *theory*. It could not be challenged with less than a theory.

Learning theory was an obvious choice: first, because there is a history of suggested therapeutic applications of learning principles, from Thorndike and Pavlov through Mowrer and Guthrie; and second, because the heart of any *psycho*therapy is changing people's behavior without changing their body structure or gross functions—which means, in plain language, teaching them and getting them to learn.

Even so, the evolution of behavior modification did not go so neatly. It could not make much use of learning theory, except for the broadest principles of learning, because most of the principles either do not yet have any really systematic application to disorders or because they are much more in dispute than naive students realize.

The polemics actually used attacked evident flaws in psychoanalytic and other psychiatric formulations, sometimes also getting a little professional jealousy of psychologists for doctors into the act. Their main points were *(a)* an attack on "the medical model"; *(b)* the insistence that the origins of disorder were in *learning* instead of biochemical or genetic events; *(c)* the proposition that effective therapeutics should treat symptoms instead of their causes, that is, that disorders are identical with their symptoms; and finally, *(d)* the demand that even the name of the game should be changed from psychotherapy to behavior therapy, so no one thinks we are mentalistic or unscientific, as other therapies obviously are (sic).

This description is not exaggerated at all. Eysenck's (1959) tabulation of "the more important differences between Freudian Psychotherapy and Behavior Therapy," for instance, says that Freudian therapy is "based on inconsistent theory never properly formulated in postulate form," while behavior therapy is "based on consistent, properly formulated theory leading to testable deducations." Similarly, Freudian practice is "derived from clinical observations made without necessary control, observation or experiment," while behavior therapy is "derived from experimental studies specifically designed to test basic theory and deductions made therefrom [p. 67]." Franks (1969) is kinder than Eysenck, but even he says a decade later, "for most behavior therapists, the preferred sequence of events is from experimental observation to clinical practice. This may be contrasted with the approach of traditional psychotherapists, in which the sequence is often reversed [p. 3]."

These arguments are not entirely pointless, but they are not entirely apropos of anything either, except who is smart and who will get the last word. What makes them largely irrelevant is that explanatory concepts are only necessary to explain what is going on—and until you know that, you do not need a theory, at least not much of one. Such theory at this point in this enterprise has to be stretched to fit facts rather than tailored to them. And it is damaging in the long run because people may start believing it and making up nonsense to plead silly cases that confuse everybody and enlighten no one. Enormous time and space have been wasted in pious debates on irrelevant aspects of most of the popular polemic issues of psychotherapy.

Discussions of the medical model, for instance, often contrast learning theory approaches to psychodynamic approaches. There is a real question about the relative utility of *organic* versus *dynamic* perspectives on some behavior disorders, but all learning theory formulations are, in fact, dynamic ones. Also, there are many medical models, and the general attack on "the" medical model is only applicable to the *infectious disease* model and only usable against psychoanalysis by lamely borrowing against Freud's (1961) unfortunate statement about putting demonology inside people's heads. Medical *epidemiological* models should have some appeal to Skinnerians, in fact, with their emphasis on environmental determinants of disorder, just as psychological models of habit formation are good for understanding the course of some developmental or degenerative medical conditions like heart disease.

The controversy about (learned versus structural) origins of disorder is mostly pointless because it is mostly irrelevant to treatment. The behaviorist attack commonly assumes that a genetic or biochemical view of etiology is bad because if disorder is learned, then treatment must be a learning process. This is nonsense. Etiology and treatment have no logical connection in either direction. Anxiety, for example, may be the result of prior experience but can be alleviated chemically; or it may be aroused by essentially chemical circumstances (like fatigue plus mild arousal to danger) but can be soothed physically or verbally (Davison, 1968).

The only treatment question of relevance is that of the functional relationship between the problem and its solution. The process is what matters and nothing else.

The biggest polemic, of course, about treating symptoms versus causes has occurred largely because of the uncertain danger of symptom return or symptom substitution. Everywhere, much confusion has occurred, mostly because of confusion about the medical model—in this instance, about the exact meaning of symptom. If symptom means trouble, surely it should be treated. If not, maybe not. The polemic has been around the question of symptoms as "the main trouble"; this is because of the widespread belief, largely from psychoanalysis, in symptom return or substitution. (Buchwald & Young, 1969, point out, incidentally, that some analysts, such as Fenichel and, later, Alexander, thought that symptoms should be treated directly.)

The real issue, in any case, is the consequence of the treatment for the person's condition—or his life. Sometimes too, the issue is prophylactic or preventive rather than ameliorative. This becomes clear by comparing the infectious disease and chronic ailment models in medicine. Behavior disorders are more like chronic ailments, where medical treatment generally aims at the symptoms only. The control of diabetes, on the other hand, is not treatment of symptoms, but their prevention. Is the shaping of behavior likewise? For changing the table manners of psychotics' ward behavior, maybe not; for molding children's manners, maybe so. The same question may be addressed to assertive training or to aversion training. Is teaching someone to talk back to his mother-in-law reducing his anxiety or preventing it from happening? Is teaching a homosexual man to attend to women when aroused and to feel repugnance for sex with men relieving his symptom or preventing a disorder (which does not exist legally until he "goes for" the man), teaching a habit pattern or unteaching one, changing a life style, altering a phenomenological field, shifting ego boundaries, redirecting id impulses or superego functions, or cathexis? And if he feels different or thinks about it differently, is it still behavior therapy?

These are silly questions. The change in the homosexual is all those things, depending on how you want to talk about them. Understanding the process is what matters, not belaboring the different styles of talking about it. The only important question about systematic treatment is that of the simultaneous relevance of the treatment technique to the person's manifest trouble and to the rest of his life.

Sometimes it accounts for both at once—as when he is suicidal. Sometimes it accounts for the rest of his life but not for the symptom—which is the behavior modifier's claim against insight types' preoccupation with motivation. Sometimes it accounts for only the manifest trouble—which is the insight therapists' accusation against behavior modifiers, based on the specious presumption that everything in a person's life is integral to it.

All of these polemics were not so much meaningless as overdone. The assault on psychoanalysts and existentialists was too extreme; the scientific claims on learning were too grandiose (Buchwald & Young, 1969; Franks, 1969). Changing from psychotherapy to behavior therapy may have been useful for people brought up on mind-body dualism, but for those of us who always thought the mind hung around the brain and that behavior meant "what happened," the distinction was graceless and gratuitous.

When you eliminate the polemics and politics and gratuities, however, what remains of theory to define the field and to tell you what it is about? Not a whole lot. The definition of the field either becomes very inclusive (Lazarus, 1971; Marks, 1971; Marston, 1970; Paul, 1969; Skinner, 1971) or very narrow (Eysenck, 1960; Skinner, 1963; Wolpe, 1958). This probably makes no serious difference to anything. As Kuhn (1962) said, "Can a definition tell a man whether he is a scientist or not [p. 160]?"

But what about theory? If behavior modification lacks theory, then is it not reduced to a technology rather than a science? Yes, it is, and I believe that is what it should be, just as medicine is technology rather than science.

There is some dispute in the field about this point. The sides are well represented by Lazarus, who agrees with my view, and Franks, who does not. Lazarus (1971) said in his latest book:

> The emphasis of the volume is upon techniques rather than upon theories. . . . Methods of therapy are often effective for reasons which are at variance with the views of their inventors or discoverers. Technical eclecticism (Lazarus, 1967) does not imply a random melange of techniques taken haphazardly out of the air. It is an approach which urges therapists to experiment with empirically useful methods instead of using their theories as a priori predictors of what will and will not succeed in therapy (Eysenck, 1957, p. 271). The rationale behind the methods described in this book is predicated upon London's (1964) observation that: "However interesting, plausible, and appealing a theory may be, it is techniques, not theories, that are actually used on people. Study of the effect of psychotherapy, therefore, is always the study of the effectiveness of techniques" [p. 33].

Franks (1969) argued to the contrary:

> It would seem to be highly desirable for the therapist to aspire to be a scientist even if this goal were difficult to realize. To function as a scientist, it is necessary to espouse some theoretical framework. For reasons too obvious to detail here, this is true of the behavioral therapist. . . . How the behavior therapist practices (including his choice of technique, his approach to the problems of general strategy, and his specific relationships with his patient) thus depending both upon his explicit theoretical orientation and upon his implicit philosophical and cultural milieu [p. 21].

The argument that behavior modification should view itself as technology rather than as science is not meant to denigrate the importance of theory, either scientifically or heuristically. Scientifically, theory is valuable because it directs the systematic search for new information by interpreting and integrating what is already known. Heuristically, theory is valuable because it lays our biases out in the open and by explicating them makes it easier for us to disavow them when they are found to be inadequate.

The question with respect to behavior modification is twofold: First, is current theory very good (scientifically) in this case? Second, is any theory very useful for the current development of this field at this time? I think the answer to both questions is no.

In reality, behavior therapists never did have so much a theory as an "ideology"; in my own paraphrase of Bell (1960) and Tomkins (1964), "Ideology does not mean just ideas, but ideas to be acted on . . . [London, 1969]." What behavior therapists called theory actually served as bases for commitment or a rallying point for talking about disorder and treatment in a certain way and, more important, about acting on it within particular sets of limited operations, that is, technical limits. In this case the commitment is to the *functional analysis of problems.* And it is for this reason that the domain incorporated within the legitimate purview of the field becomes broader and broader and the polemics milder and milder—as it is recognized that even Rogerians and humanists and psychoanalysts may analyze some things functionally and act on them accordingly.

What results from the increasing functional analysis of problems is an increasing number of plausible methods for coping with them. Until the proliferation of methods is tested and found to work, no theory is really very necessary to explain *why* they work. For practitioners, none may be needed even then, if they work well. In any case, theory will largely grow from practice (Lazarus & Davison, 1971) and practice from instrumentation, in the broadest sense; this will happen to behavior modification just as it did to psychoanalysis, but with two generations' more experience, the results, hopefully, will be more scientific.

The status of theory comes largely from the belief that technique develops out of theory, that is, that science underlies engineering. But this is only partly true even among very hard sciences, less so among soft sciences, like the social and behavioral sciences, and not at all true for many endeavors where the existence of the technological capacity and the practical need is what produces the technical application and, indeed, what "nourishes" much of the theoretical development itself (Oppenheimer, 1956).

This does not mean that the alternative to rude theory is rude empiricism; rather, it suggests a close-to-the-situation functional analysis instead of a premature and precocious search for general principles from which to get overextended, or for a professional ideology to which to be committed. Such a development seems to be proceeding now, with practitioners using the techniques of behavior modification but declining the identity (Paul, 1969b) and scholars recommending heterodoxies like "technical eclecticism" without shame (Lazarus, 1971). The rest of this article spells out what this development means, so we will see clearly what we are doing, with the view to doing it better.

By deducing the intellectual condition of behavior modification from the technology it uses, there seem to be two kinds of conceptual schemes which characterize it. Borrowing from Price's (1971) book, *Abnormal Psychology: Perspectives in Conflict*, in turn derived from Kuhn's (1962) *Structure of Scientific Revolutions*, these are, first, *metaphors* or analogies, and second, *paradigms* or models.

In the conventional classification of how much we seem to know what we are talking about in science, these concepts fit the lower end of the scale of certainty whose upper rungs are called theories and laws. A scientific law, in other words, is an idea that seems absolutely to comprehend all of the facts it talks about; a theory is one that hopes to do so, but is not so compellingly known to do so. The activities involved in behavior modification are a good distance below both these points on the same continuum. A few are paradigms or models, that is, ideas that seem to explain a group of facts pretty precisely; most are metaphors or analogies, that is, ideas that look like they might fit a group of facts, where there is no clear evidence that they really do.

In general, the treatment methods derived from speculations about conditioning studies of animals are metaphorical or analogous, especially desensitization and implosion, or flooding. In general, the treatment methods that fall under the heading of education or training or, in jargon, of instrumental learning are paradigmatic or exemplary, including modeling, shaping, and possibly aversion techniques.

The difference between the metaphoric and the paradigmatic treatments is not in how well they work but only in how well their workings are understood. This, in turn, reduces to how much of the mechanics involved can be predicted or explained with what degree of precision, which reduces still further to how many of the details are visible or can be inferred with different degrees of correlation. For practical purposes, the difference is simply one of the extent to which you can see what is going on enough to figure out how variations in your approach will affect it. The more you can peer intellectually into the "black box," in other words, and the prediction proves correct, the more you are dealing with a paradigm rather than a metaphor. A paradigm in other words, is an attempt to construct a direct model or example of how something works. A metaphor is a more oblique comparison, in which the flaws in the analogy are obvious, but the similarities are still big enough to allow us to ask whether the comparison might work.[1]

Desensitization is only a metaphor or analogy to conditioning: first, because it involves a specific cognitive process (the use of language) that classical conditioning does not; second, because it involves a mechanism of sequential imagination that can only be guessed at from conditioning studies; and third, because it is subject to a variety of successful variations that could not be predicted from the situations from which the metaphor was derived in the first place. Finally, desensitization does the same thing that implosion or flooding does, though it appears to be an opposite method.

Implosion is a better analogy than desensitization because Stampfl's original experiment (London, 1964) seems to parallel both Mowrer's (1950) theoretical statement, Solomon, Kamin, and Wynne's (1953), and Black's (1958) animal experiments more closely than Wolpe fits Masserman's cats or Pavlov's dogs. Also, implosion technique does predict all of its own variants—including Watson, Gaind, and Marks' (1971) finding that practice helps to extinguish phobic reactions and that using real objects instead of imagination as fearful stimuli also is helpful—but it is metaphorical nonetheless because it is between people, and because it is administered in social situations where the pressure *not* to escape is obviously coming from the thoughts that the patient has about the situation, not from physical restraints on his action.

Shaping is more exemplary or paradigmatic than conditioning treatments because it presumes less, in the first place, on the black box—modeling, likewise. Stated differently, both shaping and modeling methods can aim for precision in establishing the conditions that will work the desired effects without having to worry much about what is going on in the person that makes them work.

Aversion treatment is more paradigmatic than metaphoric because its critical stimulus is not cognitive; that is, it hurts the patient physically. Giving a person an electric shock is much more like shocking a dog than telling scary stories to a person is like blowing air up a rat's behind; ergo, it is more paradigmatic than metaphoric.

Neither metaphors nor paradigms are scientific theories by some distance, but both of them are useful intellectual tools. Metaphor and analogy are good heuristically—they help to turn images into thoughts and inchoate hunches into articulate propositions. Paradigms are more literally useful—they model to scale what you need to do, or give a mathematical formula into which you can put specific quanta.

Notice, however, that none of this has anything to do with whether anything works for any practical problem. Desensitization may be a poor deduction from conditioning, but it is a fine treatment for phobias. Behavior shaping may be an excellent paradigm for getting autistic children to hug people, but it does not teach them syntactical speech.

Whatever scientific concern people have about the intellectual status of the field, at this point in the development of this enterprise, none of this material is yet very important to practitioners, and it is barely important to clinical research. What *is* important at this juncture is the development of systematic practice and of a technology to sustain it. My thesis is that, in the long run, scientific understanding will derive from them.

The practitioner tries to figure out what will work, for the most part, and then, if he is scientifically inclined, looks for a way to rationalize it if it does. The technologist devises machinery to support him. This is not a bad idea, even if it doesn't add up to a test-tube-pure, white-coat science. Systematic desensitization is a good example of this process because by working in the first place it has given rise to technological refinements of itself that also work and that still leave the reasons unexplained. In the long run, this must force better and better logical and experimental confrontations with the reasons for the phenomenon—which success alone would not have done.

New equipment, new drugs, new gimmickry and gadgetry should now be the basis for systematically developing new methods of behavior modification and for streamlining the established techniques with controlled experimental testing. Instead of looking for new principles or justifying worn-out ones, we should look for new applications: What could we do to treat such-and-such if we had such-and-such machinery? What would be required to build it? To test it? And then, finally, to determine what it means?

The critical point is that *good technology always undermines bad theory*. "Bad" is not meant to be pejorative here; it means metaphoric. Precise technology reveals the empirical error in metaphoric reasoning and in the operations that result from it. So Lang's (1969a, 1969b) on-line computer removes the therapist from the desensitization process; Quirk's (1970) machine removes the imagining and the relevance of the phobic subject matter; and Wolpin's (Jacobs & Wolpin, 1971; Wolpin, 1969; Wolpin & Raines, 1966) removes the need for hypnosis, for the fear hierarchy, and, indeed, for relaxation. Since the method still works, the need for explanation becomes more and more apparent (Davison, 1969), as does the inadequacy of the very plausible metaphor that launched Wolpe (1958) on the whole business.

Technology promises, in fact, more and more to turn metaphor to paradigm, if not paradigm to theory, by going directly into the black box and doing funny things to it and, increasingly, by bringing the black box out into the open where we can see more and more what has been happening in it. For the former, I refer to drug research and to the work in progress on electrical stimulation of the brain (Cohen, 1969; Delgado, 1969; London, 1969). These activities undercut specious distinctions between learned and unlearned patterns, either by manipulating the patterns out of hand or by potentiating learning so effectively that the issue of its importance disappears.

Bringing the black box out into the open is one of the main results likely to accrue from *biofeedback* research, and it is probably the best illustration one can find of technology feeding science with one hand as it enhances practice with the other. All of the biofeedback methods work on a single principle, whether they teach people to ring buzzers from a switch in their heads or to alter their blood pressure or heartbeat or skin resistance by monitoring lights and gauges. The principle is finding a means of accurately externally recording some internal process, then of projecting that record into the person's consciousness so that he can literally see or hear what his blood vessels or brain waves or heart muscles are doing. Then let him learn to manipulate his conscious sensory experience in whatever way people learn to do anything consciously—something about which we really know next to nothing.

The clinical value of biofeedback methods remains to be seen and will certainly not be what alpha-machine hucksters seem to wish—instant cool for overheated psyches. Its clinical utility is not yet the point, only its technological sophistication and the scientific potential that comes from that.

To turn the point around, I am saying that theory has worn itself out in behavior modification and that technology, essentially of treatment, should now be a primary focus, perhaps, in the long range, even for serving scientific purposes. What began with the Mowrers' quilted pad in 1938 is extending now into therapeutic on-line computers, electric pottie chairs, electronic skin braille, and an almost self-generating brace of valuable hardware for therapeutic purposes. A summary of much of it will appear soon in a book by Robert and Ralph Schwitzgebel (in press) entitled *Psychotechnology*.

But the proper development that I am suggesting is not limited to hardware and is not self-generating, but reaches to the systematic exploration of all kinds of therapeutic things without inhibition or concern as to whether they fit ostensible *principles* of learning or reinforcement or whatever, but with a singular focus on whether they fit the *facts* of human experience. No one has been more forthright or resourceful in this connection than Lazarus (1971), whose latest work, *Behavior Therapy and Beyond*, goes into such things as imagery exercises for depression; thought control, straight out, for whatever it works for; hypnosis for all kinds of things; exaggerated role taking à la the late George Kelly; differential relaxation; covert sensitization for aversive imaging; and Masters and Johnson's penis squeezing for premature ejaculation. It would take a genius or a madman to shelter this whole array of techniques under the intellectual umbrella of conditioning, or learning, or any other single psychological theory. It would take a fool to want to. The first issue, scientifically as well as clinically, is the factual one—Do they work? On whom? When? The how and why come later.

With the era of polemics virtually ended, and Skinner (1971) citing Freud over and over again in his latest work, and the American Psychoanalytic Association at a recent convention casually incorporating behavior modification into its discourses on psychotherapy, the political utility of learning theory, so called for the definition of the field, is ended. It was never really theory anyhow, as we used it, but ideology for professional purposes and mostly metaphor for clinical ones. It is time now, I think, for the remedial branch of this business to stop worrying about its scientific pretensions, in the theoretical sense, as long as it keeps its functional nose clean, and to devise a kind of engineering subsidiary, or more precisely, a systems analysis approach to its own operations. We have gotten about as much mileage as we are going to out of old principles, even correct ones, but we have barely begun to work the new technology.

REFERENCES

Bell, D. *End of ideology: Exhaustion of political ideas in the fifties.* Glencoe, Ill.: Free Press, 1960.

Black, A. H. The extinction of avoidance responses under curare. *Journal of Comparative and Physiological Psychology*, 1958, *51*, 519–524.

Buchwald, A. M., & Young, R. D. Some comments on the foundations of behavior therapy. In C. M. Franks (Ed.), *Behavior therapy: Appraisal and status.* New York: McGraw-Hill, 1969.

Cohen, S. I. Neurobiological considerations for behavior therapy. In C. M. Franks (Ed.), *Behavior therapy: Appraisal and status.* New York: McGraw-Hill, 1969.

Davison, G. C. Systematic desensitization as a counter-conditioning process. *Journal of Abnormal Psychology*, 1968, *73*, 91–99.

______. A procedural critique of "desensitization and the experimental reduction of threat." *Journal of Abnormal Psychology*, 1969, *74*, 86–87.

Delgado, J. M. R. *Physical control of the mind.* New York: Harper & Row, 1969.

Eysenck, H. J. Learning theory and behavior therapy. *Journal of Mental Science*, 1959, *105*, 61–75.

______. (Ed.), *Behavior therapy and neuroses.* London: Pergamon Press, 1960.

Franks, C. M. (Ed.), *Behavior therapy: Appraisal and status.* New York: McGraw-Hill, 1969.

Freud, S. *The standard edition of the complete psychological works of Sigmund Freud.* London: Hogarth Press, 1961.

Jacobs, A., & Wolpin, M. A second look at systematic desensitization. In *Psychology of private events.* New York: Academic Press, 1971.

Kuhn, T. S. *The structure of scientific revolutions.* Chicago: Univ. of Chicago Press, 1962.

Lang, P. J. The mechanics of desensitization and the laboratory study of human fear. In C. M. Franks (Ed.), *Behavior therapy: Appraisal and status.* New York: McGraw-Hill, 1969a.

______. The on-line computer in behavior therapy research. *American Psychologist*, 1969b, *24*, 236–239.

Lazarus, A. A. *Behavior therapy and beyond.* New York: McGraw-Hill, 1971.

Lazarus, A. A., & Davison, G. C. Clinical innovation in research and practice. In A. F. Bergin & S. L. Garfield (Eds.), *Handbook of psychotherapy and behavior change.* New York: Wiley, 1971.

London, P. *The modes and morals of psychotherapy.* New York: Holt, Rinehart & Winston, 1964.

______. *Behavior control.* New York: Harper & Row, 1969.

Marks, I. M. The future of the psychotherapies. *British Journal of Psychiatry*, 1971, *118*, 69–73.

Marston, A. Parables for behavior therapists. Address to Southern California Behavior Modification Conference, Los Angeles, October 1970.

Mowrer, O. H. *Learning theory and personality dynamics.* New York: Ronald Press, 1950.

Oppenheimer, R. Analogy in science. *American Psychologist*, 1956, *11*, 127–135.

Paul, G. L. Behavior modification research: Design and tactics. In C. M. Franks (Ed.), *Behavior therapy: Appraisal and status.* New York: McGraw-Hill, 1969a.

______. Outcome of systematic desensitization: II. Controlled investigations of individual treatment, technique variations and current status. In C. M. Franks (Ed.), *Behavior therapy: Appraisal and status.* New York: McGraw-Hill, 1969b.

Price, R. *Abnormal psychology: Positions in perspective.* New York: Holt, Rinehart & Winston, in press.

Quirk, D. A. *Stimulus conditioned autonomic response suppression: A behavioral therapy.* Toronto: Univ. of Toronto, Clarke Institute of Psychiatry, 1970.

Schwitzgebel, R. L., & Schwitzgebel, R. K. *Psychotechnology.* New York: Holt, Rinehart & Winston, in press.

Skinner, B. F. Behaviorism at fifty. *Science,* 1963, *140,* 951–958.

______. *Beyond freedom and dignity.* New York: Knopf, 1971.

Solomon, R. L., Kamin, L. J., & Wynne, L. C. Traumatic avoidance learning: The outcomes of several extinction procedures with dogs. *Journal of Abnormal and Social Psychology,* 1953, *48,* 291–302.

Tomkins, S. The psychology of knowledge. Invited address to Division 8. Presented at the meeting of the American Psychological Association, Los Angeles, September 7, 1964.

Watson, J. P. Gaind, R., & Marks, I. M. Prolonged exposure: A rapid treatment for phobias. *British Medical Journal,* 1971, *1,* 13–15.

Wolpe, J. *Psychotherapy by reciprocal inhibition.* Stanford: Stanford Univ. Press, 1958.

Wolpin, M. Guided imagining to reduce avoidance behavior. *Psychotherapy: Theory, Research and Practice,* 1969, *6,* 122–124.

Wolpin, M., & Raines, J. Visual imagery, expected roles and extinction as possible factors in reducing fear and avoidance behavior. *Behavior Research and Therapy.* 1966, *4,* 25–37.

NOTES

1. Oppenheimer (1956) distinguished analogy from metaphor because the "structural similarity" of analogous events implies more precision in their comparison than is ordinarily true of metaphoric comparisons. I am putting them together here, however, to distinguish them both from paradigm.

BEHAVIOR THEORY AND THE MODELS OF MAN

Albert Bandura, Stanford University

The views about the nature of man conveyed by behavior theory require critical examination on conceptual and social grounds. What we believe man to be affects which aspects of human functioning we study most thoroughly and which we disregard. Premises thus delimit research and are, in turn, shaped by it. As knowledge gained through study is put into practice, the images of man on which social technologies rest have even vaster implications. This is nowhere better illustrated than in growing public concern over manipulation and control by psychological

Presidential Address presented at the meeting of the American Psychological Association, New Orleans, August 1974. Requests for reprints should be sent to Albert Bandura, Department of Psychology, Stanford University, Stanford, California 94305.

Bandura, Albert. Behavior theory and the models of man. *American Psychologist,* 1974, *29,* 859–869.

methods. Some of these fears arise from expectations that improved means of influence will inevitably be misused. Other apprehensions are aroused by exaggerated claims of psychological power couched in the language of manipulation and authoritarian control. But most fears stem from views of behaviorism, articulated by popular writers and by theorists themselves, that are disputed by the empirical facts of human behavior.

In the minds of the general public and of many within our own discipline, behavior theory is equated with conditioning. Over the years the terms *behaviorism* and *conditioning* have come to be associated with odious imagery, including salivating dogs, puppetry, and animalistic manipulation. As a result, those who wish to disparage ideas or practices they hold in disfavor need only to label them as behavioristic or as Pavlovian precursors of a totalitarian state.

Contrary to popular belief, the fabled reflexive conditioning in humans is largely a myth. *Conditioning* is simply a descriptive term for learning through paired experiences, not an explanation of how the changes come about. Originally, conditioning was assumed to occur automatically. On closer examination it turned out to be cognitively mediated. People do not learn despite repetitive paired experiences unless they recognize that events are correlated (Dawson & Furedy, 1974; Grings, 1973). So-called conditioned reactions are largely self-activated on the basis of learned expectations rather than automatically evoked. The critical factor, therefore, is not that events occur together in time but that people learn to predict them and to summon up appropriate anticipatory reactions.

The capacity to learn from correlated experiences reflects sensitivity, but because Pavlov first demonstrated the phenomenon with a dog, it has come to be regarded as a base animalistic process. Had he chosen to study physiological hyperactivity in humans to cues associated with stress or the development of empathetic reactions to expressions of suffering, conditioning would have been treated in a more enlightened way. To expect people to remain unaffected by events that are frightening, humiliating, disgusting, sad, or pleasurable is to require that they be less than human. Although negative effects such as fears and dislikes can arise from paired experiences of a direct or vicarious sort, so do some of the ennobling qualities of man. The pejorative accounts of learning principles, which appear with regularity in professional and lay publications, degrade both the science of psychology and the audiences that the offensive rhetoric is designed to sway.

It is well documented that behavior is influenced by its consequences much of the time. The image of man that this principle connotes depends on the types of consequences that are acknowledged and on an understanding of how they operate. In theories that recognize only the role of proximate external consequences and contend they shape behavior automatically, people appear as mechanical pawns of environmental forces. But external consequences, influential as they often are, are not the sole determinants of human behavior, nor do they operate automatically.

Response consequences serve several functions. First, they impart information. By observing the effects of their actions, individuals eventually discern which behaviors are appropriate in which settings. The acquired information then serves as a guide for action. Contrary to the mechanistic metaphors, outcomes change behavior in humans through the intervening influence of thought.

Consequences motivate through their incentive value, as well as inform. By representing foreseeable outcomes symbolically, future consequences can be converted into current motivators of behavior. Many of the things we do are designed to gain anticipated benefits and to avert future trouble. Our choices of action are largely under anticipatory control. The widely accepted dictum that man is ruled by response consequences thus fares better for anticipated than for actual consequences. Consider behavior on a fixed-ratio schedule (say, 50:1) in which only every fiftieth response is reinforced. Since 96% of the outcomes are extinctive and only 4% are reinforcing, behavior is maintained despite its dissuading consequences. As people are exposed to variations in frequency and predictability of reinforcement, they behave on the basis of the outcomes they expect to prevail on future occasions. When belief differs from actuality, which is not uncommon, behavior is weakly controlled by its actual consequences until repeated experience instills realistic expectations (Bandura, 1971b; Kaufman, Baron, & Kopp, 1966).

Had humans been ruled solely by instant consequences, they would have long become museum pieces among the extinct species. Not that our future is unquestionably secure. The immediate rewards of consumptive life-styles vigorously promoted for short-term profit jeopardize man's long-term chances of survival. But immediate consequences, unless unusually powerful, do not necessarily outweigh deferred ones (Mischel, 1974). Our descendants shall continue to have a future only because those who foresee the aversive long-term consequences of current practices mobilize public support for contingencies that favor survival behavior. Hazardous pesticides, for example, are usually banned before populations suffer maladies from toxic residues. The information-processing capacities with which humans are endowed provide the basis for insightful behavior. Their capacity to bring remote consequences to bear on current behavior by anticipatory thought supports foresightful action.

Explanations of reinforcement originally assumed that consequences increase behavior without conscious involvement. The still prevalent notion that reinforcers can operate insidiously arouses fears that improved techniques of reinforcement will enable authorities to manipulate people without their knowledge or consent. Although the empirical issue is not yet completely resolved, there is little evidence that rewards function as automatic strengtheners of human conduct. Behavior is not much affected by its consequences without awareness of what is being reinforced (Bandura, 1969; Dulany, 1968). After individuals discern the instrumental relation between action and outcome, contingent rewards may produce accommodating or oppositional behavior depending on how they value the incentives, the influencers, and the behavior itself, and how others respond. Thus reinforcement, as it has become better understood, has changed from a mechanical strengthener of conduct to an informative and motivating influence.

People do not function in isolation. As social beings, they observe the conduct of others and the occasions on which it is rewarded, disregarded, or punished. They can therefore profit from observed consequences as well as from their own direct experiences (Bandura, 1971c). Acknowledgment of vicarious reinforcement introduces another human dimension—namely, evaluative capacities—into the operation of reinforcement influences. People weigh consequences to themselves against those accruing to others for similar behavior. The same outcome can thus become a reward or a punishment depending upon the referents used for social comparison.

Human conduct is better explained by the relational influence of observed and direct consequences than by either factor alone. However, behavior is not fully predictable from a relational coefficient because social justifications alter the impact of outcome disparities. Inequitable reinforcement is willingly accepted when people are graded by custom into social ranks and rewarded according to position rather than by performance. Arbitrary inequities are also likely to be tolerated if the underrewarded are led to believe they possess attributes that make them less deserving of equal treatment. Persuasively justified inequities have more detrimental personal effects than acknowledged unfairness because they foster self-devaluation in the maltreated. Negative reactions to inequitable reinforcement which is acknowledged to be unwarranted can likewise be diminished by temporizing. If people are led to expect that unfair treatment will be corrected within the foreseeable future, it becomes less aversive to them.

Theories that explain human behavior as the product of external rewards and punishments present a truncated image of man because people partly regulate their actions by self-produced consequences (Bandura, 1971c; Thoresen & Mahoney, 1973). Example and precept impart standards of conduct that serve as the basis for self-reinforcing reactions. The development of self-reactive functions gives humans a capacity for self-direction. They do things that give rise to self-satisfaction and self-worth, and they refrain from behaving in ways that evoke self-punishment.

After self-reinforcing functions are acquired, a given act produces two sets of consequences: self-evaluative reactions and external outcomes. Personal and external sources of reinforcement may operate as supplementary or as opposing influences on behavior. Thus, for example, individuals commonly experience conflicts when rewarded for conduct they personally devalue. When self-condemning consequences outweigh rewarding inducements, external influences are relatively ineffective. On the other hand, if certain courses of action produce stronger rewards than self-censure, the result is cheerless compliance. Losses in self-respect for devalued conduct can be abated, however, by self-exonerating justifications. I shall return to this issue shortly.

Another type of conflict between external and self-produced consequences arises when individuals are punished for behavior they regard highly. Principled dissenters and nonconformists often find themselves in this predicament. Personally valued conduct is expressed provided its costs are not too high. Should the threatened consequences be severe, one inhibits self-praiseworthy acts under high risk of penalty but readily performs them when the chances of punishment are reduced. There are individuals, however, whose sense of self-worth is so strongly invested in certain convictions that they will submit to prolonged maltreatment rather than accede to what they regard as unjust or immoral.

External consequences exert greatest influence on behavior when they are compatible with those that are self-produced. These conditions obtain when rewardable acts are a source of self-pride and punishable ones are self-censured. To enhance compatibility between personal and social influences, people select associates who share similar standards of conduct and thus ensure social support for their own system of self-reinforcement.

Individualistic theories of moral action assume that internalization of behavioral standards creates a permanent control mechanism within the person. Restraints of conscience thereafter operate as enduring controls over reprehensible conduct. The testimony of human behavior, however, contradicts this view. Much human maltreatment and suffering are, in fact, inflicted by otherwise decent moral people. And some of the most striking changes in moral conduct, as evidenced, for example, in political and military violence, are achieved without altering personality structures or moral standards. Personal control is clearly more complex and flexible than the theorizing implies.

Although self-reinforcing influences serve as regulators of conduct, they can be dissociated from censurable deeds by self-exonerating practices (Bandura, 1973). One device is to make inhumane behavior personally and socially acceptable by defining it in terms of high moral principle. People do not act in ways they ordinarily consider evil or destructive until such activities are construed as serving moral purposes. Over the years much cruelty has been perpetrated in the name of religious principles, righteous ideologies, and regulatory sanctions. In the transactions of everyday life, euphemistic labeling serves as a handy linguistic device for masking reprehensible activities or according them a respectable status. Self-deplored conduct can also be made benign by contrasting it with more flagrant inhumanities. Moral justifications and palliative comparisons are especially effective because they not only eliminate self-generated deterrents but engage self-reward in the service of reprehensible conduct. What was morally unacceptable becomes a source of self-pride.

A common dissociative practice is to obscure or distort the relationship between one's actions and the effects they cause. People will perform behavior they normally repudiate if a legitimate authority sanctions it and acknowledges responsibility for its consequences. By displacing responsibility elsewhere, participants do not hold themselves accountable for what they do and are thus spared self-prohibiting reactions. Exemption from self-censure can be facilitated additionally by diffusing responsibility for culpable behavior. Through division of labor, division of decision making, and collective action, people can contribute to detrimental practices without feeling personal responsibility or self-disapproval.

Attribution of blame to the victim is still another exonerative expedient. Victims are faulted for bringing maltreatment on themselves, or extraordinary circumstances are invoked as justifications for questionable conduct. One need not engage in self-reproof for committing acts prescribed by circumstances. A further means of weakening self-punishment is to dehumanize the victim. Inflicting harm upon people who are regarded as subhuman or debased is less likely to arouse self-reproof than if they are looked upon as human beings with sensitivities.

There are other self-disinhibiting maneuvers that operate by misrepresenting the consequences of actions. As long as detrimental effects are ignored or minimized, there is little reason for self-censure. If consequences are not easily distortable, distress over conduct that conflicts with self-evaluative standards can be reduced by selectively remembering the benefits and forgetting the harm of one's acts.

Given the variety of self-disinhibiting devices, a society cannot rely on control by conscience to ensure moral and ethical conduct. Though personal control ordinarily serves as a self-directive force, it can be nullified by social sanctions conducive to destructiveness. Indoctrination and social justifications give meaning to events and create anticipations that determine one's actions. Control through information, which is rooted in cognitive processes, is more pervasive and powerful than conditioning through contiguity of events. Cultivation of humaneness therefore requires, in addition to benevolent personal codes, safeguards built into social systems that counteract detrimental sanctioning practices and uphold compassionate behavior.

A conceptual orientation not only prescribes what facets of man will be studied in depth but also how one goes about changing human behavior. Early applications of reinforcement principles, for example, were guided by the then prevalent belief that consequences alter behavior automatically and unconsciously. Since the process supposedly operated mechanically, the reinforcers had to occur instantly to be effective. Participants in change programs were, therefore, uninformed about why they were being reinforced, and in an effort to ensure immediacy of effects, reinforcers were presented intrusively as soon as the requisite responses were emitted. The net effect was a tedious shaping process that produced, at best, mediocre results in an ethically questionable manner. In many public and professional circles, reinforcement still connotes furtive control even though reinforcement theory and practices have progressed well beyond this level.

Realization that reinforcement is an unarticulated way of designating appropriate conduct prompted the use of cognitive factors in the modification of behavior. Not surprisingly, people change more rapidly if told what behaviors are rewardable and punishable than if they have to discover it from observing the consequences of their actions. Competencies that are not already within their repertoires can be developed with greater ease through the aid of instruction and modeling than by relying solely on the successes and failures of unguided performance.

As further research revealed that reinforcers function as motivators, consequences were recognized as sources of motivation that depend heavily for their effectiveness upon the incentive preferences of those undergoing change. Hence, people do not indiscriminately absorb the influences that impinge upon them. Outcomes resulting from actions need not necessarily occur instantly. Humans can cognitively bridge delays between behavior and subsequent reinforcers without impairing the efficacy of incentive operations.

At this second evolutionary stage, reinforcement practices changed from unilateral control to social contracting. Positive arrangements affirm that if individuals do certain things they are entitled to certain rewards and privileges. In the case of negative sanctions, reprehensible conduct carries punishment costs. The process is portrayed in reinforcement terms, but the practice is that of social exchange. Most social interactions are, of course, governed by conditional agreements, though they usually are not couched in the language of reinforcement. Describing them differently does not change their nature, however.

Contingencies vary in the human qualities they embody and in the voice individuals have in decisions concerning the social arrangements that affect their lives. Reflecting the salient values of our society, reinforcement practices have traditionally favored utilitarian forms of behavior. But conditions are changing. With growing reservations about materialistic life-styles, reinforcement practices are being increasingly used to cultivate personal potentialities and humanistic qualities. These emerging changes in value commitments will probably accelerate as people devote fewer hours to working for income and have more leisure time for self-development.

Another change of some consequence is the renewed concern for individual rights. People are seeking a collaborative role in the development of societal contingencies that affect the course and quality of their lives. As part of this social trend, even the actions taken in the name of psychotherapy are being examined for their ethics and social purposes. These concerns have provided the impetus for prescripts to ensure that reinforcement techniques are used in the service of human betterment rather than as instruments of social control.

A closely related issue is the relative attention devoted to changing individuals or to altering the institutions of society to enrich life. If psychologists are to have a significant impact on common problems of life, they must apply their corrective measures to detrimental societal practices rather than limit themselves to treating the casualties of these practices. This, of course, is easier said than done. Practitioners, whatever their specialty, are reinforced more powerfully for using their knowledge and skills in the service of existing operations than for changing them. Socially oriented efforts are hard to sustain under inadequate reinforcement supports.

The methods of change discussed thus far draw heavily upon external consequences of action. Evidence that people can exercise some control over their own behavior provided the impetus for further changes in reinforcement practices. Interest began to shift from managing conduct to developing skills in self-regulation. In the latter approach, control is vested to a large extent in the hands of individuals themselves: They arrange the environmental inducements for desired behavior; they evaluate their own performances; and they serve as their own reinforcing agents (Goldfried & Merbaum, 1973; Mahoney & Thoresen, 1974). To be sure, the self-reinforcing functions are created and occasionally supported by external influences. Having external origins, however, does not refute the fact that, once established, self-influence partly determines what actions one performs. Citing historical determinants of a generalizable function cannot substitute for contemporaneous influences arising through exercise of that function.

The recognition of self-directing capacities represents a substantial departure from exclusive reliance upon environmental control. But the emerging self-influence practices are still closely rooted in physical transactions—the self-administered consequences are, for the most part, material. Eventually changes in form, as well as source, of reinforcement will appear as the insufficiency of material outcomes is acknowledged. Most people value their self-respect above commodities. They rely extensively on their own self-demands and self-approval as guides for conduct. To ignore the influential role of covert self-reinforcement in the regulation of behavior is to disavow a uniquely human capacity of man.

Proponents who recognize only external consequences restrict their research and practice to such influences and thus generate evidence that reinforces their conceptions. Those who acknowledge personal influences as well tend to select methods that reveal and promote self-directing capabilities in man. The view of man embodied in behavioral technologies is therefore more than a philosophical issue. It affects which human potentialities will be cultivated and which will be underdeveloped.

The preceding remarks addressed the need to broaden the scope of research into the reinforcement processes regulating human behavior. Much the same might be said for the ways in which human learning is conceptualized and investigated. Our theories have been incredibly slow in acknowledging that man can learn by observation as well as by direct experience. This is another example of how steadfast adherence to orthodox paradigms makes it difficult to transcend the confines of conceptual commitment. Having renounced cognitive determinants, early proponents of behaviorism advanced the doctrine that learning can occur only by performing responses and experiencing their effects. This legacy is still very much with us. The rudimentary form of learning based on direct experience has been exhaustively studied, whereas the more pervasive and powerful mode of learning by observation is largely ignored. A shift of emphasis is needed.

The capacity to represent modeled activities symbolically enables man to acquire new patterns of behavior observationally without reinforced enactment. From observing others, one forms an idea of how certain behavior is performed, and on later occasions the coded information serves as a guide for action. Indeed, research conducted within the framework of social learning theory shows that virtually all learning phenomena resulting from direct experience can occur on a vicarious basis by observing other people's behavior and its consequences for them (Bandura, 1969). The abbreviation of the acquisition process through observational learning is, of course, vital for both development and survival. Modeling reduces the burden of time-consuming performance of inappropriate responses. Since errors can produce costly, if not fatal, consequences, the prospects of survival would be slim indeed if people had to rely solely on the effects of their actions to inform them about what to do.

In many instances the behavior being modeled must be learned in essentially the same form. Driving automobiles, skiing, and performing surgery, for example, permit little, if any, departure from essential practices. In addition to transmitting particular response patterns, however, modeling influences can create generative and innovative behavior. In the latter process, observers abstract common features from seemingly diverse responses and formulate generative rules of behavior that enable them to go beyond what they have seen or heard. By synthesizing features of different models into new amalgams, observers can achieve through modeling novel styles of thought and conduct. Once initiated, experiences with the new forms create further evolutionary changes. A partial departure from tradition eventually becomes a new direction.

Some of the limitations commonly ascribed to behavior theory are based on the mistaken belief that modeling can produce at best mimicry of specific acts. This view is disputed by growing evidence that abstract modeling is a highly effective means of inducing rule-governed cognitive behavior (Bandura, 1971a; Zimmerman & Rosenthal, 1974). On the basis of observationally derived rules, people alter their judgmental orientations, conceptual schemes, linguistic styles, information-processing strategies, as well as other forms of cognitive functioning. Nevertheless, faulty evaluations continue to be mistaken for weaknesses inherent in theory.

Observational learning has recently come to be accepted more widely, but some theorists are willing to grant it full scientific respectability only if it is reduced to performance terms. As a result, enactment paradigms are used which are rooted in the traditional assumption that responses must be performed before they can be learned. Instant reproduction of modeled responses is favored, thereby minimizing dependence upon cognitive functions which play an especially influential role when retention over time is required. The issue of whether reinforcement enhances modeling is pursued to the neglect of the more interesting question of whether one can keep people from learning what they have seen.

When learning is investigated through observational paradigms, a broader range of determinants and intervening mechanisms gains prominence. Learning by observation is governed by four component processes: *(a)* attentional functions regulate sensory input and perception of modeled actions; *(b)* through coding and symbolic rehearsal, transitory experiences are transformed for memory representation into enduring performance guides; *(c)* motor reproduction processes govern the integration of constituent acts into new response patterns; and *(d)* incentive or motivational processes determine whether observationally acquired responses will be performed. Studied from this perspective, observational learning emerges as an actively judgmental and constructive rather than a mechanical copying process.

Because observational learning entails several subfunctions that evolve with maturation and experience, it obviously depends upon prior development. Differences in theoretical perspectives prescribe different methodologies for studying how the capacity for observational learning itself is acquired. When modeling is conceptualized in terms of formation of stimulus-response linkages, efforts are aimed at increasing the probability of imitative responses through reinforcement. Modeling can be increased by rewarding matching behavior, but such demonstrations are not of much help in identifying what exactly is being acquired during the process or in explaining imitation failures under favorable conditions of reinforcement. From a social learning view, the capability for observational learning is developed by acquiring skill in discriminative observation, in memory encoding, in coordinating ideomotor and sensorimotor systems, and in judging probable consequences for matching behavior. Understanding how people learn to imitate becomes a matter of understanding how the requisite subfunctions develop and operate. Capacity for observational learning is restricted by deficits and expanded by improvements in its component functions.

Over the years, proponents of the more radical forms of behaviorism not only disclaimed interest in mentation but also marshaled numerous reasons why cognitive events are inadmissible in causal analyses. It was and still is argued that cognitions are inaccessible except through untrustworthy self-reports; they are inferences from effects; they are epiphenomenal; or they are simply fictional. Advances in experimental analysis of behavior, it was claimed, would eventually show them to be unnecessary. Empirical evidence, however, has shown the opposite to be true. A large body of research now exists in which cognition is activated instructionally with impressive results. People learn and retain much better by using cognitive aids that they generate than by repetitive reinforced performance (Anderson & Bower, 1973; Bandura, 1971a).

With growing evidence that cognition has causal influence in behavior, the arguments against cognitive determinants are losing their force.

These recent developments have shifted emphasis from the study of response learning to analyses of memory and cognition. From this effort we have gained a better understanding of the mechanisms whereby information is acquired, stored, and retrieved. There is more to learning, however, than the acquisition and retention of information. Behavioristic theories addressed themselves to performance but deemphasized internal determinants, whereas the cognitive approaches remain immersed in thought but divorced from conduct. In a complete account of human behavior, internal processes must eventually be tied to action. Hence, explanations of how information eventuates in skilled performance must additionally be concerned with the organization and regulation of behavior. Social learning includes within its framework both the processes internal to the organism as well as performance-related determinants.

Speculations about man's nature inevitably raise the fundamental issues of determinism and human freedom. In examining these questions it is essential to distinguish between the metaphysical and the social aspects of freedom. Many of the heated disputes on this topic arise as much, if not more, from confusion over the dimensions of freedom being discussed as from disagreements over the doctrine of determinism.

Let us first consider freedom in the social sense. Whether freedom is an illusion, as some writers maintain, or a social reality of considerable importance depends upon the meaning given to it. Within the social learning framework, freedom is defined in terms of the number of options available to people and the right to exercise them. The more behavioral alternatives and social prerogatives people have, the greater is their freedom of action.

Personal freedom can be limited in many different ways. Behavioral deficits restrict possible choices and otherwise curtail opportunities to realize one's preferences. Freedom can therefore be expanded by cultivating competencies. Self-restraints arising from unwarranted fears and stringent self-censure restrict the effective range of activities that individuals can engage in or even contemplate. Here freedom is restored by eliminating dysfunctional self-restraints.

In maximizing freedom a society must place some limits on conduct because complete license for any individual is likely to encroach on the freedom of others. Societal prohibitions against behavior that is socially injurious create additional curbs on conduct. Conflicts often arise over behavioral restrictions when many members of society question conventional customs and when legal sanctions are used more to enforce a particular brand of morality than to prohibit socially detrimental conduct.

The issue of whether individuals should be allowed to engage in activities that are self-injurious but not detrimental to society has been debated vigorously over the years. Prohibitionists argue that it is difficult for a person, other than a recluse, to impair himself without inflicting secondary harm on others. Should self-injury produce incapacities, society usually ends up bearing the treatment and subsistence costs. Libertarians do not find such arguments sufficiently convincing to justify a specific prohibition because some of the self-injurious activities that society approves may be as bad or worse than those it outlaws. Normative changes over time regarding private conduct tend to favor an individualistic ethic. Consequently, many activities that were formerly prohibited by law have been exempted from legal sanctions.

Some groups have their freedom curtailed by socially condoned discrimination. Here, the alternatives available to a person are limited by skin color, sex, religion, ethnic background, or social class, regardless of capabilities. When self-determination is prejudicially restricted, those who are subordinated remove inequities by altering practices that compromise or temporize the professed values of society.

Freedom deals with rights as well as options and behavioral restraints. Man's struggle for freedom is principally aimed at structuring societal contingencies so that certain forms of behavior are exempted from aversive control. After protective laws are built into the system, there are certain things that a society may not do to an individual, however much it might like to. Legal prohibitions on societal control create freedoms that are realities, not simply feelings or states of mind. Societies differ in their institutions of freedom and in the number and types of behaviors that are officially exempted from punitive control. Social systems that protect journalists from punitive control, for example, are freer than those that allow authoritative power to be used to silence critics or their vehicles of expression. Societies that possess an independent judiciary ensure greater social freedom than those that do not.

In philosophical discourses, freedom is often considered antithetical to determinism. When defined in terms of options and rights, there is no incompatibility of freedom annd determinism. From this perspective, freedom is not conceived negatively as the absence of influences or simply the lack of external constraints. Rather, it is defined positively in terms of the skills at one's command and the exercise of self-influence upon which choice of action depends.

Psychological analyses of freedom eventually lead to discourses on the metaphysics of determinism. Are people partial determiners of their own behavior, or are they ruled exclusively by forces beyond their control? The long-standing debate over this issue has been enlivened by Skinner's (1971) contention that, apart from genetic contributions, human behavior is controlled solely by environmental contingencies; for example, "A person does not act upon the world, the world acts upon him" [p. 211]. A major problem with this type of analysis is that it depicts the environment as an autonomous force that automatically shapes and controls behavior. Environments have causes as do behaviors. For the most part the environment is only a potentiality until actualized and fashioned by appropriate actions. Books do not influence people unless someone writes them and others select and read them. Rewards and punishments remain in abeyance until prompted by appropriate performances.

It is true that behavior is regulated by its contingencies, but the contingencies are partly of a person's own making. By their actions, people play an active role in producing the reinforcing contingencies that impinge upon them. Thus behavior partly creates the environment, and the environment influences the behavior in a reciprocal fashion. To the oft-repeated dictum, change contingencies and you change behavior, should be added the reciprocal side, change behavior and you change the contingencies.

The image of man's efficacy that emerges from psychological research depends upon which aspect of the reciprocal control system one selects for analysis. In the paradigm favoring environmental control, investigators analyze how environmental contingencies change behavior [$B = f(E)$]. The personal control paradigm, on the other hand, examines how behavior determines the environment [$E = f(B)$]. Behavior is the effect in the former case, and the cause in the latter. Although the reciprocal sources of influence are separable for experimental purposes, in everyday life two-way control operates concurrently. In ongoing interchanges, one and the same event can thus be a stimulus, a response, or an environmental reinforcer depending upon the place in the sequence at which the analysis arbitrarily begins.

A survey of the literature on reinforcement confirms the extent to which we have become captives of a one-sided paradigm to map a bidirectional process. Environmental control is overstudied, whereas personal control has been relatively neglected. To cite but one example, there exist countless demonstrations of how behavior varies under different schedules of reinforcement, but one looks in vain for studies of how people, either individually or by collective action, succeed in fashioning reinforcement schedules to their own liking. The dearth of research on personal control is not because people exert no influence on their environment or because such efforts are without effect. Quite the contrary. Behavior is one of the more influential determinants of future contingencies. As analyses of sequential interchanges reveal, aggressive individuals actualize through their conduct a hostile environment, whereas those who display friendly responsiveness produce an amicable social milieu within the same setting (Rausch, 1965). We are all acquainted with problem-prone individuals who, through their aversive conduct, predictably breed negative social climates wherever they go.

It should be noted that some of the doctrines ascribing preeminent control to the environment are ultimately qualified by acknowledgment that man can exercise some measure of countercontrol (Skinner, 1971). The notion of reciprocal interaction, however, goes considerably beyond the concept of countercontrol. Countercontrol portrays the environment as an instigating force to which individuals react. As we have already seen, people activate and create environments as well as rebut them.

People may be considered partially free insofar as they can influence future conditions by managing their own behavior. Granted that selection of particular courses of action from available alternatives is itself determined, individuals can nevertheless exert some control over the factors that govern their choices. In philosophical analyses all events can be submitted to an infinite regression of causes. Such discussions usually emphasize how man's actions are determined by prior conditions but neglect the reciprocal part of the process showing that the conditions themselves are partly determined by man's prior actions. Applications of self-control practices demonstrate that people are able to regulate their own behavior in preferred directions by arranging environmental conditions most likely to elicit it and administering self-reinforcing consequences to sustain it. They may be told how to do it and initially be given some external support for their efforts, but self-produced influences contribute significantly to future goal attainment.

To contend, as environmental determinists often do, that people are controlled by external forces and then to advocate that they redesign their society by applying behavioral technology undermines the basic premise of the argument. If humans were in fact incapable of influencing their own actions, they could describe and predict environmental events but hardly exercise any intentional control over them. When it comes to advocacy of social change, however, thoroughgoing environmental determinists become ardent exponents of man's power to transform environments in pursuit of a better life.

In backward causal analyses, conditions are usually portrayed as ruling man, whereas forward deterministic analyses of goal setting and attainment reveal how people can shape conditions for their purposes. Some are better at it than others. The greater their foresight, proficiency, and self-influence, all of which are acquirable skills, the greater the progress toward their goals. Because of the capacity for reciprocal influence, people are at least partial architects of their own destinies. It is not determinism that is in dispute, but whether it is treated as a one-way or a two-way control process. Considering the interdependence of behavior and environmental conditions, determinism does not imply the fatalistic view that man is but a pawn of external influences.

Psychological perspectives on determinism, like other aspects of theorizing, influence the nature and scope of social practice. Environmental determinists are apt to use their methods primarily in the service of institutionally prescribed patterns of behavior. Personal determinists are more inclined to cultivate self-directing potentialities in man. The latter behavioral approach and humanism have much in common. Behavioral theorists, however, recognize that "self-actualization" is by no means confined to human virtues. People have numerous potentialities that can be actualized for good or ill. Over the years, man has suffered considerably at the hands of self-actualized tyrants. A self-centered ethic of self-realization must therefore be tempered by concern for the social consequences of one's conduct. Behaviorists generally emphasize environmental sources of control, whereas humanists tend to restrict their interest to personal control. Social learning encompasses both aspects of the bidirectional influence process.

When the environment is regarded as an autonomous rather than as an influenceable determinant of behavior, valuation of dignifying human qualities and accomplishments is diminished. If inventiveness emanates from external circumstances, it is environments that should be credited for people's achievements and chastised for their failings or inhumanities. Contrary to the unilateral view, human accomplishments result from reciprocal interaction of external circumstances with a host of personal determinants including endowed potentialities, acquired competencies, reflective thought, and a high level of self-initiative.

Musical composers, for example, help to shape tastes by their creative efforts, and the public in turn supports their performances until advocates of new styles generate new public preferences. Each succeeding form of artistry results from a similar two-way influence process for which neither artisans nor circumstances deserve sole credit.

Superior accomplishments, whatever the field, require considerable self-disciplined application. After individuals adopt evaluative standards, they expend large amounts of time, on their own, improving their performances to the point of self-satisfaction. At this level of functioning, persistence in an endeavor is extensively under self-reinforcement control. Skills are perfected as much, or more, to please oneself as to please the public.

Without self-generated influences, most innovative efforts would be difficult to sustain. This is because the unconventional is initially resisted and gradually accepted only as it proves functionally valuable or wins prestigious advocates. As a result, the early efforts of innovators bring rebuffs rather than rewards or recognition. In the history of creative endeavors, it is not uncommon for artists or composers to be scorned when they depart markedly from convention. Some gain recognition later in their careers. Others are sufficiently convinced of the worth of their work that they labor indefatigably even though their productions are negatively received during their lifetimes. Ideological and, to a lesser extent, technological advances follow similar courses. Most innovative endeavors receive occasional social support in early phases, but environmental conditions alone are not especially conducive to unconventional developments.

The operation of reciprocal influence also has bearing on the public concern that advances in psychological knowledge will produce an increase in human manipulation and control. A common response to such apprehensions is that all behavior is inevitably controlled. Social influence, therefore, is not a question of imposing controls where none existed before. This type of argument is valid in the sense that every act has a cause. But it is not the principle of causality that worries people. At the societal level their misgivings center on the distribution of controlling power, the means and purposes for which it is used, and the availability of mechanisms for exercising reciprocal control over institutional practices. At the individual level, they are uneasy about the implications of psychotechnology in programming human relations.

Possible remedies for exploitative use of psychological techniques are usually discussed in terms of individual safeguards. Increased knowledge about modes of influence is prescribed as the best defense against manipulation. When people are informed about how behavior can be controlled, they tend to resist evident attempts at influence, thus making manipulation more difficult. Awareness alone, however, is a weak countervalence.

Exploitation was successfully thwarted long before there existed a discipline of psychology to formulate principles and practices of behavior change. The most reliable source of opposition to manipulative control resides in the reciprocal consequences of human interactions. People resist being taken advantage of and will continue to do so in the future because compliant behavior produces unfavorable consequences for them. Sophisticated efforts at influence in no way reduce the aversiveness of yielding that is personally disadvantageous. Because of reciprocal consequences, no one is able to manipulate others at will, and everyone experiences some feeling of powerlessness in getting what they want. This is true at all levels of functioning, individual and collective. Parents cannot get their children to follow all their wishes, while children feel constrained by their parents from doing what they desire. At universities, the administrators, faculty, students, and alumni all feel that the other constituencies are unduly influential in promoting their self-interests but that one's own group is granted insufficient power to alter the institutional practices. In the political arena, Congress feels that the executive branch possesses excessive power, and conversely the executive branch feels thwarted in implementing its policies by congressional counteraction.

If protection against exploitation relied solely upon individual safeguards, people would be continually subjected to coercive pressures. Accordingly, they create institutional sanctions which set limits on the control of human behavior. The integrity of individuals is largely secured by societal safeguards that place constraints on improper means and foster reciprocity through balancing of interests.

Because individuals are conversant with psychological techniques does not grant them license to impose them on others. Industrialists, for example, know full well that productivity is higher when payment is made for amount of work completed rather than for length of time at work. Nevertheless, they cannot use the reinforcement system most advantageous to them. When industrialists commanded exclusive power, they paid workers at a piece-rate basis and hired and fired them at will. Reductions in power disparity between employers and employees resulted in a gradual weakening of performance requirements. As labor gained economic coercive strength through collective action, it was able to negotiate guaranteed wages on a daily, weekly, monthly, and eventually on an annual basis. At periodic intervals new contractual contingencies are adopted that are mutually acceptable. In the course of time, as better means of joint action are developed, other constituents will use their influence to modify arrangements that benefit certain segments of labor and industry but adversely affect the quality of life for other sectors of society.

As the previous example illustrates, improved knowledge of how to influence behavior does not necessarily raise the level of social control. If anything, the recent years have witnessed a diffusion of power, creating increased opportunities for reciprocal influence. This has enabled people to challenge social inequities, to effect changes in institutional practices, to counteract infringements on their rights, and to extend grievance procedures and due process of law to activities in social contexts that hitherto operated under unilateral control. The fact that more people wield power does not in and of itself ensure a humane society. In the final analysis, the important consideration is the purposes that power serves, however it might be distributed. Nor does knowledgeability about means of influence necessarily produce mechanical responsiveness in personal relations. Whatever their orientations, people model, expound, and reinforce what they value. Behavior arising out of purpose and commitment is no less genuine than improvised action.

The cliché of *1984* and its more recent kin diverts public attention from regulative influences that pose continual threats to human welfare. Most societies have instituted reciprocal systems that are protected by legal and social codes to prevent imperious control of human behavior. Although abuses of institutional power arise from time to time, it is not totalitarian rule that constitutes the impending peril. The hazards lie more in the intentional pursuit of personal gain, whether material or otherwise, than in control by coercion. Detrimental social practices arise and resist change, even within an open society, when many people benefit from them. To take a prevalent example, inequitable treatment of disadvantaged groups for private gain enjoys public support without requiring despotic rule.

Man, of course, has more to contend with than inhumanities toward one another. When the aversive consequences of otherwise rewarding life-styles are delayed and imperceptibly cumulative, people become willful agents of their own self-destruction. Thus if enough people benefit from activities that progressively degrade their environment, then barring contravening influences, they will eventually destroy their environment. Although individuals contribute differentially to the problem, the harmful consequences are borne by all. With growing populations and spread of lavish life-styles taxing finite resources, people will have to learn to cope with new realities of human existence.

Psychology cannot tell people how they ought to live their lives. It can, however, provide them with the means for effecting personal and social change. And it can aid them in making value choices by assessing the consequences of alternative life-styles and institutional arrangements. As a science concerned about the social consequences of its applications, psychology must also fulfill a broader obligation to society by bringing influence to bear on public policies to ensure that its findings are used in the service of human betterment.

REFERENCES

Anderson, J. R., & Bower, G. H. *Human associative memory.* New York: Wiley, 1973.

Bandura, A. *Principles of behavior modification.* New York: Holt, Rinehart & Winston, 1969.

———. *Social learning theory.* New York: General Learning Press, 1971b.

———. Vicarious and self-reinforcement processes. In R. Glaser (Ed.), *The nature of reinforcement.* New York: Academic Press, 1971c.

———. *Aggression: A social learning analysis.* Englewood Cliffs, N.J.: Prentice-Hall, 1973.

Bandura, A. (Ed.). *Psychological modeling: Conflicting theories.* Chicago: Aldine-Atherton, 1971a.

Dawson, M. E., & Furedy, J. J. The role of relational awareness in human autonomic discrimination classical conditioning. Unpublished manuscript. Univ. of Toronto, 1974.

Dulany, D. E. Awareness, rules, and propositional control: A confrontation with S-R behavior theory. In T. R. Dixon & D. L. Horton (Eds.), *Verbal behavior and general behavior theory.* Englewood Cliffs, N.J.: Prentice-Hall, 1968.

Goldfried, M. R., & Merbaum, M. (Eds.), *Behavior change through self-control.* New York: Holt, Rinehart & Winston, 1973.

Grings, W. W. The role of consciousness and cognition in autonomic behavior change. In F. J. McGuigan & R. Schoonover (Eds.), *The psychophysiology of thinking.* New York: Academic Press, 1973.

Kaufman, A., Baron, A., & Kopp, R. E. Some effects of instructions on human operant behavior. *Psychonomic Monograph Supplements,* 1966, *1,* 243–250.

Mahoney, M. J., & Thoresen, C. E. *Self-control: Power to the person.* Monterey, Calif.: Brooks/Cole, 1974.

Mischel, W. Processes in delay of gratification. In L. Berkowitz (Ed.), *Advances in experimental social psychology* (Vol. 7). New York: Academic Press, 1974.

Rausch, H. L. Interaction sequences. *Journal of Personality and Social Psychology,* 1965, *2,* 487–499.

Skinner, B. F. *Beyond freedom and dignity.* New York: Knopf, 1971.

Thoresen, C. E., & Mahoney, M. J. *Behavioral self-control.* New York: Holt, Rinehart & Winston, 1973.

Zimmerman, B. J., & Rosenthal, T. L. Observational learning of rule-governed behavior by children. *Psychological Bulletin,* 1974, *81,* 29–42.

5. VIOLENCE ON TELEVISION:

How Harmful?

It is one thing to suspect that violence on television produces more aggressive or violent behavior in people who view it, but it is quite another thing to prove it. The following article and letters indicate that even among professional psychologists there is no final consensus on the proper experimental procedures for testing this important hypothesis. Without question, the United States has a more violent society than we can tolerate. But in order to try to reduce the level of violence, it would be extremely helpful to understand its causes. On one hand, we were a violent society without television, and television violence certainly reflects what people want to see (as the television producers like to tell us). On the other hand, since so many people watch television so much, television programming has an almost unlimited potential to shape attitudes and behavior.

There is a vast literature on this subject, and the following articles can serve only as an introduction to some of the research and theory in this area. The particular value of the research of Leonard Eron, L. Rowell Huesmann, Monroe Lefkowitz, and Leopold Walder lies in the fact that they had, at the time of publication, more than 10 years' worth of data on a large number of subjects through the subjects' adolescence. These data describe both the subjects' aggressive behavior and their television viewing habits. One of Eron et al.'s main findings was that there is a significant relationship between boys' preference for violent television programs in the third grade and their level of aggressiveness (as rated by their peers) 10 years later. Interestingly, no correlations were found between viewing violence on television and aggressive behavior in females.

The weakness of any correlational study, of course, is that there are usually several alternative explanations for a significant correlation.

The present research is a good example of this. What are the alternative hypotheses discussed by Eron et al.? Do their arguments on these alternatives seem convincing to you? Why, or why not? In particular, consider the alternative hypothesis d in Figure 2—that aggression in the third grade (whatever its causes) contributes both to a preference for viewing violence on television and to later aggression. As you will see, the complete understanding of much of this sort of research depends on a clear understanding of correlation coefficients.

One interesting feature of scientific literature is that it allows for public disagreement, or rebuttals concerning a previously published article. Many letters of rebuttal were submitted after publication of the Eron et al. report, and some of them are reprinted here to give you the flavor of the push-and-tug nature of scientific discourse. The letters by Gilbert Becker, Robert Kaplan, Dennis Howitt, and Herbert Kay make different points regarding the original study, and in the Huesmann et al. letter the original authors defend their original conclusions. As you read these letters, try to jot down the major arguments. Who do you think made the best points? On the basis of the following article and letters, what is your conclusion about the issue? Is more research needed, or just a better understanding of the existing data? How might one design an even better study for discovering the relationship between the viewing of violence on television and aggressive behavior?

DOES TELEVISION VIOLENCE CAUSE AGGRESSION?

Leonard D. Eron, University of Illinois, Chicago Circle

Monroe M. Lefkowitz, New York State Department of Mental Hygiene, Albany

L. Rowell Huesmann, Yale University

Leopold O. Walder, Organization for Research in the Behavioral Sciences, Greenbelt, Maryland

With the increasing prominence of violence in our society, social scientists have been turning their attention to the antecedents of aggressive behavior in children and adults. Television programming with its heavy emphasis on interpersonal violence and acquisitive lawlessness has been assigned a role both in inciting aggression and teaching viewers specific techniques of aggressive behavior. The relation between overt aggression and television habits has been demonstrated in a few survey studies which, however, because of the nature of surveys have not been able to discriminate cause and effect (Bailyn, 1959; Eron, 1963; Schramm, Lyle, & Parker, 1961).

On the other hand, manipulative laboratory experiments have demonstrated an immediate effect on the extent of aggressive behavior of subjects who have witnessed aggressive displays on film (Bandura, Ross, & Ross, 1963a; Berkowitz, Corwin, & Heironimus, 1963). The latter studies, however, can be criticized for not duplicating real-life television viewing situations and possibly not accounting for anything more than a transient effect on the viewer. Hartup and Yonas (1971) stated in their review of developmental psychology in the latest *Annual Review of Psychology*,

> Current studies of the childhood determinants of aggression are not extensive. The report of a presidential commission, *Violence and the Media* (Baker & Ball, 1969), indicates that child psychologists possess much information concerning the determinants of aggression but very little stemming directly from naturalistic sources [p. 375].

This research was supported by Grant M1726 from the National Institute of Mental Health and Contract No. HSM 42-70-60 from the Surgeon General's Scientific Advisory Committee on Television and Social Behavior. Thanks are also due to the New York State Department of Mental Hygiene for their support and to Anne Karabin, Marjorie Kline, Ann McAleer, Victor Pompa, and Ann Yeager who served as research assistants. Requests for reprints should be sent to Leonard D. Eron, Department of Psychology, University of Illinois, Box 4348, Chicago, Illinois 60680.

Eron, Leonard D., Huesmann, L. Rowell, Lefkowitz, Monroe M., and Walder, Leopold O. Does television violence cause aggression? *American Psychologist*, 1972, *27*, 253–263.

One possible way of utilizing survey procedures to demonstrate cause and effect is to use a longitudinal context. By contrasting the magnitude of contemporaneous and longitudinal correlations between two sets of variables, it is possible to account more clearly for which of the variables is antecedent and which consequent. The authors have now accumulated data on both aggressive behavior and television viewing habits over a 10-year period in a large group of subjects first seen when they were 8–9 years of age. Thus we can implement such an analysis.

The hypotheses of this research are that a young adult's aggressiveness is positively related to his preference for violent television when he was 8–9 years old and, furthermore, that his preference for violent television during this critical period is one cause of his aggressiveness.

METHOD

Longitudinal data were collected on 427 teenagers of an original group of 875 children who had participated in a study of third-grade children in 1960 (Eron, 1963; Eron, Walder, & Lefkowitz, 1971). The original 875 constituted the entire third-grade population of a semirural county in New York's Hudson River Valley, while the 427 subjects were those who could be located and interviewed 10 years later.

The information collected about these subjects in both time periods falls into two classes: *(a)* measures of aggression and *(b)* potential predictors of aggression. During the third-grade interviews, four different data sources had been used: the subject, his peers, his mother, and his father. Ten years later, the data sources were the subject and his peers. For convenience, this later time period will be designated as the thirteenth grade.

The variables used in the study are listed in Table 1. Two variables are of particular importance: peer-rated aggression and preference for violent television programs. In the third grade, peer-rated aggression scores were obtained by asking each child to nominate any of his classmates as 10 "guess who" items describing aggressive behavior; for example, "Who pushes and shoves other children?" "Who takes other children's things without asking?" "Who starts a fight over nothing?" "Who says mean things?" These aggression items were interspersed among a series of other peer nomination questions. The validity and reliability of the aggression measure have been discussed elsewhere (Eron et al., 1971; Walder, Abelson, Eron, Banta, & Laulicht, 1961).

The peer rating instrument was revised slightly for the thirteenth-grade study. One item which was deemed inappropriate for 19-year-old subjects was dropped. Furthermore, since the subjects were no longer in school, the procedure was administered individually in a face-to-face interview. The number of possible peers any subject could nominate was widened beyond his own third-grade classroom to include his classmates through high school. Thus each subject was rated by a larger set

Table 1
Measures of Aggression and Potentially Related Variables Studied at Two Different Times

VARIABLE	SOURCE
Third grade	
Measure of aggression	
Child's aggression (AGG3)	Peer ratings
Variables potentially related to aggression	
Father's occupational status	Father's report
Parents' aspirations for child	Parents' report
Parents' mobility orientation	Parents' report
Ethnicity of family	Parents' report
Mother's religiosity (frequency of church attendance)	Mother's report
Parental nurturance of child	Mother's report
Parental rejection of child	Mother's report
Parental punishment of child	Mother's report
Child's identification with father	Father's and child's report
Child's identification with mother	Mother's and child's report
Child's confessing to parents	Parents' report
Father's aggressiveness	Walters-Zak test
Mother's aggressiveness	Walters-Zak test
Parental disharmony	Parents' report
Child's IQ	Test
Child's hours of watching television	Mother's report
Child's preference for watching violent television (TVVL3)	Mother's report on favorite programs and violence scores by independent raters

Table 1 (Continued)

VARIABLE	SOURCE
Thirteenth grade	
Measures of aggression	
Subject's aggression (AGG13)	Peer rating
Subject's antisocial behavior (ASB13)	Subject's report
Subject's psychological predisposition to delinquency (MMPI-49S)	Sum of Scales 4 + 9 on MMPI
Variables potentially related to aggression	
Father's occupational status	Subject's report
Subject's occupational aspirations	Subject's report
Subject's hours of watching television	Subject's report
Subject's preference for watching violent television (TVVL13)	Subject's report of favorite programs and violence scores by independent raters

of raters in the thirteenth grade which included many of the raters from the third grade.

In the third grade the children's preferences for violent television were obtained by asking each mother for her child's three favorite television programs. All programs mentioned were then categorized as violent or nonviolent by two independent raters with 94% agreement in their ratings. Differences in the remaining 6% of the programs were resolved by mutual discussion between the raters. Each subject received a score according to the number of violent television programs he was reported by his mother as favoring. Scores ranged from 1 (for no violent programs) to 4 (for three violent programs).

In the 10-year follow-up study, each subject *himself* was asked for his four current favorite television programs. All programs were then categorized for presence or absence of violence by two independent raters who were only a few years older than the subjects themselves. Scores were assigned to each program on the basis of agreement between the raters. If they both agreed a program was nonviolent, the program received a score of 0; if they both agreed it was violent, the score was 2; if they disagreed in categorization, the program was assigned a score of 1. Here again there was good agreement between the two raters. They agreed on 81% of 125 programs mentioned by the subjects. The score for each subject was the sum of the violence ratings of the four programs mentioned.

The designation by these raters of violent and nonviolent programs agreed very well with the assignment of programs by Feshbach and Singer (1971) to aggressive and nonaggressive diets in their field experiment (see below). Furthermore, the judgments of our raters were in close agreement with the results obtained by Greenberg and Gordon (1970), who did an extensive rating study in which they used as raters both established television critics (approximately 45) and 300 subjects randomly selected from the Detroit, Michigan, telephone book. Of the 20 programs which Greenberg and Gordon indicated had the highest violence ratings, 19 were selected as violent by our raters. For the 427 cases in the 10-year follow-up study, there was a correlation of .94 between the Greenberg-Gordon average ratings and our ratings.

RESULTS

The 427 subjects studied in both the third and thirteenth grades consisted of 211 males and 216 females whose modal age at the time of the thirteenth-grade interview was 19. The sample was at the higher end of the average range in intelligence with a mean IQ of 109 and was somewhat middle class in social status. (The dropout rate from participation in the study between the third and thirteenth grade was considerably higher for subjects who displayed high aggression in the third grade than for those who displayed low aggression. For example, 57% of the low quartile in aggression were retained in the follow-up sample, while only

27% of the high quartile were retained. This can be explained by a number of factors, including the finding that residential mobility was correlated significantly with aggression in the sample.

Preliminary analysis indicated that the measures of aggression distinguished the males from the females. There were statistically significant differences between males' and females' mean scores on every measure of aggression in both grades. The differences were more pronounced in the thirteenth grade. In addition, a principal component factor analysis of subjects' sex and the variables that were used in the study yielded a first principal factor whose largest loading was for the subjects' sex and whose next largest loadings were for the measures of aggression. Finally, a comparison of girls in the highest quartile revealed a difference in MMPI profiles; the high-aggressive girls were significantly more masculine in their interests and attitudes. Because of these findings, the data for males and females were analyzed separately.

Correlations between Preference for Television, Violence and Aggression

The correlations between preference for television violence and aggression at both grade levels are presented separately for boys and girls in Table 2.

Table 2
Correlations among Violence Ratings of Preferred Television Programs and Measures of Aggression at Two Different Periods

	TVVL3	AGG3	TVVL13	AGG13	ASB13	MMPI–49S13
			Boys			
TVVL3	1	.21*	.05	.31*	.10	.12
AGG3		1	.01	.38*	.14	.21
TVVL13			1	−.05	.01	.06
AGG13				1	.49*	.39*
ASB13					1	.46*
MMPI–49S13						1
			Girls			
TVVL3	1	.02	.08	−.13	−.02	−.05
AGG3		1	−.08	.47*	.01	.13
TVVL13			1	−.05	−.10	.11
AGG13				1	.23*	.28*
ASB13					1	.45*
MMPI–49S13						1

Note.—The number 3 or 13 following a variable indicates the period, third grade or thirteenth grade, when the data were obtained. TVVL is a measure of preference for television violence. AGG = peer-rated aggression; ASB = self-rating of frequency of antisocial behavior; MMPI–49S = sum of *T* scores on Scales 4 and 9 of MMPI.

* Indicates correlation is significantly different from zero beyond .01 level of confidence.

These correlations must be interpreted in light of the total number of correlations being computed for the sample of 427 subjects and the distribution of the variables. Because of the large number of potential correlations, only those with a probability less than .01 on a two-tailed test were considered significant and only those with a probability less than .001 on a two-tailed test were called highly significant. On the other hand, it should be pointed out that the unusual skewness and kurtosis of many of the variables may impose a limit on the size of their intercorrelations.

From Table 2, one can see that there is a highly significant relation between boys' preferences for violent television programs in the third grade (TVVL3) and their peer-rated aggression in the thirteenth grade (AGG13). Similarly, there is a significant contemporaneous relation between the boys' television preferences in the third grade and peer-rated aggression in the third grade (AGG3). Neither of these effects was apparent for females. While the correlation between third-grade preferences and thirteenth-grade peer-rated aggression explains only 10% of the variance in aggression, 10% is impressive when one considers the probable limitations on the size of the correlation imposed by the skewed distributions of the variable, the large number of variables affecting aggression, the comparatively small explanatory power of these other variables (see below), and the 10-year lag between measurement times. The extremely low likelihood of achieving such a correlation by chance is a good indicator of the strength of the relation between preference for violent television at age 8 years and peer-rated aggression at age 19.

As has been pointed out previously (Eron et al., 1971), when distributions are unusual, an analysis of variance may, more clearly than a product-moment correlation, reveal the relation between the two variables. Hence the male subjects were partitioned into low, medium, and high television violence groups, representing approximately the lowest 10%, the middle 80%, and the upper 10%, respectively. The results of one-way analyses of variance on this independent variable with aggression measures as the dependent variables are shown in Table 3. Now one can see that there is a highly significant relation between preference for violent television in the third grade and aggression in the thirteenth grade, whether the measure is one of peer-rated aggression or self-ratings of aggression (antisocial behavior and MMPI–49S).

Causal Analysis

Having established that there exists a highly significant relationship between a preference for violent television in the third grade and aggressive habits in the thirteenth grade, one can consider the alternative causal explanations for this phenomenon. Of course, we cannot demonstrate that a particular hypothesis is true. One can only reject untenable hypotheses and present evidence on the plausibility of the remaining hypotheses.

Table 3
Mean Aggression Scores as a Function of Television Violence Ratings of Programs Preferred by Boys in Third Grade

TVVL3	n	AGG3		AGG13		ASB		MMPI–49S	
		M	*SD*	*M*	*SD*	*M*	*SD*	*M*	*SD*
Low	31	9.06	9.91	5.14	5.05	25.58	12.12	121.97	20.50
Medium	139	11.19	11.54	8.14	9.88	22.06	12.69	122.50	19.33
High	14	21.00	13.79	16.46	13.01	30.86	14.23	135.86	18.14
Total	184	11.58	11.75	8.27	9.86	23.33	12.90	123.42	19.67
F[a]		5.43****		6.82*****	$t = 4.04$***	3.63**		3.11*	

Note.—Abbreviations: AGG = peer-rated aggression; ASB = self-rating of frequency of antisocial behavior; MMPI–49S = sum of T scores on Scales 4 and 9 of MMPI.

[a] Because of heterogeneity of variance, a t test between the two most discrepant means for AGG13 was performed. The t was conservatively evaluated by using degrees of freedom equal to the n for the smallest group, that is, 14.

*$p < .05$.

**$p < .03$.

***$p < .01$.

****$p < .005$.

*****$p < .001$.

Cross-lagged correlations. Consider the pattern of correlations diagramed in Figure 1; the correlations on the diagonals are called cross-lagged correlations. The cross-lagged correlation between a preference for violent television in the third grade and thirteenth-grade aggression was highly significant. When coupled with the lack of a relation between third-grade aggression and a preference for violent television in the thirteenth grade, this significant correlation supports the hypothesis that preferring to watch violent television is a cause of aggressive behavior. This causal hypothesis is diagramed in Figure 2a. The probability of a chance occurrence of the difference between the cross-lagged correlations is low (Fisher's $z = 3.07$, $p < .002$); however, a few rival hypotheses are seemingly consistent with the difference and deserve consideration.

One alternative hypothesis is that preference for violent television in the third grade stimulates concurrent aggression, and this aggression leads to thirteenth-grade aggression or at least is being remeasured in the thirteenth grade. The corresponding causal chain is diagramed in Figure 2b. This interpretation can be rejected because if it were true, the relation between the end points of the causal sequence would have been no stronger than the product of the relations between all adjacent intermediate points. But the correlation between the end points was .31, which was much higher than the product of the intermediate correlations.

For a similar reason, the causal chain diagramed in Figure 2c can be eliminated as an alternative hypothesis. If early aggression caused a preference for violent television which in turn contributed to later ag-

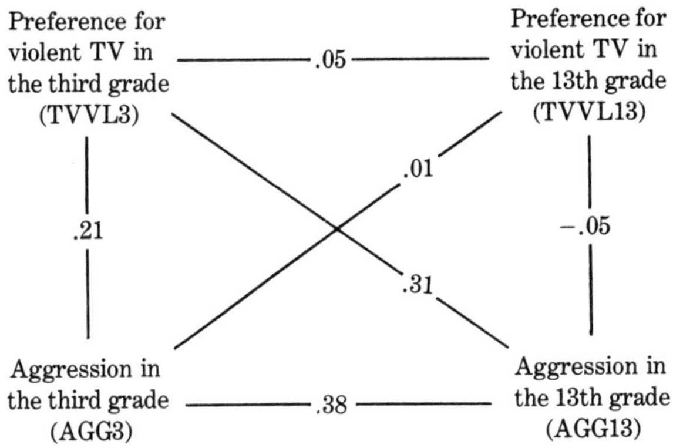

FIGURE 1. The correlations between a preference for violent television and peer-rated aggression for 211 boys over a 10-year lag.

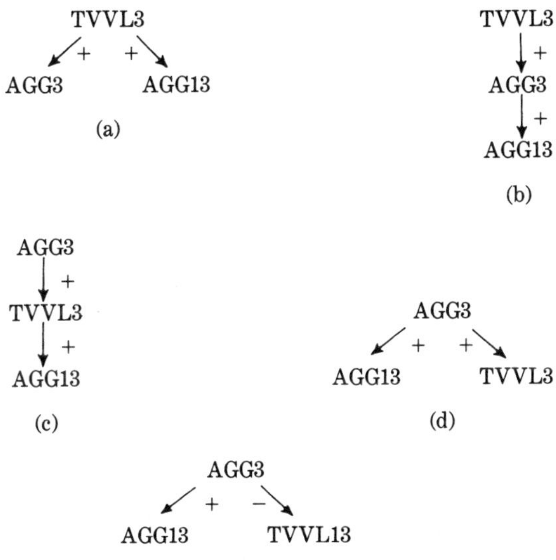

FIGURE 2. Five feasible causal hypotheses for the correlations presented in Figure 1.

gression, the correlation between early and later aggression would have been less than the product of the two intermediate correlations. It was not.

One cannot reject so easily the more realistic alternative hypothesis diagramed in Figure 2d. This causal hypothesis asserts that early aggression causes both contemporaneous preferences for violent television and later aggression. Part of this hypothesis, that early aggression contributes to later aggression, is quite probably true. What is of interest here, though, is whether or not the relation between early television preferences and later aggression can be explained as an artifact of early aggression. One can obtain evidence to refute this idea by computing the partial correlation between third-grade television violence (TVVL3) and thirteenth-grade aggression (AGG13) while controlling for third-grade aggression (AGG3). If the hypothesis diagramed in Figure 2d were the complete explanation of the correlation between early television preferences and later aggression, then the partial correlation would have been zero. But it was not. It was .25 or a distance of only .06 below the original correlation between a preference for television violence in the third grade and thirteenth-grade aggression. Hence, the hypothesis diagramed in Figure 2d is implausible as a complete causal explanation.

The final plausible alternative to be considered is that early aggression causes a diminished preference for violent television. This theory is diagramed in Figure 2e. If one views the cross-lagged correlations as deviations from the initial cross-correlation, then the zero correlation between early aggression and later television preferences might indicate that early aggression had reduced a preference for violent television. However, as Rozelle and Campbell (1969) have indicated, the most appropriate base line is not the early contemporaneous correlation but the average of the two contemporaneous correlations attenuated for the reliability of the variables. The higher the reliabilities, the less is the attenuation. With a conservative assumption of a very high temporal reliability of .70, the base line for Figure 1 would be $[(.21 + (-.05)) \times \sqrt{.70 \times .70}]/2 = .06$. With this correction, the hypothesis that aggression diminishes a preference for violent television becomes untenable, since the cross-lagged correlation from early aggression to later television preferences is very close to the base line.

As Rozelle and Campbell (1969), Kenny (in press), and others have pointed out, the validity of cross-lagged panel correlation inferences depends on the assumption that the underlying factor structure is stationary over time. If it is not, one must be very careful about the inferences drawn. The large difference between the third- and thirteenth-grade synchronous correlations is indicative of lack of stationarity and necessitates consideration of some artifactual effects.

One alternative is that the aggression measure increased in reliability between the third and thirteenth grades. Such an increase would have caused the measured correlation between third-grade television violence and thirteenth-grade aggression to increase even though the true correlation did not change. However, the reliability of the peer-rated aggression variable in the third grade was measured by a variety of methods and consistently found to be between .85 and .95 (Walder et al., 1961). Hence, an increase in reliability is not a plausible explanation of the pattern.

Similarly, a decrease in the reliability of the television violence ratings in the thirteenth grade could have caused the decrease in the correlation between third-grade aggression and thirteenth-grade television violence over the synchronous correlation. Low reliability for thirteenth-grade television violence is, in fact, plausible since thirteenth-grade television violence correlates poorly with most other variables. However, there is little evidence that third-grade television violence had much higher reliability. Furthermore, the reliability of thirteenth-grade television violence could not affect the cross-lagged correlation from television violence to aggression. Hence a decrease in the reliability of the television violence variable is not sufficient to explain the pattern of cross-lagged correlations.

Basing the causality argument on the finding that the cross-lagged correlation is greater than the initial synchronous correlation raises another question. Was the increase significant? It is not appropriate to compare the cross-lagged correlation directly with the third-grade synchronous correlation since that correlation should erode over time. Using Kenny's (in press) method for estimating erosion rates yields a rate of .605 for the correlation between television violence and aggression. Thus one should compare the cross-lagged correlation of .31 with .605 (.21) = .127. For $N = 184$, this comparison yields a Fisher's z of 2.33, which is significant at the .02 level.

On the basis of the cross-lagged correlations and the significant partial correlation between early preferences for violent television and later aggression with early aggression controlled, one concludes that the single most plausible causal hypothesis is that a preference for watching violent television in the third grade contributes to the development of aggressive habits. This does not mean that other variables are not of equal or greater importance in stimulating aggression, but only that a preference for television violence and the viewing behavior that the preference indicates probably are independent and important causes of aggressive habits.

Partial correlations. None of the data presented up to this point sheds evidence on the possibility that another variable such as IQ, social class, parental punishment, or parental aggression might have stimulated both the child's preference for violent television and his aggressiveness. However, one can test some of these hypotheses by computing the partial correlations between television violence and aggression with such variables controlled. Table 4 contains these partial correlations. Neither the child's aggression in the third grade, social class, mobility orientation of parent, IQ, parental punishment, parental aspirations for child, nor parental aggression accounts for the relationship. Nor can the relation be explained by the total number of hours of television watched by the subject in either the third or thirteenth grades.

Multiple regression. As Darlington (1968) pointed out, one can treat the standardized coefficients in a multiple regression equation as measures of the causal contributions of the predictor variables to the criterion variable. This approach assumes that all causal variables not in the regression equation are uncorrelated with those that are and that the criterion variable is not "causing" any predictor variable. While it is quite possible that these assumptions are violated, it is still worth while to examine the coefficients as approximate measures of causal contributions. Hence a multiple regression equation was computed by a stepwise method that entered the third-grade variables into the equation in order

Table 4
Partial Correlations between TVVL3 and AGG13 with Other Variables Controlled

CONTROLLED VARIABLE	n	PARTIAL CORRELATION BETWEEN TVVL3 AND AGG13
None	184	.31
Third-grade variables		
Peer-rated aggression	184	.25
Father's occupational status	140	.31
Child's IQ	179	.28
Father's aggressiveness	140	.30
Mother's aggressiveness	184	.31
Punishment administered	184	.31
Parents' aspirations for child	140	.30
Parents' mobility orientation	140	.31
Hours of television watched	184	.30
Thirteenth-grade variables		
Father's occupational status	182	.28
Subject's aspirations	149	.28
Subject's hours of television watching	183	.30

Note.—Abbreviations: TVVL3 = a measure of preference for television violence in the third grade; AGG13 = peer-rated aggression in the thirteenth grade.

of their utility in predicting the criterion variable, thirteenth-grade aggression. The regression equation shown in Table 5 predicts thirteenth-grade aggression solely from third-grade variables.

The order in which the variables were entered reveals that a preference for watching television violence was the most "useful" third-grade variable in the prediction. It explained more of the variance than any other predictor. More important, however, for a causal analysis are the standardized regression coefficients in the final regression equation. Such a coefficient can be interpreted as the contribution of the predictor variable to "causing" the criterion variable independent of the other predictor variables. The coefficients in Table 5 show that a preference for violent television in third grade is *the major contributor* to thirteenth-grade aggression among the third-grade variables. This finding supports the hypothesis that a preference for watching violent television in the third-grade time period is a cause of aggressive habits later in life independent of the other causal contributors studied.

Path analysis. A more specialized technique for using multiple regression coefficients to estimate causal effects is path analysis (Heise, 1970). The path coefficients for television and aggression are shown in Figure 3. These coefficients are standardized partial regression coefficients. In other words, the path coefficient from third-grade television violence to thirteenth-grade aggression is the coefficient of third-grade television violence in a regression equation predicting thirteenth-grade aggression

Table 5
Multiple Regression Prediction of Thirteenth-Grade Aggression (AGG13) from Third-Grade Predictors

STEP ENTERED	PREDICTOR	MULTIPLE CORRELATION	FINAL STANDARDIZED COEFFICIENTS FOR PREDICTORS
1	Television violence (TVVL3)	.31	.29
2	Parents' mobility orientation	.41	.28
3	Child's identification with mother	.44	−.03
4	Parental nurturance of child	.46	−.20
5	Parental disharmony	.47	.11
6	Parents' aspirations for child	.48	−.13
7	Child's IQ	.49	−.11
8	Mother's religiosity (frequency of church attendance)	.50	.09
9	Child's identification with father	.51	.12
10	Ethnicity of family	.51	−.09
11	Parental rejection of child	.52	.08
12	Parental punishment of child	.52	−.09
13	Child's confessing to parents	.52	−.07
14	Father's aggressiveness	.53	.06
15	Child's hours of watching television	.53	−.03
16	Mother's aggressiveness	.53	−.03
17	Father's occupational status	.53	.02

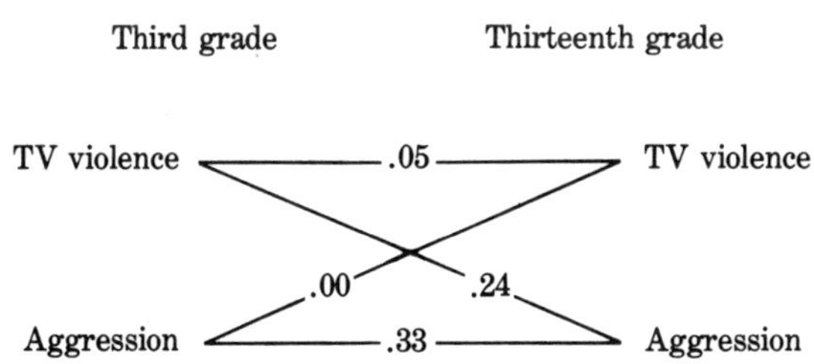

FIGURE 3: The path coefficients for a preference for watching violent television and peer-rated aggression.

with third-grade aggression controlled. The obtained pattern of path coefficients adds further credence to the argument that watching violent television contributes to the development of aggressive habits.[1]

DISCUSSION

The above results indicate that television habits established by age 8–9 years influence boys' aggressive behavior at that time and at least through late adolescence. The more violent are the programs preferred by boys in the third grade, the more aggressive is their behavior both at that time and 10 years later. This relation between early television habits and later aggression prevails both for peer-rated aggression and for self-ratings of aggression. Actually, these early television habits seem to be more influential than current viewing patterns since a preference for violent television in the thirteenth grade is not at all related to concurrent aggressive behavior, nor are early television habits related to later television habits.

It would be very difficult to explain these results as methodological artifacts. While the peer-rated aggression measure possesses demonstrated reliability (Walder et al., 1961), the thirteenth-grade scores represent more than the temporal reliability of the third-grade measure. Not only had 10 years of behavior intervened between the measurement periods, but the set of raters of each subject was substantially different as well. It is also unlikely that the findings were produced by a common method rather than content. Method refers to the form of the measuring device and the procedure for obtaining and calculating the score; content refers to what one intends to measure. Feshbach (1970), for example, warned that the

> predictive utility of sociometric, projective, and inventory measures is limited by the substantial method variance yielded by each procedure, and it is evident that the more dissimilar the test of aggression is to the aggression criterion, the weaker are the relationships obtained [p. 181].

The peer-rated aggression measure employed in this study should not be susceptible to such criticism as it has been extensively validated over a 10-year period, using a variety of techniques ranging from Campbell and Fiske's (1959) multitrait, multimethod technique to factor analysis. Peer-rated aggression scores agree closely with teacher ratings, clinical referrals, and overt behavior measured by such devices as the Iowa Aggression Machine (Williams, Meyerson, Eron, & Semler, 1967).

The ratings of the television programs for violence content also possess demonstrated reliability, as noted above, and were in close agreement with ratings made by at least two other groups (Feshbach & Singer, 1971; Greenberg & Gordon, 1970).

While only preferences for violent television were measured in both third and thirteenth grades, it is reasonable to assume that a child's preference for a television program is very highly correlated with the length of time that he attends to that program. The report of television preference in the third grade was made by the mother, who probably was strongly influenced by her child's actual viewing habits, especially since the question regarding television preference was asked immediately following the question concerning the length of time the child watched television. Hence it seems fair to conclude that a preference for violent television is indicative of viewing violent television by the child, particularly in the third grade. Furthermore, since the programs mentioned were the preferred ones, not only is it likely that they watched these programs regularly but that they also attended to the programs when they watched them. This would be a necessary condition for most theoretical explanations of a violence effect. While minor variations between preferences and watching certainly must have occurred, it is difficult to see how such variations could have enhanced our results.

These findings of a direct positive relation between the viewing of television violence and aggressive behavior on the part of the viewer corroborate in a long-term field study what has already been demonstrated as a short-term effect in the laboratory (Bandura et al., 1961, 1963b; Berkowitz, 1964; Berkowitz & Rawlings, 1963). Because the latter are manipulative studies in which systematically varied treatments were administered to randomly selected subjects under controlled conditions, statements about cause and effect relations based on their findings can be made with more confidence perhaps than those based on findings of field studies. In such studies many uncontrolled variables are unaccounted for, and observation and measurement cannot be as precise. We feel that our findings relating television violence and aggressive behavior over a 10-year period strengthen the conviction that this is indeed a real relation. The causal direction indicated for the relation is that viewing violence regularly on television at age 8 leads to more aggressive behavior on the part of the viewer at that time and also in subsequent years than does viewing nonviolent programs. Thus the significance of the laboratory studies is extended to indicate that the influence of television violence is not confined to short-term effects.

The laboratory studies of Bandura (Bandura, 1965; Bandura et al., 1961, 1963a, 1963b) furnish a theoretical model to account for these results. Bandura and his associates have demonstrated that aggressive behaviors new to the subject's repertoire of responses, as well as those already well established in his repertoire, can be evoked by observation of models performing such aggressive behaviors. The fact that the model does not get punished for the aggressive behaviors he develops serves to lower whatever inhibitions subjects have against the expression of similar behaviors. The likelihood of performance of the observed aggressive behaviors is stronger when the model is rewarded for his aggressive behavior (Bandura, 1965). It is not unusual on the more violent television programs for central characters to obtain desirable goals by violent tactics. Continued exposure to such models probably strengthens the conviction that these behaviors are permissible, and observation of acquisition of desired goals by aggressive behaviors increases the probability of performance of these behaviors by the observer. It is interesting in this regard that the more the subjects watch television at age 19 and the more violent the programs they prefer, the more likely are they to believe that situations depicted on television crime stories and westerns are realistic representations of life ($r = .28$ between judged realism of television programs and number of hours television is watched; and .36 between judged realism and television violence). Thus subjects who watch television for many hours and prefer violent programs do not consider these aggressive behaviors as deviant but as appropriate ways of solving real-life problems.

The lack of an effect of television violence on girls also corroborates the Bandura laboratory studies, which have consistently found that boys perform significantly more imitative aggression than girls (Bandura et al., 1961, 1963b). Why this is so probably has to do with the differential socialization of boys and girls in regard to aggression. Very early in life, girls learn that physical aggression is an undesirable behavior for girls, and so they acquire other behaviors more suitable to expectations for girls. Since they do not learn physical aggression as a response to instigation, they are rarely either rewarded or punished for such behavior and thus are not responsive to aggressive cues in the environment. Bandura (1965) has shown that when girls are positively reinforced for imitating aggressive behavior, they significantly increase such behavior and respond in a manner more similar to boys who are reinforced for the same behaviors. The results of Hokanson and Edelman (1966) would support this contention that lowered aggression levels in females are a function of lack of reinforcement for aggressive behavior. They found that females did not demonstrate the quickened reduction of physiological arousal after the opportunity to counteraggress against a confederate of the experimenter who had aggressed against them. However, such quickened reduction of heart rate and blood pressure to basal levels was routinely seen in male subjects. Finally, the frequency of occurrence of violently aggressive females shown on television is somewhat low. Hence the female viewer is less likely to encounter an aggressive model to imitate.

It is interesting that the aggressive girls in the present sample had significantly higher masculinity scores on the MMPI. This suggests that in the past they had been reinforced for emitting aggressive (masculine) behaviors and were thus sensitive to aggression-arousing cues in the environment in the same way that boys are.

Regardless of the theoretical explanation of the results, however, the data support the concept of a critical development period in which the child is susceptible to the influence of violent television. His preference for violent television at ages 8 and 9 influenced his current aggressiveness and his aggressiveness 10 years later, but by age 19 his current preferences were unrelated to his aggressiveness. From this, one might surmise that the role of imitation in the formation of the child's personality decreases drastically between ages 9 and 19.

One must compare the results of the current study with the somewhat different recent findings of Feshbach and Singer (1971). In a bold attempt to compromise between laboratory manipulation and a field setting, they provided findings which would indicate that the viewing of aggressive programs on television leads to a diminution of aggressive behavior on the part of some boys. Feshbach and Singer regulated the amount of television aggression viewed by their subjects over a six-week period by prescribing an aggressive or nonaggressive diet of television programs to two groups of subjects. The subjects were boys enrolled in residential private schools and homes for the underprivileged. The subjects watched television in groups of 10–18 boys at set times in specified locations. In two of the schools, participation by the subjects was compulsory. There was, of course, no voluntary choice of television programs. There are indications that at least initially this lack of preference was resented by boys assigned to the nonviolent diet since it meant they could not watch their favorite programs. In a few cases the experimenters, in order to retain the cooperation of the subjects, permitted the boys in the nonaggressive group to watch one of the aggressive programs. Although all subjects were given the same cover story, some guessed the real purpose. Feshbach and Singer found that, of the boys around 13 years old, those who were exposed to the aggressive television diet decreased in manifestations of aggression, while the control subjects increased in aggression. Feshbach and Singer's limited and special sample, their subject's ages, and their methodology all introduce factors sufficient to explain the discrepancy between their results and ours.

Actually the research of Feshbach and Singer addressed itself to a different question than did the present research, which is more concerned with the long-range effects of viewing television violence and with the consideration of more pervasive dispositions. In this regard, it is of interest that Feshbach and Singer used the peer rating measure which we had developed for our studies (Walder et al., 1961) in order to assess preexperimental aggression levels of their subjects and thereby separate them into high-aggressive and low-aggressive subsamples. They found:

> Regardless of experimental group, boys who score high on the peer aggression nomination measure display about twice as much aggressive behavior towards peers as boys who score low on the peer nomination measure [Feshbach & Singer, 1971, p. 91].

Thus any manipulation that changes the peer nomination score would indeed have powerful effects, and we have demonstrated that it is this measure which is affected by television preference. While six weeks of violent television might be expected to stimulate more aggressive behaviors, it could not be expected to have the effect on the development of aggressive habits that 5–10 years of viewing violence might have.

The weight of evidence from this study when coupled with previous laboratory studies supports the theory that during a critical period in a boy's development, regular viewing and liking of violent television lead to the formation of a more aggressive life style.

SUMMARY AND CONCLUSIONS

Among the results of a large-scale survey study of aggressive behavior in third-grade school children had been the finding that children at that age who preferred violent television programs were more aggressive in school as rated by peers than children who preferred less violent programs. In a 10-year follow-up study, 427 of the original 875 subjects, including 211 males and 216 females, were interviewed as to their television habits. They again rated their peers on aggressive behavior as well as responding to questions concerned with variables not treated extensively in the current report. It was found that the violence of programs preferred by the male subjects in Grade 3 was even more strongly related to aggression 10 years later. By the use of cross-lagged correlations, partial correlations, and multiple regression, it was demonstrated that there is a probable causative influence of watching violent television programs in early formative years on later aggression. Of course, it is not claimed that television violence is the only cause of aggressive behavior, since a number of other variables are also related to aggression, including ones in addition to the more than 20 variables we have reported on here, which could conceivably have had an influence over the 10 years covered by this longitudinal design. However, the effect of television violence on aggression is relatively independent of these other factors and explains a larger portion of the variance than does any other single factor which we studied, including IQ, social status, mobility aspirations, religious practice, ethnicity, and parental disharmony.

REFERENCES

Bailyn, L. Mass media and children: A study of exposure habits and cognitive effects. *Psychological Monographs*, 1959, *73* (1, Whole No. 471).

Baker, R. K., & Ball, S. J. *Violence and the media.* Washington, D.C.: U.S. Government Printing Office, 1969.

Bandura, A. Influence of models' reinforcement contingencies on the acquisition of imitative responses. *Journal of Personality and Social Psychology*, 1965, *1*, 589–595.

Bandura, A., Ross, D., & Ross, S. A. Transmission of aggression through imitation of aggressive models. *Journal of Abnormal and Social Psychology*, 1961, *63*, 575–582.

______. Imitation of film mediated aggressive models. *Journal of Abnormal and Social Psychology*, 1963a, *66*, 3–11.

______. Vicarious reinforcement and imitative learning. *Journal of Abnormal and Social Psychology*, 1963b, *67*, 601–607.

Berkowitz, L. Aggressive cues in aggressive behavior and hostility catharsis. *Psychological Review*, 1964, *71*, 104–122.

Berkowitz, L., Corwin, R., & Heironimus, M. Film violence and subsequent aggressive tendencies. *Public Opinion Quarterly*, 1963, *27*, 217–229.

Berkowitz, L., & Rawlings, E. Effects of film violence on inhibition against subsequent aggression. *Journal of Abnormal and Social Psychology*, 1963, *66*, 405–412.

Campbell, D. T., & Fiske, D. W. Convergent and discriminant validation by the multitrait-multimethod matrix. *Psychological Bulletin*, 1959, *56*, 81–105.

Darlington, R. D. Multiple regression in psychological research and practice. *Psychological Bulletin*, 1968, *69*, 161–182.

Eron, L. D. Relationship of television viewing habits and aggressive behavior in children. *Journal of Abnormal and Social Psychology*, 1963, *67*, 193–196.

Eron, L. D., Walder, L. O., & Lefkowitz, M. M. *Learning of aggression in children.* Boston: Little, Brown, 1971.

Feshbach, S. Aggression. In P. H. Mussen (Ed.), *Carmichael's manual of child psychology* (3rd ed., Vol. 2). New York: Wiley, 1970.

Feshbach, S., & Singer, R. D. *Television and aggression.* San Francisco: Jossey-Bass, 1971.

Greenberg, B. S., & Gordon, T. F. *Critics and public perceptions of violence in TV programs.* East Lansing: Michigan State Univ., 1970.

Hartup, W. W., & Yonas, A. Developmental psychology. In P. H. Mussen & M. R. Rosenzweig (Eds.), *Annual review of psychology,* 1971, *22,* 337–392.

Heise, D. R. Causal inference from panel data. In E. Borgatta & G. W. Bohrnstedt (Eds.), *Sociological methodology.* San Francisco: Jossey-Bass, 1970.

Hokanson, J. E., & Edelman, R. Effects of three social responses on vascular processes. *Journal of Personality and Social Psychology,* 1966, *3,* 442–447.

Kenny, D. A. Cross-lagged and synchronous common factors in panel data. In A. Goldberger & O. D. Duncan (Eds.), *Structural equation models.* New York: Seminar Press, in press.

Rozelle, R. M., & Campbell, D. T. More plausible rival hypotheses in the cross-lagged panel correlation technique. *Psychological Bulletin,* 1969, *71,* 74–80.

Schramm, W., Lyle, J., & Parker, E. B. *Television in the lives of our children.* Stanford: Stanford Univ. Press, 1961.

Walder, L. O., Abelson, R. P., Eron, L. D., Banta, T. J., & Laulicht, J. H. Development of a peer-rating measure of aggression. *Psychological Reports,* 1961, *9,* 497–556. (*Monograph Supplement,* 4–49).

Williams, J. R., Meyerson, L. J., Eron, L. D., & Semler, I. J. Peer rated aggression and aggressive responses elicited in an experimental situation. *Child Development,* 1967, *38,* 181–190.

NOTES

1. The authors are indebted to John M. Neale, State University of New York at Stony Brook, for this path analysis of our data and to David Kenny, Northwestern University, for suggestions regarding interpretation of the cross-lagged correlations.

COMMENT: CAUSAL ANALYSIS IN R-R STUDIES: TELEVISION VIOLENCE AND AGGRESSION

Gilbert Becker, University of Winnipeg

Eron, Huesmann, Lefkowitz, and Walder (1972) presented data of high interest and of apparently high internal validity which strongly suggest that 8–9-year-old males, representing the particular population sampled, who prefer to watch television programs with high violence content tend to be peer-rated high on aggression not only at that age level ($r = .21$) but also 10 years later ($r = .31$). The stated hypotheses are *(a)* early preference for watching television violence "is positively related" to later

Becker, Gilbert. Comment: Causal analyses in R-R studies: Television violence and aggression. *American Psychologist,* 1972, *27,* 967–968.

aggressiveness, and *(b)* this preference "is one cause of his aggressiveness." The authors conclude that *(a)* a positive correlation does exist and *(b)* "it was demonstrated that there is a probable causative influence of watching violent television programs . . . on later aggression." In the section headed "Causal Analysis" the authors state that alternative causal explanations can be considered but that "one cannot demonstrate that a particular hypothesis is true. One can only reject untenable hypotheses and present evidence on the plausibility of the remaining hypotheses [p. 257]."

We agree with the immediately preceding statement but add that in a context in which one uses the terms "plausibility" and "probable causative influence" interchangeably, our agreement is contingent on one very important assumption, which is that all reasonable variations within each and across all cause-and-effect directionalities are presented for examination. This may be easier said than done, but to ignore the inclusiveness of the basic directionalities by failure to consider at least one hypothesis from each is to raise strong doubts as to the legitimacy of applying a win-by-default logic.

Before continuing, we must make clear what we mean when we use the term "directionality." In any R-R study, there are three and only three directionalities of cause and effect possible associated with the two correlated responses (R_1 and R_2): *(a)* some aspect(s) of the stimulus situation associated with or predicted by R_1 can cause R_2 (initial hypothesis); *(b)* some aspect(s) of the stimulus situation associated with or predicted by R_2 can cause R_1, provided that temporal considerations do not rule that possibility out (reverse hypothesis); and *(c)* some aspect(s) of any one of a number of stimulus situations, typically not represented within the investigation, can cause both R_1 and R_2 (or some prototypical trace of R_1 or R_2) simultaneously (common-causal hypothesis). These basic (independent) directionalities can be *(a)* elaborated (some aspect[s] of the stimulus situation associated with R_1 can cause R_2, which as a stimulus-mediating response in turn can bring about R_2) and/or *(b)* combined (initial and reverse tendencies can work reciprocally, or initial and common-causal, or for that matter all three can work simultaneously).

In the Eron et al. study, elaborations are created easily because the two responses of interest are measured at two different time periods. Those elaborations tend to mask the simplicity of the three-directionalities fact. It is not surprising to find that early aggression correlates with later aggression. We would expect behaviors representing basic categories of modes of adjustment to show some consistency over time. What is surprising, to some degree, is the close to zero correlation between early preference for viewing television violence and later preference. Thus there is what we consider to be a one-sided elaboration of (later) rejected hypotheses which include, for example, the segments *(a)* early aggression causing later aggression (which we see as continuity) and *(b)* early aggression causing both later aggression and later preference (which we see as a combination of continuity and the reverse hypothesis). All five of Eron et al.'s causal paradigms are variations of either the initial or the reverse hypothesis. Not considered at all are any one of a *number* of common-causal hypotheses. (We emphasize *number* because among the three basic directionalities, only the common-causal can have more than one causal agent.) Such a common-causal variable would not come from among the two pairs of responses (preference and aggression) since those must be dependent variables according to the common-causal paradigm. Thus we see an overabundance of initial and reverse hypotheses and an underabundance (meaning complete lack) of common-causal hypotheses in which some factor other than one among the four response measures is the common-causal factor. A situation has thus been created wherein one can easily get the impression that because n possible causal hypotheses are considered and $n-1$ of those are rejected, the remaining one must be (probably) correct. This is true especially when a vicarious-reinforcement model is invoked to show what mechanisms might underlie the nonrejected hypothesis and especially when the $n-1$ hypotheses, by virtue of their lack of independence, are numerous enough so that with each rejection the accumulated effect becomes such as to "force" a win-by-default conclusion.

Let us switch from the abstract to the concrete and look at a single though complex possible directional paradigm that combines both an initial and a common-causal hypothesis. Suppose that one common-causal factor and/or another produces in at least some male children an unspecified state or predisposition such that *(a)* in certain situations, aggressive behavior is more likely to occur and *(b)* the viewing of aggressive behavior on television (and elsewhere) is more reinforcing and therefore more likely to occur. Thus far, the supposition, though lacking in detail, is sufficient to account for the r of .21 cited above. Suppose, however, that in addition, the high-"predisposition" boys who do watch more television violence become as a direct result even more aggressive over time, perhaps explainable in terms of the modeling effect cited by Eron et al. This would account for the .10 differential between early preference on the one hand and early *versus* later aggression on the other hand (which amounts to slightly over 5% "accounted-for" variance over the initially roughly 4½% found earlier in time). An alternative explanation for the differential, namely, that positively reinforced early aggression can lead to an increase in subsequent aggression, is equally tenable. An additional alternative hypothesis, following Feshbach and Singer (1971), cited by Eron et al., is that television viewing has not only a short-term effect in the opposite direction but also a long-term effect in the opposite direction, which in connection with the first alternative hypothesis suggests the possibility that if television viewing were absent altogether, the r of .31 might be substantially higher.

We conclude from our analysis that Eron et al.'s "demonstration" of a "probable causative influence" is no demonstration at all and that, therefore, Conclusion *b* cited above is gratuitous. Further, we conclude that the *positive* correlation supporting Conclusion *a* may well be masking, in terms of the "probable" initial hypothesis, a *negative* causal relationship. In a more general reference frame we add that causal analyses in R-R studies, although potentially fruitful, can easily lead to a spuriously high level of confidence in a given hypothesis and to a failure to appreciate the various combinations of cause-and-effect directionality that may be operating simultaneously in the extralaboratory world. This raw situation becomes even more raw when the directions to be taken for practical application to the problems of society depend on the outcome of such causal analyses.

REFERENCES

Eron, L. D., Huesmann, L. R., Lefkowitz, M. M., & Walder, L. O. Does television violence cause aggression? *American Psychologist,* 1972, *27,* 253–263.

Feshbach, S., & Singer, R. D. *Television and aggression.* San Francisco: Jossey-Bass, 1971.

COMMENT: ON TELEVISION AS A CAUSE OF AGGRESSION

Robert M. Kaplan, University of California, Riverside

The issue of televised violence and its relationship to aggressive behavior in children is not only one of great interest to psychologists but is of considerable import to television networks and public policy makers. During recent Senate hearings the broadcasting networks agreed to tone down the violence because the effects of such portrayals may be harmful. Since research on television and social behavior ultimately may lead to censorship, it is of paramount importance that psychologists examine research evidence with scrutiny.

The article by Eron, Huesmann, Lefkowitz, and Walder (1972) implied a causal relationship between watching violence at age 8 and behaving aggressively at age 18. A recent publication (Lefkowitz, Eron, Walder, & Huesmann, 1972) reported the same research and gave a more detailed description of the methodology. Several of the studies' design problems have been described in a recent report to the Surgeon General by the Surgeon General's Scientific Advisory Committee on Television and Social Behavior (1972). One problem is in the use of the peer rating instrument. The questions for the original study were phrased in the present tense, while the questions on the 10-year follow-up peer rating form were phrased in the past tense. In the follow up, they asked about aggression at a prior time. In reference to old schoolmates they might

Kaplan, Robert M. Comment: On television as a cause of aggression. *American Psychologist,* 1972, *27,* 968–969. Reprinted by permission.

ask, "Who started fights over nothing?" or "Who used to say mean things?" There are a number of reasons why this measure is inadequate for evaluating current aggression. First, a person may have had little or no contact with his former classmates. In the Eron et al. study, nearly half of the original subjects no longer lived in the area. It is quite likely that an individual was rated by peers he had not seen in years. A more important problem was that the structure of the questions made it impossible to make inferences about aggressive behavior at present. Respondents were asked about their peers' previous behavior but not about their current behavior. Still another problem was that mothers' reports were used to determine each child's favorite programs in the third grade. These reports are clearly incompatible with self-report measures used to make the same assessments in the 10-year follow-up. Thus the results of the Eron et al. study should be interpreted with some caution.

Robert D. Singer and I recently have completed a comprehensive review of the television and aggression literature. We have found that the majority of the experimental studies showed that witnessing violence can instigate "aggressive" behavior. These experiments, however, most frequently gained their effectiveness through the intentional arousal of subjects and the use of dependent measures that removed ordinary sanctions against aggression. Instigation effects were rarely found in studies or experimental conditions in which the subjects were not aroused intentionally. When the measure of aggression has been some naturally occurring behavior, it has been shown that television violence either has no effect (Feshbach & Singer, 1971; Siegel, 1956) or only affects children who were initially highly aggressive (Stein, Friedrich, & Vondracek, 1971). Thus we would argue that the link between televised violence and aggression has not been established clearly.

REFERENCES

Eron, L. D., Huesmann, L. R., Lefkowitz, M. M., & Walder, L. O. Does television violence cause aggression? *American Psychologist*, 1972, *27*, 253–263.

Feshbach, S., & Singer, R. D. *Television and aggression*. San Francisco: Jossey-Bass, 1971.

Lefkowitz, M., Eron, L., Walder, L., & Huesmann, L. R. Television violence and child aggression: A follow-up study. In G. A. Comstock & E. A. Rubinstein (Eds.), *Television and social behavior*. Vol. 3. *Television and adolescent aggressiveness*. Washington, D.C.: U.S. Government Printing Office, 1972.

Siegel, A. E. Film-mediated fantasy aggression and strength of aggressive drive. *Child Development*, 1956, *27*, 355–378.

Stein, A. H., Friedrich, I. K., & Vondracek, F. Television content and young children's behavior. In J. P. Murray, E. A. Rubinstein, & G. A. Comstock (Ed.), *Television and social behavior*. Vol. 2. *Television and social learning*. Washington, D.C.: U.S. Government Printing Office, 1971.

Surgeon General's Scientific Advisory Committee on Television and Social Behavior. *Television and growing up: The impact of televised violence* (Report to the Surgeon General, United States Public Health Service). Washington, D.C.: U.S. Government Printing Office, 1972.

COMMENT: TELEVISION AND AGGRESSION: A COUNTERARGUMENT

Dennis Howitt, University of Leicester, England

Eron, Huesmann, Lefkowitz, and Walder (1972) have offered evidence to suggest that television violence causes aggression. They repeat well-founded criticisms of the experimental research into the effects of exposure to television violence and argue that the longitudinal survey approach to the problem has several advantages, especially when provision is made for causal explanations. The present note is intended to indicate some of the limitations of this particular piece of research against the backdrop of the research literature in this area.

Table 1 gives a breakdown of the surveys of mass media exposure effects on actual violent and delinquent behavior. Excluded from the table are the many studies that emphasize the effects of mass media on attitudes to violence since the concern is solely with overt behavior. The remarkable thing about the table is that the studies supporting the hypothesis that exposure to the mass media increases aggression have done so essentially in terms of exposure to the cinema and comic books—television and radio being unimportant in this context. On the basis of these data, it might be argued that a subcultural explanation of the relationship between mass media and aggression or delinquency might be the best. That is, the media of cinema and comic books might be conceived of as essential elements in delinquent subculture. As R. I. Whitley (cited in Forman, 1935, pp. 259–260) has pointed out, the cinema can be an essential meeting ground for delinquents and an active site for delinquent behavior. Comic books, since these are transported readily, might serve as a coin of exchange among those engaged in the delinquent subculture. The findings of Dembo (1972) that street culture orientation (i.e., accepting the tenets of the street gang) was associated strongly with motion picture attendance and that this association disappeared when peer-rated aggression was partialed out further support the subcultural view.

The data of Eron et al. clearly do not support the above argument at face value (although the original article by Eron, 1963, indicated that the amount of exposure to television in itself is correlated negatively with aggressiveness). Since certain of the studies described in Table 1 deal with violence exposure as does the Eron et al. study, the disparity cannot be explained in terms of the difference between simple exposure and exposure to mass media violence. It is suspected that the major difference between the Eron et al. study and some of the others described is that it deals with favorite television programs and the amount of aggression contained in these rather than with the actual amount of exposure to

Howitt, Dennis. Comment: Television and aggression: A counterargument. *American Psychologist*, 1972, *27*, 969–970.

Table 1
Mass Media Exposure and Aggression Studies Summarized

SOURCE	METHOD	IMPORTANT RELATIONSHIPS
Cressey & Thrasher (1933)	Compared delinquents and normals on cinema attendance.	Delinquents attend more frequently.
Pfuhl (1960)	Examined relationship between violent media exposure (cinema, books, radio, television, and comic books) and self-reported delinquency.	Movie attendance and exposure to "dangerous" comic books correlated with delinquency.
Halloran, Brown, & Chaney (1971)	Considered probationers and controls in terms of their television usage.	Probationers and controls did not differ in amount of viewing.
Hoult (1949)	Compared the comic book exposure of delinquents and nondelinquents.	Comic book exposure highest in delinquents.

television violence (which is somewhat in line with Halloran, Brown, and Chaney's 1971 finding that delinquents tended to prefer what might be termed exciting programs). Since aggressive programs tend to be very popular (witness the viewing figures of television programs) and since a heavy viewer must watch nearly all programs rather than discriminate, a ready explanation is available of why aggressive youngsters watch less television and have a tendency to have greater preferences for aggressive programs. Certainly, the research of Eron et al. is interesting, but in the total context of mass media research it seems unlikely that their one longitudinal study finally could answer the question of the effects of television violence on real-life aggression.

REFERENCES

Cressey, P. G., & Thrasher, F. M. *Boys, movies, and city streets.* New York: Macmillan, 1933.

Dembo, R. *Aggression and media use among English working-class youths.* Unpublished manuscript, Centre for Mass Communication Research, Univ. of Leicester, England, 1972.

Eron, L. D. Relationship of TV viewing habits and aggressive behavior in children. *Journal of Abnormal and Social Psychology,* 1963, *67,* 193–196.

Eron, L. D., Huesmann, L. R., Lefkowitz, M. M., & Walder, L. O. Does television violence cause aggression? *American Psychologist,* 1972, *27,* 253–263.

Forman, H. J. *Our movie made children.* New York: Macmillan, 1935.

Halloran, J., Brown, R., & Chaney, D. *Television and delinquency.* Leicester, England: Univ. of Leicester Press, 1971.

Hoult, T. F. Comic books and juvenile delinquency. *Sociology and Social Research,* 1949, *33,* 279–284.

Pfuhl, E. *The relationship of mass media to reported delinquent behavior* (Doctoral dissertation, Washington State University). (University Microfilms, 1960, No. 61-1308).

COMMENT: WEAKNESSES IN THE TELEVISION-CAUSES-AGGRESSION ANALYSIS BY ERON ET AL.

Herbert Kay, Herbert Kay Research, Inc., Montclair, New Jersey

In asking, "Does Television Violence Cause Aggression?" Eron, Huesmann, Lefkowitz, and Walder (1972) concluded that it probably does:

> By the use of cross-lagged correlations, partial correlations, and multiple regression, it was demonstrated that there is a probable causative influence of watching violent television programs in early formative years on later aggression [p. 263].

But there are serious weaknesses in the report that the authors failed to deal with in reaching their conclusion. The following comments are strictly a methodological evaluation of this one longitudinal study and make no brief either for or against the television-causes-aggression theory in general.

Although both boys and girls were studied, the authors' conclusion is supported by data *only from the boys*, not from the girls. They reported *r*s between *(a)* assumed preference for violent television shows in the third grade and *(b)* peer-rated aggressive behavior in the thirteenth grade of .31 for boys but −.13 for girls. Their brief explanation for this curious result seems illogical and internally contradictory. They said that it

> corroborates the Bandura laboratory studies which have consistently found that boys perform significantly more imitative aggression than girls. . . . Why this is so probably has to do with the differential socialization of boys and girls in regard to aggression. Very early in life, girls learn that physical aggression is an undesirable behavior for girls, and . . . thus are not responsive to aggressive cues in the environment [p. 261].

If the differential-socialization hypothesis is true—and there is historical support for it—Eron et al. seem to have misread its implication. (They reported a lower correlation among girls but failed to report whether they also found a lower incidence of aggression among girls; however, the reported "corroboration," together with a reading of a key Bandura [1963] report, implies that a lower incidence of aggression also was obtained.)

Unless Eron et al. are suggesting that television is a far more crucial socialization influence than "significant others" such as parents—which would be farfetched—the socialization hypothesis implies that the key factor is whether or not parents condone or even encourage aggression in the child's formative years. If they do, aggressive behavior and also viewing of televised violence would be likely results—that is, effects.

Kay, Herbert. Comment: Weakness in the television-causes-aggression analysis by Eron et al. *American Psychologist*, 1972, *27*, 970–973.

If they do not condone it, then exposure to "aggressive cues" such as television violence would not increase the production of aggressive behavior, as Eron et al. themselves suggested. But this analysis robs television violence of any real causative role.

Moreover, their own data accord with this analysis. If viewing of TV violence were a *cause* of aggressive behavior, greater "socialization" of girls than of boys might have involved a lower *incidence* of aggression for girls but *not* a lower *correlation* between whatever aggression was observed and television viewing. Yet Eron et al. reported virtually zero correlations between television violence and both early and later aggression among girls.

They pointed out that nonnormality of the distributions could have held down the size of various correlations. But they reported an even higher correlation between early and later aggression among girls (.47) than among boys (.38). So nonnormality does not explain why the girls' aggression (both early and later) had roughly zero correlation with early television viewing.

The only conclusion that seems tenable is that both the data and the socialization hypothesis presented by Eron et al. confute rather than support the validity of their conclusion that early viewing of television violence probably induces later aggression.

There is a further internal discrepancy. As part of their socialization hypothesis, they alluded to "observation of models" performing aggressive behavior. The context implied that the modeling is done only by television characters, but it is well accepted that parents are fully as important, if not more so, as models.

The investigators reported that measures (obtained when the children were in third grade) of father's and mother's aggressiveness, and parental punishment or rejection of child, yielded multiple-correlation beta weights of magnitude .09–.03, and that their measurements of these variables failed to improve the multiple-correlation prediction of thirteenth-grade aggression by more than .02 correlation points (i.e., from .51 to .53).

What is strange is not just that these data are inconsistent with a tenable version of a modeling hypothesis, but that the data imply that aggression in the home has no material effect on the child's later aggression—a finding certainly not supported by current data on the "battered child" syndrome, for example.

The most likely resolution of these paradoxes is that the validity of the parental-aggression data is faulty. Mother's and father's aggression was determined by the Walters-Zak test. But no validity data or source reference for that test were provided by the investigators. Nor could I find it listed in the *Mental Measurements Yearbook* or *Personality Tests and Reviews*, both by Buros. Theoretically, then, it is of unknown validity to us. But because most psychometric devices, reports Zedeck (1971, p. 295), still have predictive validities that rarely exceed .50, the statistical odds are that the data from the Walters-Zak test likewise are not likely to have greater than .50 validity—which, of course, means 25% accuracy.

The source of other aggression-oriented data on parent-child relationships was described as "Mother's report" or "Parents' report." With no further explication, we must presume that the investigators relied on the parents to report such matters accurately—that the parents neither lied deliberately to the interviewer nor unwittingly to themselves on these delicate issues. That assumption simply is untenable. Meehl and Hathaway (1946), Rokeach (1970), and Kay (undated) are some of those who have pointed out the serious errors that occur in psychometric and survey data when superficial self-ratings and opinion statements are accepted at face value. Shortly, some evidence will be presented on the questionable accuracy of mothers' reports when used simply to determine what their children watch on television.

With no validity data to the contrary, the most probable conclusion is that the parental-aggression data collected by the investigators have serious error variances. To the extent that those data conflict with the socialization hypothesis, the former should be held suspect.

Eron et al. obtained another strange result: the virtually zero correlations between early and late "preference" for television violence (.05 for boys, .08 for girls). They found moderate positive correlations between early and late aggression for both boys and girls (.38 and .47, respectively). Why not a similar pattern for viewing of violence?

The authors' explication rested mainly on inferences drawn from cross-lagged correlations. Sandell (1971) appears less sanguine than Eron et al. about such inferences when measurements are taken at only two points in time rather than three. Eron et al. focused on the possibility of a drop in reliability of the thirteenth-grade viewing data.

But a more likely reason is that the data on the *third*-grade viewing of violence were of low *validity*. The investigators used the mother, not the child, as the source of those data: she was asked to report the child's three favorite television programs. Eron et al. stated their belief that the mothers' reports "probably" were reasonably accurate. Although ascertainment of children's viewing tastes and behavior most commonly seems to be done by questioning the mother (major broadcast-ratings services do this), at least one empirical study has cast serious doubt on the validity of this approach.

A pilot study (Kay, report in preparation) involved 40 households in which both the mother and her child (in the 6–11-year-old range, a range that would include third graders) were interviewed. Prior research indicated not only that children typically will give useful, candid viewing reports but also that the mother frequently gives inaccurate viewing reports for her children: however, these surveys did not indicate the prevalence of such error. So on the present study, while the interviewer questioned the child orally, the mother was requested to go into another room and fill out a self-administered questionnaire at the *same time* her child was being interviewed. The purpose was to minimize the danger of the mother and child contaminating each other's responses.

When asked, program by program, whether or not the child watches that show "at least once in awhile," the mothers' answers agreed with their children's answers only 62% of the time for the 22 shows. An incongruent answer was defined as a mother's "don't know" or a viewing assertion not supported by the child's response; both types of responses reflect an inability of the mother to report the child's viewing. Because of the prior survey findings that led to the present study, as well as other data (e.g., the general unreliability of second-person "hearsay" reports), most of the incongruency was attributed to mother error rather than child error.

Analysis by sex of child revealed a significant F ratio between the mother-boy and mother-girl variances (due, it seems likely, to deviant, lazy, blanket "don't know" responses from a few girls' mothers) but no significant differences between the means. The most defensible conclusion thus far is that even if mothers should prove slightly more accurate in the relative sense in reporting boys' than girls' viewing, this difference would seem minuscule compared with the absolute magnitude of reporting error for children of either sex.

Using this one study as a benchmark, it appears reasonable to conclude that the error variance in mothers' reports of the third-grade child's viewing preferences was at least two or three times larger than the coefficients of determination obtained by Eron et al. in relating early viewing to later aggression among the boys (10%) and the girls (2%). The possibility of a significant interaction between third-grade television reporting error and other variables is large enough to suggest great caution in interpreting the correlations between early "viewing" and later aggression.

Still another problem is that programs apparently were categorized as being violent or nonviolent on the basis of manifest rather than latent content—that is, without determining whether the children would *react* to the programs as portraying realistic aggression. Himmelweit, Oppenheim, and Vince (1960) concluded that, unlike crime thrillers, violence in Westerns is stylized, not realistic, and "it is likely that the majority of children can enjoy them without fear by the time they are about 7." With the "violent" programs made up of a mixture of unrealistic violence and realistic violence, we have still another confounding varible which may have affected the findings. (The investigators did assert that the 19-year-olds who watch a lot of crime and Westerns use those shows as realistic models for their own behavior—but the supporting data were not actually relevant.)

In short, there were so many serious loopholes not mentioned in the report by Eron et al. that one is justified in rejecting as insufficiently supported their conclusion from this particular study that viewing of television violence when young probably causes later aggressive behavior.

REFERENCES

Bandura, A. Vicarious reinforcement and imitative learning. *Journal of Abnormal and Social Psychology*, 1963, *67*, 601–607.

Eron, L. D., Huesmann, L. R., Lefkowitz, M. M., & Walder, L. O. Does television violence cause aggression? *American Psychologist*, 1972, *27*, 253–263.

Himmelweit, H. T., Oppenheim, A. N., & Vince, P. *Television and the child.* London: Oxford Univ. Press, 1960.

Kay, H. Five fatal fallacies in attitude research, and how to avoid them: The a posteriori approach. In American Marketing Association, *Attitude research reaches new heights*, undated (Proceedings of conference held in Mexico City, March 1970).

Meehl, P. E., & Hathaway, S. R. The A factor as a suppressor variable in the MMPI. *Journal of Applied Psychology*, 1946, *40*, 525–564.

Rokeach, M. *Beliefs, attitudes, and values.* San Francisco: Jossey-Bass, 1970.

Sandell, R. G. Note on choosing between competing interpretations of cross-lagged panel correlations. *Psychological Bulletin*, 1971, *75*, 367–368.

Zedeck, S. Problems with the use of "moderation" variables. *Psychological Bulletin*, 1971, *76*, 295–310.

COMMENT: TELEVISION VIOLENCE AND AGGRESSION: THE CAUSAL EFFECT REMAINS

L. Rowell Huesmann, Yale University

Leonard D. Eron, University of Illinois, Chicago Circle

Monroe M. Lefkowitz, New York State Department of Mental Hygiene, Albany

Leopold O. Walder, Organization for Research in the Behavioral Sciences, Greenbelt, Maryland

In the October 1972 *American Psychologist*, a series of letters were printed that were critical of the Eron, Huesmann, Lefkowitz, and Walder article, "Does Television Violence Cause Aggression?" which appeared in the April 1972 *American Psychologist*. While many of the Comments were representative of criticisms communicated elsewhere, a few of them were new. In this Comment, we review both the old and the new criticisms, showing that some of them are based on misunderstandings, some of them are contradicted by our data, and the remaining valid points are covered adequately by the careful wording of our conclusions.

Huesmann, L. Rowell, Eron, Leonard D., Lefkowitz, Monroe M., and Walder, Leopold O. Comment: Television violence and aggression: The causal effect remains. *American Psychologist*, 1973, *28*, 617–620.

With any socially relevant research project like the Surgeon General's study of television violence, there is always the danger that passions will dominate rational thought. The specters of exploitation of children or censorship of the media loom large in the back of many peoples' minds. Yet we have not dealt with such issues nor have we proposed any solutions, and we do not wish to reply to criticisms of this nature. Instead we shall stick to questions of scientific substance.

The major conclusions of our article were that

> the weight of evidence from this study when coupled with previous laboratory studies supports the theory that during a critical period in a body's development, regular viewing and liking of violent television lead to the formation of a more aggressive life style [p. 262]

and

> it was demonstrated that there is a probable causative influence of watching violent television programs in early formative years on later aggression [p. 263].

These conclusions were based on results obtained from applying a variety of specialized statistical techniques (e.g., cross-lagged panel correlations, path analysis) to data collected on 427 children when they were in the third grade and again one year after they had graduated from high school (called the thirteenth-grade period). The major findings, relating television violence to aggression, are presented in Figure 1 and Table 1. Table 1 did not appear in the original article, but it shows clearly how post-high-school aggression increases as a function of television violence, regardless of the subject's level of aggression in the third grade.

THE WEIGHT OF EVIDENCE

In evaluating our conclusions, it is important to note our qualifying phrases "when coupled with previous laboratory studies" and "probable causative influence." Yet many critics who feel our conclusion is too strong respond as if it were the only study in this area. As Chaffee (1972)

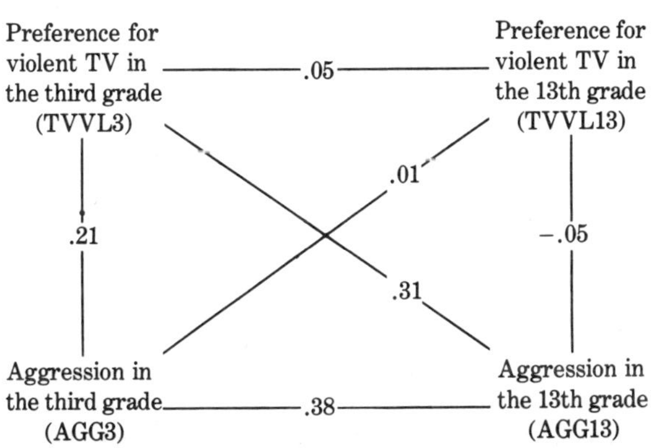

FIGURE 1. Correlations between a preference for violent television and peer-rated aggression for 211 boys over a 10-year lag. (Reprinted from the April 1972 American Psychologist.*)*

Table 1
Mean Aggression Scores for Boys in the Thirteenth Grade

LEVEL OF AGGRESSION IN THE THIRD GRADE	PREFERENCE FOR TELEVISION VIOLENCE IN THE THIRD GRADE			
	High (>80%)	*Medium*	*Low (<17%)*	$\bar{X}$
High (>75%)	165.8 (N = 13)	116.9 (N = 27)	60.6 (N = 5)	114.4 (N = 45)
Medium	103.3 (N = 15)	89.5 (N = 59)	58.7 (N = 17)	83.8 (N = 91)
Low (<26%)	110.8 (N = 8)	19.0 (N = 31)	32.4 (N = 9)	54.1 (N = 48)
$\bar{X}$	126.6 (N = 36)	75.1 (N = 117)	50.6 (N = 31)	

Note. Test of television violence in the third grade: $F = 6.63$, $df = 2/175$, $p < .005$.

reported, the majority of field studies have found significant positive correlations between viewing of violent television and aggression, and as Kaplan (1972) admitted in his Comment, the great majority of laboratory experiments have revealed short-term increases in aggression following exposure to media violence. To attack our results as though they were isolated from other research is to suggest our findings are anomalous. On the contrary, they are consistent. We are willing to defend the contribution of our own study to our conclusions, but we would not have stated the conclusions without supportive evidence from other field and laboratory studies.

THE PEER-RATING PROCEDURE

A common methodological criticism leveled against our study by many, including Kaplan (1972), is that the measure of peer-rated aggression used in the thirteenth grade (post high school) was only a remeasure of third-grade aggression. This criticism has emerged because the questions used on the peer rating instrument in the thirteenth grade were stated in the past tense, for example, "Who started fights over nothing?" Such a criticism has face validity, but other factors argue against its legitimacy. First, during the administration of the peer rating questionnaire in a face-to-face setting, the subject was instructed to "base your answers on what you *last* knew of each person from personal observation and contact." More important, however, we have data that allow us to test the validity of the thirteenth-grade peer ratings, since we also collected self-ratings of aggression in the thirteenth grade. If the thirteenth-grade peer-rated aggression score was mostly a remeasure of third-grade aggression, then it should correlate only a little higher with the thirteenth-grade self-ratings than would the third-grade peer rating of aggression.

Table 2
Correlations between the Peer Ratings of Aggression and the Thirteenth-Grade Self-Ratings of Aggression for Boys

THIRTEENTH-GRADE SELF-RATINGS OF AGGRESSION	THIRD-GRADE PEER RATING OF AGGRESSION	THIRTEENTH-GRADE PEER RATING OF AGGRESSION
Antisocial behavior	.444	.478
Aggressive habits	.159	.503
Total aggressive environment	.165	.508
MMPI-49-sum	.206	.391

As Table 2 reveals, thirteenth-grade peer-rated aggression correlates much more highly with every thirteenth-grade self-report measure than does third-grade aggression. Hence the argument that the thirteenth-grade score is only a remeasure of third-grade score does not seem to hold much water. But Kaplan (1972) also argued that "it is quite likely that an individual was rated by peers he had not seen in years." Here, Kaplan is simply wrong. Perhaps he misunderstood the design of the study. Only those 427 subjects who were reinterviewed in the thirteenth grade were rated or used as raters. All of these subjects still lived in the area. The great majority of them graduated from high school in the same class. Only a small number might not have been seen by the other subjects "in years." Finally, since the third-grade ratings had been done only by children within the subject's classroom, the thirteenth-grade ratings were performed by a quite different set of raters from the third grade, many of whom did not even know the subject at the earlier time.

"VAGUE" METHODOLOGICAL PROBLEMS

Kaplan's Comment included the statement that "several of the studies' design problems have been described in a recent report to the Surgeon General by the Surgeon General's Scientific Advisory Committee on Television and Social Behavior." If Kaplan would care to state a particular problem, we would be happy to respond, but we can hardly answer such a vague statement as this. If one reads the critiques of the two consultants hired by the Surgeon General's Committee to analyze our results (Kenny, 1972; Neale, 1972), one finds some legitimate criticisms but general agreement with our conclusions. However, Kaplan may be excused if he has been misled by Chapter 7 of the summary of the Surgeon General's report. The distortions in that chapter have been detailed elsewhere (Pastore, 1972), and it has been reported (Paisley, 1972) that the chapter was written almost entirely by a consultant for CBS Television.

REPORTS OF TELEVISION BEHAVIOR

Another criticism leveled by Kaplan and elaborated on by Kay (1972) concerns the fact that the mother's reports were used to ascertain the child's favorite television programs in the third grade, while the subject's own reports were used in the thirteenth grade. Kaplan simply said "these [mother's] reports are clearly incompatible with self-report measures used . . . in the 10-year follow-up." To whom this incompatibility is supposed to be clear is unclear. Kay (1972), on the other hand, offered a great deal of argument to support his contention that the mother's reports are invalid. Unfortunately, most of Kay's argument is based on one pilot study of his own that he has never published. In this one study he apparently gave a list of 22 programs to 40 mothers and asked them if their child watched each program "at least once in a while." He reports that on the average a mother's answer agreed with her child's on only 62% of the 22 shows. But Kay assumes the child is always right and includes "don't know" answers by the mother as disagreements. In other words, a mother could always be right in the programs she says her child watches and still have a low agreement score. Kay's conclusion that mothers cannot accurately report their child's *favorite programs*, as they were asked to do in our study, hardly seems justified from this meager evidence. Finally, Kay's assumption that our results should be rejected if the error variance in the television violence scores was greater than the variance in the aggression variable that is explained by the television violence scores has no mathematical basis.

Much of Kay's dissatisfaction with the television violence measure seems to originate in his feeling that the lack of a correlation between third-grade and thirteenth-grade television violence is "strange." If he had consulted our referenced paper in the Surgeon General's Report, he would have found that the partial data collected on our subjects in the eighth grade ($N = 64$) indicate that preference for television violence does correlate with itself over shorter time periods. The third–eighth correlation for "preference for viewing TV violence" was .16, while the eighth–thirteenth correlation was .21. The existence of such correlations refutes the claim that the mother and child's reports are "incompatible."

USE OF INVALID MEASURES

Several critics' difficulties in understanding some of the variables used in our study might also have been alleviated if they had consulted the referenced sources for validity and reliability data (Eron, Lefkowitz, & Walder, 1971). We must agree with Kay (1972) that a few of our variables did not turn out to be good measures, for example, the Walter-Zak aggression scale. However, any insinuation that this and other scales were unvalidated and unreferenced is not true.

MALE-FEMALE DIFFERENCES

Kay's (1972) best argument concerns the inadequacy of the theory he quotes to account for the differences between the results for boys and girls. However, the theory he quotes is *not* ours. He seems to have missed our assertion that "the frequency of occurrence of violently aggressive females shown on television is somewhat low [Eron et al., 1972, p. 261]," certainly lower than for males. Hence "the female viewer is less likely to encounter an aggressive model to imitate [pp. 261–262]." It is this lack of models, coupled with differential socialization, that mitigates the violence effect in girls.

Kay's (1972) two remaining criticisms, which are respectively irrelevant and untrue, seem to be *(a)* Himmelweit, Oppenheim, and Vince (1960) *said* "it is likely that the majority of children can enjoy them [violent television Westerns] without *fear* [italics added] by the time they are about 7"; *(b)* if Eron et al. admit that parents have any influence on how television violence affects the child (which, of course, we do), then this "robs television of any real causative role" (which, of course, is untrue).

THIRD VARIABLES

Perhaps no other criticism has been directed more frequently against our study than that a "third" variable causes both aggression and a preference for viewing of violent television. Becker's (1972) Comment focused on this point. His central thesis was that we considered only hypotheses of the nature "viewing television violence causes aggression" or "aggression causes viewing of television violence" and ignored the third possibility that some other variable caused both. We would be the first to admit that we have not covered the scope of all third-variable hypotheses but neither have we ignored all. The correlations between a preference for viewing violent television and aggression were shown, for example, to be mostly independent of a child's aggression level in the third grade, socioeconomic status, IQ, parental punishment, parental aggressiveness, parental aspirations for child, parental mobility orientations, and hours of television watched by the child.

Becker argued that the "$n-1$" hypotheses we reject are "small" compared to the "number" (and by "number" he must mean infinity) of hypotheses that exist. Since $(n-1)$ divided by infinity is zero, he would be right no matter how many we investigated (short of infinity); though exactly what this proves is unclear. If Becker would propose some real alternative theories, we would gladly consider them. Becker's one attempt at a "concrete" alternative included no suggestion as to what third variable might be relevant and is untestable as stated. We find Becker's concluding criticism that our "demonstration was not a demonstration at all" not a conclusion at all but a non sequitur. It could more aptly have been applied to his own wishful conclusion that in our data "the *positive* correlation . . . may well be masking . . . a *negative* causal relationship" between television violence and aggression.

CONCLUSION

In any longitudinal study, given the opportunity to repeat it, the investigators would probably change many elements of the design. We certainly wish we had done many things differently. Nevertheless, we do not find any of the criticisms leveled against the study, either alone or in concert, sufficient for us to change our conclusions. Adding up the evidence, we find no reason to change our conclusion that the most plausible hypothesis to explain our findings (and the other studies and experiments in this area) is that early exposure to television violence probably has a causal influence on aggression in males.

REFERENCES

Becker, G. Causal analysis in R-R studies: Television violence and aggression. *American Psychologist,* 1972, *27,* 967–968.

Chaffee, S. H. Television and adolescent aggressiveness. In G. A. Comstock & E. A. Rubinstein (Eds.), *Television and social behavior.* Vol. 3. *Television and adolescent aggressiveness.* Washington, D.C.: U.S. Government Printing Office, 1972.

Comstock, G. A., & Rubinstein, E. A. (Eds.). Summary and conclusions. Vol. 1. In *Television and social behavior.* Washington, D.C.: U.S. Government Printing Office, 1971.

Eron, L. D., Huesmann, L. R., Lefkowitz, M. M., & Walder, L. O. Does television violence cause aggression? *American Psychologist,* 1972, *27,* 253–263.

Eron, L. D., Walder, L. O., & Lefkowitz, M. M. *Learning of aggression in children.* Boston: Little, Brown, 1971.

Himmelweit, H. T., Oppenheim, A. N., & Vince, P. *Television and the child.* London: Oxford Univ. Press, 1960.

Kaplan, R. M. On television as a cause of aggression. *American Psychologist,* 1972, *27,* 968–969.

Kay, H. Weaknesses in the television-causes-aggression analysis by Eron et al. *American Psychologist,* 1972, *27,* 970–973.

Kenny, D. A. Threats to the internal validity of cross-logged panel inference as related to "Television violence and child aggression: A followup study." In G. A. Comstock & E. A. Rubinstein (Eds.), *Television and social behavior.* Vol. 3. *Television and adolescent aggressiveness.* Washington, D.C.: U.S. Government Printing Office, 1972.

Lefkowitz, M. M., Eron, L. D., Walder, L. O., & Huesmann, L. R. Television violence and child aggression: A followup study. In G. A. Comstock & E. A. Rubinstein (Eds.), *Television and social behavior.* Vol. 3. *Television and adolescent aggressiveness.* Washington, D.C.: U.S. Government Printing Office, 1972.

Neale, J. M. Comment on "Television violence and child aggression: A followup study." In G. A. Comstock & E. A. Rubinstein (Eds.), *Television and social behavior.* Vol. 3. *Television and adolescent aggressiveness.* Washington, D.C.: U.S. Government Printing Office, 1972.

Paisley, M. B. *Report on the Surgeon General's Committee.* Available from Institute for Communication Research. Stanford Univ., March 1972.

Pastore, J. O. (Chm.). Hearings on the Surgeon General's report by the Scientific Advisory Committee on Television and Social Behavior before the Subcomittee on Communications of the Committee on Commerce of the United States Senate (Serial No. 95–52). Washington, D.C.: U.S. Government Printing Office, 1972.

6. THE BATTERED CHILD:

Who Is Really to Blame? What Can Be Done?

One disturbing kind of human aggression is child abuse. Surprisingly perhaps, psychologists have not studied child abuse or child abusers very much. But in recent years considerable effort has been expended to bring this problem out into the open, to determine the extent of child abuse, and to try to find some explanations for it. The following two articles take rather different points of view with regard to child abuse. David Gil believes that it is the "social rather than the psychological characteristics of the parents" to which child abuse should be attributed. John Spinetta and David Rigler, on the other hand, emphasize the very psychological characteristics of the child-abusing parent that Gil plays down. Which article do you feel makes the better case? Or are both Gil and Spinetta and Rigler correct, but simply pointing to different aspects of a complex problem involving both sociological and psychological causes? What are the practical implications of these two points of view? What do you think of Gil's comment that there may be some children who are more likely than "normal" children to provoke abusive attacks against themselves? How could one test such a hypothesis?

In survey data such as Gil reports, how serious do you think is the possible reporting bias that Gil mentions? Are middle-class child abusers more or less likely to get caught than lower-class abusers? Why? How could one find out? (It is, incidentally, much easier to ask these questions than to devise satisfactory answers, but trying to devise answers may give you a feel for what it would be like to be a researcher in this area.)

Spinetta and Rigler suggest that the best predictor of whether a parent will be a child abuser is whether or not he or she was abused as a child. Assuming that this is true, for purposes of argument, how would this mesh with the causal factors that Gil cites for child abuse?

Spinetta and Rigler ask a key question: "Why is it that most deprived families do not engage in child abuse, though subject to the same economic and social stresses as those families who do abuse their children?" Granting that most human behavior has many contributing causes, what is Spinetta and Rigler's main point about the causes of child abuse? Can you think of possible means of identifying and preventing potential child abuse?

PHYSICAL ABUSE OF CHILDREN: FINDINGS AND IMPLICATIONS OF A NATIONWIDE SURVEY

David G. Gil, Florence Heller Graduate School for Advanced Studies in Social Welfare, Brandeis University

One of the basic obstacles to the development of effective countermeasures against accidental injury is the fact that the intensity of public concern over a particular type of injury-producing episode bears little relationship to its prevalence or to the seriousness of its consequences. An aircraft accident that takes 40 lives receives national attention through the mass media, whereas the fact that 150 persons died on the highways on the same day (and on every subsequent day) goes virtually unnoticed. The entrapment of a handful of children in discarded refrigerators has produced major changes in federal, state, and local laws; the death and injury of fifty times that number from accidental gunshot wounds has failed to produce even minimally effective legislation for the regulation of firearms. The "box office" appeal of various types of accidents would make an interesting study; certainly in the absence of some knowledge of this phenomenon the cost-effectiveness principle is almost impossible to apply to accident countermeasures.

The following paper deals very productively with this problem. For a number of years the "abused" or "battered" child has elicited very strong concern on the part of professionals in law, medicine, social work, and child care. And one consequence of this concern has been the establishment of legislative machinery and a reporting system. Good epidemiological research reveals, however, that child abuse, despite the intense response that it has aroused, has, in fact, relatively low prevalence and that, by implication, the funds and manpower that it now absorbs more appropriately be devoted to a more significant cause of

Gil, David G. Physical abuse of children: Findings and implications of a nationwide survey. *Pediatrics*, 1969, *44*, 857–864. Reprinted with permission of the publisher.

childhood injury. Unfortunately, legislative and administrative routines, once established, tend to perpetuate themselves. It will be interesting to note whether, in the light of the epidemiological findings, the reporting requirements will be withdrawn.

Another major contribution of this paper is its attribution of child abuse to the social rather than the psychological characteristics of the parents. Although the past decade has witnessed an increasing concern with poverty and the poor, virtually no attention has been devoted to the differential vulnerability to accidental injury of children in various socio-economic levels and subcultural groups. Our increased understanding of cultural deprivation and of lower-class life style gives us ample material for speculation about this differential, but such speculation is hazardous, and systematic empirical research must be undertaken.

Children in our own society and in many others have always been subjected to a wide range of physical and nonphysical abuse by parents and other caretakers, including teachers and child-care personnel and not infrequently by society as a whole.[1] Abusive treatment of children seems to be inherent in the basic inequality of physical make-up and social status between adults and children and in culturally determined permissive or even encouraging attitudes toward the use of physical force as a legitimate means for rearing and socializing the young.

In the course of centuries, progress has been made in protecting the interests and well-being of children in comparison with earlier periods when parents tended to wield absolute power over their offspring's life and death and when children were frequently abandoned to die of exposure, legally bartered and sold, mutilated to enhance their pity-inciting appeal as beggars, or thrashed by schoolmasters with ferrules, rods, and the cat-o'-nine tails.[2] Despite considerable social and legal progress in the protection of children, the problem of their physical abuse continues to cause serious concern in present-day American society. The extent of this concern is reflected in the fact that since 1940 several hundred professional articles and books concerning this phenomenon were published by roentgenologists, pediatricians, psychiatrists, educators, social workers, social and behavioral scientists, and lawyers.[3] Numerous papers on this subject have been presented at professional conferences of social workers and physicians in recent years, and the mass media have provided ample coverage for this phenomenon.

Professional and public interest in physical abuse of children has been stimulated by observations of roentgenologists of cases of unexplained multiple fractures of the long bones in young children found in conjunction with subdural hematomas.[4] Subsequent intensive clinical studies of these cases by social workers, pediatricians, and psychiatrists in children's hospitals, clinics, and child protective agencies in many communities throughout the country led to the suspicion and eventual confirmation that these unexplained injuries of children were often inflicted by their own parents and caretakers.[5–13] As a result of these and many other studies, physical abuse of children came to be recognized as a fairly widespread phenomenon which often resulted in serious, irreversible damage to the physical well-being and emotional development of children and which at times was even the immediate cause of their death.

The types of injuries inflicted upon children were found to range from minor, superficial bruises and cuts through burns, scaldings, fractures, and internal injuries, to intentional starvation, dismemberment, and severe injuries to the brain and central nervous system. The circumstances under which the injuries were inflicted were equally varied and ranged from simple disciplinary measures through uncontrollable angry outbursts, often under the influence of alcohol, to premeditated murderous attacks. As for the underlying causes of the phenomenon, many investigators concluded that physical abuse of children was an expression of severe personality disorders on the part of the perpetrators who attacked the children in their care. Many students of the phenomenon also noted that severe pathology of family relationships as well as environmental strains and stresses such as those related to poverty were significantly associated with incidents of child abuse. Finally, some investigators also noted that some children, because of unusual congenital or acquired characteristics, may occasionally be more likely to provoke abusive attacks against themselves than other, more "normal" children.[14]

The growing awareness of and the increasing interest in the phenomenon of child abuse on the part of physicians, educators, social workers, and lawyers, as well as of the public at large, led during the 1960s to the enactment by all the states of laws requiring or recommending to medical personnel and others to report incidents of suspected physical abuse of children to appropriate local and state authorities.[15, 16] The swift passage of these laws throughout the United States, in spite of controversy concerning details, was the result of an intensive promotional effort by the U.S. Children's Bureau and many national, state, and local professional and service organizations. Dean Monrad Paulsen of the University of Virginia Law School in referring to child abuse legislation commented that "few legislative proposals in the history of the United States have been so widely adopted in so little time."[17]

A major objective of reporting legislation is to improve mechanisms for case finding and to assure protective services for the abused child, his siblings, and his parents. A secondary purpose is to obtain a better understanding of the extent and nature of the phenomenon than was possible when only a few selected cases came to the notice of health, education, welfare, and law-enforcement authorities.

The provisions of reporting legislation vary from state to state, and physicians and hospital administrators should, therefore, familiarize themselves with legislation in effect in their own communities. Reporting is mandatory in all states except Alaska, Missouri, New Mexico, North Carolina, Texas, and Washington, where it is left to the discretion of those responsible for reporting. However, all states grant immunity from civil and criminal liability to persons making reports of abuse cases in good faith. The laws differ in the following respects: (1) the age of the child up to which injuries are reportable, (2) the conditions which are reportable, (3) the professional groups that are required to make reports, (4) the authorities on the local and state level to whom reports are to be made, (5) the rights and responsibilities of the persons making the report, (6) the responsibilities of the authorities receiving the reports, (7) the establishment of central registries for the state, and (8) the penalties for failing to report in accordance with the law. The differences between the various state laws concerning the foregoing items are described and tabulated for easy reference in the already cited publications of the U.S. Children's Bureau.[15, 16]

It has been mentioned that a secondary purpose of reporting legislation is to provide a broad basis for the study of the reported phenomenon. Prior to the enactment of reporting legislation it was possible to study relatively small local samples of abused children in hospitals, clinics, and child protective agencies. Once all the states had enacted reporting legislation it became feasible to design a nationwide epidemiologic study of all legally reported incidents of child abuse. Such a study was launched in 1965 by Brandeis University in cooperation with the U.S. Children's Bureau under the direction of this writer.[18, 19] The purpose of the study was to obtain systematic information on the number of legally reported incidents of child abuse throughout the United States, the distribution patterns of these incidents, the characteristics of the children, families, and perpetrators involved in the incidents, the circumstances surrounding the incidents, and the measures taken by health, welfare, and law-enforcement authorities in dealing with the reported incidents. All cases reported throughout 1967 were to be studied, and all cases reported during that year in 38 representative sample communities were to be subjected to a more comprehensive investigation and analysis.

Before examining some of the findings of the nationwide survey, it should be noted that legally reported incidents may constitute only part of the total universe of child abuse incidents, the real size and characteristics of which are likely to remain unknown. Since abuse incidents tend to occur in the privacy of a family's home, not all of them do come to the attention of individuals or institutions who are required to report, and not all incidents that are known to such persons and institutions are actually reported. It is possible also that the selection of incidents which are eventually reported is subject to systematic bias. It is known, for instance, that many physicians in private practice are less ready than physicians in public hospitals to report incidents that come to their attention.[20] Consequently, incidents from middle- and upper-class families may be under-reported to a greater extent than incidents from economically deprived families. Such factors as differences in administrative procedures and their effectiveness may also affect compliance with reporting requirements and reporting rates. These limitations of the data basis for the survey must be kept in mind in reviewing the following findings.

During 1967 a total of 5,993 physically abused children was reported through local channels. The geographic distribution of these reported incidents corresponded approximately to the population distribution among the states. Reporting rates remained fairly stable throughout the year.

Slightly more than half the children were boys. Their ages were as follows: about one-quarter, under 2 years of age; one-quarter, between 2 and 6 years; one-quarter, between 6 and 10 years; and one-quarter, 10 years or older. Two-thirds of all the children were white, and about one-third were non-white. However, in the metropolitan areas less than 40% of the children were white.

Nearly 30% of the children displayed noticeable deviations in social and behavioral functioning during the year preceding the abuse incident. Among the school-age children, 79% were in grades appropriate for their age; 13% were in grades below their age level or in classes for retarded children; and about 3% had never attended school.

Approximately 60% of the children had been abused prior to the incident reported in 1967. Nearly 30% of the children lived in families without a father or father substitute, and about 20% had a stepfather in the home. Only 46% lived with their own father, whereas 87% lived with their own mother. Over 10% of the children's mothers were single; nearly 20% were separated, divorced, or widowed; and about 70% were living with a spouse.

The educational level and the occupational status of the parents were very low. Only 52% of the fathers worked throughout the year. At the time of the incident about 12% of the fathers were unemployed, a rate about three times as high as the nationwide unemployment rate. The income of the families was very low. Nearly 38% earned less than $3,500 per year, and about 52% earned less than $4,500. About 45% earned between $4,500 and $10,000 and less than 5% earned over $10,000. Nearly 40% of the families were receiving Aid for Dependent Children or other public assistance at the time of the abusive incident, and nearly 60% had received such assistance during or prior to the study year.

The number of children in the families tended to be higher than in the total population. Nearly 40% of the families had four or more children compared to 20% of families with children under 18 in the United States. The families revealed a high mobility rate. Nearly 50% had lived 1 year or less in the home they occupied at the time of the abuse incident.

Over 40% of the mothers and over 45% of the fathers were rated deviant in social and behavioral functioning, and over 15% of the fathers were known to have a criminal record. At least 14% of the mothers and 7% of the fathers were known to have been abused during their childhood, and 32% of mothers and 40% of fathers were known to have abused children in the past.

Nearly 48% of the children were abused by their mothers, and over 39% by their fathers. However, since nearly 30% of the children lived in fatherless homes, the involvement rate in abuse of fathers or father substitutes who were living in the children's homes was actually higher than that of mothers. In over 17% the abuse was committed by a male caretaker while the mother was temporarily absent from her home.

The injuries of the children were rated "not serious" in over 53% of the incidents. In 37% they were rated serious without permanent damage. Nearly 5% of the injuries were rated serious with permanent damage, and under 4% were fatal. It is known, however, that the fatality rate is under-reported because fatalities are not specifically mentioned as reportable in all but three states. Nearly 60% of the children did not require hospitalization following the incident, and 25% did not require any medical treatment. Over 21% required hospitalization beyond 1 week. Nearly 14% were considered "battered children" in accordance with the conditions described by Dr. Kempe and his colleagues (Kempe et al., 1962).

In over 21% of the incidents the perpetrators themselves initiated help for the children subsequent to the incident. In 36%, other members of the victim's household initiated help. Schools initiated help in over 16% of the incidents, and in over 30% neighbors, visiting relatives, and others initiated help.

Over 36% of the abused children were removed from their families subsequent to the abuse, and in over 15% of the incidents siblings of the abused child were also removed. Courts were involved in 46% of the incidents; the police in 53%; and social agencies in 87%. Over 13% of the perpetrators were convicted by courts, and over 7% were jailed.

As to the circumstances surrounding the abuse incidents reported in the survey, it was found that 63% developed out of disciplinary action taken by a parent. In 34% it was found that the child was psychologically resented and rejected by the abusive parent. In nearly 25% the child was considered atypical in his behavior. In over 11% the abuse developed out of a quarrel between the parents. In 31% the perpetrator considered himself to be an authoritarian person; in over 46% the perpetrator was viewed by others as suffering marked emotional deviations, and in nearly 8% the abuse involved sadistic components. Abuse coincided with neglect in nearly 34%, and in 13% the perpetrator was intoxicated with alcohol at the time of the abuse. In 59%, perpetrators were subject to mounting stress as due to life circumstances.

It should be noted that the percentages in the foregoing crude classification of circumstances of child abuse incidents do not add up to 100% since many incidents fall into more than one class of the typology.

The findings of the nationwide survey reported above and of a preceding nationwide survey of public knowledge, attitudes, and opinions about physical child abuse in the United States suggest the following conclusions.[21]

The physical abuse of children can be conceptualized schematically as a multidimensional phenomenon rather than a uniform phenomenon with one set of causal factors. Its basic level upon which all other factors are superimposed is the general culturally permitted use of a measure of physical force in caretaker-child interaction and the related absence of clear-cut legal prohibitions and sanctions against this particular form of interpersonal violence. The next level is determined by specific child-rearing traditions and practices of different social classes and ethnic and nationality groups, and the different attitudes of these groups toward physical force as an acceptable measure for the achievement of the child-rearing objectives. A third level is determined by environmental chance circumstances which may transform an "acceptable" disciplinary measure into an "unacceptable" outcome. A fourth level is a broad range of environmental stress factors which may weaken or even paralyze temporarily a person's psychological mechanisms of self-control or impulse control. In this way such environmental stress factors may be indirectly conducive to the uninhibited discharge of aggressive and destructive impulse and desires toward children, who are perceived, for real or imaginary reasons, to be the causes of stress. The final level is various forms of physical, social, intellectual, and emotional deviance and pathology of caretakers and/or children in their care, as well as of entire family units to which they belong.

Substantive findings from the nationwide surveys provide support for the foregoing conceptual scheme. The culturally determined attitude permitting acts of physical violence against children and the tolerant attitude toward the perpetrators of such acts were brought out in the opinions expressed by a majority of the respondents to the public opinion survey. Moreover, a vast majority of the nearly 6,000 abusive incidents reported through legal channels during 1967 were the result of more or less "acceptable" disciplinary measures taken by caretakers in response to actual or perceived misconduct of children in their care and did not result in serious injury. The data also reveal that a large majority of the families involved in these reported abuse incidents belonged to socio-economically deprived segments of the population. Moreover, families from ethnic minority groups were over-represented in the study group. Environmental chance factors were often found to have been decisive in transforming an otherwise "acceptable" disciplinary measure into an incident of "physical abuse" resulting in relatively severe injury, and a vast array of real environmental stress situations were a precipitating element in a large proportion of the incidents. Finally, a higher than "normal" proportion of the abused children, their abusers, and their families revealed a wide range of deviance and pathology in areas of physical, social, intellectual, and emotional functioning.

Some additional comments seem indicated concerning the substantive findings of the nationwide surveys. Although no claim can be made that the nationwide survey has uncovered the true incidence rate of physical abuse of children, it seems clear, nevertheless, that the magnitude of the phenomenon has been exaggerated. Six thousand reported cases of physical abuse per year in a nation of 200 million, in spite of under-reporting, do not constitute a major social problem, at least in relative terms, tragic as every single incident may be.

To move from quantitative to qualitative considerations, it may be suggested that reported cases are likely to be the more serious portion of the phenomenon, since the degree of severity of the injury may be an important criterion in the chain of complicated decisions which affect the selection of cases entering official reporting channels. If then, the 6,000 reported cases represent as a group the more severe segment of the physical abuse spectrum, it follows that in qualitative terms physical abuse is by and large not very serious as reflected by the data on the extent and types of injury suffered by the children in the study cohort. The classical "battered child syndrome" is a relatively infrequent occurrence. Even if allowance is made for the gross under-reporting of fatalities, physical abuse cannot be considered a major killer and maimer of children.

It must also be stressed from an epidemiologic perspective that the phenomenon was found to be concentrated among the poor; it seems to be one aspect of the style of life associated with the poverty syndrome. Although it is certainly valid to argue, on the basis of much evidence, that the poor are more likely to be reported for anything they do or fail to do and that their over-representation among the reported cases of child abuse may be in part a function of this kind of reporting bias, it must not be overlooked, nevertheless, that life in poverty generates many additional stressful experiences which, as pointed out above, are likely to become precipitating factors of child abuse. The poor are subject to the same psychological conditions which may cause violent behavior toward children as are the nonpoor; but, in addition to this, they are subject to the special environmental stresses and strains associated with socioeconomic deprivation. Moreover, they have fewer alternatives and escapes than the nonpoor for dealing with aggressive impulses toward their children. Finally, there is an additional factor, the tendency toward more direct, less inhibited expression and discharge of aggressive impulses, a tendency learned apparently through lower-class socialization, which differs in this respect from middle-class socialization.

Of considerable interest are also findings concerning the troubled past history of many abused children, their parents, and their abusers—the relatively high rates of deviance and pathology in areas of biopsychosocial functioning which was frequently noted during the period preceding the actual abusive incident and the high rate of deviance in family structure which is reflected in a high proportion of female-headed households and households in which the biological father is absent.

Measures aimed at the prevention or the gradual reduction of the incidence and prevalence of specified social phenomena can achieve their purpose when they are designed and executed in a manner which assures intervention on the causal level. Applying this model of preventive intervention to the phenomenon of physical abuse of children and proceeding on an as yet untested conceptualization of the etiology of the phenomenon which was presented above, the following approaches can be suggested.

Since the cultural attitude permitting the use of physical force in child rearing seems to constitute the common core of all physical abuse of children in American society, systematic educational efforts aimed at (a) gradually changing this particular aspect of the prevailing child-rearing philosophy, and (b) developing clear-cut cultural prohibitions and legal sanctions against the use of physical force as a means for rearing children are likely to produce the strongest possible reduction in the incidence and prevalence of physical abuse of children.

The multiple links between poverty and physical abuse of children suggest that one important route toward reducing the incidence and prevalence of child abuse is the elimination of poverty from the midst of America's affluent society and the assurance of economic security as a right to all individuals and families by means of "mother's wages,"[22] "children's allowances,"[23] a "negative income tax,"[23] or some other mechanism. No doubt this is only a partial answer to the complex issue of preventing violence toward children, but perhaps a very important part of the total answer, and certainly that part without which other preventive efforts may be utterly futile.

Deviance and pathology in the physical, social, intellectual, and emotional functioning of individuals and of family units has been suggested as another set of forces which may contribute to the incidence and prevalence of physical abuse of children. Certain measures aimed at the prevention and alleviation of these conditions and at the strengthening of individual and family functioning are mentioned here. Their availability in every community seems desirable in efforts to reduce the incidence of physical abuse of children and also for helping individuals and families after abuse has occurred.

The availability of comprehensive family planning programs and liberalized legislation concerning medical abortions is likely to reduce considerably the number of unwanted children, who are known to be frequently victims of severe physical abuse and even infanticide.

Family-life education and counseling programs for adolescents and adults in preparation for and after marriage should be offered within the public school system of communities in order to avoid their becoming identified in the public mind with deviance-focused agencies.

A comprehensive high-quality, neighborhood-based, national health service, financed through the social security system or from general tax revenue, should be geared not only to the treatment of acute and chronic illness but also to the promotion and assurance of maximum feasible physical and mental health for every citizen.

A range of social services should be geared to the reduction of environmental stresses on family life and especially on mothers who carry major responsibility for the child-rearing function. No mother should be expected to care for her children around the clock, 365 days a year. Substitute-care mechanisms should be routinely available to offer mothers opportunities for carefree rest and recreation.

Finally, every community needs a system of social services geared to assisting families and children who cannot live together because of severe relationship and/or reality problems. Physically abused children belong frequently to this category, and in such situations the welfare of the child and the family may require temporary or permanent separation.

The administration of all such services must be based on a constructive and therapeutic rather than a punitive philosophy if they are to serve the ultimate objective—the reduction of the general level of violence and the raising of the general level of human well-being throughout our entire society.

REFERENCES

1. Bossard, J. H. S., & Boll, E. S. *The sociology of child development* (4th ed.). New York: Harper and Brothers, 1966.
2. Radbill, S. X. A history of child abuse and infanticide. In R. E. Helfer & C. H. Kempe (eds.), *The Battered Child.* Chicago: Univ. of Chicago Press, 1968.
3. U.S. Children's Bureau, Clearinghouse for Research in Child Life. *Bibliography on the battered child.* Washington, D.C.: U.S. Government Printing Office, 1966.
4. Caffey, Jr. Multiple fractures in the long bones of infants suffering from chronic hematoma. *American Journal of Roentgenology, Radium Therapy, and Nuclear Medicine,* 1946, *56,* 163.
5. Elmer, E. Abused young children seen in hospitals. *Social Work,* 1960, *5,* 98.
6. Boardman, H. E. A project to rescue children from inflicted injuries. *Social Work,* 1962, *7,* 43.
7. Kempe, C. H., Silverman, F. N., Steele, B. F., Droegemueller, W., & Silver, H. K. The battered-child syndrome. *Journal of the American Medical Association,* 1962, *181,* 17.
8. Kaufman, I. Psychiatric implications of physical abuse of children. In V. De Francis (Ed.), *Protecting the battered child.* Denver: American Humane Assoc., 1962.
9. Bryant, H. D., Billingsley, A., Kerry, G. A., Leefman, W. V., Merril, E. J., Senecal, G. R., & Walsh, B. G. Physical abuse of children—An agency study. *Child Welfare,* March 1963, pp. 125–130.
10. Morris, M. G., & Gould, R. W. Role reversal: A concept in dealing with the neglected/battered-child syndrome. In *The neglected/battered-child syndrome.* New York: Child Welfare League of America, 1963.
11. DeFrancis, V. *Child abuse—Preview of a nationwide survey.* Denver: American Humane Assoc., 1963.
12. Young, L. R. *Wednesday's children.* New York: McGraw-Hill, 1964.
13. Galdston, R. Observations on children who have been physically abused and their parents. *American Journal of Psychiatry,* 1965, *122,* 440.
14. Milowe, I. D., & Lonnie, R. S. The child's role in the battered child child syndrome. *Abstracts of the Society for Pediatric Research,* 1964, 1079.
15. U.S. Children's Bureau. *The abused child: Principles and suggested language on reporting the physically abused child.* Washington, D.C.: U.S. Government Printing Office, 1962.
16. U.S. Children's Bureau. *The child abuse reporting laws—A tabular view.* Washington, D.C.: U.S. Government Printing Office, 1966.
17. Paulsen, M. G. Legal protection against child abuse. *Children,* 1966, *13,* 42.
18. Gil, D. G. First steps in a nationwide study of child abuse. In A. M. Pins (Ed.), *Social work practice 1966.* New York: Columbia Univ. Press, 1966.
19. Gil, D. G. *Physical abuse of children—One manifestation of violence in American society* (a report to the Task Force on Individual Acts of Violence of the National Commission on the Causes and Prevention of Violence). Waltham, Mass.: Brandeis Univ., 1968.

20. Silver, L. B., Barton, W., & Dublin, C. C. Child abuse laws—Are they enough? *Journal of the American Medical Association*, 1967, *199*, 101.

21. Gil, D. G., & Noble, J. H. *Public knowledge, attitudes, and opinions about physical child abuse in the United States* (Papers in Social Welfare, No. 14). Waltham, Mass.: Brandeis Univ., 1967.

22. Gil, D. G. Mothers' wages—One way to attack poverty. *Children*, 1968, *15*, 229.

23. Schorr, A. L. *Poor kids*. New York: Basic Books, 1966.

THE CHILD-ABUSING PARENT: A PSYCHOLOGICAL REVIEW

John J. Spinetta, University of Southern California

David Rigler, Childrens Hospital of Los Angeles

Review of professional opinions in the literature reveals that (a) *the abusing parent was himself raised with some degree of deprivation;* (b) *the abusing parent brings to his role as parent mistaken notions of child rearing;* (c) *there is present in the parent a general defect in character structure allowing aggressive impulses to be expressed too freely; and* (d) *while socioeconomic factors might sometimes place added stresses on basic personality weakness, these stresses are not of themselves sufficient or necessary causes of abuse. A critique is made of a recent demographic survey in light of the foregoing data.*

Why does a parent physically abuse his or her own child? During the past 10 years, many attempts have been made to answer this question. An extensive literature has emerged on the medical and legal aspects of the problem of child abuse since the publication of an article by Kempe, Silverman, Steele, Droegemueller, and Silver (1962) and the pursuit of child-protective laws in California by Boardman (1962, 1963). Sociologists and social workers have contributed their share of insights, and a few psychiatrists have published their findings, but surprisingly little attention has been devoted to the problem of child abuse by the psychologist. One seeks with little success for well-designed studies of personality characteristics of abusing parents. What appears is a literature composed of professional opinions on the subject.

The authors wish to thank James Kent of the Division of Psychiatry, Childrens Hospital of Los Angeles, for his critical reading of earlier versions and for his helpful suggestions and support during the research. Request for reprints should be sent to John J. Spinetta or David Rigler, who are now at Division of Psychiatry, Childrens Hospital of Los Angeles, 4650 Sunset Boulevard, Los Angeles, California 90054.

Spinetta, John J., and Rigler, David. The child-abusing parent: A psychological review. *Psychological Bulletin*, 1972, *77*, 296–304.

The aim of this review is to bring together professional opinions of this decade on the psychological characteristics of the abusing parent in order to determine from the most commonly held opinions what generalizations can be induced and thus to lay the groundwork for systematic testing of hypotheses.

DEFINITION

What is child abuse? Kempe et al. (1962) limited their study to children who had received serious physical injury, in circumstances which indicated that the injury was caused willfully rather than by accident. They coined the term "battered child" to encompass their definition. Zalba (1966), after a brief review of definitions, likewise addressed himself primarily to those cases in which physical injury was willfully inflicted on a child by a parent or parent substitute.

Because of the difficulty of pinpointing what is emotional or psychological or social neglect and abuse, and because of the extent of the literature on physical abuse alone, this review, following Kempe's and Zalba's lead, limits the term "child abuse" to the concept of physical injury to the child, willfully inflicted. The review omits studies of parents who neglect their children—emotionally, socially, or psychologically—and adults who sexually molest them.

MEDICAL AND LEGAL HISTORY

Literature on the medical and legal aspects of the problem of child abuse is extensive. The edited volume of Helfer and Kempe (1968) contains a general overview, as do the articles by Paulson and Blake (1967), Silver (1968), and Zalba (1966). Legal aspects are delineated in De Francis (1970), McCoid (1965), and the various articles by Paulsen (1966a, 1966b, 1967, 1968a, 1968b). Simons and Downs (1968) gave an overview of patterns, problems, and accomplishments of the child-abuse reporting laws. A thorough bibliography on child abuse was published by the United States Department of Health, Education and Welfare (1969).

This review is not concerned with the medical and legal aspects of the problem and refers only to those articles that gave more than a passing mention to the psychological and social determinants of parental abuse of children.

REVIEW OF THE LITERATURE

Most of the studies of child abuse are subject to the same general criticism. First, the studies that set out to test specific hypotheses are few. Many start and end as broad studies with relatively untested commonsense assumptions. Second, in most studies in this area the researchers used samples easily available from ready-at-hand local populations, and thus the samples were not truly representative. We shall have to rely on the convergence of conclusions from various types of sampling to establish generalizations. Third, practically all of the research in child abuse is ex post facto. What is left unanswered and still to be tested is whether one can determine prior to the onset of abuse which parents are most likely to abuse their children or whether high-risk groups can only be defined after at least one incident of abuse has occurred.

In spite of these criticisms, the studies of child abuse do give general data that can furnish hypotheses for more rigorous research design and for a more differentiated approach to the question of why parents abuse their children.

Demographic Characteristics

In an attempt to discover whether or not various social or economic stresses make abuse more likely, many of the studies have described demographic characteristics of abusing families. Kempe et al. (1962) found in the abusing families a high incidence of divorce, separation, and unstable marriages, as well as of minor criminal offenses. The children who were abused were very young, often under one year of age. In many of the families, children were born in very close succession. Often one child would be singled out for injury, the child that was the victim of an unwanted pregnancy.

Various other studies enter figures from their own samples, generally repeating Kempe's findings (Birrell & Birrell, 1968; Cameron, Johnson, & Camps, 1966; Ebbin, Gallub, Stein, & Wilson, 1969; Elmer & Gregg, 1967; Gregg & Elmer, 1969; Helfer & Pollock, 1967; Johnson & Morse, 1968; Nurse, 1964; Schloesser, 1964; Skinner & Castle, 1969).

Elmer (1967) and Young (1964) add to Kempe's findings the factors of social and economic stress, lack of family roots in the community, lack of immediate support from extended families, social isolation, high mobility, and unemployment.

While pointing to the role that economic and social stresses play in bringing out underlying personality weaknesses, the majority of the foregoing authors caution that economic and social stresses alone are neither sufficient nor necessary causes for child abuse. They point out that although in the socially and economically deprived segments of the population there is generally a higher degree of the kinds of stress factors found in abusing families, the great majority of deprived families do not abuse their children. Why is it that most deprived families do not engage in child abuse, though subject to the same economic and social stresses as those families who do abuse their children?

A study that sheds light on the fact that social and economic factors have been overstressed as etiological factors in cases of child abuse is that of Steele and Pollock (1968), whose sample of abusers consisted mainly of middle-class and upper-middle-class families. Though social and economic difficulties may have added stress to the lives of the parents, Steele and Pollock considered these stresses as only incidental intensifiers of personality-rooted etiological factors.

Simons, Downs, Hurster, and Archer (1966) conducted a thorough study delineating abusing families as multiproblem families in which, not the socioeconomic factors alone, but the interplay of mental, physical, and emotional stresses underlay the abuse.

Allowing that child abuse in many cases may well be the expression of family stress, Adelson (1961), Allen, Ten Bensel, and Raile (1969), Fontana (1968), Holter and Friedman (1968), and Kempe et al. (1962) considered psychological factors as of prime importance in the etiology of child abuse. There is a defect in character structure which, in the presence of added stresses, gives way to uncontrolled physical expression.

Paulson and Blake (1969) referred to the deceptiveness of upper- and middle-class abusers and cautioned against viewing abuse and neglect as completely a function of educationally, occupationally, economically, or socially disadvantaged parents or as due to physical or health impoverishment within a family.

If it is true that the majority of parents in the socially and economically deprived segments of the population do not batter their children while some well-to-do parents engage in child abuse, then one must look for the causes of child abuse beyond socioeconomic stresses. One of the factors to which one may look is parental history.

Parental History

One basic factor in the etiology of child abuse draws unanimity: Abusing parents were themselves abused or neglected, physically or emotionally, as children. Steele and Pollock (1968) have shown a history of parents having been raised in the same style that they have recreated in the pattern of rearing their own children. As infants and children, all of the parents in the groups were deprived both of basic mothering and of the deep sense of being cared for and cared about from the beginning of their lives.

Fontana (1968) also viewed the parents as emotionally crippled because of unfortunate circumstances in their own childhood. The parents reacted to their children in keeping with their own personal experiential history of loneliness, lack of protection, and lack of love. Many authors corroborated the hypotheses of Steele and Pollock and of Fontana.

In a study surveying 32 men and 7 women imprisoned for cruelty to their children, Gibbins and Walker (1956) concluded that it was rejection, indifference, and hostility in their own childhood that produced the cruel parents.

Ten years later, Tuteur and Glotzer (1966) studied 10 mothers who were hospitalized for murdering their children and found that all had grown up in an emotionally cold and often overtly rejecting family environment in which parental figures were either absent or offered little opportunity for wholesome identification when present.

Komisaruk (1966) found as the most striking statistic in his study of abusing families the emotional loss of a significant parental figure in the early life of the abusive parent.

Perhaps the most systematic and well-controlled study in the area of child abuse, that of Melnick and Hurley (1969), compared two small, socioeconomically and racially matched groups on 18 personality variables. Melnick and Hurley found, among other things, a probable history of emotional deprivation in the mothers' own upbringing.

Further support for the hypothesis that the abusing parent was once an abused or neglected child is found in Bleiberg (1965), Blue (1965), Corbett (1964), Curtis (1963), Easson and Steinhilber (1961), Fairburn and Hunt (1964), Fleming (1967), Green (1965), Harper (1963), Kempe et al. (1962), McHenry, Girdany, and Elmer (1963), Morris, Gould, and Matthews (1964), Nurse (1964), Paulson and Blake (1969), Silver, Dublin, and Lourie (1969b), and Wasserman (1967).

In a summary statement, Gluckman (1968), repeating the findings of earlier observers, set up a 10-point differential diagnosis category. His main point, and the point of this section of the review, is that the child is the father of the man. The capacity to love is not inherent; it must be taught to the child. Character development depends on love, tolerance, and example. Many abusing parents were raised without this love and tolerance.

Parental Attitudes toward Child Rearing

In addition to concurring on the fact that many abusing parents were themselves raised with some degree of abuse or neglect, the authors agreed that the abusing parents share common misunderstandings with regard to the nature of child rearing and look to the child for satisfaction of their own parental emotional needs.

Steele and Pollock (1968) found that the parents in their study group expected and demanded a great deal from their infants and children and did so prematurely. The parents dealt with their children as if older than they really were. The parents felt insecure and unsure of being loved and looked to their children as sources of reassurance, comfort, and loving response, as if the children were adults capable of providing grown-up comfort and love.

Melnick and Hurley (1969) in their well-controlled study of personality variables also found in the mothers severely frustrated dependency needs and an inability to empathize with their children.

Galdston (1965) concurred that abusing parents treated their children as adults, and he added that the parents were incapable of understanding the particular stages of development of their children.

Bain (1963), Gregg (1968), Helfer and Pollock (1967), Hiller (1969), Johnson and Morse (1968), Korsch, Christian, Gozzi, and Carlson (1965), and Morris and Gould (1963) also reported that abusing parents have a high expectation and demand for the infant's or child's performance and a corresponding disregard for the infant's or child's own needs, limited abilities, and helplessness. Wasserman (1967) found that the parents not only considered punishment a proper disciplinary measure but strongly defended their right to use physical force.

In a 1969 study, Gregg and Elmer, comparing children accidentally injured with those abused, judged that the mother's ability to keep up the personal appearance of the child when well and her ability to provide medical care when the child was moderately ill sharply differentiated the abusive from the nonabusive mothers.

The authors seem to agree that abusing parents lack appropriate knowledge of child rearing and that their attitudes, expectations, and child-rearing techniques set them apart from nonabusive parents. The abusing parents implement culturally accepted norms for raising children with an exaggerated intensity and at an inappropriately early age.

Presence of Severe Personality Disorders

There has been an evolution in thinking regarding the presence of a frank psychosis in the abusing parent. Woolley and Evans (1955) and Miller (1959) posited a high incidence of neurotic or psychotic behavior as a strong etiological factor in child abuse. Cochrane (1965), Greengard (1964), Platou, Lennox, and Beasley (1964) and Simpson (1967, 1968) concurred. Adelson (1961) and Kaufman (1962) considered only the most violent and abusive parents as having schizophrenic personalities. Kempe et al. (1962), allowing that direct murder of children betrayed a frank psychosis on the part of the parent, found that most of the abusing parents, though lacking in impulse control, were not severely psychotic. By the end of the decade the literature seemed to support the view that only a few of the abusing parents showed severe psychotic tendencies (Fleming, 1967; Laupus, 1966; Steele & Pollock, 1968; Wasserman, 1967).

Motivational and Personality Variables: A Typology

A review of opinions on parental personality and motivational variables leads to a conglomerate picture. While the authors generally agree that there is a defect in the abusing parent's personality that allows aggressive impulses to be expressed too freely (Kempe et al., 1962; Steele & Pollock, 1968; Wasserman, 1967), disagreement comes in describing the source of the aggressive impulses.

Some authors claim that abuse is a final outburst at the end of a long period of tension (Nomura, 1966; Ten Have, 1965) or that abuse stems from an inability to face life's daily stresses (Heins, 1969). Some claim that abuse stems from deep feelings of inadequacy or from parental inability to fulfill the roles expected of parenthood (Cohen, Raphling, & Green, 1966; Court, 1969; Fontana, 1964; Johnson & Morse, 1968; Komisaruk, 1966; Silver, 1968; Steele & Pollock, 1968). Others described the parents as immature, self-centered, and impulse-ridden (Cochrane, 1965; Delaney, 1966; Jacobziner, 1964; Ten Bensel, 1963).

Some authors consider a role reversal between the spouses as a prime factor in the etiology of child abuse. A home in which the father is unemployed and the mother has taken over the financial responsibility of the family is considered a breeding ground for abuse (Galdston, 1965; Greengard, 1964; Nathan, 1965; Nurse, 1964).

Finally, there are those authors who considered low intelligence as a prime factor in the etiology of child abuse (Fisher, 1958; Simpson, 1967, 1968), although this point is disputed in the findings of Cameron et al. (1966), Holter and Friedman (1968), Kempe et al. (1962), and Ounsted (1968).

Is there a common motivational factor behind child abuse? Is there only one "type" of abusing parent? Realization that each of the above described characteristics was found to exist at least in some individual circumstances has led some authors to group together certain characteristics in clusters, and to evolve a psychodynamic within each cluster. The first major attempt at a typology was made by Merrill (1962). Because Merrill's typology is the most often quoted, it is summarized in some detail.

Merrill identified three distinct clusters of personality characteristics that he found to be true both of abusing mothers and fathers, and a fourth that he found true of the abusing fathers alone. The first group of parents seemed to Merrill to be beset with a continual and pervasive hostility and aggressiveness, sometimes focused, sometimes directed at the world in general. This was not a controlled anger and was continually with the parents, with the only stimulation needed for direct expression being normal daily difficulties. This angry feeling stemmed from conflicts within the parents and was often rooted in their early childhood experiences.

The second group Merrill identified by personality characteristics of rigidity, compulsiveness, lack of warmth, lack of reasonableness, and lack of pliability in thinking and in belief. These parents defended their right to act as they had in abusing their child. Mothers in this group had marked child-rejection attitudes, evidenced by their primary concern with their own pleasures, inability to feel love and protectiveness toward their children, and in feelings that the children were responsible for much of the trouble being experienced by themselves as parents. These fathers and mothers were extremely compulsive in their behavior, demanding excessive cleanliness of their children. Many of their parents had great difficulty in relaxing, in expressing themselves verbally, and in exhibiting warmth and friendliness.

Merrill's third group of parents showed strong feelings of passivity and dependence. Many of these parents were people who were unassuming, reticent about expressing their feelings and desires, and very unagressive. They were individuals who manifested strong needs to depend on others for decisions. These mothers and fathers often competed with their own children for the love and attention of their spouses. Generally depressed, moody, unresponsive, and unhappy, many of these parents showed considerable immaturity.

Merrill's fourth grouping or cluster of personality characteristics included a significant number of abusing fathers. These fathers were generally young, intelligent men with acquired skills who, because of some physical disability, were now fully or partially unable to support their families. In most of these situations, the mothers were working, and the fathers stayed at home, caring for the children. Their frustrations led to swift and severe punishment, to angry, rigid discipline.

Two further attempts at classification, Delsordo (1963) and Zalba (1967), with slight modifications, can be reduced to Merrill's categories.

The use of categories seems simple, unifying, and time saving. If further work can be done in refining the categories, validating them in field research, perhaps they or similar clusters shown to be empirically valid can be used as an aid in the determination of high-risk parents.

In this section we have seen a conglomerate picture of parental motivational and personality variables, with one author's attempt to cluster the characteristics into a workable unity. One basic fact of agreement emerges from the studies in this section. The authors feel that a general defect in character—from whatever source—is present in the abusing parent, allowing aggressive impulses to be expressed too freely. During times of additional stress and tension the impulses express themselves on the helpless child.

CRITIQUE OF A SURVEY

Of the studies surveying the demographic characteristics of families in which child abuse has occurred, the most extensive in scope was the national survey undertaken by Gil (1968a, 1968b, 1969).[1] In 1969, Gil reported that the phenomenon of child abuse was highly concentrated among the socioeconomically deprived segments of the population. Concluding that "physical abuse is by and large not very serious as reflected by the data on the extent and types of injury suffered by the children in the study cohort [p. 862]," Gil placed his intervention strategy in the general betterment of society. For Gil the cultural attitude permitting the use of physical force in child rearing is the common core of all physical abuse of children in American society. Since he found the socioeconomically deprived relying more heavily on physical force in rearing children, he recommended systematic educational efforts aimed at gradually changing this cultural attitude and the establishment of clear-cut cultural prohibitions against the use of physical force as a means of rearing children. He viewed this educational effort as likely to produce the strongest possible reduction in the incidence and prevalence of physical abuse of children.

For Gil, child abuse is ultimately the result of chance environmental factors. While admitting to various forms of physical, social, intellectual, and emotional deviance and pathology in caretakers and in the family units to which they belong, Gil stressed a global control of environmental factors as the solution to the problem of child abuse. He suggested: *(a)* the elimination of poverty from the midst of America's affluent society; *(b)* the availability in every community of resources aimed at the prevention and alleviation of deviance and pathology; *(c)* the availability of comprehensive family planning programs and liberalized legislation concerning medical abortions, to reduce the number of unwanted children; *(d)* family-life education and counseling programs for adolescents and adults in preparation for and after marriage, to be offered within the public school system; *(e)* a comprehensive, high-quality, neighborhood-based national health service, to promote and assure maximum feasible physical and mental health for every citizen; *(f)* a range of social services geared to the reduction of environmental stresses on family life; and *(g)* a community-based system of social services geared to assisting families and children who cannot live together because of severe relationship problems. Gil's ultimate objective is "the reduction of the general level of violence, and the raising of the general level of human well-being throughout our entire society [p. 863]."

While one must praise the efforts of the Gil study in data collection and the ultimate objective of reducing the general level of violence and raising the general level of human well-being in our entire society, one cannot help but feel that Gil did not address himself to the question of child abuse. If there really does exist as strong a link as Gil suggests between poverty and physical abuse of children, why is it that all poor parents do not batter their children, while some well-to-do parents engage in child abuse? Eliminating environmental stress factors and bettering the level of society at all stages may reduce a myriad of social ills and may even prove effective, indirectly, in reducing the amount of child abuse. But there still remains the problem, insoluble at the demographic level, of why some parents abuse their children, while others under the same stress factors do not.

Other authors throughout the decade have allowed for the types of services outlined by Gil, but less globally and in a manner less disregarding of parental personality factors. That raising the general educational and financial level of families that are socioeconomically deprived is of long-range value in the lessening of the prevalence of child abuse is generally agreed upon and finds support throughout the literature. However, most of the authors explicitly caution against considering abuse, as does Gil, as a function solely of educational, occupational, economic, or social stresses. This point is made by Adelson (1961), Allen et al. (1969), Elmer (1967), Fontana (1968), Helfer and Pollock (1967), Holter and Friedman (1968), Kempe (1968), Kempe et al. (1962), Paulson and Blake (1967), Silver et al. (1969a, 1969b), and Steele and Pollock (1968).

The great majority of the authors cited in this review have pointed to psychological factors within the parents themselves as of prime importance in the etiology of child abuse. They see abuse as stemming from a defect in character leading to a lack of inhibition in expressing frustration and other impulsive behavior. Socioeconomic factors sometimes place added stress on the basic weakness in personality structure, but these factors are not of themselves sufficient or necessary causes of abuse.

CONCLUSIONS

The purpose of this review has been to bring together the published professional opinions on the psychological characteristics of the abusing parent, in order to determine from the most commonly held opinions what generalizations can be induced and thus to lay the groundwork for more systematic testing of hypotheses.

The psychologist, both as a specialist in the functioning of the human as an individual, and as a scientist trained in research methodology, is in a unique position to test the hypotheses raised by professionals in the fields of medicine and social work, in the study of the personality characteristics of the abusing parent.

Certainly, one would hope that research can eventually develop criteria to distinguish those inadequate parents who, with professional help, can meet the needs of their children, from those who cannot. We need eventually to be able to identify the high-risk families prior to the onset of abuse, but should be satisfied for the time being if we can help determine after the fact of abuse which families must receive the most attention to assure the further safety of their child.

REFERENCES

Adelson, L. Slaughter of the innocents: A study of forty-six homicides in which the victims were children. *New England Journal of Medicine*, 1961, *264*, 1345–1349.

Allen, H. D., Ten Bensel, R. W., & Raile, R. B. The battered child syndrome. *Minnesota Medicine*, 1969, *52*, 155–156.

Bain, K. Commentary: The physically abused child. *Pediatrics*, 1963, *31*, 895–898.

Birrell, R. G., & Birrell, J. H. W. The maltreatment syndrome in children. *Medical Journal of Australia*, 1968, *2*, 1023–1029.

Bleiberg, N. The neglected child and the child health conference. *New York State Journal of Medicine*, 1965, *65*, 1880–1885.

Blue, M. T. The battered child syndrome from a social work viewpoint. *Canadian Journal of Public Health*, 1965, *56*, 197–198.

Boardman, H. E. A project to rescue children from inflicted injuries. *Social Work*, 1962, *7*, 43–51.

______. Who insures the child's right to health? *Child Welfare*, 1963, *42*, 120–124.

Cameron, J. M., Johnson, J. R. M., & Camps, F. E. The battered child syndrome. *Medicine, Science, and the Law*, 1966, *6*, 2–21.

Cochrane, W. The battered child syndrome. *Canadian Journal of Public Health*, 1965, *56*, 193–196.

Cohen, M. I., Raphling, D. L., & Green, P. E. Psychologic aspects of the maltreatment syndrome of children. *Journal of Pediatrics*, 1966, *69*, 279–284.

Corbett, J. T. A psychiatrist reviews the battered child syndrome and mandatory reporting legislation. *Northwest Medicine*, 1964, *63*, 920–922.

Court, J. The battered child: Historical and diagnostic reflections, reflections on treatment. *Medical Social Work*, 1969, *22*(1), 11–20.

Curtis, G. Violence breeds violence—perhaps. *American Journal of Psychiatry*, 1963, *120*, 386–387.

De Francis, V. *Child abuse legislation in the 1970's.* Denver: American Humane Assoc., 1970.

Delaney, D. W. The physically abused child. *World Medical Journal,* 1966, *13,* 145–147.

Delsordo, J. D. Protective casework for abused children. *Children,* 1963, *10,* 213–218.

Easson, W. M., & Steinhilber, R. M. Murderous aggression by children and adolescents. *Archives of General Psychiatry,* 1961, *4,* 1–10.

Ebbin, A. J., Gollub, M. H., Stein, A. M., & Wilson, M. G. Battered child syndrome at the Los Angeles County General Hospital. *American Journal of the Diseases of Children,* 1969, *118,* 660–667.

Elmer, E. *Children in jeopardy: A study of abused minors and their families.* Pittsburgh: Univ. of Pittsburgh Press, 1967.

Elmer, E., & Gregg, G. S. Developmental characteristics of abused children. *Pediatrics,* 1967, *40,* 596–602.

Fairburn, A. C., & Hunt, A. C. Caffey's "third syndrome": A critical evaluation. *Medicine, Science, and the Law,* 1964, *4,* 123–126.

Fisher, W. H. Skeletal manifestations of parent-induced trauma in infants and children. *Southern Medical Journal,* 1958, *51,* 956–960.

Fleming, G. M. Cruelty to children. *British Medical Journal,* 1967, *2,* 421–422.

Fontana, V. J. *The maltreated child: The maltreatment syndrome in children.* Springfield, Ill.: Charles C. Thomas, 1964.

______. Further reflections on maltreatment of children. *New York State Journal of Medicine,* 1968, *68,* 2214–2215.

Galdston, R. Observations on children who have been physically abused and their parents. *American Journal of Psychiatry,* 1965, *122,* 440–443.

Gibbins, T. C. N., & Walker, A. *Cruel parents.* London: Institute for the Study and Treatment of Delinquency, 1956.

Gil, D. G. California pilot study. In R. E. Helfer & C. H. Kempe (Eds.), *The battered child.* Chicago: Univ. of Chicago Press, 1968a.

______. Incidence of child abuse and demographc characteristics of persons involved. In R. E. Helfer & C. H. Kempe (Eds.), *The battered child.* Chicago: Univ. of Chicago Press, 1968b.

______. Physical abuse of children: Findings and implications of a nationwide survey. *Pediatrics,* 1969, *44,* 857–864.

Gluckman, L. K. Cruelty to children. *New Zealand Medical Journal,* 1968, *67,* 155–159.

Green, K. Diagnosing the battered child syndrome. *Maryland State Medical Journal,* 1965, *14*(9), 83–84.

Greengard, J. The battered-child syndrome. *American Journal of Nursing,* 1964, *64*(6), 98–100.

Gregg, G. S. Physicians, child-abuse reporting laws, and the injured child: Psychosocial anatomy of childhood trauma. *Clinical Pediatrics,* 1968, *7,* 720–725.

Gregg, G. S., & Elmer, E. Infant injuries: Accident or abuse? *Pediatrics,* 1969, *44,* 434–439.

Harper, F. V. The physician, the battered child, and the law. *Pediatrics,* 1963, *31,* 899–201.

Heins, M. Child abuse: Analysis of a current epidemic. *Michigan Medicine,* 1969, *68,* 887–891.

Helfer, R. E., & Kempe, C. H. (Eds.). *The battered child.* Chicago: Univ. of Chicago Press, 1968.

Helfer, R. E., & Pollock, C. B. The battered child syndrome. *Advances in Pediatrics,* 1967, *15,* 9–27.

Hiller, R. B. The battered child: A health visitor's point of view. *Nursing Times*, 1969, *65*, 1265–1266.

Holter, J. C., & Friedman, S. B. Principles of management in child abuse cases. *American Journal of Orthopsychiatry*, 1968, *38*, 127–136.

Jacobziner, H. Rescuing the battered child. *American Journal of Nursing*, 1964, *64*(6), 92–97.

Johnson, B., & Morse, H. A. Injured children and their parents. *Children*, 1968, *15*, 147–152.

Kaufman, I. Psychiatric implications of physical abuse of children. In V. De Francis (Ed.), *Protecting the battered child.* Denver: American Humane Assoc., 1962.

Kempe, C. H. Some problems encountered by welfare departments in the management of the battered child syndrome. In R. E. Helfer & C. H. Kempe (Eds.), *The battered child.* Chicago: Univ. of Chicago Press, 1968.

Kempe, C. H., Silverman, F. N., Steele, B. F., Droegemueller, W., & Silver, H. K. The battered-child syndrome. *Journal of the American Medical Association*, 1962, *181*, 17–24.

Komisaruk, R. Clinical evaluation of child abuse: Scarred families, a preliminary report. *Juvenile Court Judges Journal* (Wayne County, Mich.), 1966, *17*(2), 66–70.

Korsch, B. M., Christian, J. B., Gozzi, E. K., & Carlson, P. V. Infant care and punishment: A pilot study. *American Journal of Public Health*, 1965, *55*, 1880–1888.

Laupus, W. E. Child abuse and the physician. *The Virginia Medical Monthly*, 1966, *93*(1), 1–2.

McCoid, A. H. The battered child and other assaults upon the family. *Minnesota Law Review*, 1965, *50*, 1–58.

McHenry, T., Girdany, B. R., & Elmer, E. Unsuspected trauma with multiple skeletal injuries during infancy and childhood. *Pediatrics*, 1963, *31*, 903–908.

Melnick, B., & Hurley, J. R. Distinctive personality attributes of child-abusing mothers. *Journal of Consulting and Clinical Psychology*, 1969, *33*, 746–749.

Merrill, E. J. Physical abuse of children: An agency study. In V. DeFrancis (Ed.), *Protecting the battered child.* Denver: American Humane Assoc., 1962.

Miller, D. S. Fractures among children: Parental assault as causative agent. *Minnesota Medicine*, 1959, *42*, 1209–1213.

Morris, M. G., & Gould, R. W. Role reversal: A concept in dealing with the neglected/battered-child syndrome. In *The neglected/battered-child syndrome: Role reversal in parents.* New York: Child Welfare League of America, 1963.

Morris, M. G., Gould, R. W., & Matthews, P. J. Toward prevention of child abuse. *Children*, 1964, *11*, 55–60.

Nathan, H. Abused children. *American Journal of Psychiatry*, 1965, *122*, 443.

Nomura, F. M. The battered child "syndrome". A review. *Hawaii Medical Journal*, 1966, *25*, 387–394.

Nurse, S. Familial patterns of parents who abuse their children. *Smith College Studies in Social Work*, 1964, *35*, 11–25.

Ounsted, C. Review of *Battered baby syndrome* by K. Simpson. *Developmental Medicine and Child Neurology*, 1968, *10*, 133–134.

Paulsen, M. G. Legal protection against child abuse. *Children*, 1966a, *13*, 43–48.

______. The legal framework for child protection. *Columbia Law Review*, 1966b, *66*, 679–717.

______. Child abuse reporting laws: The shape of the legislation. *Columbia Law Review*, 1967, *67*, 1–49.

———. A summary of child-abuse legislation. In R. E. Helfer & C. H. Kempe (Eds.), *The battered child.* Chicago: Univ. of Chicago Press, 1968a.

———. The law and abused children. In R. E. Helfer & C. H. Kempe (Eds.), *The battered child.* Chicago: Univ. of Chicago Press, 1968b.

Paulson, M. J., & Blake, P. R. The abused, battered, and maltreated child: A review. *Trauma,* 1967, *9*(4), 3–136.

———. The physically abused child: A focus on prevention. *Child Welfare,* 1969, *48,* 86–95.

Platou, R. V., Lennox, R., & Beasley, J. D. Battering. *Bulletin of the Tulane Medical Faculty,* 1964, *23,* 157–165.

Schloesser, P. T. The abused child. *Bulletin of the Menninger Clinic,* 1964, *28,* 260–268.

Silver, L. B. Child abuse syndrome: A review. *Medical Times,* 1968, *96,* 803–820.

Silver, L. B., Dublin, C. C., & Lourie, R. S. Child abuse syndrome: The "gray areas" in establishing a diagnosis. *Pediatrics,* 1969a, *4,* 594–600.

———. Does violence breed violence? Contributions from a study of the child abuse syndrome. *American Journal of Psychiatry,* 1969b, *126,* 404–407.

Simons, B., & Downs, E. F. Medical reporting of child abuse: Patterns, problems, and accomplishments. *New York State Journal of Medicine,* 1968, *68,* 2324–2330.

Simons, B., Downs, E. F., Hurster, M. M., & Archer, M. Child abuse: Epidemiologic study of medically reported cases. *New York State Journal of Medicine,* 1966, *66,* 2783–2788.

Simpson, K. The battered baby problem. *Royal Society of Health Journal,* 1967, *87,* 168–170.

———. The battered baby problem. *South African Medical Journal,* 1968, *42,* 661–663.

Skinner, A. E., & Castle, R. L. *78 battered children: A retrospective study.* London: National Society for the Prevention of Cruelty to Children, 1969.

Steele, B. F., & Pollock, C. B. A psychiatric study of parents who abuse infants and small children. In R. E. Helfer & C. H. Kempe (Eds.), *The battered child.* Chicago: Univ. of Chicago Press, 1968.

Ten Bensel, R. W. The battered child syndrome. *Minnesota Medicine,* 1963, *46,* 977–982.

Ten Have, R. A preventive approach to problems of child abuse and neglect. *Michigan Medicine,* 1965, *64,* 645–649.

Tuteur, W., & Glotzer, J. Further observations on murdering mothers. *Journal of Forensic Sciences,* 1966, *11,* 373–383.

U.S. Department of Health, Education, and Welfare. *Bibliography on the battered child.* Washington, D.C.: U.S. Government Printing Office, 1969.

Wasserman, S. The abused parent of the abused child. *Children,* 1967, *14,* 175–179.

Woolley, P. V., & Evans, W. A. Significance of skeletal lesions in infants resembling those of traumatic origin. *Journal of the American Medical Association,* 1955, *158,* 539–543.

Young, L. *Wednesday's children: A study of child neglect and abuse.* New York: McGraw-Hill, 1964.

Zalba, S. R. The abused child: A survey of the problem. *Social Work,* 1966, *11*(4), 3–16.

———. The abused child: A typology for classification and treatment. *Social Work,* 1967, *12*(1), 70–79.

NOTES

1. Gil's book reporting his national findings (*Violence against children: Physical child abuse in the United States.* Cambridge, Mass.: Harvard Univ. Press, 1970) appeared after the present review was accepted for publication. Although the book offers greater detail, the findings and conclusions are identical to those in the cited references.

7. ON BEING SANE IN INSANE PLACES

The following two articles discuss the question of mental illness, or insanity. The article by D. L. Rosenhan is a stunning (and frightening) report on what happened to eight pseudopatients who recently faked their way into psychiatric hospitals across the United States. Despite the fact that on entry they ceased to fake any symptoms of abnormality and were both cooperative and friendly, none were detected as fakes by any of the staff (although several patients recognized their deception). The effect of being labeled "schizophrenic" on entry was profound. It appears that as far as a hospital staff in concerned, "once crazy, always crazy." This indictment of our mental institutions is crushing. Rosenhan's data raise serious questions about the legitimacy of psychiatric care as it exists, even in our best mental hospitals. The powerlessness and depersonalization of inmates of mental institutions is tragic, as Rosenhan illustrates: "I have records of patients who were beaten by staff for the sin of having initiated verbal contact. During my own experience, for example, one patient was beaten in the presence of other patients for having approached an attendant and told him, 'I like you.'"

Patients in mental hospitals become invisible as humans, a condition that can do little to help them recover from mental problems: "A nurse unbuttoned her uniform to adjust her brassiere in the presence of an entire ward of viewing men. One did not have the sense that she was being seductive. Rather, she didn't notice it. A group of staff persons might point to a patient in the dayroom and discuss him animatedly, as if he were not there."

According to Rosenhan, "it is clear that we cannot distinguish the sane from the insane in psychiatric hospitals." The hospital itself becomes an "insane place" in which a patient, once labeled "insane," stands virtually no chance of ever being treated as a whole human being again. Rosenhan seems to understate the case by saying that the "consequences to patients hospitalized in such an environment—the powerlessness, depersonalization, segregation, mortification, and self-labeling—seem undoubtedly countertherapeutic."

The idea that we may not be able to distinguish sanity from insanity in "insane places" such as our mental hospitals does not necessarily mean that insanity does not exist (although, as Roger Brown points out, there are individuals who are proposing that). If there really is such a thing as schizophrenia, what are its outstanding characteristics? If psychosis doesn't exist, for example, why are there antipsychotic drugs, such as the phenothiazines, which are consumed by literally millions of people around the world?

Brown develops the notion that the inevitable mark of schizophrenia is "delusion," of which there are almost infinite variations. How can we reconcile Rosenhan's view that psychiatrists cannot distinguish the sane from the insane (although patients can) with Brown's report that "naive" college undergraduates are quite able to make reliable judgments (compared with Ph.D. clinical psychologists) about the degree of "schizophrenicity" by examining short samples of language from a patient? There is, of course, the cynical answer: The years of medical and psychological training add nothing to one's ability to deal with schizophrenia. But Brown prefers a less pessimistic explanation. What is it? Are you convinced by Brown's argument that there is a shared cultural view about "what constitutes adequate reality testing and rational coherence" and that in our culture this allows "us, sane ones" to detect the insanity in the language production of "them, the insane ones"? If not, what are we to do with our concepts of insanity and, more important, individuals whose view of reality is so different from ours as to impair either their own safety or ours or both? Perhaps the answer will not be in the hands of psychologists anyway. As Brown suggests, the biochemists may be the first to develop "a precise etiology and an effective therapy."

ON BEING SANE IN INSANE PLACES

D. L. Rosenhan, Stanford University

If sanity and insanity exist, how shall we know them?

The question is neither capricious nor itself insane. However much

Portions of these data were presented to colloquiums of the psychology departments at the University of California at Berkeley and at Santa Barbara; University of Arizona, Tucson; and Harvard University, Cambridge, Massachusetts.

we may be personally convinced that we can tell the normal from the abnormal, the evidence is simply not compelling. It is commonplace, for example, to read about murder trials wherein eminent psychiatrists for the defense are contradicted by equally eminent psychiatrists for the prosecution on the matter of the defendant's sanity. More generally, there are a great deal of conflicting data on the reliability, utility, and meaning of such terms as "sanity," "insanity," "mental illness," and "schizophrenia" *(1)*. Finally, as early as 1934, Benedict suggested that normality and abnormality are not universal *(2)*. What is viewed as normal in one culture may be seen as quite aberrant in another. Thus notions of normality and abnormality may not be quite as accurate as people believe they are.

To raise questions regarding normality and abnormality is in no way to question the fact that some behaviors are deviant or odd. Murder is deviant. So, too, are hallucinations. Nor does raising such questions deny the existence of the personal anguish that is often associated with "mental illness." Anxiety and depression exist. Psychological suffering exists. But normality and abnormality, sanity and insanity, and the diagnoses that flow from them may be less substantive than many believe them to be.

At its heart the question of whether the sane can be distinguished from the insane (and whether degrees of insanity can be distinguished from each other) is a simple matter: do the salient characteristics that lead to diagnoses reside in the patients themselves or in the environments and contexts in which observers find them? From Bleuler through Kretchmer through the formulators of the recently revised *Diagnostic and Statistical Manual* of the American Psychiatric Association the belief has been strong that patients present symptoms, that those symptoms can be categorized, and implicitly, that the sane are distinguishable from the insane. More recently, however, this belief has been questioned. Based in part on theoretical and anthropological considerations but also on philosophical, legal, and therapeutic ones, the view has grown that psychological categorization of mental illness is useless at best and downright harmful, misleading, and pejorative at worst. Psychiatric diagnoses, in this view, are in the minds of the observers and are not valid summaries of characteristics displayed by the observed *(3–5)*.

Gains can be made in deciding which of these is more nearly accurate by getting normal people (that is, people who do not have and have never suffered symptoms of serious psychiatric disorders) admitted to psychiatric hospitals and then determining whether they were discovered to be sane and, if so, how. If the sanity of such pseudopatients were always detected, there would be prima facie evidence that a sane individual can be distinguished from the insane context in which he is found. Normality (and presumably abnormality) is distinct enough that it can be recognized wherever it occurs, for it is carried within the person. If, on the other hand, the sanity of the pseudopatients were never discovered, serious difficulties would arise for those who support traditional modes of psychiatric diagnosis. Given that the hospital staff was not incompetent, that the pseudopatient had been behaving as sanely as he had been outside of the hospital, and that it had never been previously suggested that he belonged in a psychiatric hospital, such an unlikely outcome would support the view that psychiatric diagnosis betrays little about the patient but much about the environment in which an observer finds him.

This article describes such an experiment. Eight sane people gained secret admission to 12 different hospitals *(6)*. Their diagnostic experiences constitute the data of the first part of this article; the remainder is devoted to a description of their experiences in psychiatric institutions. Too few psychiatrists and psychologists, even those who have worked in such hospitals, know what the experience is like. They rarely talk about it with former patients, perhaps because they distrust information coming from the previously insane. Those who have worked in psychiatric hospitals are likely to have adapted so thoroughly to the settings that they are insensitive to the impact of that experience. And while there have been occasional reports of researchers who submitted themselves to psychiatric hospitalization *(7)*, these researchers have commonly remained in the hospitals for short periods of time, often with the knowledge of the hospital staff. It is difficult to know the extent to which they were treated like patients or like research colleagues. Nevertheless, their reports about the inside of the psychiatric hospital have been valuable. This article extends those efforts.

PSEUDOPATIENTS AND THEIR SETTINGS

The eight pseudopatients were a varied group. One was a psychology graduate student in his 20's. The remaining seven were older and "established." Among them were three psychologists, a pediatrician, a psychiatrist, a painter, and a housewife. Three pseudopatients were women; five were men. All of them employed psuedonyms, lest their alleged diagnoses embarrass them later. Those who were in mental health professions alleged another occupation in order to avoid the special attentions that might be accorded by staff, as a matter of courtesy or caution, to ailing colleagues *(8)*. With the exception of myself (I was the first pseudopatient, and my presence was known to the hospital administrator and chief psychologist and, so far as I can tell, to them alone), the presence of pseudopatients and the nature of the research program was not known to the hospital staffs *(9)*.

The settings were similarly varied. In order to generalize the findings, admission into a variety of hospitals was sought. The 12 hospitals in the sample were located in five different states on the East and West coasts. Some were old and shabby; some were quite new. Some were research-oriented; others not. Some had good staff-patient ratios; others were quite understaffed. Only one was a strictly private hospital. All of the others were supported by state or federal funds or, in one instance, by university funds.

After calling the hospital for an appointment, the pseudopatient arrived at the admissions office complaining that he had been hearing voices. Asked what the voices said, he replied that they were often unclear, but as far as he could tell they said "empty," "hollow," and "thud." The voices were unfamiliar and were of the same sex as the pseudopatient. The choice of these symptoms was occasioned by their apparent similarity to existential symptoms. Such symptoms are alleged to arise from painful concerns about the perceived meaninglessness of one's life. It is as if the hallucinating person were saying, "My life is empty and hollow." The choice of these symptoms was also determined by the *absence* of a single report of existential psychoses in the literature.

Beyond alleging the symptoms and falsifying name, vocation, and employment, no further alterations of person, history, or circumstances were made. The significant events of the pseudopatient's life history were presented as they had actually occurred. Relationships with parents and siblings, with spouse and children, with people at work and in school, consistent with the aforementioned exceptions, were described as they were or had been. Frustrations and upsets were described along with joys and satisfactions. These facts are important to remember. If anything, they strongly biased the subsequent results in favor of detecting sanity, since none of their histories or current behaviors were seriously pathological in any way.

Immediately upon admission to the psychiatric ward, the pseudopatient ceased simulating *any* symptoms of abnormality. In some cases there was a brief period of mild nervousness and anxiety, since none of the pseudopatients really believed that they would be admitted so easily. Indeed, their shared fear was that they would be immediately exposed as frauds and greatly embarrassed. Moreover, many of them had never visited a psychiatric ward; even those who had nevertheless had some genuine fears about what might happen to them. Their nervousness, then, was quite appropriate to the novelty of the hospital setting, and it abated rapidly.

Apart from that short-lived nervousness, the pseudopatient behaved on the ward as he "normally" behaved. The pseudopatient spoke to patients and staff as he might ordinarily. Because there is uncommonly little to do on a psychiatric ward, he attempted to engage others in conversation. When asked by staff how he was feeling, he indicated that he was fine, that he no longer experienced symptoms. He responded to instructions from attendants, to calls for medication (which was not swallowed), and to dining-hall instructions. Beyond such activities as were available to him on the admissions ward, he spent his time writing down his observations about the ward, its patients, and the staff. Initially these notes were written "secretly," but as it soon became clear that no one much cared, they were subsequently written on standard tablets of paper in such public places as the dayroom. No secret was made of these activities.

The pseudopatient, very much as a true psychiatric patient, entered a hospital with no foreknowledge of when he would be discharged. Each was told that he would have to get out by his own devices, essentially by convincing the staff that he was sane. The psychological stresses associated with hospitalization were considerable, and all but one of the pseudopatients desired to be discharged almost immediately after being admitted. They were, therefore, motivated not only to behave sanely but to be paragons of cooperation. That their behavior was in no way disruptive is confirmed by nursing reports, which have been obtained on most of the patients. These reports uniformly indicate that the patients were "friendly," "cooperative," and "exhibited no abnormal indications."

THE NORMAL ARE NOT DETECTABLY SANE

Despite their public "show" of sanity, the pseudopatients were never detected. Admitted, except in one case, with a diagnosis of schizophrenia *(10)*, each was discharged with a diagnosis of schizophrenia "in remission." The label "in remission" should in no way be dismissed as a formality, for at no time during any hospitalization had any question been raised about any pseudopatient's simulation. Nor are there any indications in the hospital records that the pseudopatient's status was suspect. Rather, the evidence is strong that, once labeled schizophrenic, the pseudopatient was stuck with that label. If the pseudopatient was to be discharged, he must naturally be "in remission"; but he was not sane, nor in the institution's view had he ever been sane.

The uniform failure to recognize sanity cannot be attributed to the quality of the hospitals, for although there were considerable variations among them, several are considered excellent. Nor can it be alleged that there was simply not enough time to observe the pseudopatients. Length of hospitalization ranged from 7 to 52 days, with an average of 19 days. The pseudopatients were not, in fact, carefully observed, but this failure clearly speaks more to traditions within psychiatric hospitals than to lack of opportunity.

Finally, it cannot be said that the failure to recognize the pseudopatients' sanity was due to the fact that they were not behaving sanely. While there was clearly some tension present in all of them, their daily visitors could detect no serious behavioral consequences—nor, indeed, could other patients. It was quite common for the patients to "detect" the pseudopatients' sanity. During the first three hospitalizations, when accurate counts were kept, 35 of a total of 118 patients on the admissions ward voiced their suspicions, some vigorously. "You're not crazy. You're a journalist, or a professor [referring to the continual note-taking]. You're checking up on the hospital." While most of the patients were reassured by the pseudopatient's insistence that he had been sick before he came in but was fine now, some continued to believe that the pseudopatient was sane throughout his hospitalization *(11)*. The fact that the patients often recognized normality when staff did not raises important questions.

Failure to detect sanity during the course of hospitalization may be due to the fact that physicians operate with a strong bias toward what statisticians call the type 2 error *(5)*. This is to say that physicians are more inclined to call a healthy person sick (a false positive, type 2) than a sick person healthy (a false negative, type 1). The reasons for this are not hard to find: it is clearly more dangerous to misdiagnose illness than health. Better to err on the side of caution, to suspect illness even among the healthy.

But what holds for medicine does not hold equally well for psychiatry. Medical illnesses, while unfortunate, are not commonly pejorative. Psychiatric diagnoses, on the contrary, carry with them personal, legal, and social stigmas *(12)*. It was therefore important to see whether the tendency toward diagnosing the sane insane could be reversed. The following experiment was arranged at a research and teaching hospital whose staff had heard these findings but doubted that such an error could occur in their hospital. The staff was informed that at some time during the following 3 months, one or more pseudopatients would attempt to be admitted into the psychiatric hospital. Each staff member was asked to rate each patient who presented himself at admissions or on the ward according to the likelihood that the patient was a pseudopatient. A 10-point scale was used, with a 1 and 2 reflecting high confidence that the patient was a pseudopatient.

Judgments were obtained on 193 patients who were admitted for psychiatric treatment. All staff who had had sustained contact with or primary responsibility for the patient—attendants, nurses, psychiatrists, physicians, and psychologists—were asked to make judgments. Forty-one patients were alleged, with high confidence, to be pseudopatients by at least one member of the staff. Twenty-three were considered suspect by at least one psychiatrist. Nineteen were suspected by one psychiatrist *and* one other staff member. Actually, no genuine pseudopatient (at least from my group) presented himself during this period.

This experiment is instructive. It indicates that the tendency to designate sane people as insane can be reversed when the stakes (in this case, prestige and diagnostic acumen) are high. But what can be said of the 19 people who were suspected of being “sane” by one psychiatrist and another staff member? Were these people truly “sane,” or was it rather the case that in the course of avoiding the type 2 error the staff tended to make more errors of the first sort—calling the crazy “sane”? There is no way of knowing. But one thing is certain: any diagnostic process that lends itself so readily to massive errors of this sort cannot be a very reliable one.

THE STICKINESS OF PSYCHODIAGNOSTIC LABELS

Beyond the tendency to call the healthy sick—a tendency that accounts better for diagnostic behavior on admission than it does for such behavior after a lengthy period of exposure—the data speak to the massive role of labeling in psychiatric assessment. Having once been labeled schizophrenic, there is nothing the pseudopatient can do to overcome the tag. The tag profoundly colors others’ perceptions of him and his behavior.

From one viewpoint these data are hardly surprising, for it has long been known that elements are given meaning by the context in which they occur. Gestalt psychology made this point vigorously, and Asch *(13)* demonstrated that there are "central" personality traits (such as "warm" versus "cold") which are so powerful that they markedly color the meaning of other information in forming an impression of a given personality *(14)*. "Insane," "schizophrenic," "manic-depressive," and "crazy" are probably among the most powerful of such central traits. Once a person is designated abnormal, all of his other behaviors and characteristics are colored by that label. Indeed, that label is so powerful that many of the pseudopatients' normal behaviors were overlooked entirely or profoundly misinterpreted. Some examples may clarify this issue.

Earlier I indicated that there were no changes in the pseudopatient's personal history and current status beyond those of name, employment, and, where necessary, vocation. Otherwise, a veridical description of personal history and circumstances was offered. Those circumstances were not psychotic. How were they made consonant with the diagnosis of psychosis? Or were those diagnoses modified in such a way as to bring them into accord with the circumstances of the pseudopatient's life, as described by him?

As far as I can determine, diagnoses were in no way affected by the relative health of the circumstances of a pseudopatient's life. Rather, the reverse occurred: the perception of his circumstances was shaped entirely by the diagnosis. A clear example of such translation is found in the case of a pseudopatient who had had a close relationship with his mother but was rather remote from his father during his early childhood. During adolescence and beyond, however, his father became a close friend, while his relationship with his mother cooled. His present relationship with his wife was characteristically close and warm. Apart from occasional angry exchanges, friction was minimal. The children had rarely been spanked. Surely there is nothing especially pathological about such a history. Indeed, many readers may see a similar pattern in their own experiences, with no markedly deleterious consequences. Observe, however, how such a history was translated in the psychopathological context, this from the case summary prepared after the patient was discharged.

> This white 39-year-old male . . . manifests a long history of considerable ambivalence in close relationships, which begins in early childhood. A warm relationship with his mother cools during his adolescence. A distant relationship to his father is described as becoming very intense. Affective stability is absent. His attempts to control emotionality with his wife and children are punctuated by angry outbursts and, in the case of the children, spankings. And while he says that he has several good friends, one senses considerable ambivalence embedded in those relationships also. . . .

The facts of the case were unintentionally distorted by the staff to achieve consistency with a popular theory of the dynamics of a schizophrenic reaction *(15)*. Nothing of an ambivalent nature had been described in relations with parents, spouse, or friends. To the extent that ambivalence could be inferred, it was probably not greater than is found in all human relationships. It is true the pseudopatient's relationships with his parents changed over time, but in the ordinary context that would hardly be remarkable—indeed, it might very well be expected. Clearly, the meaning ascribed to his verbalizations (that is, ambivalence, affective instability) was determined by the diagnosis: schizophrenia. An entirely different meaning would have been ascribed if it were known that the man was "normal."

All pseudopatients took extensive notes publicly. Under ordinary circumstances, such behavior would have raised questions in the minds of observers, as, in fact, it did among patients. Indeed, it seemed so certain that the notes would elicit suspicion that elaborate precautions were taken to remove them from the ward each day. But the precautions proved needless. The closest any staff member came to questioning these notes occurred when one pseudopatient asked his physician what kind of medication he was receiving and began to write down the response. "You needn't write it," he was told gently. "If you have trouble remembering, just ask me again."

If no questions were asked of the pseudopatients, how was their writing interpreted? Nursing records for three patients indicate that the writing was seen as an aspect of their pathological behavior. "Patient engages in writing behavior" was the daily nursing comment on one of the pseudopatients who was never questioned about his writing. Given that the patient is in the hospital, he must be psychologically disturbed. And given that he is disturbed, continuous writing must be a behavioral manifestation of that disturbance, perhaps a subset of the compulsive behaviors that are sometimes correlated with schizophrenia.

One tacit characteristic of psychiatric diagnosis is that it locates the sources of aberration within the individual and only rarely within the complex of stimuli that surrounds him. Consequently, behaviors that are stimulated by the environment are commonly misattributed to the patient's disorder. For example, one kindly nurse found a pseudopatient pacing the long hospital corridors. "Nervous, Mr. X?" she asked. "No, bored," he said.

The notes kept by pseudopatients are full of patient behaviors that were misinterpreted by well-intentioned staff. Often enough, a patient would go "berserk" because he had, wittingly or unwittingly, been mistreated by, say, an attendant. A nurse coming upon the scene would rarely inquire even cursorily into the environment stimuli of the patient's behavior. Rather, she assumed that his upset derived from his pathology, not from other staff members. Occasionally, the staff might assume that the patient's family (especially when they had recently visited) or other patients had stimulated the outburst. But never were the staff found to assume that one of themselves or the structure of the hospital had anything to do with a patient's behavior. One psychiatrist pointed to a group of patients who were sitting outside the cafeteria entrance half an hour before lunchtime. To a group of young residents he indicated that such behavior was characteristic of the oral-acquisitive nature of the syndrome. It seemed not to occur to him that there were very few things to anticipate in a psychiatric hospital besides eating.

A psychiatrist label has a life and an influence of its own. Once the impression has been formed that the patient is schizophrenic, the expectation is that he will continue to be schizophrenic. When a sufficient amount of time has passed, during which the patient has done nothing bizarre, he is considered to be in remission and available for discharge But the label endures beyond discharge, with the unconfirmed expectation that he will behave as a schizophrenic again. Such labels, conferred by mental health professionals, are as influential on the patient as they are on his relatives and friends, and it should not surprise anyone that the diagnosis acts on all of them as a self-fulfilling prophecy. Eventually, the patient himself accepts the diagnosis, with all of its surplus meanings and expectations, and behaves accordingly *(15)*.

The inferences to be made from these matters are quite simple. Much as Zigler and Phillips have demonstrated that there is enormous overlap in the symptoms presented by patients who have been variously diagnosed *(16)*, so there is enormous overlap in the behaviors of the sane and the insane. The sane are not "sane" all of the time. We lose our tempers "for no good reason." We are occasionally depressed or anxious, again for no good reason. And we may find it difficult to get along with one or another person—again for no reason that we can specify. Similarly, the insane are not always insane. Indeed, it was the impression of the pseudopatients while living with them that they were sane for long periods of time—that the bizarre behaviors upon which their diagnoses were allegedly predicated constituted only a small fraction of their total behavior. If it makes no sense to label ourselves permanently depressed on the basis of an occasional depression, then it takes better evidence than is presently available to label all patients insane or schizophrenic on the basis of bizarre behaviors or cognitions. It seems more useful, as Mischel *(17)* has pointed out, to limit our discussions to *behaviors*, the stimuli that provoke them, and their correlates.

It is not known why powerful impressions of personality traits, such as "crazy" or "insane," arise. Conceivably, when the origins of and stimuli that give rise to a behavior are remote or unknown or when the behavior strikes us as immutable, trait labels regarding the *behaver* arise. When, on the other hand, the origins and stimuli are known and available, discourse is limited to the behavior itself. Thus I may hallucinate because I am sleeping, or I may hallucinate because I ingested a peculiar drug. These are termed sleep-induced hallucinations, or dreams, and drug-induced hallucinations, respectively. But when the stimuli to my hallucinations are unknown, that is called craziness, or schizophrenia—as if that inference were somehow as illuminating as the others.

THE EXPERIENCE OF PSYCHIATRIC HOSPITALIZATION

The term "mental illness" is of recent origin. It was coined by people who were humane in their inclinations and who wanted very much to raise the station of (and the public's sympathies toward) the psychologically disturbed from that of witches and "crazies" to one that was akin to the physically ill. And they were at least partially successful, for the treatment of the mentally ill *has* improved considerably over the years. But while treatment has improved, it is doubtful that people really regard the mentally ill in the same way that they view the physically ill. A broken leg is something one recovers from, but mental illness allegedly endures forever *(18)*. A broken leg does not threaten the observer, but a crazy schizophrenic? There is by now a host of evidence that attitudes toward the mentally ill are characterized by fear, hostility, aloofness, suspicion, and dread *(19)*. The mentally ill are society's lepers.

That such attitudes infect the general population is perhaps not surprising, only upsetting. But that they affect the professionals—attendants, nurses, physicians, psychologists, and social workers—who treat and deal with the mentally ill is more disconcerting, both because such attitudes are self-evidently pernicious and because they are unwitting. Most mental health professionals would insist that they are sympathetic toward the mentally ill, that they are neither avoidant nor hostile. But it is more likely that an exquisite ambivalence characterizes their relations with psychiatric patients, such that their avowed impulses are only part of their entire attitude. Negative attitudes are there too and can easily be detected. Such attitudes should not surprise us. They are the natural offspring of the labels patients wear and the places in which they are found.

Consider the structure of the typical psychiatric hospital. Staff and patients are strictly segregated. Staff have their own living space, including their dining facilities, bathrooms, and assembly places. The glassed quarters that contain the professional staff, which the pseudopatients came to call "the cage," sit out on every dayroom. The staff emerge primarily for caretaking purposes—to give medication, to conduct a therapy or group meeting, to instruct or reprimand a patient. Otherwise, staff keep to themselves, almost as if the disorder that afflicts their charges is somehow catching.

So much is patient-staff segregation the rule that, for four public hospitals in which an attempt was made to measure the degree to which staff and patients mingle, it was necessary to use "time out of the staff cage" as the operational measure. While it was not the case that all time spent out of the cage was spent mingling with patients (attendants, for example, would occasionally emerge to watch television in the dayroom), it was the only way in which one could gather reliable data on time for measuring.

The average amount of time spent by attendants outside of the cage was 11.3 percent (range, 3 to 52 percent). This figure does not represent only time spent mingling with patients, but also includes time spent on such chores as folding laundry, supervising patients while they shave, directing ward cleanup, and sending patients to off-ward activities. It was the relatively rare attendants who spent time talking with patients or playing games with them. It proved impossible to obtain a "percent mingling time" for nurses, since the amount of time they spent out of the cage was too brief. Rather, we counted instances of emergence from the cage. On the average, daytime nurses emerged from the cage 11.5 times per shift, including instances when they left the ward entirely (range, 4 to 39 times). Late afternoon and night nurses were even less available, emerging on the average 9.4 times per shift (range, 4 to 41 times). Data on early morning nurses, who arrived usually after midnight and departed at 8 a.m., are not available because patients were asleep during most of this period.

Physicians, especially psychiatrists, were even less available. They were rarely seen on the wards. Quite commonly, they would be seen only when they arrived and departed, with the remaining time being spent in their offices or in the cage. On the average, physicians emerged on the ward 6.7 times per day (range, 1 to 17 times). It proved difficult to make an accurate estimate in this regard, since physicians often maintained hours that allowed them to come and go at different times.

The hierarchical organization of the psychiatric hospital has been commented on before *(20)*, but the latent meaning of that kind of organization is worth noting again. Those with the most power have least to do with patients, and those with the least power are most involved with them. Recall, however, that the acquisition of role-appropriate behaviors occurs mainly through the observation of others, with the most powerful having the most influence. Consequently, it is understandable that attendants not only spend more time with patients than do any other members of the staff—that is required by their station in the hierarchy—but also, insofar as they learn from their superiors' behavior, spend as little time with patients as they can. Attendants are seen mainly in the cage, which is where the models, the action, and the power are.

I turn now to a different set of studies, these dealing with staff response to patient-initiated contact. It has long been known that the amount of time a person spends with you can be an index of your significance to him. If he initiates and maintains eye contact, there is reason to believe that he is considering your requests and needs. If he pauses to chat or actually stops and talks, there is added reason to infer that he is individuating you. In four hospitals the pseudopatient approached the staff member with a request which took the following form: "Pardon me, Mr. [or Dr. or Mrs.] X, could you tell me when I will be eligible for grounds privileges?" (or ". . . when I will be presented at the staff meeting?" or ". . . when I am likely to be discharged?"). While the content of the question varied according to the appropriateness of the target and the pseudopatient's (apparent) current needs, the form was always a courteous and relevant request for information. Care was taken never to approach a particular member of the staff more than once a day, lest the staff member become suspicious or irritated. In examining these data, remember that the behavior of the pseudopatients was neither bizarre nor disruptive. One could indeed engage in good conversation with them.

The data for these experiments are shown in Table 1, separately for physicians (column 1) and for nurses and attendants (column 2). Minor differences between these four institutions were overwhelmed by the degree to which staff avoided continuing contacts that patients had initiated. By far, their most common response consisted of either a brief response to the question, offered while they were "on the move" and with head averted, or no response at all.

The encounter frequently took the following bizarre form: (pseudopatient) "Pardon me, Dr. X. Could you tell me when I am eligible for grounds privileges?" (physician) "Good morning, Dave. How are you today?" (Moves off without waiting for a response.)

It is instructive to compare these data with data recently obtained at Stanford University. It has been alleged that large and eminent universities are characterized by faculty who are so busy that they have no time for students. For this comparison, a young lady approached individual faculty members who seemed to be walking purposefully to some meeting or teaching engagement and asked them the following six questions.

1) "Pardon me, could you direct me to Encina Hall?" (at the medical school: ". . . to the Clinical Research Center?").

2) "Do you know where Fish Annex is?" (there is no Fish Annex at Stanford).

3) "Do you teach here?"

4) "How does one apply for admission to the college?" (at the medical school: ". . . to the medical school?").

5) "Is it difficult to get in?"

6) "Is there financial aid?"

Without exception, as can be seen in Table 1 (column 3), all of the questions were answered. No matter how rushed they were, all respondents not only maintained eye contact but stopped to talk. Indeed, many of the respondents went out of their way to direct or take the questioner to the office she was seeking, to try to locate "Fish Annex," or to discuss with her the possibilities of being admitted to the university.

Similar data, also shown in Table 1 (columns 4, 5, and 6), were obtained in the hospital. Here too, the young lady came prepared with six questions. After the first question, however, she remarked to 18 of her respondents (column 4). "I'm looking for a psychiatrist," and to 15 others (column 5), "I'm looking for an internist." Ten other respondents received no inserted comment (column 6). The general degree of cooperative responses is considerably higher for these university groups than it was for pseudopatients in psychiatric hospitals. Even so, differences are apparent within the medical school setting. Once having indicated that

Table 1.
Self-initiated contact by pseudopatients with psychiatrists and nurses and attendants, compared to contact with other groups.

CONTACT	PSYCHIATRIC HOSPITALS		UNIVERSITY CAMPUS NONMEDICAL	UNIVERSITY MEDICAL CENTER PHYSICIANS		
	(1) Psychiatrists	*(2) Nurses and attendants*	*(3) Faculty*	*(4) "Looking for a psychiatrist"*	*(5) "Looking for an internist"*	*(6) No additional comment*
Responses						
Moves on head averted (%)	71	88	0	0	0	0
Makes eye contact (%)	23	10	0	11	0	0
Pauses and chats (%)	2	2	0	11	0	10
Stops and talks (%)	4	0.5	100	78	100	90
Mean number of questions answered (out of 6)	*	*	6	3.8	4.8	4.5
Respondents (No.)	13	47	14	18	15	10
Attempts (No.)	185	1283	14	18	15	10

*Not applicable.

she was looking for a psychiatrist, the degree of cooperation elicited was less than when she sought an internist.

POWERLESSNESS AND DEPERSONALIZATION

Eye contact and verbal contact reflect concern and individuation; their absence, avoidance and depersonalization. The data I have presented do not do justice to the rich daily encounters that grew up around matters of depersonalization and avoidance. I have records of patients who were beaten by staff for the sin of having initiated verbal contact. During my own experience, for example, one patient was beaten in the presence of other patients for having approached an attendent and told him, "I like you." Occasionally, punishment meted out to patients for misdemeanors seemed so excessive that it could not be justified by the most radical interpretations of psychiatric canon. Nevertheless, they appeared to go unquestioned. Tempers were often short. A patient who had not heard a call for medication would be roundly excoriated, and the morning attendants would often wake patients with, "Come on, you m———f———s, out of bed!"

Neither anecdotal nor "hard" data can convey the overwhelming sense of powerlessness which invades the individual as he is continually exposed to the depersonalization of the psychiatric hospital. It hardly matters *which* psychiatric hospital—the excellent public ones and the very plush private hospital were better than the rural and shabby ones in this regard, but again, the features that psychiatric hospitals had in common overwhelmed by far their apparent differences.

Powerlessness was evident everywhere. The patient is deprived of many of his legal rights by dint of his psychiatric commitment *(21)*. He is shorn of credibility by virtue of his psychiatric label. His freedom of movement is restricted. He cannot initiate contact with the staff but may only respond to such overtures as they make. Personal privacy is minimal. Patient quarters and possessions can be entered and examined by any staff member for whatever reason. His personal history and anguish is available to any staff member (often including the "grey lady" and "candy striper" volunteer) who chooses to read his folder, regardless of their therapeutic relationship to him. His personal hygiene and waste evacuation are often monitored. The water closets may have no doors.

At times, depersonalization reached such proportions that pseudopatients had the sense that they were invisible, or at least unworthy of account. Upon being admitted, I and other pseudopatients took the initial physical examinations in a semipublic room, where staff members went about their own business as if we were not there.

On the ward, attendants delivered verbal and occasionally serious physical abuse to patients in the presence of other observing patients, some of whom (the pseudopatients) were writing it all down. Abusive behavior, on the other hand, terminated quite abruptly when other staff members were known to be coming. Staff are credible witnesses. Patients are not.

A nurse unbuttoned her uniform to adjust her brassiere in the presence of an entire ward of viewing men. One did not have the sense that she was being seductive. Rather, she didn't notice us. A group of staff persons might point to a patient in the dayroom and discuss him animatedly, as if he were not there.

One illuminating instance of depersonalization and invisibility occurred with regard to medications. All told, the pseudopatients were administered nearly 2100 pills, including Elavil, Stelazine, Compazine, and Thorazine, to name but a few. (That such a variety of medications should have been administered to patients presenting identical symptoms is itself worthy of note.) Only two were swallowed. The rest were either pocketed or deposited in the toilet. The pseudopatients were not alone in this. Although I have no precise records on how many patients rejected their medications, the pseudopatients frequently found the medications of other patients in the toilet before they deposited their own. As long as they were cooperative, their behavior and the pseudopatients' own in this matter, as in other important matters, went unnoticed throughout.

Reactions to such depersonalization among pseudopatients were intense. Although they had come to the hospital as participant observers and were fully aware that they did not "belong," they nevertheless found themselves caught up in and fighting the process of depersonalization. Some examples: a graduate student in psychology asked his wife to bring his textbooks to the hospital so he could "catch up on his homework"—this despite the elaborate precautions taken to conceal his professional association. The same student, who had trained for quite some time to get into the hospital and who had looked forward to the experience, "remembered" some drag races that he had wanted to see on the weekend and insisted that he be discharged by that time. Another pseudopatient attempted a romance with a nurse. Subsequently, he informed the staff that he was applying for admission to graduate school in psychology and was very likely to be admitted, since a graduate professor was one of his regular hospital visitors. The same person began to engage in psychotherapy with other patients—all of this as a way of becoming a person in an impersonal environment.

THE SOURCES OF DEPERSONALIZATION

What are the origins of depersonalization? I have already mentioned two. First are attitudes held by all of us toward the mentally ill—including those who treat them—attitudes characterized by fear, distrust, and horrible expectations on the one hand and benevolent intentions on the other. Our ambivalence leads, in this instance as in others, to avoidance.

Second and not entirely separate, the hierarchical structure of the psychiatric hospital facilitates depersonalization. Those who are at the top have least to do with patients, and their behavior inspires the rest of the staff. Average daily contact with psychiatrists, psychologists, residents, and physicians combined ranged from 3.9 to 25.1 minutes, with an overall mean of 6.8 (six pseudopatients over a total of 129 days of hospitalization). Included in this average are time spent in the admissions interview, ward meetings in the presence of a senior staff member, group and individual psychotherapy contacts, case presentation conferences, and discharge meetings. Clearly, patients do not spend much time in interpersonal contact with doctoral staff. And doctoral staff serve as models for nurses and attendants.

There are probably other sources. Psychiatric installations are presently in serious financial straits. Staff shortages are pervasive; staff time at a premium. Something has to give, and that something is patient contact. Yet, while financial stresses are realities, too much can be made of them. I have the impression that the psychological forces that result in depersonalization are much stronger than the fiscal ones and that the addition of more staff would not correspondingly improve patient care in this regard. The incidence of staff meetings and the enormous amount of record-keeping on patients, for example, have not been as substantially reduced as has patient contact. Priorities exist, even during hard times. Patient contact is not a significant priority in the traditional psychiatric hospital, and fiscal pressures do not account for this. Avoidance and depersonalization may.

Heavy reliance upon psychotropic medication tacitly contributes to depersonalization by convincing staff that treatment is indeed being conducted and that further patient contact may not be necessary. Even here, however, caution needs to be exercised in understanding the role of psychotropic drugs. If patients were powerful rather than powerless, if they were viewed as interesting individuals rather than diagnostic entities, if they were socially significant rather than social lepers, if their anguish truly and wholly compelled our sympathies and concerns, would we not *seek* contact with them, despite the availability of medications? Perhaps for the pleasure of it all?

THE CONSEQUENCES OF LABELING AND DEPERSONALIZATION

Whenever the ratio of what is known to what needs to be known approaches zero, we tend to invent "knowledge" and assume that we understand more than we actually do. We seem unable to acknowledge that we simply don't know. The needs for diagnosis and remediation of behavioral and emotional problems are enormous. But rather than acknowledge that we are just embarking on understanding, we continue to label patients "schizophrenic," "manic-depressive," and "insane," as if in those words we had captured the essence of understanding. The facts of the matter are that we have known for a long time that diagnoses are often not useful or reliable, but we have nevertheless continued to use them. We now know that we cannot distinguish insanity from sanity. It is depressing to consider how that information will be used.

Not merely depressing, but frightening. How many people, one wonders, are sane but not recognized as such in our psychiatric institutions?

How many have been needlessly stripped of their privileges of citizenship, from the right to vote and drive to that of handling their own accounts? How many have feigned insanity in order to avoid the criminal consequences of their behavior, and conversely, how many would rather stand trial than live interminably in a psychiatric hospital—but are wrongly thought to be mentally ill? How many have been stigmatized by well-intentioned but nevertheless erroneous diagnoses? On the last point, recall again that a type 2 error in psychiatric diagnosis does not have the same consequences it does in medical diagnosis. A diagnosis of cancer that has been found to be in error is cause for celebration. But psychiatric diagnoses are rarely found to be in error. The label sticks, a mark of inadequacy forever.

Finally, how many patients might be "sane" outside the psychiatric hospital but seem insane in it—not because craziness resides in them, as it were, but because they are responding to a bizarre setting, one that may be unique to institutions which harbor nether people? Goffman *(4)* calls the process of socialization to such institutions "mortification"—an apt metaphor that includes the processes of depersonalization that have been described here. And while it is impossible to know whether the pseudopatients' responses to these processes are characteristic of all inmates—they were, after all, not real patients—it is difficult to believe that these processes of socialization to a psychiatric hospital provide useful attitudes or habits of response for living in the "real world."

SUMMARY AND CONCLUSIONS

It is clear that we cannot distinguish the sane from the insane in psychiatric hospitals. The hospital itself imposes a special environment in which the meanings of behavior can easily be misunderstood. The consequences to patients hospitalized in such an environment—the powerlessness, depersonalization, segregation, mortification, and self-labeling—seem undoubtedly countertherapeutic.

I do not, even now, understand this problem well enough to perceive solutions. But two matters seem to have some promise. The first concerns the proliferation of community mental health facilities, of crisis intervention centers, of the human potential movement, and of behavior therapies that, for all of their own problems, tend to avoid psychiatric labels, to focus on specific problems and behaviors, and to retain the individual in a relatively nonpejorative environment. Clearly, to the extent that we refrain from sending the distressed to insane places, our impressions of them are less likely to be distorted. (The risk of distorted perceptions, it seems to me, is always present, since we are much more sensitive to an individual's behaviors and verbalizations than we are to the subtle contextual stimuli that often promote them. At issue here is a matter of magnitude. And as I have shown, the magnitude of distortion is exceedingly high in the extreme context that is a psychiatric hospital.)

The second matter that might prove promising speaks to the need to increase the sensitivity of mental health workers and researchers to the

Catch-22 position of psychiatric patients. Simply reading materials in this area will be of help to some such workers and researchers. For others, directly experiencing the impact of psychiatric hospitalization will be of enormous use. Clearly, further research into the social psychology of such total institutions will both facilitate treatment and deepen understanding.

I and the other pseudopatients in the psychiatric setting had distinctly negative reactions. We do not pretend to describe the subjective experiences of true patients. Theirs may be different from ours, particularly with the passage of time and the necessary process of adaptation to one's environment. But we can and do speak to the relatively more objective indices of treatment within the hospital. It could be a mistake, and a very unfortunate one, to consider that what happened to us derived from malice or stupidity on the part of the staff. Quite the contrary, our overwhelming impression of them was of people who really cared, who were committed, and who were uncommonly intelligent. Where they failed, as they sometimes did painfully, it would be more accurate to attribute those failures to the environment in which they, too, found themselves than to personal callousness. Their perceptions and behavior were controlled by the situation, rather than being motivated by a malicious disposition. In a more benign environment, one that was less attached to global diagnosis, their behaviors and judgments might have been more benign and effective.

REFERENCES

1. Ash, P., *Journal of Abnormal and Social Psychology*, 1949, *44*, 272; Beck, A. T., *American Journal of Psychiatry*, 1962, *119*, 210; Boisen, A. T., *Psychiatry*, 1938, *2*, 233; Kreitman, N., *Journal of Mental Science*, 1961, *107*, 876; Kreitman, N., Sainsbury, P., Morrisey, J., Towers, J., & Scrivener, J., *Journal of Mental Science*, 1961, *107*, 887; Schmitt, H. O., & Fonda, C. P., *Journal of Abnormal and Social Psychology*, 1956, *52*, 262; Seeman, W., *Journal of Nervous and Mental Disease*, 1953, *118*, 541. For an analysis of these artifacts and summaries of the disputes, see Zubin, J., *Annual Review of Psychology*, 1967, *18*, 373; Phillips, L., & Draguns, J. G., *Annual Review of Psychology*, 1971, *22*, 447.
2. Benedict, R., *Journal of General Psychology*, 1934, *10*, 59.
3. See in this regard Becker, H., *Outsiders: Studies in the sociology of deviance*, New York: Free Press, 1963; Braginsky, B. M., Braginsky, D. D., & Ring, K., *Methods of madness: The mental hospital as a last resort*, New York: Holt, Rinehart & Winston, 1969; Crocetti, G. M., & Lemkau, P. V., *American Sociological Review*, 1965, *30*, 577; Goffman, E., *Behavior in public places*, New York: Free Press, 1964; Laing, R. D., *The divided self: A study of sanity and madness*, Chicago: Quadrangle, 1960; Phillips, D. L., *American Sociological Review*, 1963, *28*, 963; Sarbin, T. R., *Psychology Today*, 1972, *6*, 18; Schur, E., *American Journal of Sociology*, 1969, *75*, 309; Szasz, T., *Law, liberty, and psychiatry*, New York: Macmillan, 1963, and *The myth of mental illness: Foundations of a theory of mental illness*, New York: Hoeber Harper, 1963. For a critique of some of these views, see Gove, W. R., *American Sociological Review*, 1970, *35*, 873.
4. Goffman, E. *Asylums*. Garden City, N.Y.: Doubleday, 1961.
5. Scheff, T. J. *Being mentally ill: A sociological theory*. Chicago: Aldine, 1966.
6. Data from a ninth pseudopatient are not incorporated in this report because, although his sanity went undetected, he falsified aspects of his personal history, including his

marital status and parental relationships. His experimental behaviors therefore were not identical to those of the other pseudopatients.

7. Barry, A., *Bellevue is a state of mind,* New York: Harcourt Brace Jovanovich, 1971; Belknap, I., *Human problems of a state mental hospital,* New York: McGraw-Hill, 1956; Caudill, W., Redlich, F. C., Gilmore, H. R., & Brody, E. B., *American Journal of Orthopsychiatry,* 1952, *22,* 314; Goldman, A. R., Bohr, R. H., & Steinberg, T. A., *Professional Psychology,* 1970, *1,* 427; *Roche Report,* 1971, *1*(13), 8.

8. Beyond the personal difficulties that the pseudopatient is likely to experience in the hospital, there are legal and social ones that, combined, require considerable attention before entry. For example, once admitted to a psychiatric institution, it is difficult, if not impossible, to be discharged on short notice, state law to the contrary notwithstanding. I was not sensitive to these difficulties at the outset of the project, nor to the personal and situational emergencies that can arise, but later a writ of habeas corpus was prepared for each of the entering pseudopatients and an attorney was kept "on call" during every hospitalization. I am grateful to John Kaplan and Robert Bartels for legal advice and assistance in these matters.

9. However distasteful such concealment is, it was a necessary first step to examining these questions. Without concealment, there would have been no way to know how valid these experiences were; nor was there any way of knowing whether whatever detections occurred were a tribute to the diagnostic acumen of the staff or to the hospital's rumor network. Obviously, since my concerns are general ones that cut across individual hospitals and staffs, I have respected their anonymity and have eliminated clues that might lead to their identification.

10. Interestingly, of the 12 admissions, 11 were diagnosed as schizophrenic and one, with the identical symptomatology, as manic-depressive psychosis. This diagnosis has a more favorable prognosis, and it was given by the only private hospital in our sample. On the relations between social class and psychiatric diagnosis, see Hollingshead, A. deH., & Redlich, F. C., *Social class and mental illness: A community study,* New York: Wiley, 1958.

11. It is possible, of course, that patients have quite broad latitudes in diagnosis and therefore are inclined to call many people sane, even those whose behavior is patently aberrant. However, although we have no hard data on this matter, it was our distinct impression that this was not the case. In many instances, patients not only singled us out for attention, but came to imitate our behaviors and styles.

12. Cummings, J., & Cummings, E., *Community Mental Health,* 1965, *1,* 135; Farina, A., & Ring, K., *Journal of Abnormal Psychology,* 1965, *70,* 47; Freeman, H. E., & Simmons, O. G., *The mental patient comes home,* New York: Wiley, 1963; Johannsen, W. J., *Mental Hygiene,* 1969, *53,* 218; Linsky, A. S., *Social Psychology,* 1970, *5,* 166.

13. Asch, S. E., *Journal of Abnormal and Social Psychology,* 1946, *41,* 258, and *Social Psychology,* New York: Prentice-Hall, 1952.

14. See also Mensh, I. M., & Wishner, I., *Journal of Personality,* 1947, *16,* 188; Wishner, I., *Psychological Review,* 1960, *67,* 96; Bruner, J. S., & Tagiuri, R., in G. Lindzey (Ed.), *Handbook of social psychology* (Vol. 2), Cambridge, Mass.: Addison-Wesley, 1954; Bruner, J. S., Shapiro, D., & Tagiuri, R., in R. Tagiuri & L. Petrullo (Eds.), *Person perception and interpersonal behavior,* Stanford, Calif.: Stanford Univ. Press, 1958.

15. For an example of a similar self-fulfilling prophecy, in this instance dealing with the "central" trait of intelligence, see Rosenthal, R., & Jacobson, L., *Pygmalion in the classroom,* New York: Holt, Rinehart & Winston, 1968.

16. Zigler, E., & Phillips, L., *Journal of Abnormal and Social Psychology,* 1961, *63,* 69. See also Freudenberg, R. K., & Robertson, J. P., *A.M.A. Archives of Neurological Psychiatry,* 1956, *76,* 14.

17. Mischel, W. *Personality and assessment.* New York: Wiley, 1968.

18. The most recent and unfortunate instance of this tenet is that of Senator Thomas Eagleton.

19. Sarbin, T. R., & Mancuso, J. C., *Journal of Clinical and Consulting Psychology*, 1970, *35*, 159; Sarbin, T. R., *Journal of Clinical and Consulting Psychology*, 1967, *31*, 447; Nunnally, J. C., Jr., *Popular conceptions of mental health*, New York: Holt, Rinehart & Winston, 1961.

20. Stanton, A. H., & Schwartz, M. S. *The mental hospital: A study of institutional participation in psychiatric illness and treatment.* New York: Basic Books, 1954.

21. Wexler, D. B., & Scoville, S. E., *Arizona Law Review*, 1971, *13*, 1.

22. I thank W. Mischel, E. Orne, and M. S. Rosenhan for comments on an earlir draft of this manuscript.

SCHIZOPHRENIA, LANGUAGE, AND REALITY

Roger Brown, Harvard University

The longest playing movie in the history of the city of Cambridge is a French film called the *King of Hearts.* I felt that I ought to see a movie so successful in the city where I live, and so last December I did. Although it is about World War I, set in a small town in France that has been deserted by Allied troops and not yet reached by an advancing German army, the *King of Hearts* is a comedy. And a pleasant one, made with considerable art. But nothing in it seemed to me to account for its great popularity, after more than a year, with audiences largely made up of students. Nothing, that is, except its last scene.

When the French town in the film is evacuated, the gateway of the asylum for the insane, the *aliénés*, is unlocked, and the inmates move out into the town which they now possess and where they are free to act out their fantasies. One thinks he is a prince of the church; another a great diplomat; another a general; and several old people think they are very small children. All dress and act accordingly and cooperate in one another's delusions in such a way as to yield a bizarre but harmless and happy communal life. In the last scene a platoon of Allied soldiers returns to the town just as an advance platoon of Germans arrives. The two forces meet in the Town Square, dutifully line up in opposed ranks, raise their rifles on command, and shoot one another dead—without remainder. All this is observed by the insane, and as the film closes, they slowly

This article was presented as the Presidential Address at the annual meeting of the Eastern Psychological Association, Boston, April 1972. Requests for reprints should be sent to Roger Brown, Department of Psychology, Harvard University, 1270 William James Hall, Cambridge, Massachusetts 02138.

Brown, Roger. Schizophrenia, language, and reality. *American Psychologist*, 1973, *28*, 395–403.

trail back to the asylum, and when all are inside, a hand snakes out between the bars and locks the gate—against the world.

In December when I saw the *King of Hearts*, I was reading several of the books of Thomas Szasz, who argues that the notion of mental illness is a myth and that institutional psychiatry bears a close functional resemblance to the medieval Inquisition (Szasz, 1961, 1963, and elsewhere), being a social mechanism for disposing of people whose ideas constitute a threat to established powers. I had already read R. D. Laing (1960, and others), though with very uneven understanding, and had become acquainted with the notion that psychotics may have access to truths that are closed to the rest of us. Then I had seen an occasional leaflet of the Insane Liberation Movement—which is just that. All of these things together suggested that the ideas about psychoses, especially schizophrenia, which I had absorbed in graduate school some 20 years ago and which had not seemed to be challenged in any fundamental way by the professional reading I had done since, were nevertheless no longer considered beyond dispute. Was it the phenothiazines, I wondered, that had made it possible to think so differently about schizophrenia, or were the new ideas mainly extreme manifestations of the surge of egalitarianism evident now in all human studies? In any case I felt that the introductory psychology course at Harvard had some obligation to include these ideas, and so I decided to take on schizophrenia for a month this spring term, even though my lack of clinical experience made me obviously incompetent. Still, I thought, the class can read more competent people, not just Szasz (1963) and Laing (1960), but Brendan Maher (1966) and Norman Cameron (1947) and many others. However, I felt that I could not talk about the subject from bookish experience alone; there are in any field many things that are so well known to the practitioner or experimenter that no one thinks it worthwhile to add them to the literature, and yet some of these things are important to know if you are going to think about the subject. The fall-term reading period gave me just three free weeks in which to get out of my office and arrange something like a period of total immersion in schizophrenia. With the help of friends, psychiatrists, psychologists, and others, I was able to arrange to observe research on a family interaction research project at one local hospital and at the same hospital to have private conversations with a wide variety of schizophrenic patients who were willing to talk with me, to attend psychiatric rounds several times, and so on. I was also told that I would be welcome to attend a weekly meeting of the Cambridge Chapter of Schizophrenics Anonymous, which I did. Another hospital very generously allowed me to spend the daytime hours of one week at a particular house on their grounds where 24 patients live as a community with some degree of patient government, and with group meetings both therapeutic and task oriented as part of the regimen. The patients there ranged from student age to the early seventies: some had been hospitalized as long as 40 years; some only a few months; some were about to be discharged; some might never be discharged. Their diagnoses ran the range of subtypes of schizophrenia. I should add that everything I was allowed to do had the advance approval of the patients and that care was taken to see that I understood the importance of medical confidentiality and would observe it.

The experience was absurdly brief and biased in many ways. I took part in no therapeutic sessions. The patients I talked with were all receiving medication, and they were just those who chose to talk with me. Except for the session with Schizophrenics Anonymous, the patients were all in expensive private hospitals widely regarded as particularly good ones. I do not expect that experienced clinical psychologists can learn anything from my observations but, on the contrary, am sure they can straighten me out on many things. Of course, I learned a great deal, but that is because I started from a base line close to zero. The experience in general was sad, sometimes psychologically stressful, but above all, fascinating to a psychologist whose experience had been limited to the laboratory and classroom. I presume to impose it on you only because there must be many psychologists like me and because the problems that appear to the eye of the cognitive social psychologist are somewhat different from those that are most salient to the psychologist who does therapy.

There are some obvious things that one learns very quickly. Twenty years of reading experimental studies that contrast performance on some laboratory task of normals and schizophrenics had, without my realizing it, in the case of the latter group, though not the former, built up a preconception of a homogeneous population, a monolith, bearing the mark of "schizophrenicity." What I discovered after a few conversations, of course, is that persons called schizophrenic are as diverse as persons called normal. But, one thinks, they must have some common quality or qualities, or else why are they labeled with one term, and I kept trying to find it as I talked with one person after another. In the first few days I found my mind was doing something that my reason certainly rejected. It was trying to find some perceptual property common to schizophrenics, some special look or sound that the distance receptors, the eye and ear, could make use of in the future. In time, all hypotheses failed—there seemed to be no reliable stigma. Indeed, when that fact first came home to me, it was with a certain shock because one then recognizes that anyone, however he looks or talks in ordinary situations, may have unuttered thoughts that could qualify him as schizophrenic.

DELUSIONS

The one thing I eventually did find with the people I talked to, and I feel supported enormously by the fact that Norman Cameron with his great experience said the same thing, is that however normal the patient was in talking about most subjects, eventually one came upon an area of *delusion*. What delusions are is a difficult question to which I want to return. Here I want only to record that when the patient hit such an area, my reaction was generally quite sharp and unequivocal. In effect I said to myself: "I have followed you perfectly well thus far, but now you are saying things I cannot agree with." For example, one young man who came on as very happy-go-lucky and who made one positively envy his sunny outlook said that when he left the hospital he would go directly to Scotland, where they were making the movie of *Fiddler on the Roof*, because he wanted to try out for the lead. A young girl, who had once been a student of mine, talked pleasantly on a number of subjects familiar to both of us and then began to look so frightened I asked her if anything were wrong. She said, "I feel this room is being bugged." "By whom?" I asked. "Big Brother?" was her suggestion. An intense young married woman, very religious, said she let the Bible guide her life. I asked for an example, and she told me of the day she put her finger down at random on a page, landing on the word *God* and noticed that *God* was *dog* spelled backward. For this impiety she felt the family dog must die, and she killed him.

Without inquiring into the nature of delusions but simply postulating that they often are identified easily as such by most people in a society, notice that the three I have cited and indeed delusions generally do not seem to have the properties they should have if the *King of Hearts* were to be taken seriously. Delusions are as idiosyncratic as individual schizophrenics or normals. They generally do not overlap or complement one another. And patients do not generally go along with one another's delusions; they are perfectly able and, by my observation, often do act as reality checks on one another. I have seen groups of patients where the delusions of each member were confidently and unanimously rejected by the group as crazy—no words were minced—even though each member had his own area of delusion that he would not relinquish lightly. In addition, most patients seemed very unhappy in their delusions; some clearly suffered terribly. So I do not think the population of a French asylum, set at liberty, would actually lead the kind of coordinated happy life that the *King of Hearts* portrays.

Delusions also do not seem to be quite as they should be if institutional psychiatry were really a modern Inquisition. There seems to be nothing like a standard set of heresies, but only endless variety. And the beliefs held are not generally such as to threaten either the state or any powerful institution. They chiefly threaten the one who holds them and a few people close to him.

PATIENT GOVERNMENT

I will mention one more lesson one learns easily, though one does not learn what to do about it. Patient government is something like student government in the colleges and like inmate government in prisons. It is never complete and probably cannot be. Perhaps it was most nearly so in Laing's Kingsley Hall, where patients and doctors are said to have lived as equals for the five years the experiment lasted. It was, unfortunately, an experiment that we never shall be really able to evaluate. Some reports are sympathetic; some are unsympathetic. Laing himself moved out after about a year. Normal neighbors broke down the doors, and normal kids smashed the windows. Some patients seemed to get better, while others smeared the walls with feces. However, the same kind of thing is being tried elsewhere, and results may be produced that are easier to evaluate.

Most hospitals find that the best they can manage is patient government—up to a point. Suppose the various privileges a patient requests are intended to be granted or not, according to the vote of his fellow patients. I saw a likable young student-age patient test this system by asking for every privilege in the book, including going home on weekends. It turned out that the other patients were not willing to say no to him, and in the end the psychiatrist had to. The last time the young man went home, he had smuggled in LSD when he returned and passed it out to a couple of other patients, with one becoming so agitated she had to be put in packs and another attempting suicide. The limits of patient government, like the limits of student government and inmate government, are not lost on those to whom some but not full power has been given. In varying degree they lend a quality of make-believe to what goes on, a quality that I think they find somewhat depressing. Probably, however, limited power is less depressing than none at all.

SCHIZOPHRENIC SPEECH

Throughout my three weeks I kept my ears cocked for what has been called *schizophrenic speech,* a kind of speech still often called *regressed,* which suggests childlike, though not everyone who uses the term intends that sense. While I fairly often heard patients spoken to with what I call nursery school intonation, a kind of exaggerated prosody that most adults use with small children, I have to report that in my three weeks I never heard anything childlike from a patient nor indeed anything that I would want to set apart as schizophrenic speech. As far as my experience goes and within the limits of a particular definition of speech, I would have to conclude that there is no such thing as schizophrenic speech. I hasten to add that I encountered plenty of schizophrenic thought, but that is another matter.

Since speech or, more generally, language is the principal vehicle for making thought public, I know that many authors who have written of schizophrenic language have intended what I will call *thought,* perhaps favoring the term *language* because it is closer to the observable behavioral level. I do not know how to make a deep distinction between language and thought, but only a preliminary working distinction. My suggestion is that we confine the word *language* to just those systems that linguistic science has thus far found it possible to characterize in terms of general rules. These systems would be most clearly the phonological, including the inventory of phonemic contrasts as well as the rules of phonotactics, describing how sounds may be combined, and the grammatical, including rules of word formation and of sentence formation. The conquest of semantics, or meaning, is but little advanced in linguistics. Katz and Fodor (e.g., Katz, 1964; Katz & Fodor, 1963) in various papers have described a scheme for the representation of the kind of maximally general semantic information that gets entered in dictionaries. Information on this level, if it appears also in our mental dictionaries, could serve, as Katz and Fodor have shown, to account for a limited but important set of semantic skills possessed by the adult native speaker—such skills as the disambiguation of word meanings on the basis of sentence context, the identification of semantic anomalies, and of contradictions and synonymies. Their scheme, for instance, would mark "John astonished the rock" as anomalous through a set of rules representing the fact that *astonish* is a verb requiring in everyday literal usage a grammatical object marked as animate. Their scheme would with a sentence like "John hit the ball," select the "physical object" sense of *ball* rather than the "social event" sense. Katz and Fodor (1963) are careful to point out that their scheme, and it is still only a scheme rather than an accomplished program, has nothing at all to say about the vast domain of semantics that seems less lawful and general and that they call simply "knowledge of the world." This knowledge, they suspect, is simply too complex ever to yield to an explicit description.

With regard to the development of speech in preschool children in what we call State I (Brown, 1973), which is the first stage of sentence construction, quite a lot is known about phonology, grammar, and even referential semantics. Since there is now at least some information on about 30 languages from 10 different language families, there are statements that can claim some generality. Here, for instance, are four of the more obvious ones:

1. Sentences start short and only very gradually get longer.
2. Consonant clusters, an aspect of phonotactics, are reduced or simplified in regular ways.
3. Functional morphemes, like inflections for person and number, case endings, articles, prepositions, and so forth, are almost always omitted, even in contexts in which they are obligatory in the adult language.
4. Semantically, Stage I speech is limited almost entirely to the sensorimotor world; it concerns objects, actors, actions, locations, nominations, recurrence, disappearance, attribution, and a few other things. Notably lacking is talk about emotions, personalities, personal relationships, religion, and all of the things schizophrenics talk about.

I do not want to belabor the obvious and so will just note that, of course, the speech of adults called *schizophrenic* has none of the above properties of child speech. Near the end of my three weeks, not having heard so much as a single reduced consonant cluster or even one omitted or incorrect inflection, I got rather desperate in my quest for regressed schizophrenic language. "Isn't there a single patient in this hospital," I asked a friend, "whose language is disturbed?" Well, there was supposed to be one very old lady, and we went in search of her in the old people's ward, but she turned out to be home for the weekend. While there, we conversed with a number of other elderly patients. To be sure, they sometimes did not speak up quite loudly enough, but if you put your ear close, everything strictly linguistic was in perfect working order. Sometimes they were egocentric or autistic in taking for granted too much knowledge in the listener, and that is indeed something children do, but so do teachers and so at times do all of us. Maybe the phenothiazines have cured regressed schizophrenic speech, but I suspect not; I suspect it never existed in the sense I have described and that it was never childlike in its formal expressive mechanisms. I have found nothing in the literature from the prephenothiazine era to suggest that it was.

REALITY TESTING

But obviously there is something wrong with some of the things schizophrenics say and write. Not with all by any means, since schizophrenics are not always being schizophrenic but are only so on occasion. I have given three examples of assertions that I took to be deluded, and probably most of you agreed with me. The journals and the psychiatric wards echo with thousands of others, mostly more bizarre than my examples. But what exactly is wrong with such a statement as, "When I get out of here, I'm going to fly to Scotland, where they are making the movie of *Fiddler on the Roof*, because I'd really like to try out for the lead"? Clearly whatever is wrong is in the domain of meaning. Equally clearly, it is not today in the domain of linguistics; nothing general enough to go in a dictionary or a representation of adult semantic knowledge marks the quoted sentence as deviant.

The troubles seem to begin with the knowledge of the world: *(a)* the movie *Fiddler on the Roof* has already been made; *(b)* Scotland was never a likely location for that movie; and *(c)* the patient speaking was far too young to play the lead. But ignorance of particular facts cannot be the whole story. Any of us might be ignorant of one or all of them. The problem of the delusion goes deeper than factual information.

Notice in the first place that the assertion must be intended seriously. Any schizophrenic statement, however deluded, ceases to be schizophrenic if it is prefaced simply by the words "I dreamt that . . ." Clearly, we are applying criteria we do not apply to dream reports; the central one seems to be that the assertion is offered as serious enough to serve as a basis of action. The speaker may not act now or for years, but he speaks with a seriousness that implies the possibility. When the action implied seems imminent and would endanger the speaker or others, then, of course, the question of institutional commitment comes up.

At this point a contrast with the fantasies or delusions of childhood is instructive. They can be very vivid, as we know, and in addition they may serve as the ground of action, but the action stays generally within playful limits. The child who says, "Look, I'm a bird," and jumps from the second step of the front porch is one thing; the child who says the same and jumps from the roof of the house is quite another.

What, then, is wrong with the *Fiddler on the Roof* assertion as a serious statement? It is not, I think, simply the ignorance it reflects of one or more of three facts, though that is part of the problem. It is rather that we have a sense that the true state of affairs on these three salient points is obtained easily and disseminated quite widely in our society; most of us are familiar with at least one of them; many with all. It seems to us that a young men entertaining so large an enterprise as a trip to Scotland ought to have looked into the matter at least far enough to have discovered that some of the propositions he is building on are false. In fact, we have a sense that his reality testing, to use an old phrase that still seems right to me, has been insufficient for the costs of the venture he has in mind. If it had been sufficient, he would have easily turned up some of the relevant truths. If we ourselves were totally ignorant of the truths, we would have to feel less confident in calling the assertion deluded, and yet, even in this case, we might judge that the probability of an unknown young man getting a lead in any movie is scarcely large enough to justify a trip to Scotland.

This is only one example of what can lie behind the identification of a belief as deluded, and no two that I have thought about involve just the same processes. What they do seem to have in common is a judgment that reality testing, as we conceive it in this society at this time, has been insufficient to justify the risks attendant upon the action contemplated. It must be, I think, a culturally and historically relative notion of reality testing that is deficient. One cannot say instead simply that the patient is "out of touch with reality" as if reality were something we knew, something always the same, like a good solid block of wood. Schizophrenic delusions seem to be identifiable in all cultures today and to have been identifiable throughout history. But reality is not constant across any such range. What seems deluded at one time and place certainly may not at another. Albert Schweitzer (1948) in his little book *The Psychiatric Study of Jesus* based much of his criticism of those psychiatrists who had written that the seemingly deluded Jesus was insane, on a failure to enter sufficiently into the "mind world" of the time when the imminence of the Kingdom of God and of the appearance of the Messiah were widely held beliefs.

Reality testing of religious beliefs is not, of course, easy and is often impossible. Only very naive prophets like Marian Keech (Festinger, Riecken, & Schachter, 1956), who predicted that Chicago would be destroyed by flood on a certain date, make predictions vulnerable to easy disproof. With religious beliefs we should perhaps pay some attention to the level of moral reasoning and action that has characterized the person, perhaps using the work of Kohlberg and his associates (e.g., Kohlberg & Kramer, 1969) as a guide. One of the Szasz's (1963) most horrifying tales is of a widow who was committed involuntarily by her relatives and a couple of compliant psychiatrists because she was using the fortune inherited from her husband to help poverty-stricken strangers in remote lands. For people who reason morally at Kohlberg's Stage II, in terms simply of satisfying one's own needs and the needs of friends and relatives, this might seem insane behavior. On the other hand, it is also behavior that corresponds with the highest level of moral reasoning, Kohlberg's Stage VI, where all human lives are held to be of equal value and always more valuable than property. One should perhaps require that psychiatrists and relatives who testify at commitment hearings be at least as advanced in their moral reasoning and action as the potential patient. Schweitzer could have made the same argument since the quite consistently Stage VI moral reasoning of Jesus may have seemed insane to certain psychiatrists mainly because they were unable to think on his moral level.

EXPERIMENTAL RESEARCH ON SCHIZOPHRENIA

In the experimental literature I have read on schizophrenic language and thought, there is one general finding, repeatedly confirmed for about 15 years, that particularly fascinates me. I think William Hunt (Hunt, Jones, & Hunt, 1957) and Nelson Jones (1959) at Northwestern University originated in the late 1950s the kind of experiment I have in mind. There have been later related but significant additions made by Alan Cohen in 1961, Brendan Maher and his associates in 1966, and probably quite a few others. In extracting the general result I want to concentrate on, I cannot describe exactly the detailed procedures and results of any one of the particular experiments, and I apologize for the violence I do them. But I think the essence of the procedure and the outcome is supported by them all, and this seems also to be the opinion of Brendan Maher (Maher, McKean, & McLaughlin, 1966). In the first place, one is dealing in these experiments only with the linguistic products of patients diagnosed as schizophrenic, or in one experiment, psychotic in other ways. Linguistic productions of normals do not enter the picture. In the second place, it is necessary to recognize, as all clinicians do, that only some of the linguistic productions of schizophrenics appear either disorganized or deluded; very many do not. Basically, what is done in these experiments is to take some short stretch of language produced by a schizophrenic, bizarre or not, perhaps 50 words or so, sometimes spontaneously written or spoken, sometimes a response to a Wechsler-Bellevue vocabulary item. These short stretches are put on separate slips of paper with no identifying information whatever, but with, I would suppose, some automatic implication that they were seriously intended and not playful. Judges are then given the slips of paper and asked to sort them, sometimes on a 7-point scale of degree of schizophrenicity, sometimes simply into disordered or deluded as opposed to normal. The judges typically have been of two sorts: PhD clinical psychologists with some years of experience and college undergraduates whom we unaccountably still call "naive."

I think there are three results of considerable interest:

1. Most significantly, the interjudge reliability of both clinicians and undergraduates is consistently high, from about .70 on up, but furthermore, the reliability of the clinicians is only slightly higher than that of undergraduates, always higher to be sure but not much so, and the correlations between the judgments of the two groups are consistently very high.

2. Sometimes an effort has been made to study the validity of the judgments as well as the reliability, but this is not easy since the criterion is difficult to fix in view of the substantial unreliability of psychiatric diagnoses. Still, efforts have been made. One study (Cohen, 1961), for example, used the pooled assessments of three highly experienced and respected clinicians, who furthermore had access to all case history data, as a criterion of degree of schizophrenicity. With respect to validity, both clinician judges and undergraduate judges do fairly well, but the correlations are lower than in the case of interjudge reliabilities, and the difference between clinicians and undergraduates greater.

3. Several studies, such as Alan Cohen's (1961) and Brendan Maher's (Maher et al., 1966), have sought to discover the relative importance of the various sorts of cues relied on by the judges. In general summary, the formal cues of grammar and prosody seem of little or no importance; it is the meaning or content that guides the judgment.

The task of judging a short linguistic stretch out of context as deviant or not is one with which psycholinguists are familiar—but we have used it to entirely different purposes. It is a way of inquiring about the grammaticality, or well-formedness, of a sentence as well as about semantic anomaly, ambiguity, and the like. In general, it provides a test going beyond one's own intuition of the adequacy of proposed grammars and partial semantic theories. While the outcomes of such studies show that there are definite fringe areas where normal adult speakers do not agree very well, they also show, if indeed it needs showing, that there is a vast, really infinitely large area in which we do agree with one another, especially as regards grammar, and we do conform to the rules that linguists have written. If you were to read on a slip of paper "John will drive, didn't he?" or "Sally digged a holing," there is little doubt that you would find something grammatically amiss whether or not you had any explicit knowledge of the rules violated. It is my scarcely revolutionary suggestion that we as participants in this culture share also some much more complex notion of what constitutes adequate reality testing and rational coherence and share it well enough to agree quite closely on whether thought samples are deluded or disordered. And this sharing results not primarily from professional training but from general enculturation since naive undergraduates are not much different in their judgments than experienced clinicians.

Finally, our conception of adequate reality testing, like grammar, is continuously evolving, and just as some Middle English sentences would strike us as ungrammatical today, so some Middle English beliefs and reasoning might strike us as deluded or insane if put forward, not in a play, but as a basis for serious action. This does not imply, of course, that judgments of either ungrammaticality or delusion result from any sort of conspiracy to suppress dissent. Nor does it seem to me to imply that mental or neurological illness is a mistaken category for departures from what are admittedly relative standards. Especially not, since the intent of the category is to secure more humane treatment than is associated with alternative categories. The standards evolve, but a departure remains a departure even though it is not one in any absolute and eternal sense.

A difference, of course, between the ungrammatical and the delusional cases is that, with respect to the grammars, there are reasonably full, explicit formulations of the rules that govern judgment. With respect to thought, explicit formulation is very spotty and perhaps can never approach completeness. The most relevant formulations that exist are not, I think, the logic and the principles of evidence taught in schools, though these are canons to which we make ultimate appeal. But I should think the most relevant efforts to make explicit the notions of rationality on which we operate are the efforts to describe *psychological* implication, principles of affective consistency, principles of attribution, and the common fallacies of logic and of evidence evaluation. All of these seem to be efforts to describe rules we really use rather than rules we ought to use, and it seems chiefly to be the rules we use that cause propositions to be considered deluded. It is perhaps also the departures from these rules that indicate mental illness. Obviously only a small beginning has been made in the task of making explicit the rules and knowledge by which we judge rationality, but that does not prevent us from making the judgments and making them with a considerable degree of agreement.

Every sort of disease represents a deviation from a norm; in somatic diseases it is a deviation from the norms of the organs and functions of the body—norms that are often uniform for the species. In mental disease it is a deviation from the norms of action, belief, perception, and so on—norms that are, at least in part, culturally and historically variable. There have been a great many attempts to describe the nature of the basic deviation in schizophrenia: concreteness or overinclusion or privateness in concept formation; overgeneralization in learning; paralogic in thinking; associative intrusions in language; a failure to filter what is irrelevant in attention, etc. In general, that part of the vast quantity of research supporting these ideas that I have been able to read seems to me rather disappointing (with the qualification that I think a better case can be made for attention than for the others). The results seem to me generally disappointing in that they tend often to be inconsistent across studies and, even when consistent, usually yield small, barely significant differences between schizophrenics and normals. Of course, there are any number of possible reasons why the experimental outcomes should be so confused: failure to specify schizophrenic subtypes, failure to say what if any medication was in use, unreliability of diagnosis, and so on. But after reading quite a lot of this work, I cannot help wondering if there is not a more fundamental difficulty. The tasks used have typically been well-established laboratory tasks having slight and very occasional personal interest to any subject. It is as if the assumption were that schizophrenia resulted from an across-the-board, content-free impairment of a basic function like perception, learning, concept formation, or attention. If that were indeed the case, then it would make no difference what task was used to test the function, and convenience might as well dictate the selection. But is this the case? It may be that we have here been too much influenced by the disease concept. Lacking psychic organs comparable to the heart, liver, and spleen, we may have made too much of the unity of our functions. In my conversations with schizophrenics, it was not my impression that some particular function had become impaired in a content-free way. Quite the contrary, it seemed that when one hit upon or even approached the disturbed content area, any or all functions might suffer disruption. And the differences from normals were not slight. The average laboratory task, possibly any laboratory task, may elicit a lower performance from schizophrenics than from normals because it touches here and there on something that matters to one or another subject, and this will happen a bit more often and will be more disruptive for schizophrenics than for normals.

What should cause some people to break with their society's notions of reality testing and rationality in particular content areas? That, of course, is what we should like to know. David Rosenthal's (1970) review of the genetic evidence, which is the most complete and sophisticated I know, concluded that there is no reasonable doubt that genetics plays a substantial, though not simple, role. Evidently, there is something like a varying potential for each psychic innertube to blow. But genetics is far from accounting for all the variance, and in particular, it says nothing about why each inner tube should blow in one spot rather than another. My own guess is that the people studying family interaction like Theodore Lidz (Lidz, Fleck, & Cornelison, 1965) are on the right track. Though I do not think the case has been proved that some general factor like the double bind (Bateson, Jackson, Haley, & Weakland, 1956) is responsible. The double bind, a self-contradicting communication with one message in one channel and one in another, cannot be the prime etiological agent in schizophrenia because of its sheer ubiquity. It is in the first place, depending on its exact formulation, essentially the same as one or another of the forms of conflict formulated by Neal Miller and Kurt Lewin many years ago and also the same as one or another of the principles of imbalance, incongruity, and dissonance in attitude change. No one has thought to suggest that conflict or inconsistency must cause schizophrenia. And for good reason: they are with us all the time. And there are plenty of ways of responding to double binds without losing your grip on rationality. Fire back a double-bind message of your own, for instance, using a couple of the multiple channels available for communication. People do it all the time. Or leave the field. Or disregard one message. To make the etiological role of the double bind at all plausible (e.g., Weakland, 1960), one has to explain why some people cannot react in any of these ordinary ways but must feel both sides of the bind intensely, be unable to respond in kind, or leave the field. If these are the problems, however, then it is not the existence of the bind as such that causes illness. I should perhaps add that by my view of the mind-body problem, one does not deny biochemical causes in espousing family interaction causes. Of course, there are biochemical causes, and it would not surprise me at all if the biochemists got there first with a precise etiology and an effective therapy.

All of this logic chopping leaves me with the feeling that I have been able to do nothing in return for the kindness of the persons called schizophrenic whom I met during my three weeks outside the office. And I deeply regret that, because I found myself sympathetic to all of them and pained by the suffering many endure each day. I cannot forget the plaintive remark made by the young patient in the novel *I Never Promised You a Rose Garden*, a remark made to her intellectualizing psychiatrist: "Doctor, my difference is not my disease." Cognitive psychologists cannot help being interested also in the differences and must hope patients will forgive them.

REFERENCES

Bateson, G., Jackson, D. D., Haley, J., & Weakland, J. H. Toward a theory of schizophrenia. *Behavioral Science*, 1956, *1*, 251–264.

Brown, R. *A first language; The early stages*. Cambridge, Mass.: Harvard Univ. Press, 1973.

Cameron, N. *The psychology of the behavior disorders*. Boston: Houghton Mifflin, 1947.

Cohen, A. J. Estimating the degree of schizophrenic pathology from recorded interview samples. *Journal of Clinical Psychology*, 1961, *17*, 403–406.

Festinger, L., Riecken, H. W., & Schachter, S. *When prophecy fails*. Minneapolis: Univ. of Minnesota Press, 1956.

Hunt, W. A., Jones, N. F., & Hunt, E. B. Reliability of clinical judgment as a function of clinical experience. *Journal of Clinical Psychology*, 1957, *13*, 377–378.

Jones, N. F., Jr. The validity of clinical judgments of schizophrenic pathology based on verbal responses to intelligence test items. *Journal of Clinical Psychology*, 1959, *15*, 396–400.

Katz, J. J. Analyticity and contradiction in natural language. In J. A. Fodor & J. J. Katz (Eds.), *The structure of language: Readings in the philosophy of language*. Englewood Cliffs, N.J.: Prentice-Hall, 1964.

Katz, J. J., & Fodor, J. A. The structure of a semantic theory. *Language*, 1963, *39*, 170–210.

Kohlberg, L., & Kramer, R. Continuities and discontinuities in childhood and adult moral development. *Human Development*, 1969, *12*, 93–120.

Laing, R. D. *The divided self*. London: Tavistock, 1960.

Lidz, T., Fleck, S., & Cornelison, A. R. *Schizophrenia and the family*. New York: International Universities Press, 1965.

Maher, B. A. *Principles of psychopathology: An experimental approach.* New York: McGraw-Hill, 1966.

Maher, B. A., McKean, K. O., & McLaughlin, B. Studies in psychotic language. In P. J. Stone, D. C. Dunphy, M. S. Smith, & D. M. Ogilvie (Eds.), *The general inquirer: A computer approach to content analysis.* Cambridge, Mass.: M.I.T. Press, 1966.

Rosenthal, D. *Genetic theory and abnormal behavior.* New York: McGraw-Hill, 1970.

Schweitzer, A. *The psychiatric study of Jesus.* Boston: Beacon, 1948.

Szasz, T. S. *The myth of mental illness.* New York: Harper & Row, 1961.

———. *Law, liberty, and psychiatry.* New York: Macmillan, 1963.

Weakland, J. H. The double-bind hypothesis of schizophrenia and three-party interaction. In D. D. Jackson (Ed.), *The etiology of schizophrenia.* New York: Basic Books, 1960.

8. PSYCHOSURGERY:

A Multilevel Controversy

In 1936 under the direction of the Portuguese physician Egas Moniz, the first recorded psychosurgical operation on a human being was performed by Almeida Lima. This operation, termed a prefrontal leukotomy, involved the removal of several cores of brain tissue from the frontal lobe of an individual classified as schizophrenic. Although it is somewhat uncertain just what the result of this particular operation was (the patient survived), Walter Freeman and J. W. Watts introduced a modified frontal lobotomy technique into the United States the following year. It is estimated that during the period between 1936 and 1955 as many as 50,000 such operations were performed in this country for various reasons, primarily in efforts to alleviate the worst symptoms of agitated schizophrenia. However, many other conditions were also treated, including depression, homosexuality, and narcotic addiction. Psychosurgery is brain surgery performed with the intention of altering behavior. In the great majority of these cases there was no indication of any disease or damage to the brain. Brain surgery to remove diseased or damaged tissue is *not* properly termed psychosurgery.

Naturally, such radical procedures received considerable attention, but from the beginning it has been extremely difficult to obtain objective, reliable information as to the outcome of such surgical procedures. Too often, the only information available is from the neurosurgeon who performed the operation. Can you anticipate the problems of getting reliable, objective information in such cases? In many other cases preoperative data is sketchy or unavailable, and postoperative reports are simply that the patient is improved, about the same, or worse.

The authors of the following two articles address themselves to some of the issues and controversies in this area. As you will see, they deal with a wide range of issues: medical, legal, and practical issues, such as how to get adequate data in order to evaluate the effectiveness of psychosurgical procedures. Although the number of such operations has decreased in the United States since the 1935–55 period, there are still several neurosurgeons performing such operations, perhaps a few hundred a year in this country. Worldwide, psychosurgery continues in many other countries, such as West Germany, Denmark, England, Canada, India, Switzerland, Spain, France, Mexico, Japan, Sweden, Finland, Italy, and Norway.

In this country the state laws about who can perform what psychosurgical operations for what reasons and on whom vary considerably. A class project may be based on these questions: What are the laws regulating psychosurgery in your state? What is the current frequency of such surgery? How could you find out?

Bertram S. Brown, Louis A. Wienckowski, and Lyle W. Bivens review the current status of psychosurgery from a somewhat objective standpoint. Writing for the Department of Health, Education, and Welfare, they point out the recent history, current controls, and necessary safeguards for the future for patients recommended for psychosurgery. As you read this article, see if you can define the major problems in controlling psychosurgery. Also, try to define the issues that go beyond the borders of academic psychology.

The article by Vernon Mark is one of the few written by a practicing psychosurgeon for a general audience. Although technical reports on psychosurgery are available (Hitchcock, Laitinen, & Vaernet, 1972), it is difficult to find articles written for a more general audience by psychiatrists and neurosurgeons who advocate psychosurgery. One notable exception is the book by Vernon Mark and Frank Ervin called *Violence and the Brain* (1970). Another possibility for further reading is E. Valenstein's book, *Brain Control* (1973).

One of the nagging problems related to psychosurgery (and other procedures) is "informed consent." If the informed consent of the patient is required for such surgery, as many have proposed, what are some of the difficulties that may arise? What are some possible problems if informed consent is not required?

One state that has wrestled with this problem is Oregon. Oregon has a quite detailed and elaborate law regulating psychosurgery. Oregon Senate Bill 298, which took effect on July 1, 1973, may serve as a model for other state legislatures.

In addition to the legal and ethical issues, there are other points of controversy. The site of the surgery and the amount of tissue removed vary in different situations, and even what disorders can be helped is not widely agreed on. How can we best avoid what Mark calls the George Gershwin syndrome, while following a prudent course of action with respect to psychosurgery? Do you think these issues are best left to the lawyers and the doctors? What, if any, might be the role of a psychologist with regard to these controversial issues?

REFERENCES

Hitchcock, E., Laitinen, L., & Vaernet, K. (Eds.). *Psychosurgery: Proceedings of the Second International Conference on Psychosurgery*. Springfield, Ill.: Charles C. Thomas, 1972.

Mark, V. H., & Ervin, F. R. *Violence and the brain*. New York: Harper & Row, 1970.

Valenstein, E. *Brain control*. New York: Wiley, 1973.

PSYCHOSURGERY: PERSPECTIVE ON A CURRENT ISSUE

Bertram S. Brown, Director,
National Institute of Mental Health

Louis A. Wienckowski, Director,
Division of Extramural Research Programs

Lyle W. Bivens, Chief, Neuropsychology Section,
Division of Extramural Research Programs

People don't ask for facts in making up their minds. They would rather have one good, soul-satisfying emotion than a dozen facts.
—*Robert Keith Leavitt,* Voyages and Discoveries, *1939*

The control of human behavior has become an issue of considerable concern and prominence. Most of the concern is generated by a rapidly advancing biomedical and behavioral science technology that provides explicit and powerful means for controlling behavior and thus carries with it a correspondingly increased potential for abuse. Much recent publicity has focused on the control of behavior by removing or destroying portions of the human brain, a procedure usually called psychosurgery (Breggin, 1972a, 1972b; Holden, 1973). It also is called psychiatric surgery or functional neurosurgery. Psychosurgery is not a new technology. It has been used for nearly forty years to treat a variety of mental illnesses. But the dramatic and drastic nature of psychosurgery has aroused many concerns about its potential abuse. The following discussion is intended to provide an objective account of some of these concerns as well as to offset some of the misconceptions that have been fostered by recent and strongly critical publicity.

WHAT IS PSYCHOSURGERY?

Psychosurgery can be defined as surgical removal or destruction of brain tissue or the cutting of brain tissue to disconnect one part of the

Brown, Bertram S., Wienckowski, Louis A., and Bivens, Lyle W. Psychosurgery: Perspective on a current issue. National Institute of Mental Health, Alcohol, Drug Abuse, and Mental Health Administration, U.S. Department of Health, Education, and Welfare. Reprinted with permission.

brain from another with the *intent of altering behavior*. Usually it is performed in the absence of direct evidence of existing structural disease or damage in the brain.

The surgical treatment of epilepsy, while in one sense a form of psychosurgery since behavioral symptoms are altered, should be excluded from this discussion when the disease can be clearly diagnosed and there is convincing evidence that epilepsy is caused by organic pathology in the brain. Of course, any other neurosurgical treatment to repair or remove damaged brain tissue or to remove tumors is not psychosurgery.

In neuroanatomical terminology, the suffix -otomy refers to the destruction of brain tissue or the cutting of fibers in the brain. Lobotomy, therefore, is the destruction of tissue in the frontal lobes of the brain or the cutting of fibers connecting the frontal lobes with the rest of the brain. Thalamotomy refers to destruction of portions of the thalamus. The suffix -ectomy refers to the actual removal of tissue. Thus a frontal lobectomy would be the removal of the frontal lobes of the brain. Topectomy refers to selective removal of portions of the cortex, usually from the frontal region of the brain.

Ever since the first "radical" lobotomies were performed (Moniz, 1965), in which virtually all of the subcortical connections of the frontal lobe were severed, surgeons have attempted to refine the techniques to limit the brain destruction in the hope of reducing adverse side effects. Topectomy, which damaged less brain tissue than the early lobotomies, was tried. Then a further refinement of topectomy was the development of the undercutting techniques whereby the subcortical connections of a selective part of the cortex were severed but the cortex itself was left intact.

This search for limitation of destruction of brain tissue (and presumably of adverse side effects) culminated in stereotaxic techniques in which a small electrode is positioned in the brain. Geometric coordinates and x-ray inspection are used to place the electrode in a precise location, and then the tissue is destroyed at the electrode tip by passing a current through the electrode. With the development of stereotaxic techniques, structures deep within the brain become accessible for destruction, and amygdalotomy, thalamotomy, and hypothalamotomy began to replace lobotomy as psychosurgical procedures.

Psychosurgery was recommended for curing or ameliorating schizophrenia ("Lobotomy," 1969), depression (Knight, 1969), homosexuality ("Homosexuality," 1970), childhood behavior disorders (Andy, 1970), criminal behavior (Vaernet & Madsen, 1970; Koskoff & Goldhurst, 1968; Hirose, 1968), and a variety of narcotic addiction (Smolik, 1950); Scarff, 1950; Wikler, Pescor, Kalbaugh, & Angelucci, 1952), and other psychiatric problems. For a period from about 1936 to 1955, lobotomy was enthusiastically embraced by a large number of medical and psychiatric practitioners in this country and in England. The greatest proportion of psychosurgical treatments was upon schizophrenic patients, who were often difficult to manage and totally disabled in terms of functioning in society. A large number of psychosurgical procedures were performed in the United States (perhaps as many as 50,000 between 1936 and the mid-1950's). These operations were especially popular in England, and as late as 1962 an English study estimated that between 400 and 525 operations a year were being performed there (Pippard, 1962).

EVALUATIONS OF PSYCHOSURGERY

Starting with the first lobotomy by Egas Moniz in Portugal in 1935, there was considerable criticism of the technique and of the exaggerated claims by its proponents of the curative power of lobotomy. This criticism had little effect on the psychosurgeons, who continued to ignore or gloss over the side effects of their procedures and who continued to accept the view that "it is better for the patient to have a simplified intellect capable of elementary acts, than an intellect where there reigns the disorder of subtle synthesis. Society can accommodate itself to the most humble laborer, but it justifiably distrusts the mad thinker" (Freeman & Watts, 1950).

In 1947 an exhaustive study of 48 mental patients, 24 of whom had undergone some form of psychosurgery (lobotomy or topectomy) was undertaken by a group of scientists called the Columbia-Greystone Associates. An extensive series of medical, psychological, and physiological tests was conducted on these patients, and the results reported in 1949. In a follow-up report 3½ years after the original study, the status of the original patients in the study was reviewed. Neither the original nor the follow-up study was able to provide any substantial scientific evidence that these psychosurgical procedures were useful (Mettler, 1952).

A much larger project in England evaluated 10,365 patients subjected to lobotomy (Tooth & Newton, 1961). The study revealed that about half of the operated patients remained in the hospital at the time of the survey in 1957. Little or no data on psychological changes are provided, and since the operated patients spanned a wide range of psychiatric disorders, one could speculate that the patients that were discharged might have been discharged even if they had not undergone surgery, since many psychiatric problems show a tendency to disappear without (or despite) treatment.

Many smaller studies, using small numbers of patients with varied psychiatric or behavioral disorders, have been reported in the literature. Surgical techniques range from lobotomies to the implantation of radioactive pellets to destroy deep brain tissue. Although many of the published studies are deficient in methodology and clinical reporting, there are several that conclude that psychosurgery can be useful in selected cases as a "last resort treatment" (Koskoff, Dennis, Lazone, & Wheeler, 1947; Miller, 1967; Strom-Olsen & Carlisle, 1971; Tan, Marks, and Marset, 1971; "Surgical Modification," 1971; Kalinowsky, Brill, Freyhan, Cattell, & Ransohoff, 1969; Scoville, 1969; Shobe & Gildea, 1968). One study goes so far as to suggest that leucotomy may be the "treatment of choice" in certain cases, rather than being used as a last resort (Hohne & Walsh, 1970).

Although it is easy from our current vantage point to condemn the "lobotomists," it should be pointed out that they were dedicated and genuinely concerned professionals who were trying to help patients suffering from a devastatingly serious psychiatric disease. Their view that it was ethical and reasonable to change an immobile, uncommunicative, or destructively hyperactive patient into a placid "housekeeper" by psychosurgery is not entirely without merit. The most extreme symptoms of mental disease which they were faced with on a daily basis might have made the most ethically concerned and moralistic of us resort to desperate measures.

In fact, lobotomy had a clear, albeit limited, usefulness. Lobotomy was a "therapy of desperation," but it frequently improved the functioning of patients suffering from severe mental illness, either by improving their condition within the hospital or by permitting them to lead useful lives outside the hospital. The popular conception that lobotomy turns a person into a "vegetable" is not true. Many of the psychological changes produced by lobotomy are often much more subtle than is popularly believed (Smith, 1960; Poppen, Pribram, & Robinson, 1965; Smith & Kinder, 1959; Hamlin, 1970). Faced with the choice of leaving a patient raving in the back ward of a mental hospital, soiling himself with his own feces, and attacking other patients and staff or performing a lobotomy with a reasonably good chance of improving his condition so he can be moved to a ward with better conditions, many reasonable people would make the latter choice. Although in many cases lobotomized patients who were able to be discharged from the hospital functioned at a lower intellectual level than prior to the onset of their mental illness, this was better than the realistic and grim prospect of spending the rest of their lives in the hospital.

A case history of such a situation illustrates the usefulness of lobotomy: A schizophrenic woman, aged 31, had an abrupt onset of delusions that she was being followed by enemy agents and had seen and spoken with Dr. Goebbels, Winston Churchill, and the Archbishop of Canterbury. At various times she was withdrawn or dangerously assaultive. She was slovenly and dirty and resisted all nursing attention. After 28 months of illness a prefrontal lobotomy was performed. She showed immediate improvement with a marked reduction of her suspiciousness, and she became friendly and began to look after her personal hygiene. Although she remained in the hospital two years after the operation, she had ground parole and was a competent and sociable worker on the ward and in the hospital laundry. However, she was still disoriented for time and events and could only respond appropriately and effectively to her immediate environment (Partridge, 1950).

In the many case histories where lobotomy has had a beneficial effect, particularly for schizophrenic patients, this seems to be the typical pattern—improvement in personal habits, reduction of hallucinatory or delusional behavior, and improvement in social behavior. But because thought disorders and disorientation persist, the patient cannot really effectively function in the outside world and remains in the hospital environment. For other types of mental illness such as obsessive-compulsive neurosis, lobotomy more often relieved the symptoms to a sufficient degree that the person could be discharged from the hospital and return to productive work.

However, there were occasional disastrous effects of lobotomy (or of other forms of psychosurgery) on personality or intellectual function, and these cases were the source of much of the strong criticism leveled at lobotomy. An illustrative case is one from a series of medical temporal lobectomies performed on a group of schizophrenic or epileptic patients that resulted in devastating memory deficits. The case of H. M., who was operated on for relief of epilepsy, is described as follows:

> The patient was drowsy for the first few postoperative days but then, as he became more alert, a severe memory impairment was apparent. He could no longer recognize the hospital staff, apart from Dr. Scoville himself, whom he had known for many years; he did not remember and could not relearn the way to the bathroom, and he seemed to retain nothing of the day-to-day happenings in the hospital. At the same time, it was discovered that he had an extensive though patchy, retrograde amnesia, such that he did not remember the death of a favourite uncle three years before, nor anything of the period spent in the hospital three years before the operation, but did recall a few trivial incidents that had taken place just before his admission to the hospital. His early memories were seemingly vivid and intact, his speech was normal, and his social behaviour and emotional responses were entirely appropriate.
>
> Some 12 years later, the patient's condition was unchanged:
>
> . . . His mother states now, as she did in 1955, that he is unable to learn where objects constantly in use are kept; for example, although he mows the lawn regularly, and quite expertly, she still has to tell him where to find the lawnmower, even when he has been using it only the day before. His mother also observes that he will do the same jigsaw puzzles day after day without showing any practice effect, and read the same magazines over and over again without ever finding their contents familiar. The same forgetfulness applies to people he has met since the operation, even to those neighbours who have been visiting the house regularly for the past six years. He has not learned their names and he does not recognize any of them if he meets them in the street. (Milner, 1966).

Similar, but somewhat less severe memory defects were observed in other patients in the series.

But it was not the evaluations of psychosurgery or the ethical issues that led to its decreased use. The event that had the greatest impact on reducing the number of psychosurgical procedures was the introduction of chemical therapy for mental illness. With the advent of the tranquilizers in the mid-1950's, psychosurgery lost its position as the major somatic treatment for severe mental illness. Psychotic behavior that had previously been controllable only by psychosurgical treatment could now be controlled by less drastic, and usually more effective, chemical therapy.

CURRENT PSYCHOSURGERY

It is difficult to estimate the current extent of psychosurgery. Much of the psychosurgery today is performed by private practitioners, and there is no way to obtain any reasonably accurate figures. There does seem to have been some increase in the frequency of psychosurgical operations over the past 15 years, probably due to the failure of pharmacotherapy to fulfill the earlier expectations for it. Currently, psychosurgeons appear to be concentrating on destruction of portions of the limbic system of the brain, which animal research has shown to be involved in emotional behavior. Interruption of the cingulum bundle or removal of the cingulate gyrus—parts of the cortex which early workers thought to be a brain locus responsible for the experiencing of emotions—seems to be a particularly popular procedure (Ballantine, Cassidy, Flanigan, & Morino, 1967; Brown & Lighthill, 1968). Destruction of portions of the thalamus (Mark, Barry, McLardy, & Ervin, 1970) or hypothalamus (Schvarcz, Driollet, Rios, & Betti, 1972), other structures implicated in emotional behavior, has been used.

Over the past two decades, scientists have made considerable progress in defining and understanding the functional role of the frontal lobes and of various other parts of the brain (Isaacson, 1972; Thorne, 1972; Rosen, Stein & Butters, 1971; Pribram, Ahumada, Haryog, & Roos, 1964). Almost all of the basic research in this area has been conducted with animal subjects. For example, a scientist supported by the National Institute of Mental Health has localized areas in the cat brain, which, when electrically stimulated with permanently implanted electrodes, cause the cat to mount a directed and well-integrated attack on another animal subject. In the absence of such electrical stimulation, the cat remains placidly quiet. Conversely, stimulation of other brain areas can cause an animal that is performing an aggressive attack to stop and become placid. Extensive studies on stimulation and lesions of various areas of the brain of monkeys, cats, and rats have revealed a complex picture of several specific brain structures that are involved in the control of a variety of emotional and aggressive behaviors.

Taking their cue from these animal studies, psychosurgeons have attempted to eliminate violently aggressive behavior in human patients by small and localized destruction of specific brain areas or by electrical stimulation of brain areas with surgically implanted electrodes. These psychosurgical procedures are, for the most part, quite different from the lobotomy in that they are more firmly based on scientific data about the role of the brain structures, and the destruction of brain tissue is much more limited and localized. In a few instances, the psychosurgeons have, prior to destruction, tried to confirm the role of the specific brain structure they intend to lesion by first electrically stimulating the area to see if whatever behavior they are trying to eliminate can be elicited by the stimulation. In other cases, stimulation of only those brain areas thought to inhibit aggression is performed; any procedure based on stimulation is preferable, because electrical stimulation generally produces less brain damage than lesions. In any case, whether lesion or stimulation techniques are used, the modern psychosurgeon attempts to minimize the adverse side effects of the procedures by lesioning or stimulating only a small area of brain tissue, with the hope of eliminating the specific behavioral problems but not producing any undesirable changes in personality, intelligence, creativity, or motivation.

An illustrative case history is provided in a book entitled *Violence and the Brain* by Vernon H. Mark, M.D., and Frank R. Ervin, M.D. (1970). They cite the case of Julia, a 21-year-old girl who had on several occasions assaulted persons for no apparent reason. She was also subject to frequent severe temper tantrums and psychotic episodes, and she made several unsuccessful attempts at suicide. Julia's troubles can apparently be traced back to a severe attack of encephalitis following mumps before she was two years old. Since the age of 10, she had been having epileptic seizures. After several serious assaults, including stabbing another girl in the ladies lounge of a movie theater and stabbing a nurse in a mental hospital with a pair of scissors, and after numerous unsuccessful attempts to treat Julia with psychotherapy, electroshock, and a variety of drugs, she was admitted to Boston City Hospital for clinical evaluation. Electrodes were implanted in the temporal lobes of her brain, from which seizure discharges were recorded. By electrically stimulating the brain areas the attending physicians were able to elicit symptoms that were characteristic of the beginnings of her seizures. A lesion was made in the left temporal lobe, which seemed to be the side from which the symptoms could be most easily produced. However, this lesion did not seem to improve her condition. Using radio-stimulation techniques, in which an implanted electrode in the brain can be stimulated without having any wires or leads connected to the patient, the physicians stimulated the right temporal lobe and elicited fullblown rage reactions from Julia, during which she would attack the wall of her room or attack the nearest person if anyone was present. Abnormal electrical activity was also recorded just prior to the rage attacks. Another lesion was then made on the right side and in the two years since the second lesion was made, Julia has had only two mild episodes of rage. However, the epileptic seizures and her psychotic behavior have been unchanged.

Most of the above discussion has focused on aggressive behavior, rather than on the many other forms of mental illness such as schizophrenia or depression. Although psychosurgery is sometimes used in cases of severe depression or other serious mental problems, currently it is principally the uncontrollably aggressive patient who becomes the prime candidate for psychosurgery. The aggressive patient is the one most disruptive and threatening to family, friends, and hospital staff.

The serious disturbance of the patient's own life and the lives of the people around him and the potential for bodily harm that he may inflict on himself or others often leads to treatment of a drastic nature, especially when other treatments, particularly drugs, seem to fail.

PROGRAMS OF THE NATIONAL INSTITUTE OF MENTAL HEALTH

Since 1947 the National Institute of Mental Health has been strongly committed to a broadly based research program on brain function and behavior. All of the mental states of man are related to physical events occurring within the brain. Emotions such as love, fear, and hate are generally believed to be reflections of chemical and electrical activity in the billions of nerve cells that comprise the central nervous system. When man or animal eats, drinks, or engages in sexual activity, these drive states are a function of activity of the brain. The unimaginable complexity of the brain, not just of man but of lower animals as well, is a distinct challenge both to basic scientists and to scientists and practitioners devoted to the study of mental illness.

If normal behaviors are produced and controlled by physical events in the central nervous system, then pathological behaviors must be the result of these physical processes operating in pathological ways. In order to understand the root causes of mental disease, it is essential to understand the physiological events that shape and control normal behaviors. Consequently, support of basic brain-behavior research is an integral part of the activities of the National Institute of Mental Health.

One of the first grants awarded by the extramural research grant program of the NIMH was to study the basic neurological aspects involved in the learning process. Since that time the extramural support programs of the Institute have provided a continued and increasing program of support for neuropsychology (brain-behavior) research. In addition, the intramural research program of the NIMH has been in the forefront of research on the physiology of brain function and especially in the biochemical systems of the brain.

Despite the great amount of research on basic brain-behavior relationships, a great deal more needs to be done. Most of the mechanisms by which the brain controls a great deal of behavior, such as learning and the emotions, are just beginning to be understood. The brain is responsible not only for control of processes as relatively simple as the regulation of glandular, visceral, and muscular function but is also responsible for the highest mental processes involved in scientific and artistic creativity.

Moreover, there is a tremendous diversity of physical processes taking place within the brain which makes it necessary that the concerted efforts of scientists from many disciplines be brought to bear on the study of brain-behavior relationships.

Many pressing and important problems regarding brain-behavior relations are currently being investigated in research laboratories around the country. For example: What chemicals are responsible for transmission of nerve impulses within the brain, and how do these chemicals control different forms of behavior? What chemical or physical changes occur when learning takes place or when a memory is recovered from the brain? What anatomical structures and what chemicals are responsible for aggressive behavior, sexual behavior, eating behavior, drinking behavior, and for sleep and dreaming? How are the brain and central nervous system related to the autonomic nervous system, which controls many life processes such as heart rate, blood pressure, and a wide variety of visceral functions. What happens to the behavior and cognitive processes of man when portions of the brain are damaged through accident, birth injury, malnutrition, or disease? Can functions that have been lost through such disruption of the brain be recovered or taken over by other portions of the brain?

These and many other lines of research are being actively pursued by grantees of the National Institute of Mental Health and in the NIMH intramural research program. However, as each specific question is answered to some degree, several other questions arise as a result of the research. As more and more is learned about control of behavior by the brain, questions asked by brain scientists become more specific and more amenable to experimental tests. We are thus well on the way to building a solid framework for understanding mental processes.

Although most of the brain-behavior research supported by the Institute involves experiments with animal subjects, some studies involve human subjects. Most of the human studies are aimed at understanding the behavioral consequences of altered brain function as a result of war injury, accident, disease, or surgery performed because of *clinical* necessity (e.g., removal of brain tumors). Thus neurological patients are studied with behavioral tests in order to define and understand the sometimes subtle effects of insult to the brain (Sperry, 1973; Teuber, 1968). In these cases there is no experimental manipulation of the brain itself; the subjects are selected on the basis of pre-existing brain dysfunction, damage, or clinical surgery.

THE NIMH STUDY ON EPILEPSY AND VIOLENCE

The single project supported by the NIMH which came closest to psychosurgery was a contract, in the amount of $500,000 to the Neuro-Research Foundation in Boston, Massachusetts, which began on June 25, 1971, and terminated on March 31, 1973. The contract involved an attempt to understand and control violent and destructive behavior that is presumed to be a direct result of brain dysfunction.

The research being conducted under this contract was based on an hypothesis that some forms of mental illness, especially those characterized by violence or hyperactivity, are the direct result of organic brain disease. Based on evidence from animal studies showing relationships between the limbic system and emotional behavior, the limbic system of the brain is usually singled out as the area most likely to be involved (Wasman & Flynn, 1966; Ellison & Flynn, 1968). There are also some scattered and anecdotal reports in the clinical literature on the effects of damage to the limbic system by tumors or by war injury or accident in which a predominant symptom is violent behavior. A few studies have purported to show that there is a high incidence of abnormalities in the electrical brain activity (EEG) of criminal populations, particularly in those subjects who have repeatedly committed senselessly violent acts (Mark & Ervin, 1970). Unfortunately, interpretation of the EEG is a difficult task, and the meaning of any given type of "abnormality" is an open question in view of the present inadequate understanding of the electrical processes of the brain. In any case the main point is that the psychosurgeon believes that there is an organic basis for disordered behavior.

Certain forms of epilepsy, a disorder characterized by recurrent electrical seizure activity in the brain, have been used by some psychosurgeons as a model for explaining what happens in the brain during some violent behavior. The supposition is that some sort of electrical seizure takes place in a part of the brain that controls aggression or emotional behavior. In fact, there have been unconfirmed reports that the emotional and behavioral states preceding some types of epileptic seizures correspond to the behaviors exhibited by persons just prior to the commission of a violent or aggressive act. In a few cases there does appear to be a clear relation between epilepsy and violence, with patients displaying both conditions (Podolsky, 1962). However, even in a case where a patient clearly has epilepsy and is also subject to rage attacks, the nature of the relation between the two conditions is unclear. Frequent and violent seizures and the accompanying psychological phenomena are devastating experiences; it seems likely that at least some of the violent behavior exhibited by epileptics is triggered by frustration and fear and not directly by any electrical seizure activity in the brain.

Some forms of epilepsy are not characterized by overt seizures and loss of consciousness. In one form called psychomotor epilepsy, the person has periods that may last from one to several minutes during which automatic or stereotyped movements occur; he may pick at his clothing or aimlessly rummage through a bureau drawer. When questioned or spoken to, the person is often unresponsive, and after the episode he is usually amnesic for the period of the seizure. The source of this form of epilepsy is thought to be in the temporal lobes of the brain, and it is often called temporal lobe epilepsy (this is not an entirely satisfactory terminology, since other forms of epilepsy can arise from temporal lobe disturbances).

The group at the Neuro-Research Foundation hypothesized that for some of those persons who exhibit periodic uncontrollable violent behavior, a process akin to psychomotor epilepsy is responsible, but the source of such brain dysfunction lies deeper in the brain in the limbic system, and thus the primary symptoms are emotional rather than the automatic and more subtly-disturbed behaviors seen in psychomotor epilepsy. The intent of this group was to try to identify the organic dysfunction which they have presumed is responsible for violent behavior. The main technique used is to implant electrodes in various parts of the brain and to try to identify abnormalities, particularly seizure-like discharges, which will correlate with aggressive behavior. If an apparent focus of seizure activity is found, and if this seizure activity appears to correlate with outbursts of aggressive behavior, then a small lesion may be made to destroy tissue at the seizure focus. Ideally, this restricted lesion will stop the seizure activity at its source. Whether or not this surgical procedure constitutes "psychosurgery" as defined in the beginning of this paper is debatable. Although the surgery is done to treat aggressive behavior, it is primarily intended to stop the seizure activity of the brain.

There are many problems in this seemingly straightforward and relatively simple procedure. In the first place there remains some question as to whether seizure activity in the brain is directly responsible for or even correlated with aggressive behavior. There are no firm scientific data, either from animal or human studies, to demonstrate a close relationship between either focal or generalized seizures and aggression. Therefore, one of the aims of the project being conducted by the Neuro-Research Foundation was to examine the degree of correlation between electrical seizures in the brain and aggressive or violent behavior.

One factor that makes this kind of research especially difficult is that simply admitting an epileptic patient or a person exhibiting violent behavior to a hospital and placing him in a treatment environment may greatly reduce the frequency and/or severity of the symptoms, in the absence of any medical treatment or drug regimen. Thus it is difficult to study a phenomenon that often disappears or appears much less frequently than before as soon as the patient is put in a treatment environment.

Factors such as this led the research team of the Neuro-Research Foundation to focus more on defining the environmental situations that trigger seizure activity or aggression and to test the value of psychiatric treatment, such as group therapy, in helping patients to deal with and control their periodic outbursts of violent behavior. In fact, during the course of this contract no psychosurgery was carried out (although one chronically epileptic patient did receive a brain lesion). The research emphasis was on electrical recording studies, correlation of electric brain activity with various behaviors, and psychiatric treatment.

One of the primary issues in this area, as in all research projects dealing with human subjects, is the protection of the rights of the individual. A project which involves medical or surgical treatment in combination with psychiatric treatment and deals with patients who are severely debilitated in terms of their capacity to function in society presents especially thorny issues of protecting the physical and psychological well-being of the patient. An equally important ethical issue is the scientific merit of the proposed research, since if the studies are not scientifically sound and are not likely to yield important and useful data, then the human subjects have been exposed to medical or psychological risks that are not outweighed by the potential benefits. To illustrate how important these issues are, we shall outline in some detail the scientific and ethical review process involved in establishing the contract with the Neuro-Research Foundation and describe the continuous monitoring of the project.

At the FY 1970 HEW budget hearings, Dr. William H. Sweet, Chief of Neurosurgery, Massachusetts General Hospital; Dr. Vernon H. Mark, Director of Neurosurgery at the Boston City Hospital; and Dr. Frank R. Ervin, Department of Psychiatry, Harvard Medical School, appeared before the Congressional Appropriations Committee and requested funding for partial support of a facility designed to study violence in relation to temporal lobe epilepsy. The study involved the control of rage seizure through the implantation of electrodes into the brain and gradual destruction of tissue in the amygdala and other structures in the temporal lobe. Other projects planned for the program were studies of chromosomal and dermatoglyphic (fingerprint) abnormalities as possibly related to epilepsy. The Congress earmarked $500,000 from Chronic Disease Program funds for this study.

As a result of expenditure controls in FY 1970 the Neurological and Sensory Disease Program in the Chronic Disease Program, which was relevant to such a special project, was eliminated. Consequently, the funds were not awarded in the first year. However, the FY 1971 budget for the National Institute of Mental Health contained $500,000 earmarked for funding this project. The following paragraph is quoted from the *Congressional Report* making appropriations for the Departments of Labor and Health, Education, and Welfare for FY 1971:

> Last year the Congress determined that a study should be funded on the causes of violent behavior resulting in death or critical injury to others, with the objective of discovering medical means for preventing people from committing senseless violence. The Congress directed the Chronic Disease Division of the Regional Medical Programs Service to provide $500,000 for such a study. However, the project was not funded by the Administration. Two reasons were given for the failure to respond to the directive: one was that the Chronic Disease Division of the RMPS was being phased out; the other was that the study of violent behavior more properly belongs in the jurisdiction of Mental Health. The Committee accepts these views and directs that $500,000 of this [mental health] appropriation be devoted to the first year operations of a study of violent behavior, in keeping with its intent of last year. (U.S. Senate Report, 1971)

In response to this Congressional directive, staff of the NIMH began to negotiate a contract for the support of this work. Discussions were held by phone, letter, and visits with Dr. Sweet concerning the procedures he would need to follow and the materials he would have to submit in order to obtain these funds. Arrangements were made for a site visit to the Boston City Hospital; the visiting team included two outside consultants who were experts in this area of research, as well as a representative from the NIH Office of Institutional Relations, whose principal responsibility is the protection of the rights and welfare of human subjects. The visit occupied a major portion of the day and included a tour of the facilities as well as intensive interviews with all of the relevant staff.

Prior to and during the NIMH review of the project, a series of reviews were conducted by a number of internal institutional committees at Harvard Medical School, Massachusetts General Hospital, and Boston City Hospital. These reviews were necessary to fulfill a Public Health Service requirement that projects dealing with human subjects must have the approval of an institutional committee.

In all candor, it must be admitted that there was considerable controversy during the review of this project: indeed one would be concerned if there were *not* controversy in the review of a project so fraught with ethical complexities. Ultimately, however, the project was approved by a committee of five senior scientists and clinicians from the Harvard Medical School, Massachusetts General Hospital, and other hospitals in the Boston area, and some of the controversial issues that arose during the NIMH review of the project were resolved by extensive further documentation and correspondence provided by the Neuro-Research Foundation. The award was made with the proviso that there be a thorough and continuing examination of the procedures and results of the project. It also is of interest that reviewers of the proposal felt that an important byproduct of the project was an opportunity to develop procedures to provide the necessary broadening of the processes of review increasingly demanded by research and development in the behavioral and biological sciences.

The procedures established for the protection of the human subjects in this project were designed to assure that the patients had problems severe enough to consider them as candidates for drastic treatment measures, that the patients were fully informed (insofar as possible) as to the potential risks involved, and that every conceivable measure of protection of the patients' rights and well-being was exerted. For each and every patient admitted to the program, a review committee composed of scientists and physicians not associated with the Neuro-Research Foundation would review the individual case and approve or disapprove his admission to the program. If a patient were admitted to the program, it would be only for psychiatric and medical evaluation studies, possibly including depth electrode studies of brain seizure activity. If on the basis of these studies the investigators felt that any brain lesioning procedures were warranted, additional review by another outside committee would be required.

During the tenure of this contract continuous monitoring of the project was conducted by NIMH staff and outside experts, including regular quarterly reports, continued contact by phone and mail, and periodic site visits. The emphasis on nonsurgical and psychiatric treatment provided encouraging indications that at least some patients exhibiting uncontrollable violent behavior can be helped without resorting to irreversible surgical treatment.

PSYCHOSURGERY, BEHAVIOR CONTROL, AND ETHICS

With very few exceptions, medical scientists and clinicians oppose the "classical" lobotomy. As previously discussed, there is no sound evidence that it is a worthwhile procedure, and it too often has deleterious effects on personality. Actually, lobotomy is not the issue; as techniques for more refined brain recording, stimulation, and lesioning have become available, and as the literature on animal brain research has begun to define, however vaguely, functions of specific brain areas, practitioners are more frequently considering surgical treatment for behavioral problems.

As with any controversial issue, there are extreme opinions pro and con psychosurgery. Some opponents argue that psychosurgery in any form and for any behavioral or mental disturbance—regardless of its severity—should be outlawed. At the other extreme, some proponents argue that psychosurgical procedures should no longer be considered research but constitute routine and accepted treatment for a diversity of behavioral disorders ranging from childhood hyperkinesis to homosexuality. A middle stance would hold that psychosurgery might be of potential benefit and should be studied only for its use in cases of extreme mental illness, especially those that are life-threatening to the patient or those around him and that psychosurgery should be performed only after extensive attempts at alternate modes of therapy had failed. We believe that knowledge and understanding of the relation between the brain and behavioral abnormalities and of the optimal treatment of such abnormalities are still in very early stages. Even though there has been a vast amount of recent animal research, our knowledge of brain function is still insufficient for a clear understanding about what parts of the brain control what behaviors. In the literature on animal brain research, there are conflicting results and many controversial issues that will require much more basic research to resolve. It can be argued that if we cannot really know how the brain works in animals, it is unjustifiable to try to manipulate human brain function. Also, even if we understood in considerable detail how the monkey, cat, or rat brain works, this understanding could not be easily and uncritically generalized to the human brain. Although present evidence indicates that the basic principles of brain function are the same in animals and humans, evolutionary changes or other factors may be such that a given subdivision of the brain may subserve different functions in animals and humans.

Another realm of criticism stems from the ethical and moral issues involved in changing or controlling the behavior of individuals. Psychosurgery, because of its dramatic nature, has become a "lightning rod" for concern and criticism about behavioral control. Although there are clear and valid concerns about intrinsic issues of psychosurgery, this kind of behavior control has attracted and focused a diffuse "static" of concern that biomedical and behavioral sciences are eroding the freedom and dignity of man. Behavior control has always been exerted throughout human history in the form of codification of laws, reward and punishment in social and familial context, religious systems, and educational systems. However, when the techniques of behavior control become explicit and when an advancing behavioral and medical technology makes it more possible to exert behavior control, the possibilities for abuse become more likely. Although psychosurgery is a powerful means of changing behavior, the ethical problems posed by the modification of behavior with drugs or psychotherapy are probably of greater import because these means of control are available to a much wider range of potential abusers than are the techniques of psychosurgery.

These developments, and other advances such as techniques for the prolongation of life, bring with them ethical complexities heretofore unheard of. Medical ethics has never been, as some mistakenly believe, a matter of good versus evil or right versus wrong. It has always been a matter of when, where, and who draws the line as to whether a given medical procedure is helpful, harmful, or warranted and whether the potential benefits of any course of treatment outweigh the risks.

While, on the one hand, society is clamoring in certain fields for the right of every individual to treatment, an almost equally loud cry is beginning to be heard about the individual's right to death. Even more complicated ethical issues arise when the patient is part of a scientific study. While good clinical practice demands that the individual always be a patient first, scientific studies often demand the withholding of an experimental treatment from some patients while providing it to others in order to compare the effectiveness of the new treatment with older treatments or with no treatment. However, there are those who dispute the right to withhold treatment of potential value from anyone under any conditions.

There are no simple answers to these problems. There is an increased public awareness of the extent and nature of these difficulties and some enthusiasm for the establishment of bioethics commissions which would serve as watchdogs and would devise suitable guidelines. Still others believe that it is best if the professions involved establish their own ethical criteria and monitor their own activities. A middle stance would hold that while it is most appropriate for the various professions to establish their own ethical principles, in all instances this should be done with the involvement of other professions and with appropriate representation of laymen and consumers.

In addition to these ethical concerns, the securing of informed consent poses a difficult problem. Informed consent refers to making sure that the patient who is about to undergo a medical or surgical treatment that exposes him to any degree of risk is fully informed as to the potential risks involved and has a clear understanding of the procedures to be used. This also applies to any person who is a subject in a medical or behavioral experiment in which there is any possibility of adverse physical or psychological effects.

Obtaining adequate informed consent is difficult even when the human subjects or patients are of normal intelligence and are emotionally healthy and mature. It becomes infinitely more complicated when the subjects are seriously disturbed, below normal intelligence, or children and when the proposed procedures involve serious risks and irreversible consequences. But a clinical investigator or practitioner may not avoid the solemn responsibility of securing informed consent merely because it is difficult.

DEPARTMENT OF HEALTH, EDUCATION, AND WELFARE POLICY

Much of the biological, medical, and behavioral research conducted in this country is supported by funds from the Department of Health, Education, and Welfare. Recognizing the problems involved in research with human subjects, the department has established a Branch on Institutional Relations within the National Institutes of Health. This branch has the responsibility for formulating and overseeing policies intended to safeguard the rights and welfare of human subjects involved in activities supported by grants or contracts from the Department of Health, Education, and Welfare. Current DHEW policy, outlined in a pamphlet entitled *The Institutional Guide to DHEW Policy on Protection of Human Subjects* (1972), outlines three cardinal principles. They are, briefly: that the rights and welfare of the subjects involved are adequately protected, that the risks to the individual are outweighed by the potential benefit to him or by the importance of the knowledge to be gained, and that informed consent is obtained in an adequate and appropriate manner.

DHEW guidelines describe the basic elements of an informed consent as follows:

1. A fair explanation of the procedures to be followed, including an identification of those which are experimental;
2. A description of the attendant discomforts and risks;
3. A description of the benefits to be expected;
4. A disclosure of appropriate alternative procedures that would be advantageous for the subject;
5. An offer to answer any inquiries concerning the procedures; and
6. An instruction that the subject is free to withdraw his consent and to discontinue participation in the project or activity at any time.

In other words, the clinical investigator may not withhold from the subject any facts which are necessary to form the basis of an intelligent consent to the proposed investigation. In addition, it forbids the inclusion of any exculpatory language in the consent form through which the patient waives or appears to waive any of his legal rights or through which he releases the institution or investigator from liability for negligence.

All this assumes that the human subject is himself capable of giving an informed consent. While the DHEW guidelines speak of obtaining consent from the subject "or from his authorized representative," they leave to applicable local law such difficult questions as (1) who may consent for the patient when he is incapacitated—next-of-kin? court appointed guardian? (2) under what circumstances can a substitute or agent consent instead of the patient? (3) may parents ever consent to a risky procedure on behalf of a child when the benefit is primarily for science and the benefits for the child are minimal?

The DHEW guidelines require that any institution conducting contract or grant-supported research involving human subjects must establish a professional committee with responsibility for reviewing any application for support of such research to assure that the research protocol adequately fulfills the policy for protection of the subjects. The existence of the DHEW guidelines and the required institutional committees has produced a beneficial spill-over of ethical policy to research and treatment activities not supported by DHEW.

The National Institutes of Health have established a study group to review the current DHEW policy in the light of the many issues that are becoming apparent in biomedical and behavioral research. The group will assess the effectiveness of existing policy in such areas as informed consent, institutional review committees, protection of subjects in prisons or mental institutions, and the NIH review of research applications involving human subjects. The rapid advancement of biomedical and behavioral sciences creates continuously changing ethical issues, and ethical policy cannot be static or fixed but must remain flexible so that it can be adapted to new problems as they arise.

Many hospitals and research institutions have used the DHEW guidelines as a model for structuring their own policy for the protection of human subjects. Some hospitals and institutions have been drawing up very detailed and comprehensive procedures for solving these questions. They require the presence of the subject's personal physician, personal lawyer, and immediate kin with periods of time being allocated for reflection, questioning, and debate before consent is given. This is an area that will be receiving increased attention as we work with our sister agencies to refine and expand the DHEW requirements for research on human subjects.

With respect to the specific issue of psychosurgery, the NIMH and the National Institute of Neurological Diseases and Stroke have established an Inter-Institute Work Group on Brain and Behavior to examine a variety of aspects of the problem. The Inter-Institute Work Group will be responsible for the formulation of a comprehensive report containing recommendations and policies for further activities in this area.

SAFEGUARDS FOR THE FUTURE

The ethical and moral problems posed by current medical, biological, and behavioral techniques are of considerable concern to government agencies as well as the health professions, the scientific communities, religious groups, the Congress, and the lay public. Knowledge, or at least the application of knowledge to wield political or social power, has always been a potentially dangerous concomitant of scientific inquiry.

Even new knowledge which at first appears to have only beneficial consequences can create new problems. Potter in a book called *Bioethics* (1971) put it quite succinctly: ". . . once we have made the choice to open Pandora's Box of Knowledge, we can never put back its contents, and mankind must continue to search forever for the wisdom that is needed to cope with the avalanche of new knowledge that is upon us." We must somehow evolve a system of technology assessment whereby the state of knowledge can be assessed and its readiness for application can be addressed within the context of relevant social, human, and ethical issues. Such a system would assure the timely application of relevant technology and help prevent the premature use of those techniques not thoroughly explored for their human and social implications.

We believe that the answer to the dangerous use of knowledge is the creation of new knowledge, combined with a sensitive, rational, and humanitarian perspective on the applications of that knowledge. It is also important to broaden the training of scientists and practitioners to include such ethical issues and the humanities.

With regard to the specific issue of psychosurgery, the first problem one encounters when attempting to deal with the ethical issues involved in this area is the lack of any reliable data on the extent of the practice, the type of patients subjected to psychosurgery, the particular types of surgery used, or the results on patient behavior. The estimates of the current number of psychosurgical procedures performed are probably inflated by the opponents of psychosurgery and minimized by the psychosurgeons. The most systematic attempt (in this country) to assess the effects of psychosurgery on patient behavior and intellectual capacities was the Columbia-Greystone Project, which was conducted in 1947. Since then, many changes in psychiatric and medical practice have taken place: chemotherapy has dramatically changed the nature of the patient population in mental hospitals, and new surgical procedures have been introduced which are quite different from those studied by the Columbia-Greystone Project. Without this kind of recent information, the current state of knowledge is insufficient to permit a clear-cut comparison of the potential benefits and possible risks of psychosurgery. We hope that the NIMH-NINDS Inter-Institute Work Group on Brain and Behavior will develop a mechanism for obtaining this kind of needed information.

In recent years professional societies and private foundations have developed a variety of programs to deal with medical and behavioral ethics. One of the most active private groups is the Hastings Center Institute of Society, Ethics and the Life Sciences. Founded in 1969 with support from several philanthropic organizations and individuals, the Institute has organized a variety of seminars on ethical issues, has established an experimental teaching program on medical ethics at Columbia University, and has a dedicated and professional staff conducting research programs on ethical issues in the areas of behavior control, population control, death and dying, and genetic engineering. The National Science Foundation has recently provided support for the Institute's program of behavior control research. Organizations such as the Hastings

Center Institute merit continued support, both from private and governmental sources.

The National Academy of Sciences–National Research Council has established a Committee on the Life Sciences and Social Policy. This committee, composed of a prestigious group of lawyers, scientists, and historians, is concerned with identifying the issues and problems emerging from advances in the biological and medical sciences. The Committee has considered such issues as organ transplantation, behavior modification by drug administration to children, and fetal diagnosis and will issue a report of its deliberations in the near future. The prestige of the National Academy of Sciences and the eminence of the Committee members assures that this group's activities will be of considerable influence in the field of bioethics.

The American Psychological Association has just completed an extensive project to develop a set of ethical principles for the conduct of research with human participants. After four years of data-gathering from some 20,000 members of the association, a final report has been issued which goes into unprecedented detail on potential risks and recommendations for protection of human subjects. There has been a huge demand for reprints of this ethical code from other associations and private companies engaged in psychological research, and it promises to be very influential as a model for other behavioral sciences.

CONCLUSION

Continued research in medical science and the development of new medical technologies promise to present us with unprecedented ethical dilemmas that must be faced by the government, scientists, medical practitioners, and the public. The issues are and will be complex ones for which there are no easy answers, and deal with matters of law, philosophy, religion, science, consumerism, and public policy. The answers, when they do come, will not derive from either emotional attacks or a blind faith in the sanctity of science and medical practice but from a reasoned analysis of all facets of the issues by concerned, sensitive, and rational representatives of the diverse groups involved. The answers to the issues of psychosurgery will depend heavily upon scientific advances in our studies of the brain and behavior. Some day it may be possible to say that in the light of our expanded knowledge the potential benefits of psychosurgery far outweigh any possible risk to the human subjects—but that day is not yet. We are sobered by the thought of how very much more there is to know about that marvelous structure, the human brain.

REFERENCES

Andy, O. J. Thalamotomy in hyperactive and aggressive behavior. *Confinia Neurologica*, 1970, *32*, 322–325.

Ballantine, H. T., Jr., Cassidy, W., Flanigan, N., & Morino, R. Stereotaxic anterior aingulotomy for neuropsychiatric illness and intractable pain. *Journal of Neurosurgery*, 1967, *26*, 488–495.

Breggin, P. R. *Congressional Record,* March 30, 1972a. Comments inserted by Representative Cornelius Gallagher.

______. Lobotomies: An alert. *American Journal of Psychiatry,* 1972b, *129,* 97–98.

Brown, M. H., & Lighthill, J. Selective anterior cingulotomy: A psychosurgical evaluation. *Journal of Neurosurgery,* 1968, *29,* 513–519.

Ellison, G. D., & Flynn, J. P. Differential effects of electrical stimulation and lesions of the hippocampus and adjacent regions upon attack behavior in cats. *Brain Research,* 1968, *7,* 252–267.

Freeman, W., & Watts, J. *Psychosurgery in the treatment of mental disorders and intractable pain* (2nd ed.). Springfield, Ill.: Charles C. Thomas, 1950.

Hamlin, R. M. Intellectual function fourteen years after frontal lobe surgery. *Cortex: A Journal Devoted to the Study of the Nervous System and Behavior,* 1970, *6*(3), 299–307.

Hirose, S. Mentally abnormal offenders and psychosurgery. *Acta Criminologiae et Medicinae Legalis Japonica,* 1968, *34*(6), 186–195.

Hohne, H. H., & Walsh, K. W. *Surgical modification of the personality: Mental health research report* (Special Publications). Melbourne: Mental Health Authority, 1970.

Holden, C. Psychosurgery: Legitimate therapy or laundered lobotomy? *Science,* 1973, *179,* 1109–1112.

Homosexuality "burned out." *Medical World News,* 1970, *11*(39), 20–21.

The institutional guide to DHEW policy on protection of human subjects (Department of Health, Education, and Welfare Publication No. NIH 72–102). Washington, D.C.: U.S. Government Printing Office, December 1972.

Isaacson, R. L. Hippocampal destruction in man and other animals. *Neuropsychologia,* 1972, *10,* 47–64.

Kalinowsky, B., Brill, H., Freyhan, F. A., Cattell, J. P., & Ransohoff, J. Psychosurgery panel. *Diseases of the Nervous System: Supplement,* 1969, *30*(2), 53–59.

Knight, G. Stereotactic surgery for the relief of suicidal and severe depression and intractable psychoneurosis. *Postgraduate Medical Journal,* 1969, *45*(519), 1–13.

Koskoff, Y. D., Dennis, W., Lazovik, D., & Wheeler, E. T. The psychological effects of frontal lobotomy performed for the alleviation of pain. *Frontal Lobes,* 1947, *27,* 723–753.

Koskoff, Y. D., & Goldhurst, R. *The dark side of the house.* New York: Dial Press, 1968.

Lobotomy in schizophrenia: A review. In D. Sankar, *Schizophrenia: Current concepts and research.* Hicksville, N.Y.: PJD Publications, 1969.

Mark, V. H., Barry, H., McLardy, T., & Ervin, F. R. The destruction of both anterior thalamic nuclei in a patient with intractable agitated depression. *Journal of Nervous and Mental Disease,* 1970, *150,* 266–272.

Mark, V. H., & Ervin, F. R. *Violence and the brain.* New York: Harper & Row, 1970.

Mettler, F. A. (Ed.). *Psychosurgical problems.* New York: Blakiston, 1952.

Miller, A. The lobotomy patient—a decade later: A follow-up study of a research project started in 1948. *Canadian Medical Association Journal,* 1967, *96*(15), 1095–1103.

Milner, B. Amnesia following operation on the temporal lobes. In C. W. M. Whittey & O. L. Zangwill (Eds.), *Amnesia.* London: Butterworth, 1966.

Moniz, E. Attempt at surgical treatment of certain psychoses. In R. Wilkenson (Ed.), *Neurosurgical classics.* New York: Johnson Reprint Corp. (subsidiary of Academic Press), 1965.

Partridge, M. *Pre-frontal leucotomy.* Springfield, Ill.: Charles C. Thomas, 1950.

Pippard, J. Leucotomy in Britain today. *Journal of Mental Science,* 1962, *108,* 249–255.

Podolsky, E. The epileptic murderer. *Medico-Legal Journal,* 1962, *30,* 176–179.

Poppen, R. L., Pribram, K. H., & Robinson, R. S. Effects of frontal lobotomy in man on the performance of a multiple choice task. *Experimental Neurology*, 1965, *11*(2), 217–229.

Potter, V. R. *Bioethics: Bridge to the future*. Englewood Cliffs, N.J.: Prentice-Hall, 1971.

Pribram, K. H., Ahumada, A., Haryog, J., & Roos, L. A progress report on the neurological processes disturbed by frontal lesions in primates. In J. M. Warren & K. Akert, *Frontal granular cortex and behavior*. New York: McGraw-Hill, 1964.

Rosen, J., Stein, D., & Butters, N. Recovery of function after serial ablation of prefrontal cortex in the rhesus monkey. *Science*, 1971, *173*, 353–356.

Scarff, J. E. Unilateral prefrontal lobotomy for the relief of intractable pain and termination of narcotic addiction. *Journal of Nervous and Mental Disease*, 1950, *111*(3), 254–257.

Schvarcz, J. R., Driollet, R., Rios, E., & Betti, O. Stereotactic hypothalamotomy for behaviour disorders. *Journal of Neurology, Neurosurgery, and Psychiatry*, 1972, *35*, 356–359.

Scoville, W. B. Recent thoughts on psychosurgery. *Connecticut Medicine*, 1969, *33*(7), 453–456.

Shobe, F. O., & Gildea, M. C. L. Long-term follow-up of selected lobotomized private patients. *Journal of the American Medical Association*, 1968, *206*(2), 327–332.

Smith, A. Changes in porteus maze scores of brain-operated schizophrenics after an eight-year interval. *Journal of Mental Science*, 1960, *106*(444), 967–978.

Smith, A., & Kinder, E. F. Changes in psychological test performances of brain-operated schizophrenics after eight years. *Science*, 1959, *129*(3342), 149–150.

Smolik, E. A. Lobotomy in the management of intractable pain and narcotic addiction. *Diseases of the Nervous System*, 1950, *11*(11), 327–331.

Sperry, R. W. Lateral specialization of cerebral function in the surgically separated hemispheres. In F. J. McGuigan & R. A. Schoonover (Eds.), *The psychophysiology of thinking: Studies of covert processes*. New York: Academic Press, 1973.

Strom-Olson, R., & Carlisle, S. Bi-frontal stereotactic tractotomy. *British Journal of Psychiatry*, 1971, *118*(543), 141–154.

Surgical modification of the personality. *Medical Journal of Australia*, 1971, *2*(13), 643–644.

Tan, E., Marks, I. M., & Marset, P. Bimedial leucotomy in obsessive-compulsive neurosis: A controlled serial enquiry. *British Journal of Psychiatry*, 1971, *118*(543), 155–164.

Teuber, H. L. Disorders of memory following penetrating missile wounds of the brain. *Neurology*, 1968, *18*, 287–288.

Thorne, B. M. Brain lesions and affective behavior in primates: A selected review. *Journal of General Psychology*, 1972, *86*, 153–162.

Tooth, G. C., & Newton, M. A. *Leucotomy in England and Wales 1942–1954* (Ministry of Health: Reports on Public Health and Medical Subject No. 104). London: H.M. Stationery Office, 1961.

U.S. Senate Report 91–1335, Labor-HEW Appropriations Bill (H.R. 18515) for Fiscal Year 1971, pp. 18–19.

Vaernet, K., & Madsen, A. Stereotaxic amygdalotomy and basofrontal tractotomy in psychotics with aggressive behaviour. *Journal of Neurology, Neurosurgery, and Psychiatry*, 1970, *33*(6), 858–863.

Wasman, M., & Flynn, J. P. Directed attack behavior during hippocampal seizures. *Archives of Neurology*, 1966, *14*, 408–414.

Wikler, A., Pescor, M. J., Kalbaugh, E. P., & Angelucci, R. J. Effects of frontal lobotomy on the morphine-abstinence syndrome in man: An experimental study. *A.M.A. Archives of Neurology and Psychiatry*, 1952, *67*(4), 510–521.

BRAIN SURGERY IN AGGRESSIVE EPILEPTICS

Vernon H. Mark, Boston City College
and Harvard Medical School

A little over two years ago Frank Ervin, a psychiatrist, and I, a neurosurgeon, wrote a book called *Violence and the Brain*, detailing the application of brain surgery to problems of violent behavior. The public response to that book underscores with great vividness the fact that the medical issues of neurosurgery are no more interesting or vital than the issues of neurosurgery's *social role*. I would like here to offer some reflections about those social issues.

The most important problem to conjure with, from the standpoint of the sciences of human behavior, is the unfortunate dichotomy in basic approaches to behavior. Certain kinds of behavior (for instance, paralysis, blindness, and dementia) were put into the province of *organic neurology*. Physicians working in this field have been increasingly reluctant to examine other kinds of abnormal behavior, even when they are associated with obvious brain abnormalities.

On the other hand, social psychiatrists, sociologists, criminologists, and many psychologists tend to view the other behavioral abnormalities, for instance intractable depressions and aggressive assaultive behavior, as pure reflections of unusual or abnormal environmental stress. They believe that brain function or dysfunction is not an important determinant as far as abnormal behavior is concerned. To them, all human beings function with the same "normal" brains. Even those few social scientists who admit that brain function might be important in abnormal behavior feel that so little is known about brain function that it is useless to spend time and money investigating it.

Now whatever the sociological reasons for this division of labor in the scientific vineyard, any high school student can see that it results in absurd theoretical suppositions. No human behavior whatever, be it normal or abnormal, can be the consequence of the brain alone without the environment. Nor can any behavior, whatever its environmental determinants, take place without the brain freighting its mechanical impulses with emotion and culture. Therefore, any thorough investigation of abnormal, violent behavior should look not only to the environment for causes but also to the brain itself.

Yet when President Lyndon Johnson and Milton Eisenhower convened the Commission on Violence, there were over fifty consultants representing various fields of sociology, criminology, history, government,

This paper was originally presented at a meeting of the Institute of Society, Ethics, and Life Sciences.

Mark, Vernon H. Brain surgery in aggressive epileptics. *Hastings Center Report*, February 1973, pp. 1–5. Reprinted with permission of the Institute of Society, Ethics, and Life Sciences.

law, social psychiatry, and social psychology, but only two representing the brain!

Let me stress that recognition of the brain in behavior does not entail, as some critics might fear, that all behavior should be controlled through the brain. Rather it is precisely because any behavior, normal or abnormal, *could be* modified through altering the brain, at least in principle, that it is absolutely crucial to make *moral* decisions about the sort appropriate for neurosurgery and other direct brain manipulations. There are important moral issues at stake, for example, in the very definition of a problem as a medical one, for which medical therapy is appropriate. This problem is pressed further when a behavior problem is defined as a neurological one.

My own position regarding the appropriateness of neurosurgery can be illustrated in terms of three alternatives. The first two of these I unequivocally reject:

The first of these positions holds that medical means should be undertaken to improve *any* behavior, wherever possible, be the behavior normal or abnormal. Although neurosurgery is not in a position now to improve normal behavior, some people advocate the use of drugs—amphetamines, for instance—for that purpose. The advantage of this position is that it avoids the obvious difficulties in defining normality. The grave disadvantage is that it makes the medical men authorities on improvement and the good life, which they are not, at least under our present social arrangement. Moral values are social concerns, not medical ones in any presently recognized sense.

A second position holds that any *abnormal* behavior should be treated by whatever medical means are available. Often argued by psychotherapists, this position says that, regardless of any *organic* abnormality, what is undesirable in abnormal behavior is the behavior, not its organic base. The criteria for alteration should refer to the behavior, irrespective of whether the organic base is normal or abnormal. Should an unusual brain abnormality produce a 50 point I.W. *rise*, no one would suggest ablating it: its behavioral product is desirable. (With regard to neurosurgical control of violent behavior, I am *against* the principle that it could be used to treat abnormal behavior when there is no organic abnormality of the brain.)

A third position, then, is that medical procedures like neurosurgery should be used only when behavior is abnormal and bad, as the result of an abnormality in the brain. As I shall repeat below, violent behavior *not* associated with brain disease should be dealt with politically and socially, not medically.

With this brief positioning of what I take to be support for a very circumscribed domain for neurosurgical procedures, I now want to deal with some common criticisms of neurosurgery. Most of the criticisms either construe neurosurgery to be capable of more than it is or assume that it would be used in areas I believe to be inappropriate. Like any technological power, neurosurgery can be misused, and setting the limits of its use is more than a medical problem.

POLITICAL VERSUS PERSONAL VIOLENCE

Implicit in many of the criticisms of the surgical treatment of violent epileptics is the fear that this treatment will be used against political protestors. This fear is based on a semantic confusion about the word "violence." Many activities in our society are called violent. The "establishment" tends to view as violent any protest movement against the war, unfair living conditions, or the prison system. Protestors view the reaction of police and the National Guard as violent. Minority groups have indicated that social or job discrimination is a form of violence.

The kind of violent behavior for which I might approve neurosurgery, however, has a much narrower definition: *personal violent behavior; unwarranted and usually unprovoked acts that directly attempt to or actually do injure or destroy another person or thing.* And as I have said, I would not approve neurosurgery even in such cases unless the personal violence could be traced to organic brain disease and could not be treated by non-surgical methods.

Some political psychiatrists have argued that social injustice provokes individual acts of violence which seem "senseless" but which in reality are political protests against the social system. As Goebbels showed, political violence of mass proportions can be culled up without counting on people with diseased brains. However, the person whose violence is related to brain disease and is used by a Hitler or Goebbels is a danger to himself and his loved ones and cannot be counted on to rage only in politically strategic situations. Thus the morality of preventing such an individual from seeking proper medical diagnosis and care is certainly in question.

BIOLOGICAL FACTORS IN PERSONAL VIOLENCE

Many sociologists believe that brain dysfunction does not have a role in such behavioral abnormalities as intractable depression, thought disorders, paranoia, or aggressive assaultive behavior of the sort I am concerned with. In the last case, however, there is *solid* medical evidence to link aggressive behavior to focal brain disease. This behavioral symptom is often present in such clinical disorders as temporal lobe epilepsy, temporal lobe tumors, infections of the brain (such as rabies and postencephalitic syndromes), and serious brain injuries which affect the under-surfaces of the frontal lobes and the anterior tips of the temporal lobes (usually a transient phenomenon in the last disorder).

The most frequent occurrence of brain dysfunction in violent behavior is in brain poisoning, the most serious and ubiquitous of which is caused by alcohol. Alcohol is a specific brain poison, and individuals acutely poisoned with alcohol may have as much dysfunction during the poisoning as would be caused by a brain tumor, infection, or injury. The only difference between the former and the latter is that alcohol poisoning is temporary.

The violence in automobile accidents caused by drunk drivers takes a far greater toll than the violence in political protest or repression. A drunk driver suffers from a temporary brain abnormality. Although I certainly do not advocate neurosurgery for the treatment of alcoholism nor for all kinds of organic brain disease, it is clear that violence is sometimes a function of brain abnormalities and should be viewed as such.

RACISM

In the most *avant-garde* circles today the favorite critical epithet is "chauvinist." Neurosurgery seems to draw its critics from a somewhat stodgier class: neurosurgical treatment of violent epileptics has been called "racist."

Speaking to a national group of psychiatric investigators about our approach to the problem of violent behavior, a major professor of psychiatry conceded that the biological-social model of violence and the investigation of brain disease associated with violence had some merit. But he classified our project with the proposal of those psychologists who claim that black people have a constitutionally inferior IQ compared to white people. Admitting that the racial idea might have some merit too, he felt that nevertheless funding and research should not be given to such projects until all possible avenues of social and educational rehabilitation have been exhausted.

It seems to me there are really two issues here. The first concerns the political implications of a theory about violence. One of the functions of a theory is that it tells you where to look to find the phenomenon in question. Does the theory that some violence is caused by brain disease lead us to expect it is a characteristic mainly of black people? Certainly not. On the other hand, the theory that personal violence is caused exclusively by social conditions might very well lead us to look at the black ghettos. The environmental cues to personal violence may very well cluster around racially differentiated areas.

The second issue is whether there is any empirical evidence that organically based personal violence is more common among blacks than whites. In my experience there is no special correlation of violence with race. Domestic personal violence occurs in upper- and middle-class homes as well as in the ghettos. When it occurs in the ghetto, however, it may be more visible, spilling out into the streets from the very pressures of overcrowding. It may very well be that violence in ghettos more often gets reported in police records and other data available to the sociologist. But the perspective of the physician is the emergency room and clinic where the products of violence are immediate. From this perspective, claret is the predominant color, not black or white.

It is my perception that the biological-social model of violence will not concentrate on one race, ethnic group, or other social segment of our population as do the subculture theories of violence. In fact, I feel it is important in cases of violence related to brain disease to study the violent act primarily and to consider the style of violence, which is socially determined, as a secondary phenomenon.

DANGERS IN A MEDICAL MODEL OF VIOLENCE

All sorts of dire predictions have been made about the outcome of brain research directed toward the understanding and treatment of emotional disorders and especially those related to violent behavior. Shades of *1984*! "The neurosurgeons want to put electrodes in everyone's brain to keep them from protesting!" "They're going to develop a new drug that will completely destroy the will!" "Man's dignity will be shattered, and his innate human quality will be destroyed!" These would indeed be serious statements if they were true. But it is important to see just what the issues are.

It is one thing to advocate neurosurgical procedures for certain kinds of violent behavior caused by organic brain disease or dysfunction. It is quite another to advocate them as general methods of behavior control. My own belief is that no form of conditioning, drug therapy, or surgery is necessary or desirable to control normal-brained members of our society, no matter what their political views are or how they express them.

Of course it is true that behavior control techniques developed to be used in a circumscribed sphere might be adapted to widespread and immoral ends by unscrupulous people. No greater lesson is needed than that provided by Nazi Germany.

But interestingly enough, the controls Goebbels used were environmental ones, not direct alterations of the brain. No drugs were needed to seduce the German population. The S.S. storm troopers did not have little electrodes implanted in their limbic systems.

Although Joseph Goebbels might have reduplicated Skinner's experiments in the best conditioning traditions, he did so before, rather than after, the fact. As a clinician living among the German people for two years after the war, I could find nothing in them that would distinguish them from other human beings.

Can one imagine the most advanced brain electrode technology of the future or even a new and much more sophisticated group of psychic drugs that could produce a more perfect form of behavior control than that initiated by environmental "natural" factors in the Third Reich?

One of the important factors to emerge from our own research on the relative influence of deep electrical brain stimulation versus environmental "natural" stimuli is the importance, in terms of effectiveness, of the latter. Of course, effective electrical brain stimulation in target areas can produce pronounced behavioral effects. However, even in susceptible individuals with brain disease, the effect of nonconvulsing doses of electrical stimulation can be remarkably altered and suppressed by giving the subject a demanding and attention-absorbing task during electrical brain stimulation.

My thesis that behavior control through the direct manipulation of the brain is not as dangerous for mass abuse as environmental forms of control should not be taken to imply that it has no dangers whatsoever for mass abuse. But the social limitations on who performs neurosurgery or administers drugs on whom and for what reasons, ought to be set through public discussion and social decisions. My own claim is that the dangers of mass abuse are not sufficient to warrant preventing the very development of the techniques that might have very great therapeutic value for patients with organic brain disease.

MORAL PROBLEMS IN NEUROSURGERY

If neurosurgery is not much of a danger as a political tool, there still are serious problems with its medical use. I would like to address two of these.

First is the problem of neurological diagnosis. The emphasis I have been placing on the neurological side of the problem of violence ought not be taken out of the context of environmental factors also. Due to the very fundamental problem of specialization in medicine, it is very difficult to maintain a biological-social model of violence in actual practice. The neurologists are in one place, and the psychiatrists and social workers are in another.

Yet if the model is worthwhile, treatment of a patient should involve not only his brain but his family, living conditions, job, and role in society. It is very important, therefore, to embed a neurological diagnosis of problems of violence into a larger integrated approach to human behavior. The social forms for this holistic therapy are yet to be worked out, although my own group has tried to include psychiatric and social psychiatric diagnosis along with the neurological.

From my reading of the present situation, however, I believe the greater danger is that the neurological side will be left out. Recently, for example, an airplane hijacker killed one pilot and shot another before he himself was subdued with a blow to the head. Examination of this man afterward revealed he had been a neurological cripple for eleven years, ever since receiving a gunshot wound of the brain. Yet repeated tests, including hours of brainwave examinations, psychological testing, psychiatric and neurological assessment, failed to reveal the tremendous damage that had occurred in this man's emotional center or limbic brain.

The difficulties of diagnosis had their classic but tragic expression in the case of George Gershwin. This talented composer was seen and treated psychiatrically for a long time while a tumor in the limbic system of his brain grew to an unmanageable and untreatable size. The George Gershwin syndrome of the thirties is still being treated in the seventies. Recently eighteen patients were committed to a mental hospital at one of our best university centers who turned out to have tumors of their limbic brains. In some cases the true nature of this illness was not recognized until the tumor had caused the patient's death.

Second, after the diagnosis of brain disease has been confirmed, *what are the problems of proper consent to treatment?* Does the patient consent to the treatment? Does he know the dangers of the treatment and how those dangers compare with letting him pass without treatment? What are the wider factors involved in informed consent when the patient is mentally incompetent?[1]

Usually close members of their families are the sources of consent. But in cases of surgery for violence, I believe the patient and his family should have the assistance of an impartial, noninvolved professional group to determine whether surgery or other forms of treatment should be undertaken. In practical terms this means that a committee of some sort, composed of physicians, or in some cases, physicians and informed laymen should be present to monitor the medical, psychiatric, and/or surgical treatment.[2]

In my own practice, I and my group do not accept patients for treatments who do not want therapy, and we do not believe that the public good or public interest should intrude upon the personal medical model in terms of protecting the public against violent individuals.

FREE WILL AND BEHAVIOR CONTROL

Radical critics of the biological-social model of violence often construe human violence to be an expression of free will. In line with this they consider the medical correction of brain disease that would, as a secondary result, stop violent episodes to have an unnatural and degrading effect on human dignity. As a physician I find this view particularly inappropriate, not because I deny free will but because I prize the quality of human life.

Many of the patients who come to us with focal brain disease associated with violent behavior are so offended by their own actions they have attempted suicide. They feel their human dignity has been lost precisely because of uncontrollable behavior patterns they find unnatural and repugnant.

Because our work, and that of other physicians, has indicated a clinical relationship between limbic brain disease, such as temporal lobe epilepsy, and aggressive assaultive behavior, *I believe the correction of that organic condition gives the patient more, rather than less, control over his own behavior.* It enhances, and does not diminish, his dignity. It adds to, and does not detract from, his human qualities.

Finally, it is appropriate to return to the specter of a tyrannical government controlling a submissive population through neurosurgery and electrical brain stimulation. Even though this is technically unlikely now, it is a possibility to be conjured with. In the face of this possibility I still have great confidence that the neurological research in behavior control now being done will lead to a better understanding of brain mechanisms and that when this occurs, *it should be possible for brain scientists to devise techniques for making behavior control of one individual by another more difficult or even impossible.*

In other words, one of the expected benefits of increased brain research will be the creation of new techniques enabling each individual better to control or govern his or her behavior, without unwarranted or unwanted interference by other individuals or devices.

There is already enough knowledge of environmental and psychopharmacological drugs to control a vast segment of our population without invoking brain surgery or electrical brain stimulation. The great hope of emotional brain research is that it will free us from our present tyrannies and future dangers of control. To this end, brain scientists need the help of philosophers, ethicists, theologians, social scientists, and jurists, working in concert.

NOTES

1. Prison inmates suffering from epilepsy should receive only medical treatment; surgical therapy should not be carried out, because of the difficulty in obtaining truly informed consent.

2. In conjunction with Dr. David Allen, we are exploring "consumer advocacy" utilizing a group with religious, legal, and community representatives in addition to physicians.